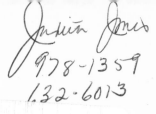

**OPERATIONS
RESEARCH**

McGRAW-HILL
BOOK COMPANY
New York
St. Louis
San Francisco
Düsseldorf
Johannesburg
Kuala Lumpur
London
Mexico
Montreal
New Delhi
Panama
Paris
São Paulo
Singapore
Sydney
Tokyo
Toronto

JAMES E. SHAMBLIN

School of Industrial Engineering and Management
Oklahoma State University

G. T. STEVENS, Jr.

School of Industrial Engineering and Management
Oklahoma State University

Operations Research

A FUNDAMENTAL APPROACH

This book was set in Times New Roman.
The editors were Thomas H. Kothman and Michael Gardner;
the cover was designed by Studio 17;
the production supervisor was Leroy A. Young.
The drawings were done by ANCO Technical Services.
The Maple Press Company was printer and binder.

Library of Congress Cataloging in Publication Data

Shamblin, James E
    Operations research: a fundamental approach.

    1. Operations research.   I.   Stevens, Gladstone
Taylor, date   joint author.   II.   Title.
T57.6.S48   658.4'034   74-3047
ISBN 0-07-056378-0

OPERATIONS RESEARCH
A Fundamental Approach

    4567890MAMM79876

To WILSON J. BENTLEY

CONTENTS

This book was written to be used as a general text in operations research at the undergraduate or lower graduate level. The purpose is to explain and interpret the mathematics of operations research. We feel that much of the basic operations research field does not require sophisticated mathematics for use or more importantly for understanding. It has been our experience that an operations research consultant or fully employed practitioner must first interpret the physical or economic environment to allow a mathematical model to be constructed. Finally the results of the mathematical manipulations must be interpreted on an economic or physical basis for these to be implemented. Thus a strong appeal has been made to the physical or economic interpretation of the mathematics instead of trying to emphasize theorems and proofs. This book has been written primarily for students who will be applying operations research concepts, and in many cases an intuitive basis for understanding is used instead of a more rigorous treatment. In some cases, notes appended to chapters provide additional rigor. These may be used at the discretion of the instructor. References at the end of each chapter will help cover more advanced extensions of the topics presented. It is believed that the coverage of topics in this text provides a foundation upon which to consider more advanced extensions.

The authors have long felt the need for a text which emphasizes explanations and interpretations and yet contains sufficient coverage to justify a quality course and not just a shallow survey of the terminology.   It is our strong contention that operations research topics can be treated with necessary rigor and still maintain readability. Mathematical developments are fully included as required but every consideration has been given to ensure that these are easily followed and readily interpreted.   In addition, these explanations have been strengthened by numerical examples throughout the text and problems at the end of each chapter.   We do not consider this as a text which has "neglected" theory but one which fully explains both how and why the mathematical concepts work without overemphasizing complex notation.

The mathematics required for this book can be covered by a course in algebra and calculus.   The student should be sufficiently familiar with quantitative topics to have no trouble in formulating problems in mathematical terms.   This ability is more important than straight mathematical expertise.   Any junior or senior in a quantitative area of a business college or an engineering college should have adequate mathematical background to make use of this text.   At the lower graduate level it may be desirable to omit or quickly review the first two chapters so that more attention might be given to the later chapters.

In writing this book, every attempt has been made to incorporate our feeling regarding the importance of teaching and sympathy for students saddled with a difficult-to-comprehend text.   At higher levels, rigor will require the increased use of abstract notation, but not at the introductory level.

Dr. Wilson J. Bentley continually demonstrated the understanding, concern, and scholarship that constitutes good teaching.   We dedicate this book to his memory as our friend, counselor, and leader.   We wish, also, to thank our wives, Jane and Norma Jeanne, for their patience and encouragement.   Finally, we appreciate the many contributions of our colleagues and students who allowed us to try out many ideas on them and worked with us until an adequate form was reached.

JAMES E. SHAMBLIN
G. T. STEVENS, Jr.

OPERATIONS
RESEARCH

THE NATURE OF OPERATIONS RESEARCH

Operations research (OR) is a scientific approach to decision making. In this context, operations research can be traced back to Frederick W. Taylor, the Gilbreths, and Henry Gantt. However, it was not until World War II that the term operations research was used to describe an approach taken by interdisciplinary groups of scientists to solve strategic and tactical problems for military management. After the war, this approach spread to industrial organizations, and with the advent of the high-speed computer it has developed into a common approach to organizational problems.

Operations research begins by describing some system by a model, and then it manipulates the model to find the best way of operating the system. The approach can be further explained by considering the major phases of an OR study (from Ref. 2):

1 Formulating the problem
2 Constructing a model to represent the system under study
3 Deriving a solution from the model
4 Testing the model and the solution derived from it
5 Establishing controls over the solution
6 Putting the solution to work: implementation

FORMULATING THE PROBLEM

It is essential in any OR study that the problem under consideration be clearly defined. It is almost impossible to obtain the "right" answer from the "wrong" problem.

In formulating the problem, objectives, alternative courses of actions, constraints, and the effect of the system under study upon related systems must be well established. There must be complete agreement on these points between the persons initiating the OR study and the persons performing the study. In addition, a measure of effectiveness must be agreed upon by the parties involved. This measure of effectiveness must be in harmony with the objectives of the total organization; i.e., an overall viewpoint must be taken in OR studies. This does not imply that the definition of a problem should explicitly include all branches of the organization but that consideration should be given to overall organizational objectives when determining a measure of effectiveness for a particular problem. For example, a company might have a primary objective of delivering its products to customers in a minimum length of time. A study which minimizes equipment idle time, although worthwhile in itself, may not be consistent with this primary objective.

CONSTRUCTING A MODEL

After formulating the problem, the next step is to construct a model of the problem or system under study. In OR work this is usually a mathematical model. There are, of course, other types of models, e.g., physical and schematic models. An example of a physical model is a scale model of a plant used for plant-layout studies. An organizational chart showing the interrelationship between various functions in a company is an example of a schematic model.

A mathematical model is a set of equations that describes a system or problem. The mathematical model usually contains two types of equations: (1) the effectiveness function and (2) the constraints. The effectiveness function, often called the *objective equation*, is a mathematical expression of the objective of the study; e.g., mathematical expression of profit or cost for a particular operation. Mathematical expressions of the limitations on an operation or system are examples of constraints. Constraints are sometimes referred to as restrictions.

The objective and constraint equations are functions of two types of variables, controllable (decision) variables and uncontrollable variables. A controllable variable is one that can be directly controlled by a decision maker. The values of these variables are to be determined. Uncontrollable variables are those which are not under the direct control of a decision maker. As a simple example of a mathematical model, consider the following situation. A company produces two products, A and B. The profit for product A is \$1,000 per unit, and the profit for product B is \$1,500 per unit. It requires 20 hours to produce a single unit of product A and 30 hours to produce a single unit of product B. The total manufacturing time available in a year is 1,200 hours. Expected demands for the two products have led to the decision that the amount of A produced should not be greater than 40 units per year and the amount of B not more than 30 units per year. If it is desired to maximize the profit for the year, the mathematical model for the situation just described is to maximize

$$1,000x_A + 1,500x_B \qquad \text{(1-1)}$$

subject to the constraints

$$20x_A + 30x_B \leq 1,200 \qquad \text{(1-2)}$$
$$x_A \leq 40 \qquad \text{(1-3)}$$
$$x_B \leq 30 \qquad \text{(1-4)}$$

where x_A and x_B are the number of units produced per year, i.e., the controllable variables. In this formulation, the profits per unit, costs per unit, production amounts, and production times are all uncontrollable variables. Equation (1-1) is the objective equation, and Eqs. (1-2) to (1-4) are the constraints.

It must be remembered that a model is an *approximation* of a real system. Consequently, all variables may not be included in the model. This is often misunderstood by persons not familiar with the OR approach. No true OR specialist will claim that his model is all-inclusive or that the answers derived from the model are infallible when they are applied to the actual system under study. In any approximating procedure there is bound to be some error. The attempt is to make the error as small as possible.

The description of a system by a model makes it possible to analyze a system and try various alternatives without interrupting the actual system. Another advantage is that a model tends to make a problem more meaningful, and it can clarify important relationships between the variables. A model will make it clear what variables are important and what data are necessary for the analysis of a system. Once a model has been formulated, it is possible to analyze the problem.

DERIVING A SOLUTION

Once a mathematical model has been established, the next step is to obtain a solution to the problem from the model. This is accomplished by determining the optimum solution to the model and then applying this solution to the actual problem. Sometimes mathematical complexities in the model make an optimum solution impossible, and a " good " answer must suffice. Even when an optimum answer can be obtained for the model, this answer is not necessarily an optimum for the problem. Since a model is an approximation of a real system or problem, the optimum solution for the model does not guarantee an optimum solution for the real problem. However, if the model has been well formulated and tested, solutions from the model will provide a good approximation to the true optimum.

Solutions for mathematical models can be obtained by using certain tools and techniques. The greater portion of this book is devoted to these subjects.

TESTING THE MODEL AND SOLUTION

After a solution for the model has been obtained, the model and solution should be tested. This can be done in two ways: (1) using past data, make a comparison of the actual performance of the system and the performance indicated by the model; (2) let the system operate without change and compare its performance with the performance of the model. The worth of the model and its solution can be judged on the basis of these comparisons.

ESTABLISHING CONTROLS

Once a model and its solution are considered acceptable, controls should be placed on the solution. These controls are established to detect any significant changes in the conditions upon which the model is based. Obviously, if conditions change so much that the model is no longer an accurate representation of the system, the model is invalidated. Consequently, some monitoring procedure must be established to detect any changes in the system as soon as possible so that the model can be revised to reflect these changes.

IMPLEMENTATION

Implementing the solution derived from the model is the last phase of an OR study. In this phase the OR group explains the solution to the management responsible for the system under study. It is important that the explanation of the solution be made in terms of procedures used in the actual system. Once there is agreement on the solution, it is the responsibility of both parties to translate the solution into an easily understood operating procedure. After the solution has been applied to the system, the OR group should observe the response of the system to the changes made. This allows the OR group to make any additional changes and modifications indicated by the performance of the system.

The amount of support received from management will determine the success of an OR study. One method of obtaining this support is by making management an active participant in all phases of the OR study.

The importance of the implementation phase cannot be overemphasized since it is from this phase that the benefits of an OR study are fully realized.

It is hoped that this discussion of the various phases of an OR study has provided a better understanding of the OR approach. This discussion serves as a procedural framework. The phases of an OR study are not rigid rules, and often they must be modified. Obviously, there is a considerable interrelationship between the various phases. By its basic nature, OR work must be approached creatively and with ingenuity.

A VIEW OF THE BOOK

This book covers such traditional OR models as replacement models, inventory models, and queuing theory. In addition, prominent tools and techniques are presented, e.g., matrix algebra, Markov chains, linear and dynamic programming, and simulation. The emphasis has been on the application of the topics presented and on explanation by numerical examples rather than vigorous mathematical proofs.

Obviously, in any introductory text, the discussion of the various topics must be terminated at some point. Entire books have been written on some of the topics considered here. The aim in this book is to provide the student with a foundation upon which to build further study of a particular topic. References which cover extended applications and more formal mathematical treatments of topics are provided at the end of each chapter.

REFERENCES

1   ACKOFF, R. L., and M. W. SASIENI: "Fundamentals of Operations Research," chaps. 1–4, John Wiley & Sons, Inc., New York, 1968.
2   CHURCHMAN, C. W., R. L. ACKOFF, and E. L. ARNOFF: "Introduction to Operations Research," John Wiley & Sons, Inc., New York, 1957, pts. I–III and IX.
3   HILLIER, F. S., and G. J. LIEBERMAN: "Introduction to Operations Research," chaps. 1 and 2, Holden-Day, Inc., Publisher, San Francisco, 1967.
4   RICHMOND, S. B.: "Operations Research for Management Decisions," chap. 1, The Ronald Press Co., New York, 1968.
5   WAGNER, H. W.: "Principles of Operations Research with Application to Managerial Decisions," chaps. 1 and 2, Prentice-Hall, Inc., Englewood Cliffs, N.J., 1969.

2

A REVIEW OF STATISTICS AND PROBABILITY

Many OR activities require a knowledge of statistics and probability. This chapter reviews some of the fundamentals in these areas.

BASIC CONCEPTS

Population and a Sample

The *population* (universe or parent distribution) is the entire collection of objects or measurements under consideration. A population may be finite or infinite. A *sample* is a group of objects taken from a population. The usual case is to estimate population characteristics (*parameters*) by determining sample characteristics (*statistics*). For example, the mean and variance of a population are often estimated on the basis of the mean and variance of a sample taken from the population.

Continuous and Discrete Data

Continuous data are data that can theoretically assume any value between two given values. Most data obtained by some measuring process are continuous. Continuous data may appear discrete due to termination of the measuring process. If data values are separate and distinct elements, the data are discrete. A counting process usually results in discrete data, e.g., the number of men required to perform a task.

Random Variable

A random variable, also known as a chance or stochastic variable, is a function whose numerical value depends on the outcome of a chance experiment. The function may be just a rule which assigns a value based upon the outcome of the experiment. As an example of a random variable, consider the experiment of taking n steel rods and measuring their lengths, $x_1, x_2, \ldots, x_i, \ldots, x_n$. In this case x_i is the random variable, and the rule might be to assign the measured values to each x_i.

Any function of a random variable is also a random variable. That is, if the lengths are used in some subsequent calculations, the results of these calculations are also random variables.

DESCRIPTIVE STATISTICS

Statistics may be divided into two general classifications, inductive and descriptive statistics. Inductive (inferential) statistics is concerned with drawing conclusions about a population on the basis of a sample taken from the population. Descriptive statistics refers to the presentation of collected data in a meaningful manner. In this chapter, only descriptive statistics is considered.

A collection of data in their raw form usually does not provide a great deal of information. For example, the data presented in Table 2-1 represent the number of

Table 2-1 NUMBER OF UNITS SOLD PER DAY

26	24	30
28	24	29
24	26	24
25	27	27
25	27	25
29	25	26
23	28	24
26	26	25
26	22	26
27	28	23

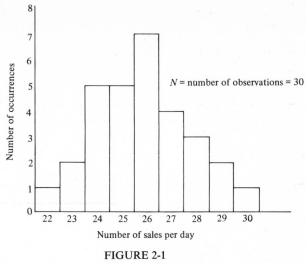

FIGURE 2-1
Histogram for the number of sales per day.

units sold per day. In this form, the data do not provide much information, but if the data are summarized as shown in Fig. 2-1, a clearer picture is obtained. Figure 2-1 is a graphical representation of the frequency distribution of the data, called a *histogram.*

Frequency Distributions

A frequency distribution separates data into classes and shows the number of occurrences in each class, or *class frequency.* In Fig. 2-1 the classes are 22, 23, 24, ..., 30, and the class frequency for the class 24 is five.

Class boundaries refer to the minimum and maximum values of a class; the class boundaries in Fig. 2-1 are 21.5, 22.5, 23.5, ..., 30.5. The class interval refers to the

Table 2-2 CONTINUOUS DATA

37.0	37.8	32.2	29.0
34.2	25.1	31.9	30.9
29.7	32.9	33.0	29.5
30.4	31.7	36.2	29.9
32.0	32.3	40.1	30.1
33.4	29.8	34.6	32.1
31.0	29.2	35.0	31.8
29.0	30.5	29.3	33.5
28.5	31.1	31.0	33.4
28.4	30.0	28.8	35.8

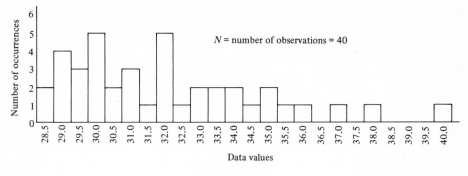

FIGURE 2-2
Histogram for data in Table 2-2 with a class interval of .5.

difference between the minimum and maximum class boundaries for a particular class, which, for the class 22, is $21.5 - 22.5 = 1.0$. Often the terms class and class interval are used synonomously; actually, however, a class interval is a representation of a class.

A decision regarding the choice of classes and class intervals is not always readily apparent. For example, consider the data shown in Table 2-2.

A histogram for these data is shown in Fig. 2-2. The classes in Fig. 2.2 are 28.5, 29.0, 29.5, ..., 40.0, and the class boundaries are 28.25, 28.75, 29.25, ..., 40.25. Figure 2-2 does not clearly show the significant features of the data because of the small class interval (.5). If classes 29.0, 30.5, 32.0, ..., 39.5 are used, Fig. 2-3 is the result; it presents a clearer picture of the data.

Separating the data into fewer classes is equivalent to a coarser rounding off of the data and results in a change of the identity of some of the original data, since the data takes on the values of the midpoints of the cell intervals. Consequently, the

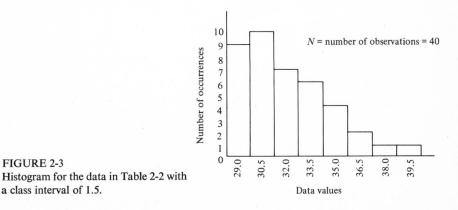

FIGURE 2-3
Histogram for the data in Table 2-2 with
a class interval of 1.5.

justification for saying Fig. 2-3 presents a clearer picture of the data lies in the assumption that those values "lost" in the process of using a larger cell interval are not repeatable; therefore, they are not representative of the underlying distribution.

There is no one best method for establishing the classes for a set of data. There are, however, certain rules of thumb which can be employed. One such rule is that the number of cell intervals should be from 8 to 20.

Classes should be chosen so that they agree with actual data. This tends to reduce errors when computing means and variances based on the frequency of values. Class boundaries should be chosen so that they do not coincide with actual data. Otherwise, problems can occur regarding the class in which a particular value should be placed.

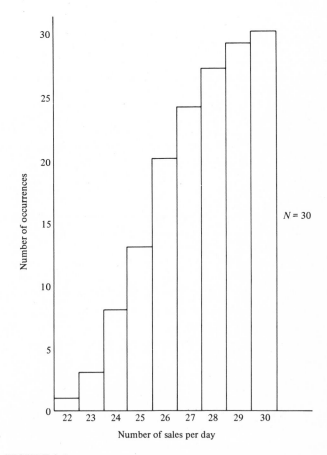

FIGURE 2-4
Cumulative frequency distribution of the number of sales per day.

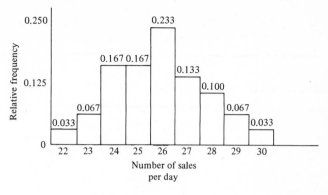

FIGURE 2-5
Relative frequency for the number of sales per day.

A cumulative frequency distribution is obtained by summing the number of occurrences in a particular class interval and the number of occurrences in all lower class intervals. This is shown in Fig. 2-4. It indicates, for example, that the number of times that sales per day were 24 or less was 8.

It is usual to convert frequency distributions into relative frequency distributions. This is accomplished by dividing the frequency of occurrences in a particular class by the total frequency of all classes. Examples of relative frequency distributions, using the data given in Table 2-1, are shown in Figs. 2-5 and 2-6.

Relative frequencies of occurrences are often interpreted in OR work as probabilities of occurrences, provided, of course, that past data are believed to predict future performance adequately. For example, the probability is .167 that the number of sales in any one day is 24 units (Fig. 2-5), and the probability is .800 (Fig. 2-6) that the number of sales in any one day is 27 or less.

Another use of a frequency distribution is to see whether the actual data can be approximated by a theoretical probability distribution, i.e., normal, Poisson, exponential, etc. The use of a theoretical distribution often makes further analysis easier.

In addition to the histogram, other measures are used to describe a mass of data. Two of these measures are central tendency and dispersion.

Central Tendency

Three common measures of central tendency are the mean, median, and mode. The mean (expected value, expectation, or average) is mathematically defined by

$$\mu = \frac{\Sigma x}{n} = \frac{x_1 + x_2 + \cdots + x_n}{n} \qquad (2\text{-}1)$$

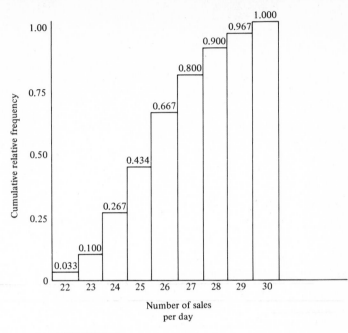

FIGURE 2-6
Cumulative relative frequency for the number of sales per day.

The mean of the data given in Table 2-1 is

$$\mu = \frac{26 + 28 + 24 + \cdots + 23}{30} = \frac{775}{30} = 25.8$$

The median is the middle value of a set of data arranged in order of magnitude. To determine the median of the data in Table 2-1, the first step is to arrange the data in the following order:

$$22, 23, 23, 24, 24, 24, 24, 24, \ldots, 30$$

Since there are 30 values, there is no clear-cut middle value.   Therefore, the median is the average of the two middle values, the fifteenth and sixteenth values in this case.   The median is $(26 + 26)/2 = 26$.   If there had been an odd number of values, the median would have been the middle value.

The mode is that value which occurs in a set of data with the greatest frequency. The mode for the data given in Table 2-1 is 26.   The mode is not necessarily unique, nor does it have to exist.   A set of data may have more than one mode, or it may have none.

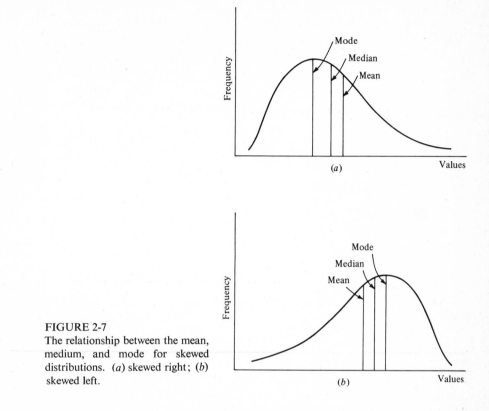

FIGURE 2-7
The relationship between the mean,
medium, and mode for skewed
distributions. (a) skewed right; (b)
skewed left.

In general, the mean, median, and mode are not the same. However, if a frequency distribution is symmetrical and decreases continuously from the center, e.g., the normal distribution, then the mean, median, and mode are the same. The approximate relationships between the three measures of central tendency for skewed distributions are shown in Fig. 2-7.

Dispersion

Three measures of dispersion are range, standard deviation, and variance. These measures describe the spread of a set of data. The range is merely the difference between the largest and smallest values in the data. One disadvantage of the range is that it does not consider the cluster of the data.

The most widely used measure of dispersion is the variance (or its square root, the standard deviation). The variance basically measures the mean squared deviations. Mathematically, the variance is defined as

$$\sigma^2 = \frac{\Sigma (x - \mu)^2}{n - 1} \qquad (2\text{-}2)$$

In some texts the denominator in Eq. (2-2) is replaced with n.   If the variance of a set of values is wanted, using n in the denominator is correct, but if the data are being used as an estimate of the variance of the population, the denominator should be $n - 1$. Since this is the usual situation in OR work, Eq. (2-2) will be used in this text unless otherwise noted.

The variance of the data given in Table 2-1 is

$$\sigma^2 = \frac{(22 - 25.8)^2 + (23 - 25.8)^2 + (23 - 25.8)^2 + \cdots + (30 - 25.8)^2}{30 - 1}$$

$$\sigma^2 = \frac{108.20}{29} = 3.73$$

and the standard deviation is

$$\sigma = \sqrt{3.73} = 1.93$$

PROBABILITY

Probability provides a means for mathematically expressing the degree of assurance or doubt of a chance event.   The probability of an event varies from 0 to 1.   An event with a probability of 0 is certain not to occur; an event with a probability of 1 is certain to occur.

Combinations and Permutations

For the solution of many probability problems, it is necessary to know how many different sets of r objects can be chosen from n objects or how many *ordered* sets of r objects can be chosen from n objects.   The first question is a combination problem and the second a permutation problem.   For example, consider a blue, a red, and a green pencil.   How many different combinations of two colors are possible from the three pencils?   The various combinations are red-green, green-blue, and blue-red, a total of three combinations.   It should be noted that the answer would be the same if the combination were listed as green-red, blue-green, and red-blue since in combinations the ordering of a set does not matter.   Mathematically, the number of combinations is

$$C_r^n = \frac{n!}{r!(n-r)!} \qquad (2\text{-}3)$$

where $n!$ is read "n factorial" and is equal to $(n)(n - 1)(n - 2) \cdots (1)$.   By definition, $0! = 1$. C_r^n is the number of combinations of n things taken r at a time.   In the pencil problem $n = 3$ and $r = 2$; therefore

$$C_2{}^3 = \frac{3!}{2!(3-2)!} = \frac{3!}{2!1!} = 3$$

Permutations are concerned with the order (arrangement) of sets.   In the pencil example there are six different ordered sets.   Mathematically, the number of different arrangements for n objects taken r at a time is

$$P_r'^n = \frac{n!}{(n-r)!} \qquad (2\text{-}4)$$

For the pencil problem, Eq. (2-4) gives

$$P_2{}^3 = \frac{3!}{(3-2)!} = 6$$

One method of distinguishing between combinations and permutations is to remember that when dealing with permutations n objects are being placed into r cells and one wants to find the number of different ways this can be accomplished.   It is also important that the significance of the word "different" be fully understood.   For example, if we want to find the number of different six-digit license plates that can be formed if the digits $0, 1, 2, \ldots, 9$ are used, there are six cells in which to place the digits 0 through 9.   If it is required that a different digit be located in each cell for each arrangement, the solution is

$$P_6{}^{10} = \frac{10!}{(10-6)!} = 151{,}200$$

However, if the repetition of digits is allowed, the solution is 10^6.   That is, there are 10 ways to put a digit in the first cell, 10 ways to put a digit in the second cell, etc. Consequently, it must be known whether repetitions are allowed in a permutation problem.   In certain types of permutation problems it is not necessary to state that repetitions are not allowed because of the nature of the objects being considered.   For example, the problem of determining the number of different ways nine people can be seated on a bench if only five people can sit on the bench at one time: obviously, one person can not be in two seats at the same time, implying that repetitions are not allowed.   Therefore, the solution is

$$P_5{}^9 = \frac{9!}{(9-5)!} = 15{,}120$$

Probability Theorems

In this section five basic probability theorems are reviewed.

Theorem 2-1   If A and B are two independent events with probabilities $P(A)$ and $P(B)$, then the probability that both events will occur is

$$P(A \text{ and } B) = [P(A)][P(B)] \qquad (2\text{-}5) \qquad ////$$

Theorem 2-2   If A and B are two dependent events, the probability that both the events will occur is the probability of the first multiplied by the probability that if the first has occurred, the second will also happen.

$$P(A \text{ and } B) = [P(A)][P(B \mid A)] \qquad (2\text{-}6)$$

where $P(B \mid A)$ is the probability of B given that A has occurred. $////$

As examples of Equations (2-5) and (2-6), consider an urn with six black and four white balls.   Suppose that two balls are drawn from an urn.   What is the probability that both are black!   If the balls are drawn one at a time and the first is replaced in the urn before drawing the second, then the events of drawing a black ball on the first draw and a black ball on the second draw are independent.   Consequently, Eq. (2-5) is applicable.

$$P(\text{black and black}) = \tfrac{6}{10}(\tfrac{6}{10}) = \tfrac{36}{100} = \tfrac{9}{25}$$

If the first ball is not replaced, the events are dependent and Eq. (2-6) gives the solution.

$$P(\text{black and black}) = \tfrac{6}{10}(\tfrac{5}{9}) = \tfrac{30}{90} = \tfrac{1}{3}$$

Theorem 2-3   If two independent events can occur simultaneously, the probability that either A or B or both A and B will occur is

$$P[A \text{ or } B \text{ or } (A \text{ and } B)] = P(A) + P(B) - [P(A)][P(B)] \qquad (2\text{-}7) \qquad ////$$

As an example, suppose the probability $P(A)$ that it will rain is .5 and the probability $P(B)$ that it will snow is .6.   What is the probability that it will rain, snow, or do both?   Since it is possible for it to rain and snow simultaneously, the answer is

$$P[A \text{ or } B \text{ or } (A \text{ and } B)] = .5 + .6 - .5\,(.6) = .8$$

Theorem 2-4   If two events are mutually exclusive, so that when one occurs the other cannot occur, the probability that A or B will occur is,

$$P(A \text{ or } B) = P(A) + P(B) \qquad (2\text{-}8) \qquad ////$$

Equation (2-8) is obtainable from Eq. (2-7) since the term $[P(A)][P(B)]$ is 0 if the events are mutually exclusive.

An urn has eight blue, four red, and three white balls. If one ball is drawn, what is the probability that the ball is either blue or red? In this problem the events are mutually exclusive. Therefore, using Eq. (2-8), the solution is

$$P(A \text{ or } B) = \tfrac{8}{15} + \tfrac{4}{15} = \tfrac{12}{15}$$

Theorem 2-5 If two events are complementary in addition to being mutually exclusive, i.e., if A does not occur, B must occur and vice versa, then the sum of the two events is 1:

$$P(A) + P(B) = 1 \qquad (2\text{-}9) \qquad ////$$

In the example of Theorem 2-4 if a blue or red ball is not drawn, then the ball drawn must be white. The probability of drawing a white ball is $\tfrac{3}{15}$. Therefore, the probability of the ball's being blue, red, or white is

$$\tfrac{12}{15} + \tfrac{3}{15} = 1.0$$

This theorem is often useful in calculating the probability of an event by calculating the probability that it will not occur and then subtracting from 1. In some types of probability problems, this approach makes calculations easier.

The two key phrases in applying the preceeding probability theorem are "independent events" and "mutually exclusive events." Events are independent, in a probability sense, when the occurrence of the event A in no way adds to our knowledge of the occurrence or nonoccurrence of event B. Events are mutually exclusive if the occurrence of event A makes the simultaneous occurrence of event B impossible.

PROBABILITY DISTRIBUTIONS

In this section some common probability distributions are reviewed. A probability distribution assigns a probability to every possible value of a random variable.

The Hypergeometric Distribution

The hypergeometric distribution is the most basic discrete probability distribution. It is applicable to the case of sampling without replacement. Consider a collection of N items, D having a certain property, and the remainder, $N - D$, not having this property. If a sample of n items is drawn without replacement, then the probability of exactly r events in the sample n is

$$P(r) = \frac{C_{n-r}^{N-D} C_r^{D}}{C_n^{N}} \qquad (2\text{-}10)$$

As an example, a bag has 20 balls; 15 are red, and 5 are white. If 3 balls are drawn together (or one at a time without replacement), what is the probability that exactly 2 balls are red? If the red balls are considered as those items having a certain property (their redness), then $D = 15$ and the solution is

$$P(r = 2) = \frac{C_{3-2}{}^{20-15} C_2{}^{15}}{C_3{}^{20}} = \frac{C_1{}^5 C_2{}^{15}}{C_3{}^{20}} = \frac{35}{76}$$

If replacement is used, i.e., a ball is drawn out, its colored noted, and then replaced, and this is done 3 times, then the probability of 2 red balls out of 3 draws is

$$P(r,r,w) + P(r,w,r) + P(w,r,r)$$

or

$$\tfrac{3}{4}(\tfrac{3}{4})(\tfrac{1}{4}) + \tfrac{3}{4}(\tfrac{1}{4})(\tfrac{3}{4}) + \tfrac{1}{4}(\tfrac{3}{4})(\tfrac{3}{4}) = \tfrac{27}{64}$$

In this case the probability of an event (drawing a red ball) is a constant ($\tfrac{3}{4}$). Consequently, the binomial distribution (discussed next) can be used to solve this case.

The Binomial Distribution

The binomial distribution is a discrete distribution described by the relationship

$$P(r) = C_r{}^n p^r q^{n-r} \qquad (2\text{-}11)$$

where

   $P(r)$ = probability of exactly r events in n finite independent trials
   p = probability of event in one trial
   $q = 1 - p$ = probability event will not occur

In order to be theoretically correct in the use of this distribution, p must be a constant. This condition can be satisfied by sampling from an infinite universe or replacing in the universe each sampled unit.

   The mean and variance of the binomial distribution are np and npq respectively.

   As an example, consider the case mentioned in the discussion of the hypergeometric distribution, where the ball was replaced after each trial. The probability in this case of drawing a red ball in one trial is a constant:

$$p = \tfrac{15}{20} = \tfrac{3}{4}$$

Therefore, using Eq. (2-11), the probability of two red balls in three draws is

$$P(r = 2) = C_2{}^3 (\tfrac{3}{4})^2 (\tfrac{1}{4}) = \tfrac{27}{64}$$

For another example, consider a manufacturing situation where the probability of an item's being defective is .05.   If a sample of 10 items is taken, the probability of fewer than three defectives in a sample is

$$P(r < 3) = P(r = 0) + P(r = 1) + P(r = 2)$$

Therefore,

$$P(r < 3) = C_0{}^{10}(.05)^0(.95)^{10} + C_1{}^{10}(.05)^1(.95)^9 + C_2{}^{10}(.05)^2(.95)^8 = .988$$

The Poisson Distribution

The Poisson distribution is a discrete distribution used in probability situations where the area of opportunity for the occurrence of an event is large but the probability of an occurrence in a particular interval or at a particular point is very small.   Some of the traditional examples of practical situations where the Poisson distribution is considered applicable are the number of defects in a length of insulated wire, typing errors made by a secretarial force, imperfections in plate glass, industrial accidents, and arrivals in queuing models.

In each of these examples the area of opportunity is considered large but the probability of an occurrence at a point is considered small.   Mathematically, the probability of exactly r occurrences of an event, using a Poisson distribution, is

$$P(r) = \frac{(c')^r e^{-c'}}{r!} = \frac{(np)^r e^{-np}}{r!} \qquad 0 \le r \le \beta \qquad (2\text{-}12)$$

where c' is the mean and equal to np.   The variance is also c' or np.

As an example, consider a manufacturing process that produces sheets of glass where the average number of defects per sheet of glass is five ($c' = 5$).   The probability that a sheet of glass will have exactly six defects is

$$P(r = 6) = \frac{5^6 e^{-5}}{6!} = .146$$

Tables provided in Appendix A for evaluating Poisson probabilities give the probability of r occurrences or less (in Appendix A the letter c is used in place of r). To solve this example, the following values are obtained from Appendix A:

$$P(r \le 6) = .762$$
$$P(r \le 5) = .616$$

Therefore, the probability of exactly six defects is

$$P(r = 6) = .762 - .616 = .146$$

Under certain circumstances, discussed later in this chapter, the Poisson distribution can be used to approximate the binomial distribution.

For example, in the discussion of the binomial distribution the probability of fewer than three defectives in a sample of 10 was found to be .988 when the probability of one item's being defective was .05. If a Poisson approximation is used for this same example, the result is

$$np = 10(.05) = .5$$

$$r = 2$$

$$P(r \leq 2) = .986$$

The Normal Distribution

One of the most widely used is the normal distribution, sometimes referred to as the gaussian distribution, normal curve, or bell-shaped distribution. The normal distribution is continuous and symmetrical about the mean and extends from minus infinity to plus infinity. Mathematically, the probability density function (PDF) of the normal distribution is defined by

$$f(x) = \frac{1}{\sigma \sqrt{2\pi}} e^{-(x-\mu)^2/2\sigma^2}, \qquad -\infty < x < \infty \qquad (2\text{-}13)$$

where $\pi = 3.141 \cdots$

$e = 2.718 \cdots$

$\mu = $ mean

$\sigma = $ standard deviation

The probability of a normally distributed random variable's being equal to or less than a is the area under the normal curve from $-\infty$ to a, as shown in Fig. 2-8. Mathematically, this probability is given by

$$P(x \leq a) = \int_{-\infty}^{a} \frac{1}{\sigma \sqrt{2\pi}} e^{-(x-\mu)^2/2\sigma^2} \, dx \qquad (2\text{-}14)$$

Similarly, the probability of a normally distributed random variable's being greater than a is

$$P(x > a) = 1 - P(x \leq a) = \int_{a}^{\infty} \frac{1}{\sigma \sqrt{2\pi}} e^{-(x-\mu)^2/2\sigma^2} \, dx \qquad (2\text{-}15)$$

Since the integration implied in Eq. (2-14) and (2-15) cannot be done directly, tables are used to determine areas under the normal curve. A set of these tables is given in Appendix B, based on a mean of 0 and a standard deviation of 1, which is

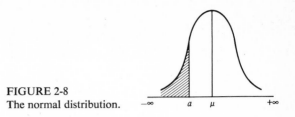

FIGURE 2-8
The normal distribution.

often referred to as the *standard form* of the normal distribution. Since, in most cases, the mean will not be 0 and the standard deviation 1, a transformation must be made. This is accomplished by the relationship (called the *standard normal variate*)

$$Z_\alpha = \frac{x - \mu}{\sigma} \qquad (2\text{-}16)$$

For example, a normal distribution has a mean of 20 and a standard deviation of 8. It is required to find the probability of a value less than 14. The formula for the normal variate gives

$$Z_\alpha = \frac{14 - 20}{8} = -.75$$

Therefore, $\alpha = .2266$.

The value $\alpha = .2266$ can also be interpreted as the proportion of values less than 14.

Rectangular Distributions

The rectangular (uniform) distribution may be either discrete or continuous. It applies to situations where the probabilities of all outcomes are equal.

In the continuous case, the PDF is

$$f(x) = \frac{1}{b - a} \qquad a \le x \le b \qquad (2\text{-}17)$$

This situation is shown in Fig. 2-9. The mean and variance for the continuous uniform distribution are $(a + b)/2$ and $(b - a)^2/12$, respectively.

In the discrete case, the PDF is

$$f(x) = \frac{1}{n + 1} \qquad \text{for } x = a, a + 1, a + 2, \ldots, a + (n - 1), a + n$$

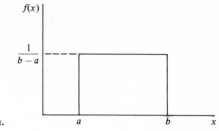

FIGURE 2-9
Rectangular distribution.

The mean and variance are

$$E(x) = a + \frac{n}{2} \qquad (2\text{-}18)$$

$$\sigma^2 = \frac{n(n + 2)}{12} \qquad (2\text{-}19)$$

As an example of the discrete case consider a random variable that can have only the values 3, 4, 5, 6, and 7.   In this example $a = 3$ and $n = 4$.   Therefore the mean is

$$E(x) = 3 + \tfrac{4}{2} = 5$$

and the variance is

$$\sigma^2 = \frac{4(4 + 2)}{12} = 2$$

The probability that a random variable will have a particular value is the same for all values.   In this example, the probability is

$$f(x) = \frac{1}{n + 1} = \frac{1}{4 + 1} = .20$$

The Exponential Distribution

The exponential distribution is a continuous distribution that is often used in operations research and reliability studies.   The PDF for the exponential distribution is given by

$$f(x) = \frac{1}{\mu} e^{-x/\mu} \qquad 0 \leq x \leq \infty \qquad (2\text{-}20)$$

This form of exponential distribution is referred to more specifically as the negative exponential distribution and in this form is often used to describe service times in queuing models.   If Eq. (2-20) is integrated between the limits 0 and x, the result is the cumulative distribution function, CDF, which is

$$\text{CDF} = F(x) = 1 - e^{-x/\mu} \qquad (2\text{-}21)$$

The mean and standard deviation of the exponential distribution are both μ.

As an example, suppose the mean service time for a unit is 2 hours and we want to find the probability of a service time of less than 3 hours.   Using Eq. (2-21), we get

$$P(x \le 3) = 1 - e^{-3/2} = 1 - e^{-1.5} = .777$$

APPROXIMATIONS

Under certain conditions probability problems can be solved by approximating the theoretically correct distribution with another distribution.   For example, a sample of 5 is taken, without replacement, from a lot of 100 items having 10 defectives.   The probability of exactly 2 defectives is

$$P(r = 2) = \frac{C_{5-2}{}^{100-10}C_5{}^{10}}{C_5{}^{100}} = .0702$$

This answer is based on a hypergeometric distribution and is the theoretically correct answer.   An approximate solution to the same problem is possible by using a binomial distribution.   For approximation purposes, the probability of an event (probability of drawing one defective in one trial) is considered a constant equal to

$$p = \frac{10}{100} = .10$$

Thus, a binomial approximation gives

$$P(r = 2) = C_2{}^5(.1)^2(.9)^3 = .0729$$

The same problem can be approximated using a Poisson distribution:

$$np = 5(.1) = .5$$
$$c = 2$$
$$P(r \le 2) = .986$$
$$np = 5(.1) = .5$$
$$c = 1$$
$$P(r \le 1) = .910$$
$$P(r = 2) = .986 - .910 = .0760$$

A normal approximation is also possible, but since the normal approximation is a continuous distribution, an adjustment must be made.   The usual adjustment is to consider the area under the normal curve from 1.5 to 2.5 as an estimate of the probability of exactly two defectives.   The area from $-\infty$ to 1.5 is

$$Z_\alpha = \frac{1.5 - 5(.1)}{\sqrt{5(.1)(.9)}} = 1.49$$

$$\alpha = .9319$$

and the area from $-\infty$ to 2.5 is

$$Z_\alpha = \frac{2.5 - 5(.1)}{\sqrt{5(.1)(.9)}} = 2.98$$

$$\alpha = .9986$$

Therefore, a normal approximation is

$$P(r = 2) = .9986 - .9319 = .0667$$

If the probability of two or more defectives in the sample is required, the answer is $1 - .9319 = .0681$ using a normal approximation. If the probability of two or fewer defectives is required, the answer is .9986.

The question that now occurs is: Under what conditions are the approximations satisfactory? The answer to this question is summarized in following statements.

1 The hypergeometric distribution can be approximated by the binomial distribution if the universe is large relative to the sample size.
2 The binomial or hypergeometric distribution can be approximated by the Poisson if the sample size is large, p is small, and $np < 5$.
3 The binomial or hypergeometric distributions can be approximated by the normal if p is close to .5 or the sample size is large $(n > 50)$ and $.20 < p < .80$.

Obviously, the greater the deviations from these conditions the greater the error in the approximation.

SOME THEOREMS FOR RANDOM VARIABLES

The following basic theorems for random variables are very useful in operations research.

Theorem 2-6 The expected value of a sum of random variables μ_T is the sum of the individual expected values. Mathematically, this theorem is expressed as

$$E(x_1 + x_2 + \cdots + x_n) = \mu_T = \sum_{i=1}^{n} \mu_i \qquad (2\text{-}22)$$

where $x_1, x_2, \ldots, x_n$ are the random variables and μ_i is the mean of the ith random variable.   ////

This theorem is true for both independent and dependent random variables.

Theorem 2-7 The variance of a sum of random variables, $\sigma_T^{\,2}$ is

$$V(x_1 + x_2 + \cdots + x_3) = \sigma_T^{\,2} = \sum_{i=1}^{n} \sigma_i^{\,2} + 2\sum_{i=1}^{n-1} \sum_{j=i+1}^{n} \sigma_{ij} \qquad (2\text{-}23)$$

where σ_i^2 is the variance of the ith random variable and σ_{ij} are the covariance terms.   ////

As an example of the expansion of Eq. (2-23), the variance of four random variables is

$$\sigma_T^2 = \sigma_1^2 + \sigma_2^2 + \sigma_3^2 + \sigma_4^2 + 2\sigma_{12} + 2\sigma_{13} + 2\sigma_{14} + 2\sigma_{23} + 2\sigma_{24} + 2\sigma_{34}$$

The covariance terms can be expressed as

$$\text{cov}\,(x_i, x_j) = \sigma_{ij} = E(x_i x_j) - E(x_i)E(x_j) \qquad (2\text{-}24)$$

A substitution often made for covariance terms is

$$\sigma_{ij} = r_{ij}\sigma_i\sigma_j \qquad (2\text{-}25)$$

where r_{ij} is the correlation coefficient for the random variables x_i and x_j. Covariance terms are 0 if the random variables are independent.

Theorem 2-8 If a random variable x with a mean μ_x is multiplied by a constant k to give the random variable $y = kx$, then the mean μy of y is

$$\mu_y = k\mu_x \qquad (2\text{-}26) \qquad ////$$

Theorem 2-9 If a random variable x with a variance of σ_x^2 is multiplied by a constant k to give the random variable $y = kx$, then the variance σ_y^2 of y is

$$\sigma_y^2 = k^2\sigma_x^2 \qquad (2\text{-}27) \qquad ////$$

In general, the preceding theorems provide an answer only for the mean and variance of the random variables. They do not provide any information about the form of the resulting probability distribution of the random variable. For the answer to this question, one must use statistical concepts beyond the scope of this book. However, in certain cases, the probability distribution resulting from the sum of random variables has been determined. For example, if independent normally distributed variables are added, the sum is normally distributed. Similar statements are also true for the binomial, chi-squared, and Poisson distributions. In addition to these statements, the central-limit theorem also provides some knowledge about the distribution resulting from the addition of random variables.

Central-Limit Theorem

The central-limit theorem is of considerable theoretical and practical significance. It says that the distribution of the sum of identically distributed independent random variables, each having a mean and finite variance, approaches the normal distribution as the number of variables becomes infinite.   The condition that the random variables be identically distributed is not essential as long as a particular few of the random variables do not dominate the sum.   This implies that the sum of a large number of random variables will be approximately normal regardless of the distribution of the individual random variables.

As an example of the use of these theorems, consider the following problem. The monthly sales of a certain product have been found to be normally distributed with a mean of 1,000 units and a standard deviation of 120 units.   Assuming that the distribution of sales for each month is the same but independent, determine the probability of yearly sales being less than 12,600 units.   From Theorems 2-6 and 2-7, the expected yearly sales are

$$\mu_T = \sum_{i=1}^{12} \mu_i = 12(1,000) = 12,000$$

and the variance is

$$\sigma_T{}^2 = \sum_{i=1}^{12} \sigma_i{}^2 = 12(120)^2 = 172,800$$

Therefore, the probability of a yearly demand less than 12,600 units is

$$Z_\alpha = \frac{12,600 - 12,000}{\sqrt{172,800}} = \frac{600}{415} = 1.45$$

$$\alpha = .9265$$

Suppose the selling price of 1 unit is $200 and we want to determine the probability of a monthly income of less than $180,000.   Using Theorems 2-8 and 2-9, we find the expected monthly income and variance to be

$$\mu = 200(1,000) = \$200,000$$
$$\sigma^2 = 200^2(120)^2 = 576 \times 10^6$$

The probability of a monthly income less than $180,000 is

$$Z_\alpha = \frac{180,000 - 200,000}{\sqrt{576 \times 10^6}} = \frac{-20,000}{24,000} \doteq -.83$$

$$\alpha = .2033$$

REFERENCES

1 AIGNER, D. J.: "Principles of Statistical Decision Making," The Macmillan Company, New York, 1968.

2 HAHN, G. J., and S. S. SHAPIRO: "Statistical Models in Engineering," John Wiley & Sons, Inc., New York, 1967.

3 LINDGREN, B. W., and G. W. MCELRATH: "Probability and Statistics," The Macmillan Company, New York, 1959.

4 MOSTELLER, F., R. E. K. ROURKE, and G. B. THOMAS: "Probability with Statistical Applications," Addison-Wesley Publishing Company, Inc., Reading, Mass., 1961.

5 SCHLAIFER, R., "Probability and Statistics for Business Decisions," McGraw-Hill Book Company, New York, 1959.

PROBLEMS

2-1 The tabulated data show the weight in pounds of a sample of 42 items manufactured by a company.

(*a*) Plot a histogram of the data using a class interval of .03; use 7.25 as the midpoint of the first class interval.

(*b*) Plot a relative frequency distribution for the data.

(*c*) Plot a relative cumulative frequency distribution for the data.

(*d*) Estimate the mean and standard deviation of the universe using the data.

DATA

7.29	7.31	7.36	7.31	7.35	7.32	7.48
7.37	7.32	7.28	7.36	7.32	7.37	7.33
7.36	7.35	7.34	7.33	7.26	7.33	7.38
7.30	7.25	7.35	7.34	7.40	7.40	7.27
7.32	7.42	7.39	7.41	7.44	7.30	7.36
7.37	7.43	7.28	7.39	7.35	7.29	7.41

2-2 What are the median and mode of the *data* given in Prob. 2-1?

2-3 Using the results of Prob. 2-1, answer the following questions:

(*a*) What is the probability that the weight of an item is 7.30?

(*b*) What is the probability that the weight of an item is 7.35 or less?

(*c*) What is the probability that the weight of an item is 7.36 or greater?

2-4 Evaluate the following:

(*a*) $C_2{}^6$

(*b*) $P_2{}^6$

(*c*) $P_3{}^8$

(*d*) $C_4{}^7$

(*e*) If $P_4{}^n = 5{,}040$, find $C_4{}^n$.

(*f*) If $C_4{}^n = 70$, find $P_4{}^n$.

2-5 Determine whether each of the following is a combination or permutation problem and solve.

(*a*) In how many different ways can seven books be arranged in a bookcase if there is room for only five books?

(*b*) How many ways can a different committee of five people be formed from ten people available?

(*c*) How many different hands of 13 cards can be dealt from a pack of 52 different cards?

(*d*) In how many ways can a committee of three Democrats and two Republicans be selected from a group of seven Democrats and six Republicans?

2-6 How many different sums can be formed from the digits 5, 8, 3, 6 using any number of digits at a time?

2-7   A bookshelf has space for six books.   There are five different mathematics books and six different English books.   If three mathematics books and three English books are placed on the shelf, how many arrangements are possible keeping all mathematics and English books together?

2-8   If each symbol consists of three letters in succession, how many different symbols can be formed using the letters a, b, c, d, e, f if:

(*a*) No letter can be repeated in the same symbol?

(*b*) Repetitions are allowed?

2-9   Considering the network shown, determine the number of paths from point *A* to point *B*, each path being of the smallest possible length.

PROB. 2-9   *A*

2-10   A machine consist of two parts, *A* and *B*.   If either part fails, the machine fails.   If the probability that part *A* will fail is .2 and the probability that part *B* will fail is .3:

(*a*) What is the probability that the machine will fail?

(*b*) What is the probability that the machine will fail due to the failure of part *A* alone? *B* alone?

(*c*) What is the probability that the machine will fail due to the failure of either part?

(*d*) What is the probability that both parts will fail together?

2-11   Two bags contain the distribution of balls shown.

Bag 1	Bag 2
10 black 6 white	7 black 4 orange 3 white

(*a*) If two balls are taken from bag 2, what is the probability that the first is black and the second orange?

(*b*) If one ball is taken from each bag, what is the probability that of the two balls, one is black and one is white?

(*c*) If two balls are taken from each bag, what is the probability that of the four balls three are black and one is white?

2-12   Suppose one of the bags in Prob. 2-11 is chosen at random and then two balls are taken from the selected bag.   What is the probability that both balls will be white?

2-13   In a multiple-choice test, each question is to be answered by selecting one out of four different proposed answers, only one of which is correct.   If there are 10 questions on the test, what is the probability of:

(*a*) Getting a grade of exactly 60 percent by pure guesswork?

(*b*) Getting a grade of at least 60 percent by pure guesswork?

(*c*) Getting a grade of less than 60 percent by pure guesswork?

2-14   If a random variable is normally distributed with a mean of 4.63 and a standard deviation of .86, determine:
(a) The probability of a value of 3.52 or less.
(b) The probability of a value of 4.50 or greater.
(c) The probability of a value of between 3.52 and 4.50.
(d) If 500 values of these are considered, how many would you expect to be between 4.63 and 4.80?

2-15   The number of units sold in a day is normally distributed with a mean of 120 units and a standard deviation of 16 units.   How many units should be on hand at the beginning of the day for the probability of a shortage (no units available for sale) to be .10?

2-16   If a random variable is Poisson distributed with a mean of 5.2, determine:
(a) The probability that the random variable will have a value of 4 or less.
(b) The probability that the random variable will have a value of exactly 5.
(c) The probability that the random variable will have a value greater than 6.
(d) The standard deviation of this random variable.

2-17   A bag contains a total of 100 balls. If 10 balls are black and the remaining 90 balls are white and a sample of 15 balls is taken, determine:
(a) The probability of one or two black balls in a sample using the hypergeometric distribution.
(b) Repeat part (a) using a binomial approximation.
(c) Repeat part (a) using a Poisson approximation.
(d) Repeat part (a) using a normal approximation.

2-18   If a random variable is exponentially distributed with a mean of 4, determine:
(a) The variance of the random variable.
(b) The probability of a value of 4 or less.
(c) The probability of a value greater than 6.

2-19   Adjust Eqs. (2-18) and (2-19) to take care of the case $x = a$, $a + k$, $a + 2k$, $a + 3k$, $\ldots$, $a + (n - 1)k$, $a + nk$, where k is the cell interval.   From your results, what is the mean for 20, 25, 30, 35, 40, 45, 50?

2-20   The distribution of two random variables, x and y, is tabulated.   Use these data to solve the following problems:

Random variable x	Random variable y
30	5
20	17
20	11
10	14
40	20
30	14
50	8
30	8
40	14
10	21
40	11

(a) Using the random variable x and a constant of 5, show that Eq. (2-26) and (2-27) are correct.

(b) Show that Eqs. (2-22) and (2-23) are correct. (Note that these variables are not necessarily independent.)

(c) Reverse the random variable y to 11, 21, 14, ..., 5 and repeat part (b).

(d) Explain any differences that occur in the results of parts (b) and (c).

2-21 A company sells products A, B, and C. The demands for these three products are independent and normally distributed with the means and standard deviations tabulated.

Product	Mean units/year	Standard deviation, units/year
A	10,000	2,000
B	20,000	4,000
C	15,000	3,000

(a) What is the probability that the demand for all three products will be greater than 50,000 units in a year?

(b) If the selling price for 1 unit of product A is $60, what is the probability that the income from the sale of product A will be less than $450,000 in a year?

(c) If the selling prices for products A, B, and C are $60, $50, and $20 per unit, respectively, what is the probability that the yearly income from the sale of all three products will be less than $2,200,000?

3

MATRIX ALGEBRA APPLIED TO SYSTEMS OF LINEAR EQUATIONS

INTRODUCTION

This chapter is concerned with the application of matrix algebra to systems of linear equations, especially as this concept is used in such OR topics as linear programming and Markov chains. As a result, concepts of linear algebra which are more often applied in other fields of mathematics are skimmed over or omitted. Treatment of these topics will be found in the references. With regard to systems of linear equations, matrix algebra is a convenient way of handling large amounts of data, allowing rapid addition, subtraction, multiplication, and (in a loose sense) division. These manipulations can be used to solve sets of linear equations, thus the matrix algebra.

PHYSICAL CONCEPT OF VECTORS AND MATRICES

Matrices and vectors present data in a condensed form. Suppose that a plant manager tabulates the materials required to make 1 unit of a product:

$$\text{Product } A \begin{cases} \text{Steel} = 5 \text{ lb} \\ \text{Castings} = 10 \text{ lb} \\ \text{Bolts} = 30 \text{ units} \end{cases}$$

These data can be presented in a more condensed form by grouping and omitting the units.

$$\begin{matrix} \text{Steel} \\ \text{Castings} \\ \text{Bolts} \end{matrix} \begin{bmatrix} 5 \\ 10 \\ 30 \end{bmatrix}$$

In this form the data are referred to as a *vector* (actually a column vector since it is in column form).   This column vector is a 3×1 vector since it has 3 rows (data elements) and only 1 column.   All vectors and matrices are described in this manner, rows $\times$ columns.   If the type of material is represented by y_i, that is, y_1 = steel, y_2 = castings, and y_3 = bolts, and if the amount needed is represented by b_i, where $b_1 = 5$, $b_2 = 10$, and $b_3 = 30$, the example becomes

$$\begin{bmatrix} y_1 \\ y_2 \\ y_3 \end{bmatrix} = \begin{bmatrix} b_1 \\ b_2 \\ b_3 \end{bmatrix}$$

Suppose the plant makes four products, *A, B, C, D*, each requiring different amounts of these three materials.   The plant manager tabulates the steel requirements for each product.

	A	B	C	D
Steel required	5 lb	7 lb	10 lb	3 lb

These data can be rewritten as a row vector.

$$\text{Steel required} = \begin{bmatrix} 5 & 7 & 10 & 3 \end{bmatrix}$$

This is a 1×4 row vector since it is a single row having 4 elements, or columns.

If the material requirements for all products are tabulated, the result is a 3×4 matrix, i.e., a matrix of 3 rows and 4 columns.

$$\begin{matrix} \text{Steel} \\ \text{Castings} \\ \text{Bolts} \end{matrix} \begin{bmatrix} 5 & 7 & 10 & 3 \\ 10 & 9 & 12 & 5 \\ 30 & 22 & 40 & 15 \end{bmatrix}$$

In condensed form this becomes

$$\text{requirements/unit} = \begin{bmatrix} 5 & 7 & 10 & 3 \\ 10 & 9 & 12 & 5 \\ 30 & 22 & 40 & 15 \end{bmatrix}$$

Vectors are viewed a special type of matrix.   Thus a row vector is simply a $1 \times n$ matrix having 1 row and n columns.   A column vector is a $m \times 1$ matrix having m rows and only 1 column.   A matrix having m rows and n columns is called an $m \times n$ matrix.

EXAMPLE 3-1 [2 6 3 9 4 5] is a row vector of six components, or a 1 × 6 matrix.

$$\begin{bmatrix} 5 \\ 4 \\ 3 \\ 2 \end{bmatrix}$$ is a column vector or a 4 × 1 matrix.

$$\begin{bmatrix} 2 & 9 & 14 & -7 & 3 \\ 6 & 15 & 0 & 1 & 2 \\ -3 & 7 & 4 & 12 & 6 \end{bmatrix}$$ is a 3 × 5 matrix.   ////

The size of a vector or matrix is indicated by its order.   Thus the last matrix in Example 3-1 is of 3 × 5 order.   The order or size is indicated by first noting the number of rows and then the number of columns.

$$\text{Order} = \text{rows} \times \text{columns}$$

A square matrix has as many rows as columns.   A square matrix having n rows and columns is of nth order.

Matrices and vectors are a means of displaying data in a convenient, condensed form.   Actually the data displayed in this manner may be either numeric or symbolic but they still have the same meaning.   The data may represent units of weight, dimension, dollars, people, velocities, forces, a mathematical constant, or even some undefined variable x or y.

MATRIX MANIPULATIONS

Addition and Subtraction

Addition and/or subtraction can be performed on vectors or matrices in two ways: (1) by adding or subtracting a constant to the matrix or vector and (2) by adding or subtracting two matrices or vectors.

Adding a constant, called a scalar, to a vector simply means adding the same constant to every data element in the vector:

$$2 + \begin{bmatrix} 3 \\ 4 \\ -1 \\ 1 \end{bmatrix} = \begin{bmatrix} 3+2 \\ 4+2 \\ -1+2 \\ 1+2 \end{bmatrix} = \begin{bmatrix} 5 \\ 6 \\ 1 \\ 3 \end{bmatrix} \tag{3-1}$$

$$2 + [5 \quad 0 \quad -3 \quad 10] = [7 \quad 2 \quad -1 \quad 12] \tag{3-2}$$

Subtraction occurs in the same manner.

$$\begin{bmatrix} 3 \\ 4 \\ -1 \\ 1 \end{bmatrix} - 2 = \begin{bmatrix} 1 \\ 2 \\ -3 \\ -1 \end{bmatrix} \qquad (3\text{-}3)$$

$$[5 \quad 0 \quad -3 \quad 10] - 2 = [3 \quad -2 \quad -5 \quad 8] \qquad (3\text{-}4)$$

This actually is accomplished by adding two vectors together, where one vector is composed entirely of 2s:

$$\begin{bmatrix} 2 \\ 2 \\ 2 \\ 2 \end{bmatrix} + \begin{bmatrix} 3 \\ 4 \\ -1 \\ -1 \end{bmatrix} \text{ (see the discussion on the addition of vectors).}$$

The same process is used in adding or subtracting a constant and a matrix.

EXAMPLE 3-2   In these examples, [2] and [a] stand for a 2 × 2 matrix of all 2s or a's.

$$[2] + \begin{bmatrix} 3 & -1 \\ 0 & 4 \end{bmatrix} = \begin{bmatrix} 5 & 1 \\ 2 & 6 \end{bmatrix}$$

$$\begin{bmatrix} 3 & -1 \\ 0 & 4 \end{bmatrix} - [2] = \begin{bmatrix} 1 & -3 \\ -2 & 2 \end{bmatrix}$$

$$[a] + \begin{bmatrix} 15 & 6 \\ b & -3 \end{bmatrix} = \begin{bmatrix} 15+a & 6+a \\ b+a & -3+a \end{bmatrix} \qquad ////$$

Vectors can be added or subtracted like matrices, but they *must* both be of the same order. That is, only a 1 × 5 row vector can be added to another 1 × 5 row vector. Only a 5 × 7 matrix can be added to another 5 × 7 matrix. In adding two vectors of the same order, each element of one vector is added to the corresponding element of the other vector. The same rules apply to matrices.

$$\begin{bmatrix} 14 \\ -5 \\ 7 \\ 1 \\ 4 \end{bmatrix} + \begin{bmatrix} 3 \\ 9 \\ -5 \\ 0 \\ -9 \end{bmatrix} = \begin{bmatrix} 17 \\ 4 \\ 2 \\ 1 \\ -5 \end{bmatrix} \qquad (3\text{-}5)$$

$$\begin{bmatrix} 14 \\ -5 \\ 7 \\ 1 \\ 4 \end{bmatrix} - \begin{bmatrix} 3 \\ 9 \\ -5 \\ 0 \\ 9 \end{bmatrix} = \begin{bmatrix} 11 \\ -14 \\ 12 \\ 1 \\ -5 \end{bmatrix} \qquad (3\text{-}6)$$

$$[a \quad 17 \quad -4 \quad 35 \quad 3] + [16 \quad -21 \quad -b \quad 0 \quad 8] = [a + 16 \quad -4 \quad -4 - b \quad 35 \quad 11]$$

(3-7)

$$[a \quad 17 \quad -4 \quad 35 \quad 3] - [16 \quad -21 \quad -b \quad 0 \quad 8] = [a - 16 \quad 38 \quad -4 + b \quad 35 \quad -5]$$

(3-8)

$$\begin{bmatrix} 8 & 3 \\ 14 & 27 \\ 6 & -15 \end{bmatrix} + \begin{bmatrix} 14 & -1 \\ 7 & 4 \\ -8 & 0 \end{bmatrix} = \begin{bmatrix} 22 & 2 \\ 21 & 31 \\ -2 & -15 \end{bmatrix}$$

(3-9)

$$\begin{bmatrix} 8 & 3 \\ 14 & 27 \\ 6 & -15 \end{bmatrix} - \begin{bmatrix} 14 & -1 \\ 7 & 4 \\ -8 & 0 \end{bmatrix} = \begin{bmatrix} -6 & 4 \\ 7 & 23 \\ 14 & -15 \end{bmatrix}$$

(3-10)

$$\begin{bmatrix} a & b & c \\ d & e & f \end{bmatrix} + \begin{bmatrix} e & m & m \\ 0 & p & q \end{bmatrix} = \begin{bmatrix} a+e & b+m & c+m \\ d+0 & e+p & f+q \end{bmatrix}$$

(3-11)

$$\begin{bmatrix} a & b & c \\ d & e & f \end{bmatrix} - \begin{bmatrix} e & m & n \\ 0 & p & q \end{bmatrix} = \begin{bmatrix} a-e & b-m & c-n \\ d-0 & e-p & f-q \end{bmatrix}$$

(3-12)

$$[3 \quad 4 \quad 0] + \begin{bmatrix} 4 \\ 5 \\ 2 \end{bmatrix} \qquad \text{not possible}$$

(3-13)

$$[3 \quad 4 \quad 0] + [4 \quad 5 \quad 2 \quad 7] \qquad \text{not possible}$$

(3-14)

$$\begin{bmatrix} 8 & 3 \\ 14 & 27 \end{bmatrix} + \begin{bmatrix} 14 & -1 \\ 7 & 4 \\ -8 & 0 \end{bmatrix} \qquad \text{not possible}$$

(3-15)

Multiplication

Matrices and vectors can be multiplied but with somewhat more restrictions. As an illustration, the plant manager's data will be extended. Recall that the data matrix used to display the material requirements for each of the four products made consisted of the following 3×4 matrix:

		Product		
Material	A	B	C	D
Steel	5	7	10	3
Castings	10	9	12	5
Bolts	30	22	40	15

Suppose that the daily production of each product is 100 units of A, 50 units of B, 80 units of C, and 200 units of D.   How much material should be supplied each day? This is an extremely simple problem in algebra.

Steel requirements = lb A × no. of A + lb B × no. of B
$\qquad$ + lb C × no. of C + lb D × no. of D

Castings requirement = lb A × no. of A + lb B + no. of B
$\qquad$ + lb C × no. of C + lb of D + no. of D

Bolt requirements = lb A × no. of A + lb B × no. of B
$\qquad$ + lb C × no. of C + lb D × no. of D.

Steel requirements = 5 × 100 + 7 × 50 + 10 × 80 + 3 × 200
$\qquad$ = 500 + 350 + 800 + 600
$\qquad$ = 2250 lb of steel

Castings requirements = 10 × 100 + 9 × 50 + 12 × 80 + 5 × 200
$\qquad$ = 1,000 + 450 + 960 + 1,000
$\qquad$ = 3,410 lb of castings

Bolt requirements = 30 × 100 + 22 × 50 + 40 × 80 + 15 × 200
$\qquad$ = 3,000 + 1,100 + 3,200 + 3,000
$\qquad$ = 10,300 bolts

The total requirements can then be expressed as a vector

$$\begin{matrix} \text{Steel} \\ \text{Casting} \\ \text{Bolts} \end{matrix} \begin{bmatrix} 2,250 \\ 3,410 \\ 10,300 \end{bmatrix}$$

This illustrates the basic procedures and restrictions required for matrix multiplication.

$$\begin{bmatrix} 5 & 7 & 10 & 3 \\ 10 & 9 & 12 & 5 \\ 30 & 22 & 40 & 15 \end{bmatrix} \begin{bmatrix} 100 \\ 50 \\ 80 \\ 200 \end{bmatrix} = \begin{bmatrix} 2,250 \\ 3,410 \\ 10,300 \end{bmatrix} \qquad (3\text{-}16)$$

Note that to obtain the steel requirements of 2,250 lb of steel, the top row in the matrix was multiplied by the column vector and the result summed.

$$[5 \quad 7 \quad 10 \quad 3] \begin{bmatrix} 100 \\ 50 \\ 80 \\ 200 \end{bmatrix} = (5 \times 100) + (7 \times 50) + (10 \times 80) + (3 \times 200) = 2,250 \quad (3\text{-}17)$$

In algebraic symbols this is represented as

$$[a \quad b \quad c \quad d]\begin{bmatrix} p \\ q \\ r \\ s \end{bmatrix} = (a \times p) + (b \times q) + (c \times r) + (d \times s) \qquad (3\text{-}18)$$

This illustrates the basic rule of matrix multiplication.   Two vectors may be multiplied only if the first, *a row vector*, contains as many columns as the second, *a column vector*, contains rows.   In other words, only a $1 \times n$ vector can be multiplied by a $n \times 1$ vector.   Some examples are presented below

$$[3 \quad 5 \quad 2]\begin{bmatrix} 4 \\ 9 \\ 1 \end{bmatrix} = (3 \times 4) + (5 \times 9) + (2 \times 1) = 59 \qquad \overset{\text{equal}}{1 \times 3 \times 3 \times 1}$$

$$[2 \quad 6]\begin{bmatrix} 5 \\ 4 \end{bmatrix} = (2 \times 5) + (6 \times 4) = 34 \qquad \overset{\text{equal}}{1 \times 2 \times 2 \times 1}$$

$$[3 \quad 1 \quad 5]\begin{bmatrix} 2 \\ 6 \end{bmatrix} \qquad \text{not possible} \qquad \overset{\text{not equal}}{1 \times 3 \times 2 \times 1}$$

Notice also that in the first two examples, the result has 1 row and 1 column, i.e., is a single number.   This fact will be referred to later in more detail.

When multiplying two matrices, the same basic rule applies; the first matrix must have as many *columns* as the second matrix has rows.   In this case the result will be another matrix instead of a single number.

EXAMPLE 3-3

$$\begin{bmatrix} 2 & 3 \\ 1 & 4 \end{bmatrix}\begin{bmatrix} 4 & 5 \\ 7 & 3 \end{bmatrix}$$

This may be thought of as the multiplication of two row vectors by two column vectors.

$$[2 \quad 3]\begin{bmatrix} 4 \\ 7 \end{bmatrix} = (2 \times 4) + (3 \times 7) = 29$$

$$[1 \quad 4]\begin{bmatrix} 4 \\ 7 \end{bmatrix} = (1 \times 4) + (4 \times 7) = 32$$

$$[2 \quad 3]\begin{bmatrix} 5 \\ 3 \end{bmatrix} = (2 \times 5) + (3 \times 3) = 19$$

$$[1 \quad 4]\begin{bmatrix} 5 \\ 3 \end{bmatrix} = (1 \times 5) + (4 \times 3) = 17$$

If each of these individual results is placed in a matrix in its correct position, the result is the product of the multiplication.

$$\begin{bmatrix} 2 & 3 \\ 1 & 4 \end{bmatrix}\begin{bmatrix} 4 & 5 \\ 7 & 3 \end{bmatrix} = \begin{bmatrix} 29 & 19 \\ 32 & 17 \end{bmatrix}$$

Note that the product of row 1 × column 1 gives the element (1,1) in the resultant matrix.   Similarly row 1 × column 2 gives the element (1,2), etc.   ////

EXAMPLE 3-4

$$\begin{bmatrix} 5 & 2 & 1 \\ 6 & 9 & -2 \\ 4 & -1 & 0 \end{bmatrix}\begin{bmatrix} -3 & 9 & 7 \\ 4 & 0 & 8 \\ 2 & -5 & 7 \end{bmatrix}$$

$$= \begin{bmatrix} (5 \times -3) + (2 \times 4) + (1 \times 2) & (5 \times 9) + (2 \times 0) + (1 \times -5) \\ (6 \times -3) + (9 \times 4) + (-2 \times 2) & (6 \times 9) + (9 \times 0) + (-2 \times -5) \\ (4 \times -3) + (-1 \times 4) + (0 \times 2) & (4 \times 9) + (-1 \times 0) + (0 \times -5) \end{bmatrix}$$

$$\begin{matrix} (5 \times 7) + (2 \times 8) + (1 \times 7) \\ (6 \times 7) + (9 \times 8) + (-2 \times 7) \\ (4 \times 7) + (-1 \times 8) + (0 \times 7) \end{matrix}$$

$$= \begin{bmatrix} -5 & 40 & 58 \\ 14 & 64 & 100 \\ -16 & 36 & 20 \end{bmatrix}$$ ////

The order of the two matrices gives the order of the product.   Thus, the product of a 2 × 3 and a 3 × 4 matrix will be matrix having 2 rows and 4 columns.

$$\overset{\text{equal}}{2 \times 3 \times 3 \times 4}$$
$$\text{Rows} \quad \text{Columns}$$

$$\begin{bmatrix} 2 & 7 & 3 \\ 7 & -8 & 1 \end{bmatrix}\begin{bmatrix} 4 & 2 & -3 & 6 \\ 5 & 6 & 4 & 0 \\ -1 & 0 & 9 & -4 \end{bmatrix}$$

$$= \begin{bmatrix} 8 + 35 - 3 & 4 + 42 + 0 & -6 + 28 + 27 & 12 + 0 - 12 \\ 28 - 40 - 1 & 14 - 48 + 0 & -21 - 32 + 9 & 42 - 0 - 4 \end{bmatrix}$$

$$= \begin{bmatrix} 40 & 46 & 49 & 0 \\ -13 & -34 & -44 & 38 \end{bmatrix} \qquad (3\text{-}19)$$

This means that it is possible for the product of two vectors to be a matrix.

$$\begin{bmatrix} 4 \\ 7 \end{bmatrix}\begin{bmatrix} 2 & 3 \end{bmatrix} = \begin{bmatrix} 4 \times 2 & 4 \times 3 \\ 7 \times 2 & 7 \times 3 \end{bmatrix} = \begin{bmatrix} 8 & 12 \\ 14 & 21 \end{bmatrix} \qquad (3\text{-}20)$$

$$\overset{\text{equal}}{2 \times 1 \quad 1 \times 2}$$
$$\text{Rows} \quad \text{Columns}$$

Similarly, the product of a matrix and a vector may either be a vector or a matrix, depending on the alignment of the multiplication

$$\begin{bmatrix} 4 \\ 7 \end{bmatrix}\begin{bmatrix} 4 & 5 \\ 7 & 3 \end{bmatrix} \qquad \text{not possible} \qquad 2 \times \overset{\text{not equal}}{1 \times 2} \times 2 \qquad (3\text{-}21)$$

$$[2 \quad 3]\begin{bmatrix} 4 & 5 \\ 7 & 3 \end{bmatrix} = [8 + 21 \quad 10 + 9] = [29 \quad 19] \qquad 1 \times \overset{\text{equal}}{2 \ \times \ 2} \times 2 \qquad (3\text{-}22)$$
$$\text{Rows} \quad \text{Columns}$$

$$\begin{bmatrix} 4 & 5 \\ 7 & 3 \end{bmatrix}\begin{bmatrix} 4 \\ 7 \end{bmatrix} = \begin{bmatrix} 16 + 35 \\ 28 + 21 \end{bmatrix} = \begin{bmatrix} 51 \\ 49 \end{bmatrix} \qquad 2 \times \overset{\text{equal}}{2 \ \times \ 2} \times 1 \qquad (3\text{-}23)$$
$$\text{Rows} \quad \text{Columns}$$

$$\begin{bmatrix} 4 & 5 \\ 7 & 3 \end{bmatrix}[2 \quad 3] \qquad \text{not possible} \qquad 2 \times \overset{\text{not equal}}{2 \times 1} \times 2 \qquad (3\text{-}24)$$

The student should verify the following statement:

$$\begin{bmatrix} 4 & 5 \\ 7 & 3 \end{bmatrix}\begin{bmatrix} 2 & 5 \\ -3 & 7 \end{bmatrix} \neq \begin{bmatrix} 2 & 5 \\ -3 & 7 \end{bmatrix}\begin{bmatrix} 4 & 5 \\ 7 & 3 \end{bmatrix}$$

EXAMPLE 3-5 Let $A = \begin{bmatrix} 2 & 3 \\ 4 & 1 \end{bmatrix}$ and $B = \begin{bmatrix} 1 & 0 \\ 3 & 2 \end{bmatrix}$.

$$AB = \begin{bmatrix} 2 & 3 \\ 4 & 1 \end{bmatrix}\begin{bmatrix} 1 & 0 \\ 3 & 2 \end{bmatrix} = \begin{bmatrix} 2+9 & 0+6 \\ 4+3 & 0+2 \end{bmatrix} = \begin{bmatrix} 11 & 6 \\ 7 & 2 \end{bmatrix}$$

$$BA = \begin{bmatrix} 1 & 0 \\ 3 & 2 \end{bmatrix}\begin{bmatrix} 2 & 3 \\ 4 & 1 \end{bmatrix} = \begin{bmatrix} 2+0 & 3+0 \\ 6+8 & 9+2 \end{bmatrix} = \begin{bmatrix} 2 & 3 \\ 14 & 11 \end{bmatrix}$$

and so

$$AB \neq BA$$

Let $C = \begin{bmatrix} 3 & 1 & 2 \\ 0 & 4 & 3 \end{bmatrix}$. Show that $(A + B)C = AC + BC$

$$\left(\begin{bmatrix} 2 & 3 \\ 4 & 1 \end{bmatrix} + \begin{bmatrix} 1 & 0 \\ 3 & 2 \end{bmatrix}\right)\begin{bmatrix} 3 & 1 & 2 \\ 0 & 4 & 3 \end{bmatrix} = \begin{bmatrix} 3 & 3 \\ 7 & 3 \end{bmatrix}\begin{bmatrix} 3 & 1 & 2 \\ 0 & 4 & 3 \end{bmatrix} = \begin{bmatrix} 9 & 15 & 15 \\ 21 & 19 & 23 \end{bmatrix}$$

$$\begin{bmatrix} 2 & 3 \\ 4 & 1 \end{bmatrix}\begin{bmatrix} 3 & 1 & 2 \\ 0 & 4 & 3 \end{bmatrix} + \begin{bmatrix} 1 & 0 \\ 3 & 2 \end{bmatrix}\begin{bmatrix} 3 & 1 & 2 \\ 0 & 4 & 3 \end{bmatrix}$$

$$= \begin{bmatrix} 6 & 14 & 13 \\ 12 & 8 & 11 \end{bmatrix} + \begin{bmatrix} 3 & 1 & 2 \\ 9 & 11 & 12 \end{bmatrix} = \begin{bmatrix} 9 & 15 & 15 \\ 21 & 19 & 23 \end{bmatrix}$$

Note again that CA or CB is not possible.
Let

$$L = \begin{bmatrix} 1 & 3 \\ 2 & 1 \end{bmatrix} \qquad M = \begin{bmatrix} 2 & 4 \\ 1 & 0 \end{bmatrix} \qquad N = \begin{bmatrix} 3 & 1 \\ 2 & 2 \end{bmatrix}$$

Then

$$LMN = LM \times N = L \times MN$$

$$\begin{bmatrix} 1 & 3 \\ 2 & 1 \end{bmatrix}\begin{bmatrix} 2 & 4 \\ 1 & 0 \end{bmatrix}\begin{bmatrix} 3 & 1 \\ 2 & 2 \end{bmatrix} = \begin{bmatrix} 5 & 4 \\ 5 & 8 \end{bmatrix}\begin{bmatrix} 3 & 1 \\ 2 & 2 \end{bmatrix} = \begin{bmatrix} 23 & 13 \\ 31 & 21 \end{bmatrix}$$

$$\begin{bmatrix} 1 & 3 \\ 2 & 1 \end{bmatrix}\begin{bmatrix} 2 & 4 \\ 1 & 0 \end{bmatrix}\begin{bmatrix} 3 & 1 \\ 2 & 2 \end{bmatrix} = \begin{bmatrix} 1 & 3 \\ 2 & 1 \end{bmatrix}\begin{bmatrix} 14 & 10 \\ 3 & 1 \end{bmatrix} = \begin{bmatrix} 23 & 13 \\ 31 & 21 \end{bmatrix}$$ ////

SYMBOLIC REPRESENTATION

Convenient as matrix notation is, it is common practice to condense the notation further by representing the matrices and vectors by algebraic symbols. Matrices are commonly represented by capital letters and vectors by lowercase letters. Thus AB indicates the multiplication of matrices A and B; and $c + d$ indicates the addition of vectors c and d.

The data elements for components within a matrix may be identified by subscripts. Thus the lowercase term a_{ij} would represent the element in the ith row and the jth column in matrix A while the term c_i or d_j would represent the ith element in a row vector of c and the jth element in the column vector d respectively.

$$\begin{bmatrix} a_{11} & a_{12} & a_{13} & \cdots & a_{1j} & \cdots & a_{1n} \\ a_{21} & a_{22} & a_{23} & \cdots & a_{2j} & \cdots & a_{2n} \\ \cdot & \cdot & \cdot & & \cdot & & \cdot \\ a_{i1} & a_{i2} & a_{i3} & \cdots & a_{ij} & \cdots & a_{in} \\ \cdot & \cdot & \cdot & & \cdot & & \cdot \\ a_{m1} & a_{m2} & a_{m3} & \cdots & a_{mj} & \cdots & a_{mn} \end{bmatrix}$$

$$\begin{bmatrix} c_1 \\ c_2 \\ \vdots \\ c_j \\ \vdots \\ c_m \end{bmatrix} \qquad [d_1 \quad d_2 \quad \cdots \quad d_j \quad \cdots \quad d_n]$$

Sometimes it is convenient to refer to a matrix A by using the general form of the elements. This is indicated as $\|a_{ij}\|$. The a_{ij} refers to any element at row i column j and the bars represent an entire matrix.

Matrices and Linear Systems

Matrix notation can be used to express linear systems. Two vectors or matrices are said to be equal only if each component in one is equal to the corresponding component in the other. This allows systems of linear equations to be represented in matrix notation. Consider the matrix equation

$$\begin{bmatrix} 5 & 7 & 3 \\ 4 & 1 & 2 \end{bmatrix} \begin{bmatrix} x_1 \\ x_2 \\ x_3 \end{bmatrix} = \begin{bmatrix} 35 \\ 20 \end{bmatrix} \qquad (3\text{-}25)$$

If the left side of the equation is expanded by matrix multiplication, the result is

$$\begin{bmatrix} 5x_1 + 7x_2 + 3x_3 \\ 4x_1 + 1x_2 + 2x_3 \end{bmatrix} = \begin{bmatrix} 35 \\ 20 \end{bmatrix} \qquad (3\text{-}26)$$

Since the two vectors are equal, by definition their corresponding components must be equal.

$$5x_1 + 7x_2 + 3x_3 = 35$$

$$4x_1 + x_2 + 2x_3 = 20$$

Thus a system of linear equations can be represented in either matrix notation or algebraic notation.

To convert from matrix notation to algebraic notation requires performing the indicated matrix manipulations. Referring to the previous example, it can be seen that a system of equations may be represented by a matrix and two column vectors as indicated below.

$$a_{11}x_1 + a_{12}x_2 + a_{13}x_3 = b_1$$

$$a_{21}x_1 + a_{22}x_2 + a_{23}x_3 = b_2$$

$$a_{31}x_1 + a_{32}x_2 + a_{33}x_3 = b_3$$

$$\begin{bmatrix} a_{11} & a_{12} & a_{13} \\ a_{21} & a_{22} & a_{23} \\ a_{31} & a_{32} & a_{33} \end{bmatrix} \begin{bmatrix} x_1 \\ x_2 \\ x_3 \end{bmatrix} = \begin{bmatrix} b_1 \\ b_2 \\ b_3 \end{bmatrix} \qquad (3\text{-}27)$$

The reader may expand the matrices by performing the indicated multiplication to verify this expression. In general, then, linear equations are expressed in matrix form as follows:

$$[m \times n \text{ matrix of coefficients}] \begin{bmatrix} n \times 1 \\ \text{vector} \\ \text{of} \\ \text{variables} \end{bmatrix} = \begin{bmatrix} m \times 1 \\ \text{vector} \\ \text{of} \\ \text{constants} \end{bmatrix}$$

Using symbolic notation, these equations can be written

$$Ax = b \qquad (3\text{-}28)$$

where A represents the $m \times n$ matrix of coefficients, x represents the $n \times 1$ column vector of variables, and b represents the $m \times 1$ column vector of constants.

IDENTITY MATRIX

Division, as normally conceived in algebra, is not possible in matrix algebra. For the purposes of this book, an identity matrix I will be a square matrix (one having as many rows as columns) which has a major diagonal of 1s and 0s elsewhere:

$$\begin{bmatrix} 1 & 0 \\ 0 & 1 \end{bmatrix} \qquad \begin{bmatrix} 1 & 0 & 0 & 0 & 0 \\ 0 & 1 & 0 & 0 & 0 \\ 0 & 0 & 1 & 0 & 0 \\ 0 & 0 & 0 & 1 & 0 \\ 0 & 0 & 0 & 0 & 1 \end{bmatrix}$$

$$A\ 2 \times 2 \qquad\qquad A\ 5 \times 5$$
$$\text{identity matrix} \qquad \text{identity matrix}$$

In matrix multiplication, an identity matrix has similar properties to a 1 in regular multiplication. That is, any matrix multiplied by an identity matrix has as its product the original matrix.

$$\begin{bmatrix} 2 & 5 \\ -3 & 7 \end{bmatrix} \begin{bmatrix} 1 & 0 \\ 0 & 1 \end{bmatrix} = \begin{bmatrix} 2+0 & 0+5 \\ -3+0 & 0+7 \end{bmatrix} = \begin{bmatrix} 2 & 5 \\ -3 & 7 \end{bmatrix} \qquad (3\text{-}29)$$

$$\begin{bmatrix} 5 & 6 \\ -2 & 0 \end{bmatrix} \begin{bmatrix} 1 & 0 \\ 0 & 1 \end{bmatrix} = \begin{bmatrix} 5+0 & 0+6 \\ -2+0 & 0+0 \end{bmatrix} = \begin{bmatrix} 5 & 6 \\ -2 & 0 \end{bmatrix} \qquad (3\text{-}30)$$

In symbolic form this becomes

$$AI = A \qquad (3\text{-}31)$$

$$IA = A \qquad (3\text{-}32)$$

and

$$AI = IA \qquad (3\text{-}33)$$

Although it is *not* possible to perform division in matrix algebra, it is possible to achieve results that are very similar. This requires the creation of an *inverse*, which has properties similar to a reciprocal. The analogy has definite limits and should not be extended too far. However, the concept of the analogy is valid and does allow an easier interpretation of the technique. To solve the algebraic expression below for b, one would simply divide both sides of the equation by a:

$$ab = c$$

$$\frac{ab}{a} = \frac{c}{a} \quad \text{or} \quad \frac{1}{a}\ ab = \frac{1}{a}\ c$$

$$b = \frac{c}{a}$$

Since it is not possible to perform matrix division directly, the following matrix equations suggest use of the same reciprocal and multiplying:

$$AB = C$$

$$\frac{1}{A}AB = \frac{1}{A}C$$

$$B = \frac{1}{A}C$$

What is needed is a matrix term having similar properties to a reciprocal.   This is an *inverse*, denoted by the negative exponent:

$$\text{Inverse of } A = A^{-1}$$

An inverse can be defined only for a square matrix.   An inverse has the following property:

$$A^{-1}A = AA^{-1} = I \qquad (3\text{-}34)$$

as indicated by

$$A = \begin{bmatrix} 1 & 2 \\ 4 & 6 \end{bmatrix} \qquad A^{-1} = \begin{bmatrix} -3 & 1 \\ 2 & -\frac{1}{2} \end{bmatrix}$$

$$AA^{-1} = \begin{bmatrix} 1 & 2 \\ 4 & 6 \end{bmatrix}\begin{bmatrix} -3 & 1 \\ 2 & \frac{1}{2} \end{bmatrix} = \begin{bmatrix} 1 & 0 \\ 0 & 1 \end{bmatrix} = I$$

$$A^{-1}A = \begin{bmatrix} -3 & 1 \\ 2 & -\frac{1}{2} \end{bmatrix}\begin{bmatrix} 1 & 2 \\ 4 & 6 \end{bmatrix} = \begin{bmatrix} 1 & 0 \\ 0 & 1 \end{bmatrix} = I$$

The reader should verify this property by completing the indicated multiplication.

A generalized way of obtaining an inverse can be described by first understanding row operations.   Row operations on a matrix consist of multiplying (or dividing) every component in a row by a constant or by adding one row to another.   Actually these steps may be combined once they are understood.   When this is done to both sides of a matrix equation, the equality is still valid.   For example,

$$A = \begin{bmatrix} 2 & 3 \\ 4 & 1 \end{bmatrix} \qquad \text{a } 2 \times 2 \text{ matrix}$$

$$B = \begin{bmatrix} 1 & 0 & 2 \\ 2 & -1 & 4 \end{bmatrix} \qquad \text{a } 2 \times 3 \text{ matrix}$$

$$C = \begin{bmatrix} 8 & -3 & 16 \\ 6 & -1 & 12 \end{bmatrix} \qquad \text{a } 2 \times 3 \text{ matrix}$$

In matrix A, if the first row is multiplied by 2, the matrix becomes

$$\begin{bmatrix} 4 & 6 \\ 4 & 1 \end{bmatrix}$$

If the first row is then added to the second row, the result is

$$\begin{bmatrix} 4 & 6 \\ 8 & 7 \end{bmatrix}$$

In matrix B, if the second row is multiplied by -2 and added to the first row, the answer is

$$\begin{bmatrix} -3 & 2 & -6 \\ 2 & -1 & 4 \end{bmatrix}$$

For this example, the following matrix equation is a true statement:

$$AB = C$$

$$\begin{bmatrix} 2 & 3 \\ 4 & 1 \end{bmatrix} \begin{bmatrix} 1 & 0 & 2 \\ 2 & -1 & 4 \end{bmatrix} = \begin{bmatrix} 8 & -3 & 16 \\ 6 & -1 & 12 \end{bmatrix}$$

First multiply the first row in the left matrix (A) by 2 and the first row in the right matrix (C) by 2. The result is still an equality.

$$\begin{bmatrix} 4 & 6 \\ 4 & 1 \end{bmatrix} \begin{bmatrix} 1 & 0 & 2 \\ 2 & -1 & 4 \end{bmatrix} = \begin{bmatrix} 16 & -6 & 32 \\ 6 & -1 & 12 \end{bmatrix}$$

Next add the first row to the second row in both A and C. The result is still an equality.

$$\begin{bmatrix} 4 & 6 \\ 8 & 7 \end{bmatrix} \begin{bmatrix} 1 & 0 & 2 \\ 2 & -1 & 4 \end{bmatrix} = \begin{bmatrix} 16 & -6 & 32 \\ 22 & -7 & 44 \end{bmatrix}$$

This illustrates the principle that if identical row operations are performed on the left-hand and right-hand matrices (A and C in this case), the equality still holds.[1]

Row operations can be performed to obtain the inverse of a matrix. Recalling the properties of an identity matrix I

$$A = AI \qquad (3\text{-}31)$$

and an inverse A^{-1}

$$A^{-1}A = I = AA^{-1} \qquad (3\text{-}35)$$

suggests a procedure for obtaining an inverse. Refer to Eq. (3-31) defining the properties of I.

If row operations are carried out on the A matrix on the left side of the equation and upon the identity matrix on the right side of the equation, the equality is maintained. Suppose that these row operations were selected to convert the A matrix into an identity matrix.

$$A = IA \qquad (3\text{-}31)$$

$$I = AX \qquad (3\text{-}36)$$

---

[1] In a similar manner, column operations on both matrices located where B and C are will maintain the equality. The reader may verify this for his own interest.

By the properties previously defined, X must be the inverse of A or A^{-1}.   Actually it is not necessary to carry this equals sign along during this conversion.

$$A = \begin{bmatrix} 2 & 4 \\ 4 & 6 \end{bmatrix}$$

Find A^{-1}.

$$\begin{bmatrix} 2 & 4 \\ 4 & 6 \end{bmatrix} \quad \begin{bmatrix} 1 & 0 \\ 0 & 1 \end{bmatrix}$$

First perform multiplication or division to obtain a 1 in the uppermost left-hand corner of A (position 1) in this case, divide the first row by 2.

$$\begin{bmatrix} 1 & 2 \\ 4 & 6 \end{bmatrix} \quad \begin{bmatrix} \frac{1}{2} & 0 \\ 0 & 1 \end{bmatrix}$$

Next, perform multiplication and addition to achieve 0s in the remaining rows in the first column.   Here multiply the first row by -4 and add the result to the second row.

$$\begin{bmatrix} 1 & 2 \\ 0 & -2 \end{bmatrix} \quad \begin{bmatrix} \frac{1}{2} & 0 \\ -2 & 1 \end{bmatrix}$$

Now, perform multiplication to obtain a 1 in the second column of the second row, i.e., multiply by $-\frac{1}{2}$

$$\begin{bmatrix} 1 & 2 \\ 0 & 1 \end{bmatrix} \quad \begin{bmatrix} \frac{1}{2} & 0 \\ 1 & -\frac{1}{2} \end{bmatrix}$$

Finally obtain 0s in all other rows in the second column to achieve an identity matrix. Multiply the second row by -2 and add the result to the first row.

$$\begin{bmatrix} 1 & 0 \\ 0 & 1 \end{bmatrix} \quad \begin{bmatrix} -\frac{3}{2} & 1 \\ 1 & -\frac{1}{2} \end{bmatrix}$$

Thus,

$$A^{-1} = \begin{bmatrix} -\frac{3}{2} & 1 \\ 1 & -\frac{1}{2} \end{bmatrix}$$

EXAMPLE 3-6   Obtain the inverse of the following 3×3 matrix.   Perform row operations to convert this matrix into an identity matrix.

$$\begin{bmatrix} 2 & 1 & 4 \\ -4 & 0 & -2 \\ 6 & 2 & 0 \end{bmatrix} \quad \begin{bmatrix} 1 & 0 & 0 \\ 0 & 1 & 0 \\ 0 & 0 & 1 \end{bmatrix}$$

STEP 1   Multiply row 1 by $\frac{1}{2}$ to obtain a 1 in position (1,1):

$$\begin{bmatrix} 1 & \frac{1}{2} & 2 \\ -4 & 0 & -2 \\ 6 & 2 & 0 \end{bmatrix} \quad \begin{bmatrix} \frac{1}{2} & 0 & 0 \\ 0 & 1 & 0 \\ 0 & 0 & 1 \end{bmatrix}$$

STEP 2   Multiply row 1 by 4 and add to row 2 to obtain a zero in (2,1):

$$\begin{bmatrix} 1 & \frac{1}{2} & 2 \\ 0 & 2 & 6 \\ 6 & 2 & 0 \end{bmatrix} \quad \begin{bmatrix} \frac{1}{2} & 0 & 0 \\ 2 & 1 & 0 \\ 0 & 0 & 1 \end{bmatrix}$$

STEP 3   Multiply row 1 by -6 and add to row 3 to obtain a zero in (3,1):

$$\begin{bmatrix} 1 & \frac{1}{2} & 2 \\ 0 & 2 & 6 \\ 0 & -1 & -12 \end{bmatrix} \quad \begin{bmatrix} \frac{1}{2} & 0 & 0 \\ 2 & 1 & 0 \\ -3 & 0 & 1 \end{bmatrix}$$

STEP 4   Multiply row 2 by $\frac{1}{2}$ to obtain a 1 in (2,2):

$$\begin{bmatrix} 1 & \frac{1}{2} & 2 \\ 0 & 1 & 3 \\ 0 & -1 & -12 \end{bmatrix} \quad \begin{bmatrix} \frac{1}{2} & 0 & 0 \\ 1 & \frac{1}{2} & 0 \\ -3 & 0 & 1 \end{bmatrix}$$

STEP 5   Multiply row 2 by $-\frac{1}{2}$ and add to row 1 to obtain a zero in (1,2):

$$\begin{bmatrix} 1 & 0 & \frac{1}{2} \\ 0 & 1 & 3 \\ 0 & -1 & -12 \end{bmatrix} \quad \begin{bmatrix} 0 & -\frac{1}{4} & 0 \\ 1 & \frac{1}{2} & 0 \\ -3 & 0 & 1 \end{bmatrix}$$

STEP 6   Add row 2 to row 3 to obtain a zero in (3,2):

$$\begin{bmatrix} 1 & 0 & \frac{1}{2} \\ 0 & 1 & 3 \\ 0 & 0 & -9 \end{bmatrix} \quad \begin{bmatrix} 0 & -\frac{1}{4} & 0 \\ 1 & \frac{1}{2} & 0 \\ -2 & \frac{1}{2} & 1 \end{bmatrix}$$

STEP 7   Multiply row 3 by $-\frac{1}{9}$ to obtain a 1 in (3,3):

$$\begin{bmatrix} 1 & 0 & \frac{1}{2} \\ 0 & 1 & 3 \\ 0 & 0 & 1 \end{bmatrix} \quad \begin{bmatrix} 0 & -\frac{1}{4} & 0 \\ 1 & \frac{1}{2} & 0 \\ \frac{2}{9} & -\frac{1}{18} & -\frac{1}{9} \end{bmatrix}$$

STEP 8   Multiply row 3 by $-\frac{1}{2}$ and add to row 1 to obtain a zero in (1,3):

$$\begin{bmatrix} 1 & 0 & 0 \\ 0 & 1 & 3 \\ 0 & 0 & 1 \end{bmatrix} \quad \begin{bmatrix} -\frac{1}{9} & -\frac{8}{36} & \frac{1}{18} \\ 1 & \frac{1}{2} & 0 \\ \frac{2}{9} & -\frac{1}{18} & -\frac{1}{9} \end{bmatrix}$$

STEP 9   Multiply row 3 by -3 and add to row 2 to obtain a zero in (2,3):

$$\begin{bmatrix} 1 & 0 & 0 \\ 0 & 1 & 0 \\ 0 & 0 & 1 \end{bmatrix} \qquad \begin{bmatrix} -\frac{1}{9} & -\frac{8}{36} & \frac{1}{18} \\ \frac{1}{3} & \frac{2}{3} & \frac{1}{3} \\ \frac{2}{9} & -\frac{1}{18} & -\frac{1}{9} \end{bmatrix}$$

Thus the inverse[1] is

$$\begin{bmatrix} -\frac{1}{9} & -\frac{8}{36} & \frac{1}{18} \\ \frac{1}{3} & \frac{2}{3} & \frac{1}{3} \\ \frac{2}{9} & -\frac{1}{18} & -\frac{1}{9} \end{bmatrix} \qquad ////$$

Not every matrix has an inverse.   A matrix which has no inverse is said to be *singular*.   For those familiar with determinants we add that a singular matrix has a determinant value of 0.   This situation is equivalent to trying to find the intersection of two parallel lines.   A matrix is said to be nonsingular if an inverse exists.   If an inverse does exist for a matrix, it is unique and no other inverse exists.   It is not always possible to tell ahead of time whether a matrix is singular; however, it will not be possible to continue the calculations used to obtain an inverse.   If A is singular, one eventually either tries to divide by zero or obtains a null row (all zeros).

$$\begin{bmatrix} 2 & 4 & 1 \\ 2 & 1 & 1 \\ 4 & 5 & 2 \end{bmatrix} \qquad \begin{bmatrix} 1 & 0 & 0 \\ 0 & 1 & 0 \\ 0 & 0 & 1 \end{bmatrix}$$

$$\begin{bmatrix} 1 & 2 & \frac{1}{2} \\ 0 & -3 & 0 \\ 0 & -3 & 0 \end{bmatrix} \qquad \begin{bmatrix} \frac{1}{2} & 0 & 0 \\ -1 & 1 & 0 \\ -2 & 0 & 1 \end{bmatrix}$$

$$\begin{bmatrix} 1 & 0 & \frac{1}{2} \\ 0 & 1 & 0 \\ 0 & 0 & 0 \end{bmatrix} \qquad \begin{bmatrix} -\frac{1}{6} & \frac{2}{3} & 0 \\ \frac{1}{3} & -\frac{1}{3} & 0 \\ -1 & -1 & 1 \end{bmatrix}$$

Note that in this case, row 3 is a linear combination (sum) of rows 1 and 2.

The inverse can be used to solve simultaneous linear equations.   Consider the following problem:

$$2x_1 + 4x_2 = 8$$
$$4x_1 + 6x_2 = 10$$

[1] This is the augmented-matrix method of inverting a matrix.   The actual procedure used is called a Gauss-Jordon elimination and can easily be programmed.   Several other methods of matrix inversion are described in the references.

This can be described in general matrix form.

$$Ax = b$$

$$A = \begin{bmatrix} 2 & 4 \\ 4 & 6 \end{bmatrix} \qquad \text{matrix of coefficients}$$

$$x = \begin{bmatrix} x_1 \\ x_2 \end{bmatrix} \qquad \text{column vector of variables}$$

$$b = \begin{bmatrix} 8 \\ 10 \end{bmatrix} \qquad \text{column vector of constants}$$

In the equation $Ax = b$ if both sides are multiplied by the inverse A^{-1}

$$A^{-1}Ax = A^{-1}b$$

the result becomes

$$Ix = A^{-1}b \qquad \text{or} \qquad x = A^{-1}b$$

This is the solution to the vector of variables x.   Thus,

$$Ax = b$$

$$\begin{bmatrix} 2 & 4 \\ 4 & 6 \end{bmatrix}\begin{bmatrix} x_1 \\ x_2 \end{bmatrix} = \begin{bmatrix} 8 \\ 10 \end{bmatrix}$$

From a prior example

$$A^{-1} = \begin{bmatrix} -\frac{3}{2} & 1 \\ 1 & -\frac{1}{2} \end{bmatrix}$$

and

$$\begin{bmatrix} x_1 \\ x_2 \end{bmatrix} = \begin{bmatrix} -\frac{3}{2} & 1 \\ 1 & -\frac{1}{2} \end{bmatrix}\begin{bmatrix} 8 \\ 10 \end{bmatrix} \qquad \text{or} \qquad \begin{aligned} A^{-1}Ax &= A^{-1}b \\ Ix &= A^{-1}b \\ x &= A^{-1}b \end{aligned}$$

$$x_1 = -\tfrac{3}{2}(8) + 1(10) = -2$$
$$x_2 = 1(8) + -\tfrac{1}{2}(10) = 3$$

EXAMPLE 3-7   Let

$$A = \begin{bmatrix} 2 & 4 \\ 1 & 0 \end{bmatrix} \qquad B = \begin{bmatrix} 3 & 1 \\ 2 & 2 \end{bmatrix} \qquad C = \begin{bmatrix} 14 & 10 \\ 3 & 1 \end{bmatrix}$$

Then

$$AB = C$$

The reader should verify this statement.

Solve for AB.

$$A^{-1}AB = A^{-1}C$$

$$A^{-1} = \begin{bmatrix} 0 & 1 \\ \frac{1}{4} & -\frac{1}{2} \end{bmatrix}$$

The reader may also want to verify this statement.

$$IB = A^{-1}C$$

$$B = A^{-1}C$$

$$\begin{bmatrix} 3 & 1 \\ 2 & 2 \end{bmatrix} = \begin{bmatrix} 0 & 1 \\ \frac{1}{4} & -\frac{1}{2} \end{bmatrix}\begin{bmatrix} 14 & 10 \\ 3 & 1 \end{bmatrix} = \begin{bmatrix} 3 & 1 \\ 2 & 2 \end{bmatrix}$$

$$A^{-1}AB \neq CA^{-1}$$

$$IB \neq CA^{-1}$$

$$B \neq CA^{-1}$$

$$\begin{bmatrix} 3 & 1 \\ 2 & 2 \end{bmatrix} \neq \begin{bmatrix} 14 & 10 \\ 3 & 1 \end{bmatrix}\begin{bmatrix} 0 & 1 \\ \frac{1}{4} & -\frac{1}{2} \end{bmatrix} = \begin{bmatrix} \frac{10}{4} & 9 \\ \frac{1}{4} & \frac{5}{2} \end{bmatrix}$$

Solve for A.

$$ABB^{-1} = AB^{-1}B = CB^{-1}$$

$$AI = CB^{-1}$$

$$A = CB^{-1} \qquad B^{-1} = \begin{bmatrix} \frac{1}{2} & -\frac{1}{4} \\ -\frac{1}{2} & \frac{3}{4} \end{bmatrix}$$

$$\begin{bmatrix} 2 & 4 \\ 1 & 0 \end{bmatrix} = \begin{bmatrix} 14 & 10 \\ 3 & 1 \end{bmatrix}\begin{bmatrix} \frac{1}{2} & -\frac{1}{4} \\ -\frac{1}{2} & \frac{3}{4} \end{bmatrix} = \begin{bmatrix} 7-5 & -\frac{14}{4}+\frac{30}{4} \\ \frac{3}{2}-\frac{1}{2} & -\frac{3}{4}+\frac{3}{4} \end{bmatrix} = \begin{bmatrix} 2 & 4 \\ 1 & 0 \end{bmatrix}$$

$$ABB^{-1} \neq B^{-1}C$$

$$A \neq B^{-1}C$$

$$\begin{bmatrix} 2 & 4 \\ 1 & 0 \end{bmatrix} \neq \begin{bmatrix} \frac{1}{2} & -\frac{1}{4} \\ -\frac{1}{2} & \frac{3}{4} \end{bmatrix}\begin{bmatrix} 14 & 10 \\ 3 & 1 \end{bmatrix} = \begin{bmatrix} 6\frac{1}{4} & 4\frac{3}{4} \\ -4\frac{3}{4} & 4\frac{1}{4} \end{bmatrix}$$

$$B^{-1}AB \neq ABB^{-1}$$

$$\begin{bmatrix} \frac{1}{2} & -\frac{1}{4} \\ -\frac{1}{2} & \frac{3}{4} \end{bmatrix}\begin{bmatrix} 2 & 4 \\ 1 & 0 \end{bmatrix}\begin{bmatrix} 3 & 1 \\ 2 & 2 \end{bmatrix} \neq \begin{bmatrix} 2 & 4 \\ 1 & 0 \end{bmatrix}\begin{bmatrix} 3 & 1 \\ 2 & 2 \end{bmatrix}\begin{bmatrix} \frac{1}{2} & -\frac{1}{4} \\ -\frac{1}{2} & \frac{3}{4} \end{bmatrix}$$

$$\begin{bmatrix} 6\frac{1}{2} & 4\frac{3}{4} \\ -4\frac{3}{4} & 4\frac{1}{4} \end{bmatrix} \neq \begin{bmatrix} 2 & 4 \\ 1 & 0 \end{bmatrix}$$

Care should be taken in solving matrix equations with regard to placement of matrices for multiplication.   ////

The algebraic analogy can be seen in the following example.   Solve by algebra

$$2x_1 + 4x_2 = 8$$
$$4x_1 + 6x_2 = 10$$

Divide the first equation by 2:

$$x_1 + 2x_2 = 4$$
$$4x_1 + 6x_2 = 10$$

Multiply the first equation by -4 and add to the second equation:

$$x_1 + 2x_2 = 4$$
$$0x_1 - 2x_2 = -6$$

Multiply the second equation by $-\frac{1}{2}$:

$$x_1 + 2x_2 = 4$$
$$0x_1 + 1x_2 = 3$$

Multiply the second equation by -2 and add to the first equation:

$$x_1 + 0x_2 = -2$$
$$0x_1 + x_2 = 3$$

These are the same steps previously used to invert the 2×2 matrix $\begin{bmatrix} 2 & 4 \\ 4 & 6 \end{bmatrix}$.   Matrix algebra is illustrated here as a convenient and condensed way of handling data to provide a solution.   The use of matrices lends itself to computer techniques as well as allowing a more condensed notation form for mathematics.

REFERENCES

1 GERE, JAMES M., and WILLIAM WEAVER, JR.: "Matrix Algebra for Engineers," D. Van Nostrand Company, Inc., Princeton, N.J., 1965.
2 HADLEY, G.: "Linear Algebra," Addison-Wesley Publishing Company, Inc., Reading, Mass., 1961.
3 HOHN, FRANZ E.: "Elementary Matrix Algebra," The Macmillan Company, New York, 1958.
4 KEMENY, JOHN G., HAZELTON MIRKEL, J. LAURIE SNELL, and GERALD L. THOMPSON: "Finite Mathematical Structures," pp. 205–336, Prentice-Hall, Inc., Englewood Cliffs, N.J., 1959.
5 LEVIN, RICHARD I., and CHARLES A. KIRKPATRICK: "Quantitative Approaches to Management," 2d ed., pp. 274–306, McGraw-Hill Book Company, New York, 1971.

PROBLEMS

3-1 Given the matrices

$$X = \begin{bmatrix} 3 & 2 \\ 4 & 1 \\ 6 & 2 \end{bmatrix} \qquad Y = \begin{bmatrix} 2 & 1 \\ 4 & 3 \\ 6 & 2 \end{bmatrix} \qquad Z = \begin{bmatrix} 1 & 2 \\ 2 & 0 \\ 1 & 4 \end{bmatrix}$$

determine:

(a) $X + Y + Z$ (b) $2X$

(c) $3Z - 4Y$ (d) $X + 2Y - 3Z$

3-2 Given the vectors

$$L = [1 \quad 2 \quad 3] \qquad M = [4 \quad 0 \quad 2] \qquad N = \begin{bmatrix} 6 \\ 1 \\ 1 \end{bmatrix} \qquad P = \begin{bmatrix} 2 \\ 6 \\ 1 \end{bmatrix}$$

determine the following *if* possible:

(a) $L + M$ (b) $M - N$ (c) MP

(d) $LN - MP$ (e) $L - M + N - LP$ (f) PL

3-3 Given the matrices and vectors in Probs. 3-1 and 3-2, determine:

(a) LX (b) $MX - MZ$ (c) PLY

3-4 If A is a 2×4 matrix, B a 4×3 matrix, C a 3×3 matrix, and D a 3×2 matrix, what size would the following products be?

(a) AB (b) BC (c) BD

(d) DA (e) DAB (f) $ABCD$

(g) BC^2D

3-5 If $\begin{bmatrix} x \\ y \\ z \end{bmatrix} + \begin{bmatrix} 3 \\ 1 \\ 2 \end{bmatrix} = \begin{bmatrix} 7 \\ 9 \\ 4 \end{bmatrix}$, what does $\begin{bmatrix} x \\ y \\ z \end{bmatrix}$ equal?

3-6 Find the inverse of the following matrices if possible.

(a) $\begin{bmatrix} 1 & 1 \\ 1 & 1 \end{bmatrix}$ (b) $\begin{bmatrix} 1 & 2 \\ 4 & 3 \end{bmatrix}$ (c) $\begin{bmatrix} 1 & 4 & 6 \\ 2 & 2 & 4 \\ 2 & 1 & 1 \end{bmatrix}$ (d) $\begin{bmatrix} 2 & 1 & 3 \\ 2 & 0 & 4 \\ 4 & 1 & 7 \end{bmatrix}$

3-7 If $A = \begin{bmatrix} 2 & 4 \\ 1 & 3 \end{bmatrix}$ and $C = \begin{bmatrix} 2 \\ 1 \end{bmatrix}$, given that $AX = C$, what must X be? Find X if $A^2 X = C$.

3-8 If $A = \begin{bmatrix} 2 & 2 \\ 1 & 4 \end{bmatrix}$ and $C = \begin{bmatrix} 8 & 8 \\ 13 & 10 \end{bmatrix}$, given that $AX = C$, what must X be?

3-9 Express the following equations in terms of the product of matrices (like $AX = C$).

$$2x_1 + 4x_2 - 3x_3 = 6$$
$$x_1 + x_2 + x_3 = 8$$
$$5x_2 + x_3 = 18$$

3-10 Solve the following equations by matrix methods.

(a) $2x_1 + 4x_2 = 6$
    $x_1 - 2x_2 = 2$

(b) $2x_1 + 6x_2 = 20$
    $x_2 + x_3 = 5$
    $x_1 - x_3 = -1$

(c) $x_1 - x_2 + x_3 = 2$
    $2x_1 - x_2 + 3x_3 = 6$
    $x_2 + 4x_3 = 2$

3-11 A company makes five products, numbered 1 to 5. These products require processing times in each of the three departments A, B, and C. Item 1 takes 2 hours in A, 3 hours in B and .5 hour in C. Item 2 takes 2 hours in each department. Item 3 takes 4 hours in A, 2 hours in B, and 1 hour in C. Item 4 takes 1 hour in A, 2 hours in B, and 2 hours in C. Item 5 takes 1 hour in A, 4 hours in B, and 3 hours in C. The cost of processing in department A is \$7.50 per hour, in B is \$8 per hour and in C \$10 per hour. Use matrix methods to find:

(a) The cost of each item.
(b) The department requirements if the daily demand is for 100 of item 1, 200 of item 2, 50 of item 3, 80 of item 4, and 250 of item 5.
(c) The total daily cost.

4

FORMULATION AND ANALYSIS OF FIRST-ORDER MARKOV CHAINS

DESCRIPTION OF THE PROBLEM

First-order Markov chains can be used to model a physical or economic process with the following properties:

> *1* The set of possible outcomes is finite.
> *2* The probability of the next outcome depends only on the outcome immediately before.[1]
> *3* These probabilities are constant over time.

Each individual outcome is called a *state*. Thus there will be as many states as there are possible outcomes. For purposes of notation, S_i will signify the ith state out of a total of m possible states, where $\infty > m \geq 2$. Each time a new result or outcome occurs, the process is said to have *stepped* or incremented one step. This can be repeated over and over as many times as desired. A step may represent a time period or any other condition which would result in another possible outcome. The

---

[1] If the outcome depends on other than the immediately prior result, it is a higher-order chain. For example, a second-order chain describes a process in which an outcome depends upon the two previous outcomes, etc.

symbol n will be used to indicate the number of steps or increments. If $n = 0$, this represents the present; if $n = 1$, this represents the possible outcome next time; and if $n = 2$, this represents the outcome time after next.

As an example, consider the following hypothetical situation. A customer may purchase a Ford, Chevrolet, or Plymouth. For simplicity, assume that this covers all possibilities. His next purchase is controlled by the car he presently owns. A step occurs each time a new car is purchased. There are $m = 3$ possible states, purchase of a Ford, Chevrolet, or Plymouth. Using the suggested notation, this process is described by the table. At present, $n = 0$, S_1, S_2, or S_3 represents the

State notation	Physical description
S_1	Customer buys a Ford
S_2	Customer buys a Chevrolet
S_3	Customer buys a Plymouth

present state, i.e., what kind of car the customer now owns. At $n = 1$, next time, S_1, S_2, or S_3 represent all possible results of his next purchase.

EXAMPLE 4-1   The status of a machine might be described as a Markov chain. In this case, a state can describe the condition of the machine—running, awaiting repair, or being repaired. Each state is discrete, and in at least some cases the probability of the machine condition at the next observation depends upon its present status.

State notation	Physical description
S_1	Machine running, in production
S_2	Machine idle, waiting repair
S_3	Machine idle, being repaired

////

Markov chains are used to analyze problems of this type. Actually, this is a probability problem, and theoretically it can be analyzed using the fundamentals of classical probability theory. The concepts of Markov chains offer a more suitable method of performing this analysis. Initially, it may be convenient to think of a

Markov chain as an analysis technique suitable for a special case of probability problems. Many OR problems consist of discrete outcomes which depend on a prior result. In these cases, Markov chains may be used to advantage in both modeling and analysis. Some examples of these are replacement problems, inventory, queuing, and marketing models. Formulation of some of these problems will be demonstrated in a later section of this chapter.

FORMULATION OF A PROCESS AS A MARKOV CHAIN

Suppose that the three automobile manufacturers had maintained the following data regarding customer purchases. This table represents the probability that a customer

Present purchase ($n = 0$)	Next purchase ($n = 1$)		
	% buying Ford	% buying Chevrolet	% buying Plymouth
Ford	40	30	30
Chevrolet	20	50	30
Plymouth	25	25	50

now owning a Ford (S_1), $n = 0$, will buy a Ford, Chevrolet, or Plymouth next time, i.e., at the next step, $n = 1$. Similar information is provided for all possible states. As such, this table gives the probability that a customer now in state S_i will go to state S_j at the next step (next purchase). For purposes of notation, S_i typically indicates that the process is now in the ith state and S_j indicates that at some later step (usually next time) the process will be in the jth state.

If this same information is rewritten as simply a table of probabilities, it is called a *transition matrix*, denoted as P.

$$P = \begin{array}{c} \\ S_1 \\ S_2 \\ S_3 \end{array} \begin{array}{ccc} S_1 & S_2 & S_3 \\ \begin{bmatrix} .40 & .30 & .30 \\ .20 & .50 & .30 \\ .25 & .25 & .50 \end{bmatrix} \end{array}$$

Each element in this table represents a probability of going from one state to another. For notation purposes, an element in a transition matrix will be called p_{ij}. This is the conditional probability that if the process is now in state i, it will be in state j on the next step. For example, $p_{13} = .30$ means that the probability that a customer now owning a Ford (S_1 at $n = 0$) will purchase a Plymouth next time (S_3 at $n = 1$) is .30.

For convenience, a transition matrix can be viewed as a from-to table which gives the probabilities of the process going *from* state i *to* state j in one step.

	To		
From	S_1	S_2	S_3
S_1			
S_2			
S_3			

$$P =$$

EXAMPLE 4-2 What is the probability that a Plymouth owner buys a Ford next time?

$$\text{Plymouth purchase} = S_3$$
$$\text{Ford purchase} \quad = S_1$$

At $n = 0$, the state is S_3, and at $n = 1$, the state is S_1; thus the probability is p_{ij} or $p_{31} = .25$. ////

A transition matrix must meet the following conditions:

1 Each element must be a probability, i.e., it must be between 1 and 0. This simply reflects the fact that it is impossible to have a negative probability or to have a probability value larger than 1.
2 Each row must sum to exactly 1. If one sums the probabilities of *all possible* outcomes, obviously this sum must equal 1.

If this transition matrix is written using general notation, it appears as follows:

$$P = \begin{array}{c} S_1 \\ S_2 \\ \\ S_m \end{array} \begin{bmatrix} p_{11} & p_{12} & \cdots & p_{1m} \\ p_{21} & p_{22} & \cdots & p_{2m} \\ \cdots & \cdots & & \cdots \\ p_{m1} & p_{m2} & & p_{mm} \end{bmatrix}$$

where $0 \leq p_{ij} \leq 1$

$$\sum_{j=1}^{m} p_{ij} = 1, \, i = 1, 2, \ldots, m$$

Note that for a given state at $n = 0$, a row exhaustively enumerates all possible courses of action (states) that the customer (process) can take. Thus a row is a *probability vector*. This is to be expected since a vector is simply a $1 \times m$ matrix. For purposes of notation, a row vector will be labeled as V_i to represent the ith row. For example, $V_2 = [.20 \quad .50 \quad .30]$. A probability vector must meet requirements similar to those for a transition matrix.

1   Each element must be a probability, that is,

$$0 \le p_{ij} \le 1 \qquad (4\text{-}1)$$

2   The sum of the elements in the vector must equal 1:

$$\sum_{j=1}^{m} p_{ij} = 1 \qquad (4\text{-}2)$$

Thus a transition matrix P is a matrix composed of rows of probability vectors V_i.

PROBABILITY ANALYSIS BY MARKOV CHAINS

The transition matrix can be used to determine the probability of an outcome after n steps, given some specified starting state S_i. This can be demonstrated by a simple example using the data already presented.

Suppose the following question is asked. If a customer has just purchased a Ford, $S_i = S_1$ at $n = 0$, what is the probability that he will purchase a Chevrolet time after next, $S_j = S_2$ at $n = 2$? First this question will be analyzed by the techniques of classical probability theory. It is possible to enumerate the various ways that a customer now owning a Ford can end up buying a Chevrolet in two steps. This is illustrated by means of the tree in Fig. 4-1.

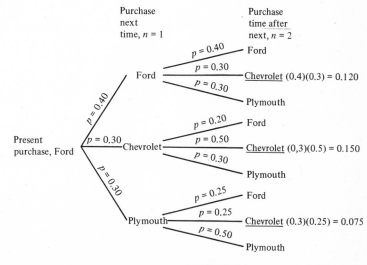

FIGURE 4-1
Possible outcomes in two steps, $n = 2$.

Purchase at $n = 1$ (next time)	Purchase at $n = 2$ (time after next)
Ford	Chevrolet
Chevrolet	Chevrolet
Plymouth	Chevrolet

When the probabilities of all of these possibilities are summed, they give the result tabulated.

Purchase at $n = 1$		Purchase at $n = 2$		Joint probability
State	Probability	State	Probability	
Ford	.40	Chevrolet	.30	.40 (.30) = .120
Chevrolet	.30	Chevrolet	.50	.30 (.50) = .150
Plymouth	.30	Chevrolet	.25	.30 (.25) = .075
				.345

Thus the probability that a Ford owner, S_1 at $n = 0$, purchases a Chevrolet time after next, S_2 at $n = 2$, is .345.

This can be obtained using the analysis technique provided by Markov chains. First consider exactly what the probability vector V_i means. For state S_1, $V_1 = [.4 \quad .3 \quad .3]$. This says that if the present state is S_1, the probability that the next state is S_1 is $p_{11} = .4$, S_2 is $p_{12} = .3$, and S_3 is $p_{13} = .3$. Thus the vector gives the probabilities of outcomes for the next step, $n = 1$, given a specified present state at $n = 0$. For purposes of notation, let V_i^n be the probability vector which describes the probabilities of possible outcomes in n steps if the present state is S_i. The question being considered will be answered if V_1^2 can be obtained. This gives the probabilities of all purchases two steps from now given that the customer now owns a Ford, S_1 at $n = 0$. This information is obtained from the product of V_1^1 and P.

$$V_1^2 = V_1^1 P = [.4 \quad .3 \quad .3] \begin{bmatrix} .40 & .30 & .30 \\ .20 & .50 & .30 \\ .25 & .25 & .50 \end{bmatrix}$$
$$= [.4(.4) + .3(.2) + .3(.25) \quad .4(.3) + .3(.5) + .3(.25) \quad .4(.3) + .3(.3) + .3(.5)]$$
$$= [.295 \quad .345 \quad .360]$$

This says that if the present state is S_1 at $n = 0$, two steps later ($n = 2$) the probability of being in state S_1 is $p_{12} = .295$, in state S_2 is $p_{12} = .345$, and in state S_3 is $p_{13} = .360$. Note that the middle term, the one relating to state S_2, has exactly the same elements as used in the analysis by probability concepts. Thus far, Markov chains simply provide a technique for formulating and analyzing a special case of probability problems.

EXAMPLE 4-3   If the present state is a Plymouth, S_3 at $n = 0$, what are the probabilities of being in each of the respective states at $n = 1$ and at $n = 2$?

$$V_3{}^1 = [.25 \quad .25 \quad .50]$$

$$V_3{}^2 = V_3{}^1 P = [.25 \quad .25 \quad .50] \begin{bmatrix} .40 & .30 & .30 \\ .20 & .50 & .30 \\ .25 & .25 & .50 \end{bmatrix} = [.275 \quad .325 \quad .400] \qquad ////$$

In terms of the defined notation, the following has been demonstrated to be true.

$$V_i{}^0 = [p_{i1} \quad p_{i2} \quad \cdots \quad p_{ii} \quad \cdots \quad p_{im}] \qquad \text{and} \qquad p_{ii} = 1$$

At time 0 (right now) we know exactly what the state is; thus there is a probability of 1 that state i exists.

$$V_i{}^1 = V_i{}^0 P = [p_{i1} \quad p_{i2} \quad \cdots \quad p_{im}]$$

the ith row in the P matrix, the probability vector i.

$$V_i{}^2 = V_i{}^1 P$$

The probability for results or outcomes in two steps is the product of the probability vector $V_i{}^1$ and the transition matrix P.   This then indicates that the following analysis can be made.

$$V_i{}^3 = V_i{}^2 P = (V_i{}^1 P)P = V_i{}^1 P^2$$
$$V_i{}^4 = V_i{}^3 P = (V_i{}^1 P^2)P = V_i{}^1 P^3$$
$$V_i{}^n = V_i{}^{n-1} P = (V_i{}^1 P^{n-2})P = V_i{}^1 P^{n-1} \qquad (4\text{-}3)$$

Thus the probabilities of outcomes n steps from now can be determined using the probability vector V_i and some power of the transition matrix P.

EXAMPLE 4-4   If the customer now owns a Chevrolet, what are the probabilities associated with his fourth purchase?

$$V_2 = [.20 \quad .50 \quad .30]$$
$$V_2{}^4 = V_2 P^3$$

$$P^3 = \begin{bmatrix} .277 & .351 & .372 \\ .269 & .359 & .372 \\ .275 & .345 & .380 \end{bmatrix}$$

$$V_2 P^3 = [.2 \quad .5 \quad .3] \begin{bmatrix} .277 & .351 & .372 \\ .269 & .359 & .372 \\ .275 & .345 & .380 \end{bmatrix}$$

$$= [.2724 \quad .3532 \quad .3744] \qquad ////$$

Actually, if the result after n steps is desired, P^n gives even more complete information since it is composed of all the individual vectors V_i^n. Thus P^n gives the probabilities of being in any given state for all possible starting conditions or states.

EXAMPLE 4-5   Find the probabilities of purchase in four steps.

$$P^4 = \begin{bmatrix} .2740 & .3516 & .3744 \\ .2724 & .3532 & .3744 \\ .2740 & .3500 & .3760 \end{bmatrix}$$

The first row gives the probabilities associated with a starting state S_1. The second row gives the probabilities associated with a starting state S_2, and the third row gives the probabilities associated with a starting state S_3.   ////

ERGODIC MARKOV CHAINS

If the system or process being modeled as a Markov chain has certain properties, it is possible to determine the probabilities of outcomes after steady-state conditions have been reached. After the process has been in operation for a long time, a given outcome will result x percent of the time. It is often desirable to be able to determine these percentages. Perhaps the most detrimental assumed condition in this case is the requirement that the transition matrix contain probabilities which are constant over time. This requirement should always be kept in mind when this analysis is being made to ensure that the results obtained are properly interpreted.

To ensure that steady-state conditions are reached, the chain must be *ergodic* (sometimes this is called an irreducible chain).[1] An ergodic chain mathematically describes a process in which it is possible to go from one state to any other state. It is not necessary for this to be possible in just one step, but it must be possible for any outcome to be reached regardless of the present state.

For example, Joe is driving in an area with the streets laid out as indicated in Fig. 4-2. Every time Joe comes to a corner, he makes a turn or goes straight with equal probability. That is, if he is at corner 2 as indicated in Fig. 4-2, he may go next to corner 1, 3, or 5 with a probability of $\frac{1}{3}$. If he is at corner 5, he may go next to corner 2, 4, 6, or 8 with a probability of $\frac{1}{4}$, etc. A state describes the corner Joe is at

[1] For proof of this statement, see Refs. 3 and 4.

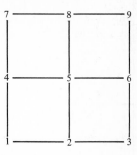

FIGURE 4-2
Layout of streets for Joe to drive.

when he makes his decision. Thus there are nine possible states. The transition matrix for this situation is

$$
\begin{array}{c c}
 & \begin{array}{ccccccccc} 1 & 2 & 3 & 4 & 5 & 6 & 7 & 8 & 9 \end{array} \\
\begin{array}{c} 1 \\ 2 \\ 3 \\ 4 \\ 5 \\ 6 \\ 7 \\ 8 \\ 9 \end{array} &
\left[\begin{array}{ccccccccc}
0 & \frac{1}{2} & 0 & \frac{1}{2} & 0 & 0 & 0 & 0 & 0 \\
\frac{1}{3} & 0 & \frac{1}{3} & 0 & \frac{1}{3} & 0 & 0 & 0 & 0 \\
0 & \frac{1}{2} & 0 & 0 & 0 & \frac{1}{2} & 0 & 0 & 0 \\
\frac{1}{3} & 0 & 0 & 0 & \frac{1}{3} & 0 & \frac{1}{3} & 0 & 0 \\
0 & \frac{1}{4} & 0 & \frac{1}{4} & 0 & \frac{1}{4} & 0 & \frac{1}{4} & 0 \\
0 & 0 & \frac{1}{3} & 0 & \frac{1}{3} & 0 & 0 & 0 & \frac{1}{3} \\
0 & 0 & 0 & \frac{1}{2} & 0 & 0 & 0 & \frac{1}{2} & 0 \\
0 & 0 & 0 & 0 & \frac{1}{3} & 0 & \frac{1}{3} & 0 & \frac{1}{3} \\
0 & 0 & 0 & 0 & 0 & \frac{1}{2} & 0 & \frac{1}{2} & 0
\end{array}\right]
\end{array}
$$

Obviously Joe can eventually get to any given location (state) from any present location (state). Thus this is an ergodic chain.

The transition matrix can be inspected to see whether it describes an ergodic chain. Simply check to see if it is possible to get from every starting or present state to all other states. (Sometimes one may go directly from s_1 to s_2 but not directly from s_2 to s_1.) Consider the transition matrix

$$
\begin{array}{c c}
 & \begin{array}{ccccc} 1 & 2 & 3 & 4 & 5 \end{array} \\
\begin{array}{c} 1 \\ 2 \\ 3 \\ 4 \\ 5 \end{array} &
\left[\begin{array}{ccccc}
X & X & 0 & X & X \\
0 & X & X & 0 & X \\
0 & 0 & 0 & X & X \\
X & 0 & X & 0 & X \\
X & X & 0 & 0 & 0
\end{array}\right]
\end{array}
$$

Let X equal some positive p_{ij} value. From state 1, it is possible to go directly to every state except 3; however, it is possible to go from 1 to 2 then to 3. Thus it is possible to go from state 1 to any other state. Now check to all other states, it is only necessary to show that it is possible to get to state 1 since that implies that it is possible to go to all other states.

State 2: go to 5, then from 5 to 1
State 3: go to 5, then from 5 to 1
State 4: go to 1
State 5: go to 1

This, then, is a transition matrix for an ergodic chain.

A more restricted case of an ergodic chain is a *regular* chain. A regular chain is defined as a chain having a transition matrix P which for some power of P has only positive probability elements (no zeros). Using the same transition matrix as before, the easiest way to check to see if a chain is regular is to keep squaring the matrix until all zeros are removed or until a pattern develops making it obvious that at least one zero will never be removed. As the example below illustrates, this was also a regular chain. Note that all regular chains will be ergodic but the reverse is not necessarily true. Not all ergodic chains are regular.

$$P = \begin{bmatrix} X & X & 0 & X & X \\ 0 & X & X & 0 & X \\ 0 & 0 & 0 & X & X \\ X & 0 & X & 0 & X \\ X & X & 0 & 0 & 0 \end{bmatrix} \quad P^2 = \begin{bmatrix} X & X & X & X & X \\ X & X & X & X & X \\ X & X & X & 0 & X \\ X & X & 0 & X & X \\ X & X & X & X & X \end{bmatrix} \quad P^4 = \begin{bmatrix} X & X & X & X & X \\ X & X & X & X & X \\ X & X & X & X & X \\ X & X & X & X & X \\ X & X & X & X & X \end{bmatrix}$$

EXAMPLE 4-6   Test each transition matrix to see if the chain is (a) regular and (b) ergodic.

$$P = \begin{array}{c} 1 \\ 2 \\ 3 \end{array}\begin{bmatrix} X & X & 0 \\ X & 0 & X \\ 0 & X & X \end{bmatrix} \quad P^2 = \begin{bmatrix} X & X & X \\ X & X & X \\ X & X & X \end{bmatrix} \quad \text{regular (thus ergodic)}$$

with column headers $\begin{array}{ccc} 1 & 2 & 3 \end{array}$ above P.

Check:
From 1 go to 1 or 2 directly, then from 2 to 3. From 2 go to 1. From 3 go to 2, then to 1. Thus ergodic.

$$P = \begin{array}{c} 1 \\ 2 \\ 3 \\ 4 \end{array}\begin{bmatrix} X & 0 & X & 0 \\ 0 & X & 0 & X \\ X & 0 & X & 0 \\ 0 & X & 0 & X \end{bmatrix} \quad P^2 = \begin{bmatrix} X & 0 & X & 0 \\ 0 & X & 0 & X \\ X & 0 & X & 0 \\ 0 & X & 0 & X \end{bmatrix} \quad P^4 = \begin{bmatrix} X & 0 & X & 0 \\ 0 & X & 0 & X \\ X & 0 & X & 0 \\ 0 & X & 0 & X \end{bmatrix}$$

with column headers $\begin{array}{cccc} 1 & 2 & 3 & 4 \end{array}$ above P.

This matrix will continually repeat this pattern for all real powers of P; therefore it is *not regular*.

From 1 to 1 or 3, and from 3 to 3 or 1; thus cannot get from 1 to 2 or 4. *Not ergodic.*

$$P = \begin{array}{c} \\ 1 \\ 2 \\ 3 \\ 4 \end{array} \overset{\begin{array}{cccc} 1 & 2 & 3 & 4 \end{array}}{\begin{bmatrix} X & 0 & X & 0 \\ 0 & X & X & 0 \\ X & 0 & 0 & X \\ 0 & X & X & 0 \end{bmatrix}} \quad P^2 = \begin{bmatrix} X & 0 & X & X \\ X & X & X & X \\ X & X & X & 0 \\ X & X & X & X \end{bmatrix} \quad P^4 = \begin{bmatrix} X & X & X & X \\ X & X & X & X \\ X & X & X & X \\ X & X & X & X \end{bmatrix} \quad \text{regular}$$

From 1 to 1 or 3 directly, from 3 to 4, from 4 to 2. From 2 to 3 to 1. From 3 to 1. From 4 to 3 to 1. Ergodic.

$$P = \begin{array}{c} \\ 1 \\ 2 \\ 3 \\ 4 \end{array} \overset{\begin{array}{cccc} 1 & 2 & 3 & 4 \end{array}}{\begin{bmatrix} 0 & X & X & 0 \\ X & 0 & 0 & X \\ X & 0 & 0 & X \\ 0 & X & X & 0 \end{bmatrix}} \quad P^2 = \begin{bmatrix} X & 0 & 0 & X \\ 0 & X & X & 0 \\ 0 & X & X & 0 \\ X & 0 & 0 & X \end{bmatrix}$$

$$P^4 = \begin{bmatrix} X & 0 & 0 & X \\ 0 & X & X & 0 \\ 0 & X & X & 0 \\ X & 0 & 0 & X \end{bmatrix} \quad P^8 = \begin{bmatrix} X & 0 & 0 & X \\ 0 & X & X & 0 \\ 0 & X & X & 0 \\ X & 0 & 0 & X \end{bmatrix}$$

Note that P raised to an even-numbered power gives the result above, while P raised to an odd-numbered power will give the original matrix. All have some nonpositive elements, *not regular.*

From 1 to 2 or 3, from 2 to 1 or 4. From 2 to 1. From 3 to 1. From 4 to 2 to 1. *Ergodic.* ////

DETERMINATION OF STEADY-STATE CONDITIONS

The existence of steady-state conditions in a regular ergodic chain can be demonstrated most easily by computing P^n for various values of n. Table 4-1 presents the values of P^n from the automobile-customer example for values of $n = 1$ to 8. Note that as n becomes larger, the values p_{ij} tend to a fixed limit and each probability vector V_i^n tends to become equal for all values of i. This suggests the following statements.

1 For a sufficiently large value of n, the probability vector V_i^n becomes equal for all i and does not change for larger values of n.

2 Since $V_i^{n+1} = V_i^n P$ and $V_i^{n+1} = V_i^n$, there exists a vector V^* such that $V^* = V^*P$.

For a more rigorous statement of this theorem, see Refs. *3* and *4*; a proof is presented in Ref. *4*.

The vector V^* contains the probabilities which exist at steady-state conditions. Statement 2 provides an analytical method of obtaining these values. Let v_j be the jth element in the probability vector V^*. Since V^* is still a probability vector, the following condition must still exist:

$$\sum_{j=1}^{m} v_j = 1 \qquad (4\text{-}4)$$

And from statement 2,

$$[v_1 \quad v_2 \quad v_3 \quad \cdots \quad v_m]P = [v_1 \quad v_2 \quad v_3 \quad \cdots \quad v_m] \qquad (4\text{-}5)$$

If this matrix product is expanded, there will be m equations. When added to the requirement that the sum of the probabilities equals 1, there are $m + 1$ equations and m unknowns. These can be solved for the m unknowns by discarding any one of the latter m equations. The equation $\sum_{j=1}^{m} v_j = 1$ cannot be discarded since the remaining m equations may be satisfied if all $v_j = 0$.

As an example, find the steady-state probabilities for the automobile-customer problem, using eqs. 4-4 and 4-5.

$$\sum_{j=1}^{3} v_j = 1$$

$$[v_1 \quad v_2 \quad v_3]P = [v_1 \quad v_2 \quad v_3]$$

$$v_1 + v_2 + v_3 = 1$$

$$.4v_1 + .2v_2 + .25v_3 = v_1$$

$$.3v_1 + .5v_2 + .25v_3 = v_2$$

$$.3v_1 + .3v_2 + .5v_3 = v_3$$

Table 4-1.   Values of P^n

$$P = \begin{bmatrix} .4 & .3 & .3 \\ .2 & .5 & .3 \\ .25 & .25 & .5 \end{bmatrix} \qquad P^2 = \begin{bmatrix} .295 & .345 & .360 \\ .255 & .385 & .360 \\ .275 & .325 & .400 \end{bmatrix}$$

$$P^3 = \begin{bmatrix} .277 & .351 & .372 \\ .269 & .359 & .372 \\ .275 & .345 & .380 \end{bmatrix} \qquad P^4 = \begin{bmatrix} .2740 & .3516 & .3744 \\ .2724 & .3532 & .3744 \\ .2740 & .3500 & .3760 \end{bmatrix}$$

$$P^5 = \begin{bmatrix} .27352 & .35160 & .37488 \\ .27320 & .35192 & .37488 \\ .27360 & .35120 & .37520 \end{bmatrix} \qquad P^6 = \begin{bmatrix} .273448 & .351576 & .374976 \\ .273384 & .351640 & .374976 \\ .273480 & .35140 & .375040 \end{bmatrix}$$

$$P^7 = \begin{bmatrix} .2734384 & .3515664 & .3749952 \\ .2734256 & .3515792 & .3749952 \\ .2734480 & .3515440 & .3750080 \end{bmatrix} \qquad P^8 = \begin{bmatrix} .27343744 & .35156352 & .37499904 \\ .27343488 & .35156608 & .37499904 \\ .27344000 & .35155840 & .37500160 \end{bmatrix}$$

Discarding the last equation and performing algebraic manipulations gives

$$v_1 + v_2 + v_3 = 1$$
$$-.6v_1 + .2v_2 + .25v_3 = 0$$
$$.3v_1 - .5v_2 + .25v_3 = 0$$

Solving these three equations gives

$$v_1 = .273$$
$$v_2 = .352$$
$$v_3 = .375$$

Interpreting these results in terms of this problem, we can make either of two types of statement:

1 In the long run, 27.3 percent of the customers buy Fords, 35.2 percent buy Chevrolets, and 37.5 percent buy Plymouths.
2 In the long run, the probability that a given customer will buy a Ford is .273, etc.

EXAMPLE 4-7   If

$$P = \begin{bmatrix} .2 & .5 & .3 \\ .1 & .6 & .3 \\ .5 & 0 & .5 \end{bmatrix}$$

find V^*, (v_1, v_2, v_3)

$$v_1 + v_2 + v_3 = 1$$
$$.2v_1 + .1v_2 + .5v_3 = v_1$$
$$.5v_1 + .6v_2 + 0 = v_2$$
$$.3v_1 + .3v_2 + .5v_3 = v_3$$

Omit the second equation.

$$v_1 + v_2 + v_3 = 1$$
$$.5v_1 - .4v_2 = 0$$
$$.3v_1 + .3v_2 - .5v_3 = 0$$
$$v_1 = .282$$
$$v_2 = .352$$
$$v_3 = .366 \qquad ////$$

When the chain is not regular, the method of analysis is the same but the interpretation is more restrictive. For example, the transition matrix may be such that it is not possible to reach a given state on odd- (even-) numbered steps. In this case, interpretation 2 is not meaningful. However, interpretation 1 is still valid, and the vector V^* indicates the relative frequency of the process in each possible state.

ABSORBING MARKOV CHAINS

A special case of Markov chains is used to describe processes or systems which cease (or at least restart) upon reaching certain given conditions. For example, once a predetermined number of acceptable or defective parts is found, a sequential inspection stops; after x hours of operation, a machine breaks down and is either repaired or replaced, etc. Such processes can be modeled as an absorbing Markov chain. An absorbing Markov chain is defined below.

Definition 1 An *absorbing state* is one with a zero probability of leaving i.e., once entered, it is impossible to leave, and the process either stops completely or stops and is then started over from some other state.

Definition 2 A Markov chain is absorbing if: (1) it has at least one absorbing state and (2) it is possible to go from every nonabsorbing state to at least one absorbing state. It is not necessary to make this transition in one step; nor is it necessary to be able to reach every absorbing state from any one nonabsorbing state.

This case is best presented by means of a simple problem. Suppose parts are inspected according to the following sequential inspection plan: select and inspect item by item until either a defective is found (reject) or five good parts are found (accept).

In this problem, the possible states are described below.

State	Physical description		
	No. of good parts	No. of defectives	
S_1 (0,0)	0	0	Just starting
S_2 (1,0)	1	0	
S_3 (2,0)	2	0	
S_4 (3,0)	3	0	
S_5 (4,0)	4	0	
S_6 (5,0)	5	0	
S_7 (0,1)	0	1	Absorbing
S_8 (1,1)	1	1	
S_9 (2,1)	2	1	
S_{10} (3,1)	3	1	
S_{11} (4,1)	4	1	

If it is expected that 90 percent of the parts are acceptable, the transition matrix is

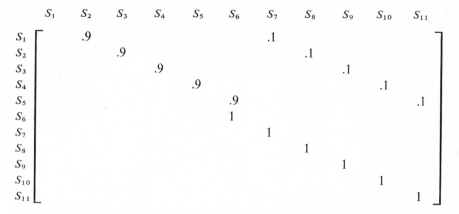

Note that once states S_6 to S_{11} are reached, the probability that the process stays in the respective state is 1.   Thus it is impossible (zero probability) to go from any of these states to any other state.   Physically this is because the inspector will make an accept-reject decision at that time and end the inspection.

ANALYSIS OF ABSORBING MARKOV CHAINS

Several kinds of pertinent information can be obtained from the analysis of this type of chain.   It is possible to determine the following data:

> *1* The expected number of steps before the process is absorbed
> *2* The expected number of times the process is in any given nonabsorbing state
> *3* The probability of absorption by any given absorbing state

The first step in the analysis is to rearrange the transition matrix so that four submatrices exist:

$$P = \left[\begin{array}{c|c} I & 0 \\ \hline A & N \end{array}\right]$$

These smaller matrices contain probability elements but taken individually do not constitute a transition matrix.   If taken individually, they contain the following information concerning probabilities.   Assume there are a absorbing states, n nonabsorbing states, and $a + n = m$ total states.

> *I* An $a \times a$ identity matrix represents the probabilities of staying within an absorbing state.   (This matrix is not used in later calculations.)
> 0 An $a \times n$ zero matrix reflects the probabilities of going from an absorbing state to a nonabsorbing state.

A An $n \times a$ matrix contains the probabilities of going from any nonabsorbing state to an absorbing state.

N An $n \times n$ matrix contains the probabilities of going from any nonabsorbing state to any other nonabsorbing state.

The revised transition matrix is

	(5,0) S_6	(0,1) S_7	(1,1) S_8	(2,1) S_9	(3,1) S_{10}	(4,1) S_{11}	(0,0) S_1	(1,0) S_2	(2,0) S_3	(3,0) S_4	(4,0) S_5
S_6 (5,0)	1						0	0	0	0	0
S_7 (0,1)		1					0	0	0	0	0
S_8 (1,1)			1				0	0	0	0	0
S_9 (2,1)				1			0	0	0	0	0
S_{10}(3,1)					1		0	0	0	0	0
S_{11}(4,1)						1	0	0	0	0	0
S_1 (0,0)	0	.1	0	0	0	0	0	.9	0	0	0
S_2 (1,0)	0	0	.1	0	0	0	0	0	.9	0	0
S_3 (2,0)	0	0	0	.1	0	0	0	0	0	.9	0
S_4 (3,0)	0	0	0	0	.1	0	0	0	0	0	.9
S_5 (4,0)	.9	0	0	0	0	.1	0	0	0	0	0

Before going into the analysis, it is important to have a good understanding of the meaning and use of two matrices N and A. As previously indicated, N gives the probabilities of going from any nonabsorbing state to another nonabsorbing state *in exactly one step*. As previously developed for the transition matrix P, N^2 gives the probabilities of going from any nonabsorbing state to another nonabsorbing state in exactly two steps. N^3 gives similar information for three steps, etc. Thus N^n gives this same information for exactly n steps. In addition, N^0 would represent the probabilities of being in a state right now. Since this is known and that state cannot be left in zero steps, N^0 is actually a $n \times n$ identity matrix.

If this problem were being worked by classical probability concepts, one way of finding the expected number of steps before the process is absorbed would be to find the *expected* number of times the process would be in each nonabsorbing state and sum them. This would total the number of steps before the process was discontinued or stopped and thus the expected number of steps to absorption.

The expected number of times the process will be in a nonabsorbing state j is the sum of the following terms:

Expected number of times in $j = 1 \times$ probability of being in j at start $+$
$$1 \times \text{probability of being in } j \text{ after } 1$$
$$\text{step} + 1 \times \text{probability of being in } j$$
$$\text{after 2 steps} + \cdots$$
$$= 1N^0 + 1N + 1N^2 + 1N^3 + \cdots$$
$$= 1N^0 + N + N^2 + N^3 + \cdots$$

The matrix N is composed of decimal fractions p_{ij}, where $0 \leq p_{ij} \leq 1$. Thus as the power n becomes large, N^n approaches zero. It can be shown that this series of matrices behaves like a power series, having for its sum the limit

$$N^0 + N + N^2 + N^3 + \cdots = (I - N)^{-1} \qquad (4\text{-}6)$$

I is an $n \times n$ identity matrix. This is analogous to the algebraic power series

$$1 + x + x^2 + x^3 + \cdots = \frac{1}{1 - x} \qquad \text{where } |x| < 1 \qquad (4\text{-}7)$$

Thus, for a given starting state, the matrix $(I - N)^{-1}$ gives the expected number of times a process is in each nonabsorbing state before absorption. Using the example which models a sequential inspection plan, this is demonstrated below.

$$I - N = \begin{bmatrix} 1 & 0 & 0 & 0 & 0 \\ 0 & 1 & 0 & 0 & 0 \\ 0 & 0 & 1 & 0 & 0 \\ 0 & 0 & 0 & 1 & 0 \\ 0 & 0 & 0 & 0 & 1 \end{bmatrix} - \begin{bmatrix} 0 & .9 & 0 & 0 & 0 \\ 0 & 0 & .9 & 0 & 0 \\ 0 & 0 & 0 & .9 & 0 \\ 0 & 0 & 0 & 0 & .9 \\ 0 & 0 & 0 & 0 & 0 \end{bmatrix}$$

$$= \begin{bmatrix} 1 & -.9 & 0 & 0 & 0 \\ 0 & 1 & -.9 & 0 & 0 \\ 0 & 0 & 1 & -.9 & 0 \\ 0 & 0 & 0 & 1 & -.9 \\ 0 & 0 & 0 & 0 & 1 \end{bmatrix}$$

Invert this matrix to obtain $(I - N)^{-1}$.

$$(I - N)^{-1} = \begin{array}{c} \\ \\ (0,0)S_1 \\ (1,0)S_2 \\ (2,0)S_3 \\ (3,0)S_4 \\ (4,0)S_5 \end{array} \begin{array}{ccccc} (0,0) & (1,0) & (2,0) & (3,0) & (4,0) \\ S_1 & S_2 & S_3 & S_4 & S_5 \\ \begin{bmatrix} 1 & .9 & .81 & .729 & .6561 \\ 0 & 1 & .9 & .81 & .729 \\ 0 & 0 & 1 & .9 & .81 \\ 0 & 0 & 0 & 1 & .9 \\ 0 & 0 & 0 & 0 & 1 \end{bmatrix} \end{array}$$

To interpret this result, start at the beginning of the inspection process, S_1; the expected number of times in this state is 1, in state 2 (1 good, 0 bad) is .9, in state 3 is .81, etc. If the process is now in state S_3 (2 good, 0 bad) the expected number of times in S_3 is 1, in S_4 is .9 and in S_5 is .81. As indicated previously, the expected number of steps before absorption is the sum of the times the process is in each non-absorbing state.

Initial state	Expected steps before absorption
S_1	$1 + .9 + .81 + .729 + .6561 = 4.0951$
S_2	$1 + .9 + .81 + .729 = 3.439$
S_3	$1 + .9 + .81 = 2.71$
S_4	$1 + .9 = 1.9$
S_5	1

EXAMPLE 4-8　Find the expected number of steps to absorption for the transition matrix

$$
\begin{array}{c@{}c}
 & \begin{array}{cccc} S_1 & S_2 & S_3 & S_4 \end{array} \\
\begin{array}{c} S_1 \\ S_2 \\ S_3 \\ S_4 \end{array} &
\left[\begin{array}{cccc}
.2 & .3 & .3 & .2 \\
0 & 1 & 0 & 0 \\
.4 & 0 & .3 & .3 \\
.4 & .2 & .2 & .2
\end{array}\right]
\end{array}
$$

Rearrange the matrix into four partitions.

$$
\begin{array}{c@{}c}
 & \begin{array}{c@{\quad}ccc} S_2 & S_1 & S_3 & S_4 \end{array} \\
\begin{array}{c} S_2 \\ \\ S_1 \\ S_3 \\ S_4 \end{array} &
\left[\begin{array}{c|ccc}
1 & 0 & 0 & 0 \\ \hline
.3 & .2 & .3 & .2 \\
0 & .4 & .3 & .3 \\
.2 & .4 & .2 & .2
\end{array}\right]
\end{array}
$$

Find $I - N$.

$$
\begin{bmatrix}
1 & 0 & 0 \\
0 & 1 & 0 \\
0 & 0 & 1
\end{bmatrix} -
\begin{bmatrix}
.2 & .3 & .2 \\
.4 & .3 & .3 \\
.4 & .2 & .2
\end{bmatrix} =
\begin{bmatrix}
.8 & -.3 & -.2 \\
-.4 & .7 & -.3 \\
-.4 & -.2 & .8
\end{bmatrix}
$$

Find $(I - N)^{-1}$.

$$
(I - N)^{-1} =
\begin{bmatrix}
2.551 & 1.429 & 1.173 \\
2.245 & 2.857 & 1.633 \\
1.837 & 1.429 & 2.245
\end{bmatrix}
$$

Starting in state S_1, the expected number of steps to absorption is $2.551 + 1.429 + 1.173 = 5.153$. Starting in state S_3, the expected number of steps to absorption is $2.245 + 2.857 + 1.633 = 6.735$. Starting in state S_4, the expected number of steps to absorption is $1.837 + 1.429 + 2.245 = 5.511$.　　　////

　　To find the probability of absorption by any given absorbing state, a similar logic is used in the analysis. Let j signify some given absorbing state; let i signify some specified nonabsorbing state; and let k be any nonabsorbing state.

　　Probability of ending in j = probability of going from i to j in 1 step
　　　　　　　　　　　　+ probability of going from i to j in 2
　　　　　　　　　　　　steps + probability of going from i to j
　　　　　　　　　　　　in 3 steps + $\cdots$

　　Probability of going from i to j in 1 step = A

Probability of going from i to j in 2 steps $=$ probability of going from i to k in 1 step $\times$ probability of going from k to j in 1 step, summed for all values of $k = NA$

Probability of going from i to j in 3 steps $=$ probability of going from i to k in 2 steps $\times$ probability of going from k to j in 1 step, summed for all values of $k = N^2 A$

Probability of going from i to j in 4 steps $= N^3 A$

Probability of going from i to j in n steps $= N^{n-1} A$

Thus the probability of going from i to j is the sum of the terms in a converging series.

$$\text{Probability of going from } i \text{ to } j = A + NA + N^2 A + N^3 A + \cdots$$
$$= IA + NA + N^2 A + N^3 A + \cdots$$
$$= (I + N + N^2 + N^3 + \cdots)A \qquad (4\text{-}8)$$

$$\text{Probability} = (I - N)^{-1} A \qquad (4\text{-}9)$$

Returning to the example of the inspection. The probability that the process will end by accepting the lot as good is the probability of being absorbed in state S_6 (five good parts).

$$(I - N)^{-1} A =
\begin{bmatrix}
1 & .9 & .81 & .729 & .6561 \\
0 & 1 & .9 & .81 & .729 \\
0 & 0 & 1 & .9 & .81 \\
0 & 0 & 0 & 1 & .9 \\
0 & 0 & 0 & 0 & 1
\end{bmatrix}
\begin{bmatrix}
0 & .1 & 0 & 0 & 0 & 0 \\
0 & 0 & .1 & 0 & 0 & 0 \\
0 & 0 & 0 & .1 & 0 & 0 \\
0 & 0 & 0 & 0 & .1 & 0 \\
.9 & 0 & 0 & 0 & 0 & .1
\end{bmatrix}$$

$$= \begin{array}{c}
S_1 \\ S_2 \\ S_3 \\ S_4 \\ S_5
\end{array}
\begin{array}{cccccc}
S_6 & S_7 & S_8 & S_9 & S_{10} & S_{11} \\
\left[\begin{array}{cccccc}
.59049 & .1 & .09 & .081 & .0729 & .06561 \\
.6561 & 0 & .1 & .09 & .081 & .0729 \\
.729 & 0 & 0 & .1 & .09 & .081 \\
.81 & 0 & 0 & 0 & .1 & .09 \\
.9 & 0 & 0 & 0 & 0 & .1
\end{array}\right]
\end{array}$$

To interpret this result, the probability of absorption in state S_6 if the initial state is S_1 is .59049. Thus the probability that the lot is accepted is .59049. The probability of rejection is the sum of the probabilities of absorption by the rejection states, S_7, S_8, S_9, S_{10}, and S_{11}.

Probability of rejection starting at $S_1 = .1 + .09 + .081 + .0729 + .06561$
$$= .40951$$

FIRST-PASSAGE TIMES FOR NONABSORBING CHAINS

At times it is of interest in a nonabsorbing chain to determine the expected number of steps before the process enters or reaches the nonabsorbing state j if it starts in state i. This is analogous to the process of absorption in an absorbing chain. Thus to determine first-passage times for a specified state j, simply modify the transition matrix so that state j appears to be an absorbing state and use the previously developed method of analysis.

As an example, using the automobile-customer problem, find the expected number of purchases before a present Ford owner (state S_1) buys a Plymouth (state S_3). The transition matrix is modified to make state S_3 (Plymouth purchase) an absorbing state:

$$
\begin{array}{c c}
 & \begin{array}{ccc} S_1 & S_2 & S_3 \end{array} \\
\begin{array}{c} S_1 \\ S_2 \\ S_3 \end{array} &
\left[\begin{array}{ccc}
.4 & .3 & .3 \\
.2 & .5 & .3 \\
0 & 0 & 1
\end{array} \right]
\end{array}
$$

Partition this matrix into four submatrices:

$$
\begin{array}{c c}
 & \begin{array}{ccc} S_3 & S_1 & S_2 \end{array} \\
\begin{array}{c} S_3 \\ \\ S_1 \\ S_2 \end{array} &
\left[\begin{array}{c|cc}
1 & 0 & 0 \\
\hline
.3 & .4 & .3 \\
.3 & .2 & .5
\end{array} \right]
\end{array}
$$

$$
I - N = \begin{bmatrix} 1 & 0 \\ 0 & 1 \end{bmatrix} - \begin{bmatrix} .4 & .3 \\ .2 & .5 \end{bmatrix} = \begin{bmatrix} .6 & -.3 \\ -.2 & .5 \end{bmatrix}
$$

$$
(I - N)^{-1} = \begin{bmatrix} 2.08 & 1.25 \\ .82 & 2.50 \end{bmatrix}
$$

This says that the expected number of times before a Ford owner first buys a Plymouth is $2.08 + 1.25 = 3.33$. In addition, the expected first-passage time from S_2 to S_3 is $.82 + 2.50 = 3.32$.

EXAMPLE 4-9 Determine the first-passage times to states S_1 and S_2.
Find the first-passage time to S_1. Make S_1 an absorbing state.

$$
\begin{array}{c}
\begin{array}{ccc} S_1 & S_2 & S_3 \end{array} \\
\begin{array}{c} S_1 \\ S_2 \\ S_3 \end{array}
\begin{bmatrix} 1 & 0 & 0 \\ .2 & .5 & .3 \\ .25 & .25 & .5 \end{bmatrix}
\end{array}
$$

$$
I - N = \begin{bmatrix} 1 & 0 \\ 0 & 1 \end{bmatrix} - \begin{bmatrix} .5 & .3 \\ .25 & .5 \end{bmatrix} = \begin{bmatrix} .5 & -.3 \\ -.25 & .5 \end{bmatrix}
$$

$$
(I - N)^{-1} = \begin{bmatrix} 2.86 & 1.71 \\ 1.43 & 2.86 \end{bmatrix}
$$

The expected number of times before a Chevrolet owner first buys a Ford is 2.86 + 1.71 = 4.57 times; for a Plymouth owner it is 1.43 + 2.86 = 4.29 times.
Find the first-passage times to S_2.

$$
\begin{array}{c}
\begin{array}{ccc} S_2 & S_1 & S_3 \end{array} \\
\begin{array}{c} S_2 \\ S_1 \\ S_3 \end{array}
\begin{bmatrix} 1 & 0 & 0 \\ .3 & .4 & .3 \\ .25 & .25 & .5 \end{bmatrix}
\end{array}
$$

$$
I - N = \begin{bmatrix} 1 & 0 \\ 0 & 1 \end{bmatrix} - \begin{bmatrix} .4 & .3 \\ .25 & .5 \end{bmatrix} = \begin{bmatrix} .6 & -.3 \\ -.25 & .5 \end{bmatrix}
$$

$$
(I - N)^{-1} = \begin{bmatrix} 2.22 & 1.33 \\ 1.11 & 2.67 \end{bmatrix}
$$

The expected number of times before a Ford owner buys a Chevrolet is 2.22 + 1.33 = 3.55; for a Plymouth owner it is 1.11 + 2.67 = 3.78.   ////

FORMULATION OF PHYSICAL OR ECONOMIC PROBLEMS AS A MARKOV CHAIN

A surprising number of physical or economic situations can be mathematically modeled by a Markov chain. This often requires ingenuity in the definition of a step or a state and a sound background in basic probabilities. The first tends to be the result of experience. A few examples are presented in this section to illustrate how Markov chains can be used.

One interesting application of Markov chains lies in the analysis of problems containing feedback or the possibility of returning to states previously occupied. As

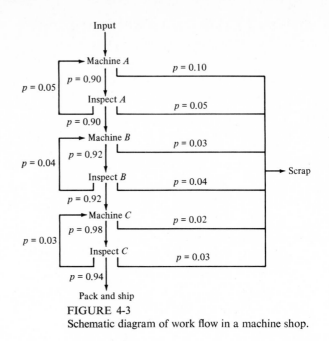

FIGURE 4-3
Schematic diagram of work flow in a machine shop.

an example, suppose a machine shop makes 100 parts; and the sequence of manu-facturing steps for each part is:

Machine *A*
Inspect *A*
Machine *B*
Inspect *B*
Machine *C*
Inspect *C*
Pack and ship

Actually the real sequence would be more complex than this since parts could be ruined during the machining step, e.g., a casting defect might be uncovered while machining, and immediately classified as defective without going to inspection. In some cases, the inspector might return the part to the earlier machine center for reworking instead of labeling it as defective. This real sequence is described in the schematic outline in Fig. 4-3, and estimated probabilities are indicated. Suppose the following questions are asked.

1 What expected fraction of parts started are completed and shipped?
2 Given data on estimated times per operation, what is the expected man-hour requirement at each station?
3 Given data on wage rates and materials costs, what are the expected direct costs?

These questions can be answered by the analysis of a problem formulated as a Markov chain.   Assume that the following additional data have been obtained.

Operation	Estimated operation time, man hours	Hourly operation
Machine A	3.0	$10
Machine B	2.5	10
Machine C	1.5	12
Inspection (all)	.25	10
Pack and ship	.10	8

The materials cost $15 per part, and scrap value is $2 per part.

The first step in the problem formulation is to define a step and a state to be used in the Markov chain.   In this problem a state will be defined as an operation center; thus machine A will be state 1, inspect A will be state 2, etc.   A step will be defined as the completion of work at an operation center.   This gives a chain having eight states:

State	Description
1	Machine A
2	Inspect A
3	Machine B
4	Inspect B
5	Machine C
6	Inspect C
7	Pack and ship
8	Scrap

Since a step is the completion of work at an operation center, the probabilities presented in Fig. 4-3 can be used to complete the transition matrix.

$$
\begin{array}{c c c c c c c c c}
 & 1 & 2 & 3 & 4 & 5 & 6 & 7 & 8 \\
1 & 0 & .90 & & & & & & .10 \\
2 & .05 & & .90 & & & & & .05 \\
3 & & & & .97 & & & & .03 \\
4 & & & .04 & & .92 & & & .04 \\
5 & & & & & & .98 & & .02 \\
6 & & & & & .03 & & .94 & .03 \\
7 & & & & & & & 1 & \\
8 & & & & & & & & 1 \\
\end{array}
$$

Notice that states 7 and 8 are absorbing states.   Once a part is completed and shipped, it will not return; similarly, once it has been scrapped, it will not be reused.

To answer the first question, the probability of absorption by state 7 is required. This will be the probability that a part is completed, packed, and shipped. This requires the analysis of an absorbing chain.

$$
N = \begin{array}{c} \\ 1 \\ 2 \\ 3 \\ 4 \\ 5 \\ 6 \end{array}
\begin{array}{cccccc}
1 & 2 & 3 & 4 & 5 & 6 \\
.9 & & & & & \\
.05 & .90 & & & & \\
& & .97 & & & \\
& .04 & & .92 & & \\
& & & & .98 & \\
& & & .03 & &
\end{array}
\qquad
A = \begin{array}{c} \\ 1 \\ 2 \\ 3 \\ 4 \\ 5 \\ 6 \end{array}
\begin{array}{cc}
7 & 8 \\
0 & .10 \\
0 & .05 \\
0 & .03 \\
0 & .04 \\
0 & .02 \\
.94 & .03
\end{array}
$$

$$
I - N = \begin{array}{c} \\ 1 \\ 2 \\ 3 \\ 4 \\ 5 \\ 6 \end{array}
\begin{array}{cccccc}
1 & 2 & 3 & 4 & 5 & 6 \\
1 & -.9 & & & & \\
-.05 & 1 & -.9 & & & \\
& & 1 & -.97 & & \\
& & -.04 & 1 & -.92 & \\
& & & & 1 & -.98 \\
& & & & -.03 & 1
\end{array}
$$

$$
(I - N)^{-1} = \begin{array}{c} \\ 1 \\ 2 \\ 3 \\ 4 \\ 5 \\ 6 \end{array}
\begin{array}{cccccc}
1 & 2 & 3 & 4 & 5 & 6 \\
1.05 & .94 & 88. & .86 & .81 & .79 \\
.05 & 1.05 & .98 & .95 & .90 & .88 \\
0 & 0 & 1.04 & 1.01 & .96 & .97 \\
0 & 0 & .04 & 1.04 & .99 & .94 \\
0 & 0 & 0 & 0 & 1.03 & 1.01 \\
0 & 0 & 0 & 0 & .03 & 1.03
\end{array}
$$

To get the probability of absorption by state 7, find the product $(I - N)^{-1}A$.

$$
(I - N)^{-1}A = \begin{array}{c} \\ 1 \\ 2 \\ 3 \\ 4 \\ 5 \\ 6 \end{array}
\begin{array}{cc}
1 & 2 \\
.75 & .25 \\
.83 & .17 \\
.88 & .12 \\
.91 & .09 \\
.95 & .05 \\
.97 & .03
\end{array}
$$

Thus for an entering part (at state 1) the probability of being successfully completed is .75. If exactly 100 parts are started, the number expected to be completed is .75(100) = 75. Not knowing the standard deviation makes it difficult to make probability statements, but if 100/.75 = 134 parts are started, 100 would be expected to be completed.

Row 1 in the matrix $(I - N)^{-1}$ provides the data needed for the analysis to answer question 2. These values represent the expected number of times an *entering part* spends in each operation center. Thus the expected time required in a center is the product of the expected number of times in that center and the estimated operation time.

ESTIMATED MAN-HOUR REQUIREMENTS PER ENTERING PART

Operation	State		Man-hours
Machine *A*	1	3.0 × 1.05	3.15
Inspect *A*	2	.25 × .94	.23
Machine *B*	3	2.5 × .88	2.20
Inspect *B*	4	.25 × .86	.22
Machine *C*	5	1.5 × .81	1.21
Inspect *C*	6	.25 × .79	.20
			7.21

In addition, .1 hours will be required for packing and shipping the completed part. To cover this information on a completed-part basis, divide all values by the probability of a successful completion.

ESTIMATED MAN-HOUR REQUIREMENTS PER COMPLETED PART

Operation		man/hours
Machine *A*	3.15/.75	4.20
Inspect *A*	.23/.75	.31
Machine *B*	2.20/.75	2.93
Inspect *B*	.22/.75	.29
Machine *C*	1.2/.75	1.61
Inspect *C*	.20/.75	.27
Pack and ship		.10
		9.71

Finally these data are used to obtain an expected direct cost of a completed part. This value will be the sum of the operation costs plus the materials cost minus any scrap value of rejected parts.

OPERATIONS COST

Operation	Hourly rate	Man-hours	Total cost
Machine *A*	10	4.20	$42.0
Inspect *A*	10	.31	3.10
Machine *B*	10	2.93	29.30
Inspect *B*	10	.29	2.90
Machine *C*	12	1.61	19.32
Inspect *C*	10	.27	2.70
Pack and ship	8	.10	.80
			$100.12

Materials cost $= \$15(1.33) - \$2(1.33)(.25) = \$19.29$.

or

Materials cost = number of parts started to complete 1 good part
− number of parts started × probability of rejection × scrap value

Accounting practices vary from firm to firm, yet this general procedure can be used to estimate product cost and manpower or machine-time requirements.

Most queuing problems can be analyzed by means of a Markov chain although other techniques may be more favorable when they apply. The use of Markov chains is particularly desirable when unusual distributions of arrival or service are required. As an example, consider the following queuing problem. This facility has a single channel and only three spaces for arriving customers to wait for service.

If a state is defined as the number in the system (either in service or waiting), the maximum value is 4; at this point arriving customers are refused and returned to the parent population. Let a step be a small increment in time Δt such that an arriving unit cannot be serviced during that time. For consistency, the following assumptions are made regarding time of arrivals and service.

1 Customers arrive at the beginning of a period.
2 Services are completed at the end of a period.

Thus, if the system is full, early arrivals are turned away even though an empty spot develops at the end of the period. The following data have been accumulated on customer arrival and service probabilities during the time period Δt.

No. of Arrivals	Probability	No. of units serviced	Probability*
0	.6	0	.5
1	.4	1	.4
2	0	2	.1

* This is a conditional probability, i.e., the probability of two units being serviced $= .1$ given that 2 units require service.

The possible states are $S_0 =$ empty, $S_1 = 1$ unit being serviced, S_2, S_3, and

$S_4 = 1$ unit being serviced and 1, 2, or 3 units waiting.   The first step will be to find the probabilities, p_{ij}, required for the transition matrix.

Probability	Description	Value
$p_{0,0}$	Empty now, empty next time; probability of no arrivals	.6
$p_{0,1}$	Empty now, one in system next time; this can occur by having one arrival	.4
$p_{0,2}$	Empty now, two in system next time, not possible	
$p_{0,3}, p_{0,4}$	Not possible	
$p_{1,0}$	One in system now, empty next time; this can occur by having no arrivals and a completed service	$.6(1-.5) = .30$
$p_{1,1}$	This can occur in two ways: a One in system, no arrivals and no services b One in system, one arrival and one service	$a + b = .6(.5) + .4(1-.5)$ $= .30 + .20 = .50$
$p_{1,2}$	One in system, one arrival, no service	$.4(1-.5) = .20$
$p_{1,3}, p_{1,4}$	Not possible	
$p_{2,0}$	Two in system, no arrivals, two services	$.6(.1) = .06$
$p_{2,1}$	a. Two in system, no arrivals, one service b. Two in system, one arrival, two services	$.6(.4) + .4(.1) = .24 + .04 = .28$
$p_{2,2}$	Two in system, no arrivals, no service Two in system, one arrival, one service	$.6(.5) + .4(.4) = .30 + .16 = .46$
$p_{2,3}$	Two in system, one arrival, no service	$.4(.5) = .20$
$p_{2,4}$	Not possible	
$p_{3,0}$	Not possible	
$p_{3,1}$	Three in system, no arrivals, two services	$.6(.1) = .06$
$p_{3,2}$	Three in system, no arrivals, one service Three in system, one arrival, two services	$.6(.4) + 4(.1) = .24 + .04 = .28$
$p_{3,3}$	Three in system, no arrivals, no service Three in system, one arrival, one service	$.6(.5) + .4(.4) = .30 + .16 = .46$
$p_{3,4}$	Three in system, one arrival, no service	$.4(.5) = .20$
$p_{4,0}$	Not possible	
$p_{4,1}$	Not possible	
$p_{4,2}$	Four in system, two services (none can arrive since they would be rejected)	.1
$p_{4,3}$	Four in system, one service	.4
$p_{4,4}$	Four in system, no service	.5

This gives the transition matrix.

$$\begin{bmatrix} .60 & .40 & 0 & 0 & 0 \\ .30 & .50 & .20 & 0 & 0 \\ .06 & .28 & .46 & .20 & 0 \\ 0 & .06 & .28 & .46 & .20 \\ 0 & 0 & .10 & .40 & .50 \end{bmatrix}$$

Since this is an ergodic chain, steady-state conditions can be determined.   Let V_i represent the individual components of the steady-state vector V^*.

$$v_0 + v_1 + v_2 + v_3 + v_4 = 1$$
$$.6v_0 + .3v_1 + .06v_2 \qquad\qquad = v_0$$
$$.4v_0 + .5v_1 + .28v_2 + .06v_3 \qquad = v_1$$
$$.2v_1 + .46v_2 + .28v_3 + .1v_4 = v_2$$
$$.20v_2 + .46v_3 + .4v_4 = v_3$$

Solving these equations gives values for v_0, v_1, v_2, v_3, and v_4.

$$V^* = [.30 \quad .36 \quad .20 \quad .10 \quad .04]$$

This says that the system is empty .30 of the time, has 1 unit in service .36 of the time, etc.   The average number in the system is $0(.30) + 1(.36) + 2(.20) + 3(.10) + 4(.04) = 1.22$.   Since $v_4 = .04$, the conditional probability that an arriving customer is turned away is .04.

REFERENCES

1 CLARK, A. BRUCE, and RALPH L. DISNEY: "Probability and Random Processes for Engineers and Scientists," John Wiley & Sons, Inc., New York, 1970.

2 HILLIER, FREDERICK S. and GERALD J. LIEBERMAN: "Introduction to Operations Research," pp. 402–438, Holden-Day, Inc., Publisher, San Francisco, 1967.

3 KEMENY, JOHN G., HAZELTON MIRKEL, J. LAURIE SNELL, and GERALD L. THOMPSON: "Finite Mathematical Structures," pp. 384–438, Prentice-Hall, Inc., Englewood Cliffs, N.J., 1959.

4 KEMENY, JOHN G., and J. LAURIE SNELL: "Finite Markov Chains," Prentice-Hall, Inc., Englewood Cliffs, N.J., 1960.

5 LEVIN, RICHARD I., and CHARLES A. KIRKPATRICK: "Quantitative Approaches To Management," 2d ed., pp. 346–367, McGraw-Hill Book Company, New York, 1971.

PROBLEMS

4-1 Two teams are to play a best of seven series; i.e., when one team wins four games, it is declared champion and the series ends. If the Cowboys have a probability of .6 of winning any one game and the Roustabouts have a probability of .4 of winning, represent this as a Markov chain and form the transition matrix P.

4-2 For each transition matrix below, find P^2 and P^3. Is it a regular chain?

(a) $\begin{bmatrix} .2 & .3 & .5 \\ 0 & 0 & 1 \\ 1 & 0 & 0 \end{bmatrix}$
$\qquad$
(b) $\begin{bmatrix} \frac{1}{4} & \frac{3}{4} \\ 1 & 0 \end{bmatrix}$
$\qquad$
(c) $\begin{bmatrix} \frac{1}{4} & \frac{3}{4} \\ 0 & 1 \end{bmatrix}$

4-3 Find the steady-state vector V^* for each of the regular matrices below.

(a) $\begin{bmatrix} \frac{1}{3} & \frac{2}{3} \\ \frac{5}{6} & \frac{1}{6} \end{bmatrix}$

(b) $\begin{bmatrix} 0 & 0 & 1 \\ \frac{1}{3} & \frac{1}{3} & \frac{1}{3} \\ \frac{1}{2} & \frac{1}{4} & \frac{1}{4} \end{bmatrix}$

(c) $\begin{bmatrix} .6 & .4 \\ .3 & .7 \end{bmatrix}$

(d) $\begin{bmatrix} .8 & .2 & .0 \\ .2 & .4 & .4 \\ 0 & .5 & .5 \end{bmatrix}$

4-4 A market survey is made on three brands of breakfast foods, X, Y, and Z. Every time the customer purchases a new package, he may buy the same brand or switch to another brand. The following estimates are obtained, expressed as decimal fractions:

$$\begin{array}{c} \text{Present} \\ \text{brand} \end{array} \begin{array}{c} \\ X \\ Y \\ Z \end{array} \overset{\begin{array}{ccc} \text{Brand just} \\ \text{purchased} \\ X \quad Y \quad Z \end{array}}{\begin{bmatrix} .7 & .2 & .1 \\ .3 & .5 & .2 \\ .3 & .3 & .4 \end{bmatrix}}$$

At this time it is estimated that 30 percent of the people buy brand X, 20 percent brand Y, and 50 percent brand Z. What will the distribution of customers be two time periods later?

4-5 Determine if the following chains are ergodic and/or regular.

(a) $\begin{bmatrix} 0 & 0 & 1 \\ 0 & .5 & .5 \\ 1 & 0 & 0 \end{bmatrix}$

(b) $\begin{bmatrix} .5 & 0 & .5 & 0 \\ 0 & .7 & 0 & .3 \\ .5 & 0 & .5 & 0 \\ 0 & .7 & 0 & .3 \end{bmatrix}$

(c) $\begin{bmatrix} 0 & 1 & 0 \\ .5 & 0 & .5 \\ 0 & 1 & 0 \end{bmatrix}$

4-6 Find the steady-state vector V^* for each of the chains in Prob. 4-5 if possible.

4-7 Two men match coins. Fred wins if the coins are the same, and Jim wins if they are not alike. Jim starts with three coins and Fred with two coins, and the game will end when either of them wins all the coins.
(a) Formulate this as a Markov chain.
(b) What is the probability that Fred wins all the coins?
(c) What is the expected number of flips that will be made before the game ends?

4-8 What is the probability that the process described by the following matrix will be in state 1?

$$\begin{array}{c} \\ 1 \\ 2 \end{array} \overset{\begin{array}{cc} 1 & 2 \end{array}}{\begin{bmatrix} .6 & .4 \\ .2 & .8 \end{bmatrix}}$$

4-9 Show that an absorbing chain is not regular.

4-10 The probability that a part will fail during a time interval Δt is .1. After failure it is replaced.
(a) Describe this as an absorbing Markov chain.
(b) Find the expected number of time intervals before replacement.

4-11 Given the transition matrix below and that the process is in state 1, what is the probability that the process ends in state 4?

$$
\begin{array}{c c}
 & \begin{array}{c c c c} 1 & 2 & 3 & 4 \end{array} \\
\begin{array}{c} 1 \\ 2 \\ 3 \\ 4 \end{array} &
\left[\begin{array}{c c c c}
.2 & .3 & .4 & .1 \\
0 & 1 & 0 & 0 \\
1 & 0 & 0 & 0 \\
0 & 0 & 0 & 1
\end{array} \right]
\end{array}
$$

4-12 P, the transition matrix for a Markov chain is given by

$$
\begin{array}{c c}
 & \begin{array}{c c c} 1 & 2 & 3 \end{array} \\
\begin{array}{c} 1 \\ 2 \\ 3 \end{array} &
\left[\begin{array}{c c c}
1 & 0 & 0 \\
0 & 1 & 0 \\
a & b & c
\end{array} \right]
\end{array}
\qquad
\begin{array}{l}
a + b + c = 1 \\
a, b, c > 0
\end{array}
$$

Find the values for a, b, and c such that starting from state 3, the average number of steps to absorption is four and the probability of being absorbed in state 2 is twice the probability of being absorbed in state 1.

4-13 In Prob. 4-1 what is the probability that the Cowboys win the championship?

4-14 Dr. Small likes to go duck hunting. He only shoots at one duck at a time regardless of how many fly by. The probability of a hit is .2. A maximum of two ducks per day are allowed. Describe this as an absorbing Markov chain. Find the expected number of shots he must take before he gets his limit.

4-15 A sequential inspection procedure is used, inspecting parts on item-by-item basis and classifying them as good or bad. The inspection plan is sketched. If 10 percent of the parts are bad, find the probability of rejecting the lot.

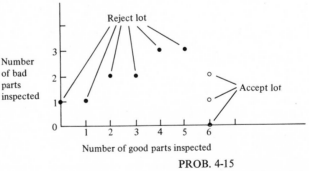

PROB. 4-15
Number of parts inspected.

4-16 A similar inspection procedure is used, but the parts are classified as *oversize, undersize,* or *within specification*. The lot is rejected when 1 unit is found oversize *or* when 1 unit is found undersize. It is accepted when 3 parts are found within the specification. If 10 percent of the parts are oversize and 5 percent are undersize, what is the probability of acceptance?

4-17 A machine operates with a probability of .3 of failure during any given time period; 60 percent of the time the failure can be fixed in exactly one period, and in all other cases it will require exactly two periods for repair. Assume failures occur at the *end* of a period. Downtime costs $50 per period.

    (*a*) Formulate as a Markov chain, describe the states and assumptions, and develop a transition matrix.

    (*b*) For $20 per time period, an extra helper can be hired so that a failure is always repaired in one period. Should this be done?

4-18 In a certain production process, items pass through two manufacturing stages. At the end of each stage, the items are junked (probability of .2), sent through the stage again for rework (probability of .3), or passed on to the next step (probability of .5).

    (*a*) Describe this as a Markov chain and set up the transition matrix.

    (*b*) What is the expected number of steps to absorption?

    (*c*) If 100 parts are started in a lot, what is the expected number of good parts that will be completed?

5

REPLACEMENT MODELS

NEED FOR REPLACEMENT

If a venture continues over an extended time, the equipment becomes worn and a decision regarding the need for replacement becomes necessary. This need for replacement may be caused by a loss of efficiency, leading to an economic decline. In this case, there is no sharp, clearly defined point when the need for replacement is obvious. An economic trade-off exists between increasing and decreasing cost functions. The decreasing cost function is that of depreciation of the original equipment; i.e., spreading the capital cost over a longer time results in a lower average cost. This favors the decision not to replace. In contrast, the increasing cost function is that of decreasing efficiency due to age or wear. This favors the decision to replace at an early age to reduce operating and maintenance cost. Minimum cost is obtained by summing both terms and determining the minimum total cost.

A separate but similar problem is the need for replacement due to failure or impending failure. The decreasing cost function is still that of depreciating the original equipment cost. The operating efficiency is not considered to change with use, but replacement is required due to a failure. After failure, no decision is required since repair or replacement is necessary. However, it may be economically advantageous to replace or repair on a scheduled basis before failure occurs.   In this case, early replacement results in decreased cost.   Thus, the problem becomes one of determining an optimal replacement interval.

REPLACEMENT DUE TO ECONOMIC DESIGN

Economic decline in the use of equipment may be the result of several factors, either individually or in combination.   The most common of these are:

> Increasing maintenance cost
> Increasing operation cost
> Technical and/or economic obsolescence

The first two factors, maintenance and operation, are generally grouped together since this is a normal result of deterioration from time and wear.   These are the easiest factors to consider since they can generally be estimated with a fair degree of accuracy.   The existence of technical or economic obsolescence is well established; yet it is very difficult to estimate, especially for a relatively short time.   For this reason, this factor is first treated as a separate case.

INCREASED OPERATION AND MAINTENANCE COST

Discrete Method of Analysis

Since both operation and maintenance costs tend to increase with the passage of time, they are grouped in presenting the method of analysis.   The effects of increased operation and maintenance costs can be evaluated by two techniques, tabular or classical optimization.   The tabular method offers two major advantages: it is simple and permits one to use discontinuous data.   Let us look at an example.

Fleet cars have increased costs as they continue in service due to increased direct operating cost (gas and oil) and increased maintenance (repairs, tires, batteries, etc.). The initial cost is $3,500, and the trade-in value drops as time passes until it reaches a constant value of $500.   The problem is to determine the proper length of service before cars should be replaced.   In this example, the time value of money will not be considered; i.e., interest will be assumed to equal zero.   Cost data are presented in Table 5-1.

If the interest rate is assumed to be zero, the comparison can be made on an average cost basis.   The total cost of owning and operating the vehicle is accumulated for n years, and this total is divided by n. Table 5-2 demonstrates this analysis. As indicated in Table 5-2, replacement every 3 years results in the lowest average annual cost, $3,200 per year. Note that this assumes a continuing requirement for this equipment.

If the effect of the time value of money is to be considered, the analysis must be based on an equivalent annual cost. To do this, all values must first be converted to a present-worth basis. These values are then accumulated as in Table 5-2, but an equivalent annual cost for n years of service life is determined instead of a strictly arithmetic average. This analysis is presented in Table 5-3. Note that the results in the final column are determined by using the equal-payment-series capital-recovery factor (Ref. 6), where

$$A = P\left[\frac{i(1 + i)^n}{(1 + i)^n - 1}\right] = P(AP^{i-n}) \qquad (5\text{-}1)$$

In this factor, A is assumed to be one of a series of equal year-end payments. Thus this comparison is based on year-end cost instead of beginning-of-the-year costs. For beginning-of-the-year costs, these values are discounted back in time for one period. The decision will be the same although the values themselves will be different.

The analysis in Table 5-3 indicates an optimum replacement period of 4 years instead of 3 years as indicated when the effect of interest was neglected. Thus the effect of interest tends to shift the decision toward an increased service life. Figure 5-1 presents a graphical comparison of the results of these two methods of analysis. As Fig. 5-1 indicates, the inclusion of an interest charge will increase the computed cost. Actually, in almost all cases the total-average-cost curve is so flat that the decision indicated by the simple analysis when $i = 0$ does not increase the cost by a significant factor. However, if i is large (above 20 percent) and applied to large investment values, the analysis should consider the time value of money.

Table 5-1   COST DATA FOR AUTOMOBILE
OPERATION

Initial price $3,500

Years of service	Year-end trade-in value	Annual operating cost	Annual Maintenance cost
1	$1,900	$1,500	$ 300
2	1,050	1,800	400
3	600	2,100	600
4	500	2,400	800
5	500	2,700	1,000

Table 5-2 TABULAR ANALYSIS, ZERO INTEREST

(1) Years of service	(2) Trade-in value	(3) Investment cost (initial minus trade-in)	(4) Yearly operation and maintenance cost	(5) Summation of operation and maintenance cost	(6) Average investment cost per year $(6) = \frac{(3)}{(1)}$	(7) Average operation plus maintenance cost per year $(7) = \frac{(5)}{(1)}$	(8) Total average annual cost $(8) = (6) + (7)$
1	$1,900	$1,600	$1,800	$1,800	$1,600	$1,800	$3,400
2	1,050	2,450	2,200	4,000	$\frac{2,450}{2} = 1,225$	$\frac{4,000}{2} = 2,000$	3,225
3	600	2,900	2,700	6,700	$\frac{2,900}{3} = 967$	$\frac{6,700}{3} = 2,233$	3,200
4	500	3,000	3,200	9,900	$\frac{3,000}{4} = 750$	$\frac{9,900}{4} = 2,475$	3,225
5	500	3,000	3,700	13,600	$\frac{3,000}{5} = 600$	$\frac{13,600}{5} = 2,720$	3,320

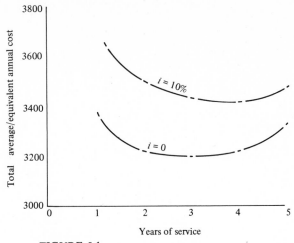

FIGURE 5-1
Comparison of results of analysis when $i = 0$, $i = 10\%$.

Note that in this example if the decision had been made to replace every 3 years, the increase in equivalent annual cost would have been only $3,431 - 3,416 = 15$. This is an error of only .4 percent, which is certainly less than the accuracy of any estimated data which might be used.

The tabular method can also be formulated as a mathematical model and optimized by this means. The case of zero interest will be presented first.

The average investment cost is the capital expense divided by the number of service periods.

$$\text{Average investment cost} = \frac{I - T_n}{n} \qquad (5\text{-}2)$$

where I = initial investment cost

T_n = trade-in value at end of nth period

n = number of service periods

The average cost of operation and maintenance is the cumulative amount spent on operation and maintenance divided by the number of service periods.

$$\text{Average operation and maintenance} = \frac{\sum_{i=1}^{n} O_i + M_i}{n} \qquad (5\text{-}3)$$

where O_i = operating cost for ith period

M_i = maintenance cost for ith period

Thus the average total cost ATC_n, for n periods is the sum of these two components.

Table 5-3 TABULAR METHOD, INTEREST –10%, COMPOUNDED ANNUALLY

(1) Years of service	(2) Present worth of trade-in, Trade-in $\times (PS10 - n)$	(3) Initial investment – present worth trade-in $3,500 - (2)$	(4) Present worth of operation + maintenance cost (Operation + maintenance) $\times (PS10 - n)$	(5) Total present worth of operation plus maintenance cost	(6) Total present worth of investment cost plus operation and maintenance $(3) + (5)$	(7) Equivalent annual cost of service $(6)(RP10 - n)$
1	$1,727	$3,500 - 1,727$ = 1,773	$1,637	$1,637	$1,773 + 1,637$ = 3,410	$3,751
2	867	$3,500 - 867$ = 2,632	1,818	$1,637 + 1,818$ = 3,455	$2,632 + 3,455$ = 6,087	3,507
3	450	$3,500 - 450$ = 3,050	2,028	$3,455 + 2,028$ = 5,483	$3,050 + 5,483$ = 8,533	3,431
4	341	$3,500 - 341$ = 3,159	2,186	$5,483 + 2,186$ = 7,669	$3,159 + 7,669$ = 10,828	3,416
5	310	$3,500 - 310$ = 3,190	2,297	$7,669 + 2,297$ = 9,966	$3,190 + 9,966$ = 13,156	3,470

If $I - T_n$ is assumed to be monotonically decreasing and $\sum_{i=1}^{n}(O_i + M_i)$ is assumed to be monotonically increasing, a means of proving an optimum value of n can be developed. In addition, decision rules for replacement can be established. Under these assumptions, there will exist a value for n that results in the minimum ATC. Let this be ATC_n. Thus $\text{ATC}_{n-1} > \text{ATC}_n < \text{ATC}_{n+1}$. From this, the two inequalities

$$\text{ATC}_{n-1} - \text{ATC}_n > 0 \qquad (5\text{-}4)$$

$$\text{ATC}_{n+1} - \text{ATC}_n > 0 \qquad (5\text{-}5)$$

can be established. This says that if ATC_n is truly a minimum, any other ATC value must be greater or equal.

From these inequalities, a basic decision rule can be derived:

$$\text{ATC}_n = \frac{1}{n}\left[I - T_n + \sum_{i=1}^{n}(O_i + M_i)\right] \qquad (5\text{-}6)$$

Rewrite for period $n + 1$.

$$\text{ATC}_{n+1} = \frac{1}{n+1}\left[I - T_{n+1} + \sum_{i=1}^{n+1}(O_i + M_i)\right] \qquad (5\text{-}7)$$

Regroup terms to allow expression in the same terms as for the nth period, see underlined terms.

$$\text{ATC}_{n+1} = \frac{1}{n+1}\left[\underline{I - T_n} + T_n - T_{n+1} + \underline{\sum_{i=1}^{n}(O_i + M_i)} + O_{n+1} + M_{n+1}\right] \qquad (5\text{-}8)$$

$$= \frac{n}{n+1}\frac{I - T_n + \sum_{i=1}^{n}(O_i + M_i)}{n} + \frac{1}{n+1}(T_n - T_{n+1} + O_{n+1} + M_{n+1}) \qquad (5\text{-}9)$$

$$= \frac{n}{n+1}\text{ATC}_n + \frac{1}{n+1}(T_n - T_{n+1} + O_{n+1} + M_{n+1}) \qquad (5\text{-}10)$$

$$\text{ATC}_{n+1} - \text{ATC}_n = \frac{n}{n+1}\text{ATC}_n - \text{ATC}_n + \frac{1}{n+1}(T_n - T_{n+1} + O_{n+1} + M_{n+1}) \qquad (5\text{-}11)$$

$$= \text{ATC}_n\frac{-1}{n+1} + \frac{1}{n+1}(T_n - T_{n+1} + O_{n+1} + M_{n+1}) \qquad (5\text{-}12)$$

Since $\text{ATC}_{n+1} > \text{ATC}_n$, then $\text{ATC}_{n+1} - \text{ATC}_n > 0$.

$$-\text{ATC}_n\frac{1}{n+1} + \frac{1}{n+1}(T_n - T_{n+1} + O_{n+1} + M_{n+1}) > 0$$

Multiply both sides by $n + 1$.

$$-\text{ATC}_n + T_n - T_{n+1} + O_{n+1} + M_{n+1} > 0$$

$$\text{ATC}_n < T_n - T_{n+1} + O_{n+1} + M_{n+1} \qquad (5\text{-}13)$$

This provides the first decision rule.

Rule 1   If the loss in trade-in value for the next period $(T_n - T_{n+1})$ plus the cost of operation and maintenance $(O_{n+1} + M_{n+1})$ is greater than ATC_n, it is economical to replace.

To obtain the second decision rule, write the expressions for ATC_{n-1} and ATC_n.

$$\text{ATC}_{n-1} = \frac{1}{n-1}\left[I - T_{n-1} + \sum_{i=1}^{n-1}(O_i + M_i)\right] \tag{5-14}$$

$$\text{ATC}_n = \frac{1}{n}\left[I - T_n + \sum_{i=1}^{n}(O_i + M_i)\right] \tag{5-15}$$

$$= \frac{1}{n}\left[I - T_{n-1} + T_{n-1} - T_n + \sum_{i=1}^{n-1}(O_i + M_i) + (O_n + M_n)\right] \tag{5-16}$$

$$= \frac{1}{n}\left[(\text{ATC}_{n-1})(n-1) - T_n + T_{n-1} + O_n + M_n\right] \tag{5-17}$$

$$\text{ATC}_n - \text{ATC}_{n-1} = \text{ATC}_{n-1}\left(\frac{n-1}{n} - 1\right) + \frac{T_{n-1} - T_n + O_n + M_n}{n} \tag{5-18}$$

$$= \text{ATC}_{n-1}\frac{n-1-n}{n} + \frac{T_{n-1} - T_n + O_n + M_n}{n} \tag{5-19}$$

$$= \frac{-\text{ATC}_{n-1} + T_{n-1} - T_n + O_n + M_n}{n} \tag{5-20}$$

Since $\text{ATC}_n < \text{ATC}_{n-1}$, then $\text{ATC}_n - \text{ATC}_{n-1} < 0$.   Thus

$$\frac{-\text{ATC}_{n-1} + T_{n-1} - T_n + O_n + M_n}{n} < 0 \tag{5-21}$$

$$\text{ATC}_{n-1} > T_{n-1} - T_n + O_n + M_n \tag{5-22}$$

This gives decision rule 2.

Rule 2   If the decrease in trade-in value plus the cost of operation and maintenance for the next period is less than the present ATC, do not replace.

Referring to Table 5-2 and applying rule 1, note that for the third period, the decrease in trade-in value plus the operation and maintenance cost is $(600 - 500) + 3{,}200 = 3{,}300$.   This value is greater than the average total cost for three periods; thus decision rule 1 says replace.   Applying rule 2, the decrease in investment value plus operation and maintenance cost for period 3, $(1{,}050 - 600) + 2{,}700 = 3{,}150$, is less than the ATC_3 ($\$3{,}200$); so decision rule 2 says not to replace at the end of period $n - 1$, that is, at the end of period 2.

A similar analysis can be made when the interest rate is considered to be a significant factor.   Here the comparison is made on the basis of equivalent annual cost (EAC). For this analysis, assume that all costs for operation and maintenance are accounted at the end of each period. If replacement is made at the end of n periods the equivalent annual cost is the present worth of all costs for n periods multiplied by the capital-recovery factor.

Present worth for replacement after n periods =

investment − discounted trade-in + sum of all operation and maintenance costs discounted to present

$$PW~(n) = I - \frac{T_n}{(1 + i)^n} + \sum_{j=1}^{n} \frac{O_j + M_j}{(1 + i)^j} \qquad (5\text{-}23)$$

where i is the interest rate per period, compounded per period.

$$EAC_n = \left[I - \frac{T_n}{(1 + i)^n} + \sum_{j=1}^{n} \frac{O_j + M_j}{(1 + i)^j} \right] \frac{i(1 + i)^n}{(1 + i)^n - 1} \qquad (5\text{-}24)$$

If n is an optimal replacement interval,

$$EAC_{n+1} > EAC_n < EAC_{n-1}$$

This results in two decision rules for optimal replacement (see Note at the end of the chapter).

Condition 1: $EAC_n < T_n(1 + i) - T_{n+1} + O_{n+1} + M_{n+1}$

where T_n is the trade-in value at the end of the nth period but valued at time $n + 1$, T_{n+1} is the trade-in value at the end of the $(n + 1)$st period, and O_{n+1} and M_{n+1} are the operation and maintenance cost for the $(n + 1)$st period. Thus the first decision rule may be expressed as follows.

Rule 1 If the equivalent annual cost for n periods of use EAC_n is less than the discounted loss in trade-in plus the operation and maintenance cost for the $(n + 1)$st period, replace.

Referring to Table 5-2, $T_4 = 500$, $T_5 = 500$, $O_5 = 2{,}700$, and $M_5 = 1{,}000$.

$$500(1 + .10) - 500 + 2{,}700 + 1{,}000 = 3{,}750$$

From Table 5-3, $EAC_4 = 3{,}416$.

Since $3{,}416 < 3{,}750$, replacement *should* occur at the end of period 4.

To obtain the second decision rule, use the same method of analysis for the equation $\mathrm{EAC}_n - \mathrm{EAC}_{n-1}$. The fact that $\mathrm{EAC}_n - \mathrm{EAC}_{n-1} < 0$, gives the following result.

Condition 2: $\mathrm{EAC}_{n-1} > T_{n-1}(1 + i) - T_n + O_n + M_n$

> **Rule 2** If the equivalent annual cost for $n - 1$ periods of use EAC_{n-1} is greater than the discounted loss in trade-in value plus the operation and maintenance cost for the nth period, do not replace.

Referring to Table 5-2, $T_3 = 600$, $T_4 = 500$, $O_4 = 2,400$, and $M_4 = 800$.

$$600(1 + .10) - 500 + 2,400 + 800 = 3,360$$

From Table 5-3, $\mathrm{EAC}_3 = 3,431$.   Since $3,431 > 3,360$, replacement *should not* occur.

Analysis Using Continuous Functions

If both the increasing and decreasing cost functions are assumed to be continuous, the problem can be optimized by normal methods of the calculus. This technique is particularly applicable for problems dealing with future predictions since the discrete method of analysis requires data points that will be available only by estimation.   If it is possible to approximate the predictions of future expenditures as a continuous function, it will be possible to optimize the total-cost equation by taking the derivative with respect to the decision variable and solving for the value of the decision variable which minimizes total average cost.   It is convenient to assume that the decision variable will be quadratic or of some lower order.   This guarantees that the cost function will be unimodal.

One valuable asset of this method of analysis is the insight it provides management into the problem and the relationships involved.   The effects of changing parameters or errors in decisions or errors in estimating data can be evaluated using the methods of sensitivity analysis (Chap. 9).   Generally this technique is most applicable to problems in which the time value of money may be ignored, thus assuming that the interest rate is equal to zero.   As previously indicated, this assumption does not generally provide a decision involving a large error cost, and the mathematical complexity is greatly reduced.

To illustrate this method of analysis, consider the following simple problem formulation.

Average total cost = average investment cost + average operation and maintenance cost

$$\mathrm{ATC} = \frac{I}{n} + \frac{n-1}{2}(O + M) + C_o + C_m \qquad (5\text{-}25)$$

where ATC = average total cost, $/year

     I = equipment investment cost, $

     n = service life of equipment or time between replacement, years

     O = rate of increase in operation cost per time period, $/year

     M = rate of increase in maintenance cost per time period, $/year

     C_o = cost of operation for the first year of service, $

     C_m = cost of maintenance for the first year of service, $

This then assumes that the average investment cost decreases according to the hyperbolic function I/n and the operation and maintenance cost increase linearly with respect to time.

To minimize this function, take the derivative with respect to n, set equal to zero, and solve for the value of n which results in the minimum average cost.

$$\frac{d(\text{ATC})}{dn} = -\frac{I}{n^2} + \frac{O+M}{2}$$

$$-\frac{I}{n^2} + \frac{O+M}{2} = 0$$

$$n^2 = \frac{2I}{O+M}$$

$$n^* = \left(\frac{2I}{O+M}\right)^{1/2} \tag{5-26}$$

The initial cost of operation and maintenance for the first year does not appear in the final solution for n^* (optimal service life) since these are constant values and exist regardless of the value of the decision variable n.

The minimum average total cost ATC* is obtained by substituting the function n^* into the original ATC equation.

$$\text{ATC*} = \frac{I}{[2I/(M+O)]^{1/2}} + \frac{1}{2}\left[\left(\frac{2I}{M+O}\right)^{1/2} - 1\right](O+M) + C_o + C_m \tag{5-27}$$

$$\text{ATC*} = [2I(M+O)]^{1/2} - \frac{O+M}{2} + C_o + C_m \tag{5-28}$$

EXAMPLE 5-1 A company maintains a pool of cars to be used by its area representatives. The following cost data have been collected or estimated.

     Investment cost I = $3,000 = purchase price − normal trade-in

     Operation cost, first year C_o = $1,500

     Yearly increase in annual operation cost O = $225

     Maintenance cost, first year C_m = $200

     Yearly increase in annual maintenance cost M = $175

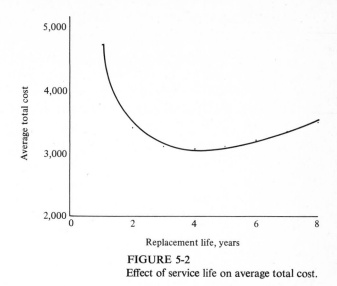

FIGURE 5-2
Effect of service life on average total cost.

Find the optimum service life n^* and the minimum average total cost ATC*.

$$n^* = \left[\frac{2(3,000)}{225 + 175}\right]^{1/2} = 3.87 \text{ years}$$

$$\text{ATC}^* = \sqrt{2(3,000)(225 + 175)} - \frac{225 + 175}{2} + 1,500 + 200$$

$$= \$3,049.19 \text{ per year} \qquad\qquad ////$$

The results of this example are presented graphically in Fig. 5-2. As indicated in this figure, the combination of a decreasing hyperbola and an increasing linear function tends to give a rather flat total-cost curve, and the decision value may vary by as much as an entire time interval without causing a significant increase in the average cost. This method of analysis is particularly desirable due to the possibility of the application of sensitivity analysis as presented in Chap. 9. Using this management tool, operating ranges for replacement life can be determined. In addition, the effects of possible errors in data can be evaluated on a cost basis.

The assumption of a linearly increasing operation and maintenance cost is not always justified. In this case, a different method of formulation and analysis is suggested. This method estimates the function which represents the average cost of operation and maintenance. It assumes that the average cost of operation and maintenance is a direct product of the first year's cost and n^k. This gives

$$\text{ATC} = \frac{I}{n} + (C_o + C_m)n^k \qquad (5\text{-}29)$$

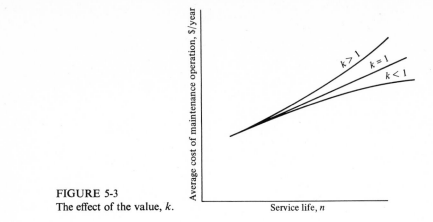

FIGURE 5-3
The effect of the value, k.

The terms are as previously indicated; k is selected to provide the best fit of the estimated cost of operation and maintenance. The major advantage of this model is the possibility of applying the techniques of sensitivity analysis. Since the term expressing average operating and maintenance cost is different from the one previously formulated, it may also fit the estimated data better. The optimal service life n^* is again found by the standard procedures of the calculus.

$$\frac{d(\text{ATC})}{dn} = -\frac{I}{n^2} + k(C_o + C_m)n^{k-1}$$

$$-\frac{I}{n^2} + k(C_o + C_m)n^{k-1} = 0$$

$$n^* = \left[\frac{I}{k(C_o + C_m)}\right]^{1/(k+1)} \tag{5-30}$$

Figure 5-3 illustrates the effects of values of k, which are either greater or less than 1. Values of k greater than 1 are used to represent operating or maintenance costs which increase over time at an increasing rate; values less than 1 represent costs which increase over time at a decreasing rate. This depends on the properties of the equipment and its environment. Increasing the value of k has the effect of decreasing the optimal service life n^*. Note that if b is selected as .5 and k as 1, this more general model is identical to the previous case, where the cost of operation and maintenance increased at a linear rate. The subtracted term is used so that the increase will not be applied to year 1.

EXAMPLE 5-2

Investment cost $I = \$3,000$
Operation cost, first year, $C_o = \$1,500$
Maintenance cost, first year, $C_m = \$200$
Best fit for constant $k = .25$

$$n^* = \left[\frac{3,000}{.25(1,500 + 200)}\right]^{1/(.25+1)} = 4.76$$

Life n, years	Average Investment cost per year	Average annual operation and maintenance cost	Total annual average cost
1	$3,000	$1,700	$4,700
2	1,500	2,022	3,522
3	1,000	2,237	3,237
4	750	2,404	3,154
5	600	2,542	3,142
6	500	2,661	3,161
7	429	2,765	3,194
8	375	2,859	3,234

Using the methods of sensitivity analysis presented in Chap. 9, find the allowable operating range for n which will not increase the variable cost more than 2 percent. From Chap. 9, the general total-cost equation is

$$Y = ax^n + \frac{b}{x^m} + c$$

and the general sensitivity term is

$$\frac{\text{TVC}}{\text{TVC*}} = \frac{1}{m+n}\left(mw^n + \frac{n}{w^m}\right)$$

Using the average total cost equation for this model,

$$\text{ATC} = \frac{I}{n} + (C_o + C_m)n^k$$

gives the tabulated equalities.

General model	Total average cost
a	$C_o + C_m$
x	n
n	$k = .25$
b	I
m	1
c	0

Table 5-4   DEVIATIONS IN COST FOR VALUES OF THE ERROR TERM

w	$\dfrac{\text{ATC}}{\text{ATC*}}$	Increase, %
1.5	1.019	1.9
1.51	1.0192	1.92
1.52	1.0199	1.99
1.53	1.020	2.0
.68	1.0205	2.05
.682	1.0202	2.02
.683	1.0201	2.01
.684	1.0199	1.99

Substituting into the general sensitivity term, we have

$$\frac{\text{ATC}}{\text{ATC*}} = \frac{1}{1+k}\left(w^k + \frac{k}{w}\right)$$

Using the value of $k = .25$ for this example, the ATC/ATC* ratio is reduced to

$$\frac{\text{ATC}}{\text{ATC*}} = \frac{1}{1.25}\left(w^{.25} + \frac{.25}{w}\right)$$

Table 5-4 presents ATC/ATC* ratios for various values of w.

Thus the error term w may range from 1.53 to .684 without exceeding the allowable increase in cost of 2 percent.   Since $n = n^*w$, the operating range of n for a maximum cost increase of 2 percent is 4.76(1.53) = 7.28 and 4.73(.684) = 3.23.

Allowable operating range (2% cost) = $7.28 \geq n \geq 3.23$ ////

REPLACEMENT UNDER CONDITIONS OF TECHNOLOGICAL AND ECONOMIC OBSOLESCENCE

It is a well-established fact that technological improvements may render equipment undesirable simply because they are no longer economically competitive with newer developments.   Thus it is feasible to replace equipment presently operating satisfactorily in a mechanical sense with newer, perhaps more expensive equipment. Analysis of problems of this type is simplified if the improvement is assumed to occur incrementally each year.   Actually, this may be inappropriate on a short-term basis since technological improvements typically occur at discrete points in time.   For example, several years may pass before a significant improvement is made in competitive equipment, then as a new model is brought out, a considerable economic disadvantage must be applied to older operating equipment.   In such a case perhaps the best method of comparison is to evaluate the economic desirability of replacement with the newer model using the standard methods of comparison discussed in engineering economy textbooks.

When equipment is expected to have an extended service life due to the extreme expense of replacement, the assumption of continuous technological improvement may be appropriate, as in the operation of oil refineries, chemical plants, etc.   Generally, historical data can be obtained for estimation of the expected rate of improvement over an extended time.   In a large, complex installation such as a refinery, the technological advance will tend to occur as a result of improvement in many separate components of the aggregate installation.   These individual improvements will generally be spread over a time span giving a net result of a more uniform technological advance of the whole operation.   Thus the assumption of an incremental improvement per time period for estimation is more appropriate.

One method of formulating this problem is to attach an economic cost to older equipment due to obsolescence.   Actually this cost is not incurred directly, but the net result is a loss in potential revenue just as though a real cost had been incurred. This gives an average total cost of operation that will be composed of three terms: investment, operation and maintenance, and economic obsolescence.   This last term is expressed by considering the potential loss in savings due to use of newer equipment as an indirect cost of continuing with present equipment.   For example, assume that the average rate of improvement is 2 percent per year, resulting in lower operation cost.   If the initial operating cost is \$100,000 per year, savings with new equipment installed 1 year from the present will be $100,000 - 100,000/(1 + .02) = \$1,961$. Inserting this term into the ATC equation provides the formulation for n years:

$$\text{ATC}_n = \frac{I + \sum_{\chi=1}^{\chi=n} (C_o + C_m)x^k + \sum_{\chi=1}^{\chi=n} C_o \left[1 - \left(\frac{1}{1+r}\right)^{x-1}\right]}{n} \qquad (5\text{-}31)$$

where r is the rate of technological improvement per year, expressed as a decimal fraction.   In this formulation, the component relating to the cost of operation and maintenance, $(C_o + C_m)n^k$, must represent the actual cost of operation and maintenance for the nth year.   If it may be assumed that *all* functions are either monotonically increasing or decreasing, then it can be shown that at the optimum service life n^*

$$\text{ATC}_n^* < (C_o + C_m)(n + 1)^k + C_o\left[1 - \left(\frac{1}{1+r}\right)^n\right] \qquad (5\text{-}32)$$

$$\text{ATC}_{n-1} > (C_o + C_m)n^k + C_o\left[1 - \left(\frac{1}{1+r}\right)^{n-1}\right] \qquad (5\text{-}33)$$

This is presented in Note 2 at the end of the chapter. These relationships allow the prediction of an optimal service life for given values of increasing operation and maintenance costs and economic obsolescence.

Interpretation of these inequations will make their application easier. In Eq. (5-32) the quantity $(C_o + C_m)(n + 1)^k$ is the cost of operation and maintenance for the $(n + 1)$st period. The quantity $C_o\{1 - [1/(1 + r)]\}^n$ represents the cost of obsolescence as a result of n periods of nonreplacement; i.e., equipment is $n + 1$ periods old. Thus n^* is an optimal service interval if the average total cost at the end of n periods is less than the sum of the operation and maintenance cost for the next period and the cost of obsolescence for the next period. Referring to Table 5-5, at $n = 16$, the $\text{ATC}_{16} = \$6,152$. The operation and maintenance cost plus obsolescence for the next period is $\$6,214$; thus the equipment should not be operated beyond 16 periods. This is verified when ATC_{17} is found to be $\$6,156$.

In the Eq. (5-33) the value n^* has been reached if the ATC at $n - 1$ is greater than the cost of operation and maintenance plus obsolescence for the coming interval. From the example, $\text{ATC}_{15} = \$6,154,000$.

$$(C_o + C_m)16^k + C_o\left[1 - \left(\frac{1}{1 + r}\right)^{15}\right] = 5,353,000 + 771,000 = 6,124,000$$

Since $6,154,000 > 6,124,000$, replacement should not occur at $n = 15$.

Table 5-5   ANALYSIS OF SERVICE LIFE FOR A REFINERY

(1)	(2)	(3)	(4)	(5)
n	ATC_n	$(C_o + C_m)(n + 1)^k$	$C_o\left[1 - \left(\frac{1}{1 + r}\right)^{m - 1}\right]$	(3) + (4)
1	18,883	3,883		3,883
2	11,535	4,127	58	4,185
3	9,165	4,309	116	4,425
4	8,031	4,455	173	4,628
5	7,386	4,579	228	4,807
6	6,983	4,686	283	4,969
7	6,717	4,781	336	5,117
8	6,534	4,866	388	5,254
9	6,406	4,943	439	5,383
10	6,316	5,015	490	5,505
11	6,253	5,081	539	5,620
12	6,209	5,142	587	5,729
13	6,180	5,200	634	5,835
14	6,163	5,254	681	5,935
15	6,154	5,305	726	6,013
16	6,152	5,353	771	6,124
17	6,156	5,400	815	6,214

EXAMPLE 5-3   A refinery is being planned, and management needs an estimate of its estimated economic service life.   The following data have been accumulated:

$$I = \$15,000,000 \qquad C_o = \$3,000,000 \qquad C_m = \$500,000$$
$$k = .15 \qquad r = .02$$

The analysis is presented in Table 5-5 using the equation previously developed for ATC.

Least cost ATC_n is at $n = 16$, $ATC_{16} = \$6,152,000$. //////

If service provided by the equipment is necessary, obviously it must be replaced when failure occurs.   The decision in this case is to determine whether the equipment should be replaced prior to failure and if so when.   In this problem, the cost trade-off exists between the lengthened service life and the accompanying lower average investment cost vs. the cost of emergency or unscheduled replacement due to failure during operation.   In many situations, shutdown costs caused by an unscheduled failure are extremely expensive due to downtime cost and the cost of expedited effort for replacement or repair.   In these cases it may be economically desirable to attempt to replace or repair the equipment just before failure.   Sometimes the cost of replacement after failure is not high enough to justify replacement until failure occurs.   This problem is meaningful only if the impending failure is probabalistic.   Should the failure time be known with certainty, the obvious answer would be to replace or schedule a repair just before failure.   However, failure in most equipment tends to be a random process and thus must be treated as probabilistic.

Generally these probabilities and their distribution can be estimated from past data of older equipment or from experimental data on prototype or test equipment. Sometimes it is necessary to alter these distributions based on judgment or as better data become available.   At any rate, past data are commonly used to predict the probability of future failures.   The method of analysis presented in this section is restricted to items which have an increasing probability of failure as time increases, i.e., with length in service.   Premature failure, often called infant mortality, during breaking-in periods will be neglected; thus we assume that the equipment has already been subjected to any necessary run-in time.

Total-Cost Equation

In most cases, this method of analysis will be applied to equipment with a relatively short span of life in terms of years.   Thus it will be assumed that the time value of money is negligible.   Since the equipment life is a variable, the total-cost equation will be expressed as an average cost per time period.   The average total cost then is the sum of the cost of the initial installment spread over the effective life of the equipment plus the expected cost of failure:

$$\text{ATC} = \frac{1}{n} + \frac{F(x)_n C}{n} \qquad (5\text{-}34)$$

where ATC = average total cost, \$/period
l = initial installment cost, \$
n = planned service life before scheduled repair or replacement periods
$F(x)_n$ = expected number of failures during time span
C = cost of failure or breakdown, \$

With this general cost equation, the major problem is that of determining the expected number of failures $F(x)_n$ during the time span n.

Determination of Expected Failures

This is most easily illustrated by means of a simple example.   Assume that a factory making tires is being run on a three-shift basis, 7 days/week.   This factory operates 10 molding machines for tire manufacture.   Periodically maintenance work on the machines and dies is necessary to continue producing an acceptable product.   Past data indicate that the probability of a malfunction increases with length of service. Company policy has been to operate equipment until a malfunction occurred and then shut down the machine and perform the required maintenance.   Data presented in Table 5-6 have been accumulated for analysis to determine whether some other maintenance program would be better.

Table 5-6   DATA RELATING SERVICE LIFE TO OCCURRENCE OF MALFUNCTION

Service time between maintenance, number of shifts	Number of malfunctions reported	Probability of malfunction pn	Conditional probability of malfunction pc_n	Conditional probability of no malfunction pr_n
1	20	$\frac{20}{200} = .10$	$\frac{20}{200} = .100$	$1 - .1 = .90$
2	30	$\frac{30}{200} = .15$	$\frac{30}{180} = .167$	$1 - .167 = .833$
3	30	$\frac{30}{200} = .15$	$\frac{30}{150} = .200$	$1 - .2 = .8$
4	60	$\frac{60}{200} = .30$	$\frac{60}{120} = .500$	$1 - .5 = .5$
5	40	$\frac{40}{200} = .20$	$\frac{40}{60} = .667$	$1 - .667 = .333$
6*	20	$\frac{20}{200} = .10$	$\frac{20}{20} = 1.00$	$1 - 1 = 0$

* No equipment has functioned satisfactorily more than six shifts without maintenance.

The problem then is of scheduling maintenance programs on a regular basis. This can be done at the beginning of any shift without incurring excessive downtime cost. The first step in analysis is to compute the expected number of failures for a potential maintenance program. This is complicated by the fact that some failures will occur between any scheduled maintenance. It is possible that equipment may fail, be repaired, and fail again before a scheduled repair occurs. This gives a cumulative effect to the expected number of failures $F(x)_n$ which becomes more complex as n becomes large.

This problem can be approached by the classical techniques of probability if n is not too large. Failures and repair will be treated as if they occurred at the end of a period. The expected number of failures during the first period is $p_1 n = .10(10) = 1$. The expected number of failures during the second period, $n = 2$, is the sum of the failures occurring for the first time during the second period plus those which failed during the first period, were repaired, and failed again during the second period.

$$F(x)_2 = np_2 + F(x)_1 p_1$$
$$= 10(.15) + 10(.10)(.10)$$
$$= 1.5 + .1 = 1.6$$

The expected number of failures during the third period, $n = 3$, is formulated in a similar manner. This is most easily followed by means of the simple table below.

POSSIBLE COMBINATIONS RESULTING IN FAILURE AT PERIOD $n = 3$

	Period		
$n = 1$	$n = 2$	$n = 3$	Probability expression
OK	OK	Fail	p_3
OK	Fail	Fail	$p_2 p_1$
Fail	OK	Fail	$p_1 p_2$
Fail	Fail	Fail	$p_1 p_1 p_1$

$$F(x)_3 = 10(p_3 + p_2 p_1 + p_1 p_2 + p_1 p_1 p_1)$$
$$= 10[.15 + .15(.10) + .10(.15) + .10(.10)(.10)]$$
$$= 1.81$$

This is actually a combinational problem, becoming increasingly complex as n becomes large. The tables below present an analysis for $n = 4$ and $n = 5$.

POSSIBLE COMBINATIONS RESULTING IN FAILURE AT PERIOD $n = 4$

	Period			Probability expression
$n = 1$	$n = 2$	$n = 3$	$n = 4$	
OK	OK	OK	Fail	p_4
OK	OK	Fail	Fail	$p_3 p_1$
OK	Fail	OK	Fail	$p_2 p_2$
Fail	OK	OK	Fail	$p_1 p_3$
OK	Fail	Fail	Fail	$p_2 p_1 p_1$
Fail	OK	Fail	Fail	$p_1 p_2 p_1$
Fail	Fail	OK	Fail	$p_1 p_1 p_2$
Fail	Fail	Fail	Fail	$p_1 p_1 p_1 p_1$

$$F(x)_4 = 10[.30 + .15(.1) + .15(.15) + .10(.15) + .15(.10)(.10)$$
$$+ .10(.15)(.10) + .10(.10)(.15) + .10(.10)(.10)(.10)]$$
$$= 3.571$$

POSSIBLE COMBINATIONS RESULTING IN FAILURE AT PERIOD $n = 5$

	Period				Probability expression
$n = 1$	$n = 2$	$n = 3$	$n = 4$	$n = 5$	
OK	OK	OK	OK	Fail	p_5
OK	OK	OK	Fail	Fail	$p_4 p_1$
OK	OK	Fail	OK	Fail	$p_3 p_2$
OK	Fail	OK	OK	Fail	$p_2 p_3$
Fail	OK	OK	OK	Fail	$p_1 p_4$
OK	OK	Fail	Fail	Fail	$p_3 p_1 p_1$
OK	Fail	OK	Fail	Fail	$p_2 p_2 p_1$
Fail	OK	OK	Fail	Fail	$p_1 p_3 p_1$
OK	Fail	Fail	OK	Fail	$p_2 p_1 p_2$
Fail	OK	Fail	OK	Fail	$p_1 p_2 p_2$
Fail	Fail	OK	OK	Fail	$p_1 p_1 p_3$
OK	Fail	Fail	Fail	Fail	$p_2 p_1 p_1 p_1$
Fail	OK	Fail	Fail	Fail	$p_1 p_2 p_1 p_1$
Fail	Fail	OK	Fail	Fail	$p_1 p_1 p_2 p_1$
Fail	Fail	Fail	OK	Fail	$p_1 p_1 p_1 p_2$
Fail	Fail	Fail	Fail	Fail	$p_1 p_1 p_1 p_1 p_1$

$$F(x)_5 = 10[.2 + .3(.1) + .15(.15) + .15(.15) + .1(.3) + .15(.1)(.1)$$
$$+ .15(.15)(.1) + .1(.15)(.1) + .15(.1)(.15) + .1(.15)(.15)$$
$$+ .1(.1)(.15) + .15(.1)(.1)(.1) + .1(.15)(.1)(.1)$$
$$+ .1(.1)(.15)(.1) + .1(.1)(.1)(.15) + .1(.1)(.1)(.1)(.1)]$$
$$= 3.1686$$

Formulation as a Markov Chain

As this simple example illustrates, the number of combinations becomes extremely large as the number of time intervals n increases. This problem is much more easily handled if it is formulated as a Markov chain. This can be done quite easily by recognizing that a step-by-step procedure exists in going from one time interval to the next. In this case, the states of the Markov chain will be the ages of the ith unit of equipment.

Included in Table 5-6 are the conditional probabilities of failure or malfunction for all possible periods of operation. This represents the probability of malfunction during the $n = 1$ period if it is known that the equipment has had a service life of n periods. Once a malfunction does occur, the unit will be repaired or replaced and thus begin the next period with a prior service life of zero. This assumes no operation in the remaining shift time. The total number of states required for a Markov chain is determined by the maximum possible service life of the equipment in question. In this example, the maximum life is six time intervals; thus the number of states is six. Based on this, a transition matrix is formulated to represent the probabilities of a unit's failing or not failing during the next period.

This transition matrix P is interpreted by saying that if a unit is now newly repaired (in state 0), the probability that it will fail (and thus be repaired) during the

Table 5-7   TRANSITION MATRIX FOR PROBABLE FAILURES: NEXT STATE

Present state (age at beginning of interval)	Age at start of next interval					
	0	1	2	3	4	5
0	pc_1	pr_1	0	0	0	0
1	pc_2	0	pr_2	0	0	0
2	pc_3	0	0	pr_3	0	0
3	pc_4	0	0	0	pr_4	0
4	pc_5	0	0	0	0	pr_5
5	pc_6	0	0	0	0	0

Present state	Next state					
	0	1	2	3	4	5
0	.100	.900	0	0	0	0
1	.167	0	.833	0	0	0
2	.200	0	0	.800	0	0
3	.500	0	0	0	.500	0
4	.667	0	0	0	0	.333
5	1	0	0	0	0	0

very next time interval is .100, similarly, if the unit has had an operating time of one shift (in state 1) the probability of failing and thus beginning the next interval in state 0 is .167.   Note that if the unit is now in state 5 (has had five shifts of operation), the probability of failure is 1 and thus it will be repaired and begin in state 0 next time.

To analyze this problem using Markov chains, define a vector X^n which represents the number of units in each state at n periods.   If all units start having just been repaired, $X^0 = [10\ \ 0\ \ 0\ \ 0\ \ 0\ \ 0]$, which says that all 10 machines are in state 0.   If this vector is multiplied by P, X^0P, the result will be X^1, or the expected number of machines in each state after 1 shift:

$$X^1 = [1\ \ 9\ \ 0\ \ 0\ \ 0\ \ 0]$$

This says that during the first shift one machine will be expected to require maintenance and thus go back to state 0.

The vectors, X^2, X^3, X^4, and X^5 represent the expected number of machines in each state after two, three, four, or five shifts if maintenance is performed only after failure.

$$X^2 = [1.60\ \ \ .90\ \ 7.50\ \ 0\ \ 0\ \ 0]$$
$$X^3 = [1.81\ \ \ 1.44\ \ \ .75\ \ 6.00\ \ 0\ \ 0]$$
$$X^4 = [3.57\ \ \ 1.63\ \ \ 1.20\ \ \ .60\ \ 3\ \ 0]$$
$$X^5 = [3.17\ \ \ 3.21\ \ \ 1.36\ \ \ .96\ \ \ .3\ \ 1]$$

In each case, the value representing the 0 state indicates the expected number of machines failing during that time period.   The techniques developed in Chap. 3 can be used to determine steady-state conditions if maintenance is provided only after failure.

$$X^*P = X^*$$

$$[x_0^*\ \ x_1^*\ \ x_2^*\ \ x_3^*\ \ x_4^*\ \ x_5^*]P = [x_0^*\ \ x_1^*\ \ x_2^*\ \ x_3^*\ \ x_4^*\ \ x_5^*]$$

$$.100x^* + .167x^* + .200x^* + .500x^* + .667x^* + x_5 = x_0^*$$
$$.900x_0^* \qquad\qquad\qquad\qquad\qquad\qquad = x_1^*$$
$$.833x_1^* \qquad\qquad\qquad\qquad\qquad = x_2^*$$
$$.800x_2^* \qquad\qquad\qquad\qquad = x_3^*$$
$$.500x_3^* \qquad\qquad\qquad = x_4^*$$
$$.333x_4^* \quad = x_5^*$$

From the last six equations, X^* is determined:

$$X^* = [2.74\ \ \ 2.47\ \ \ 2.06\ \ \ 1.64\ \ \ .82\ \ \ .27]$$

Since $x_0^* = 2.74$, this says that at steady-state conditions, an average of 2.74 of the machines will fail each shift.

Economic Analysis

To determine a least-cost replacement or maintenance policy, various feasible policies must be evaluated. Assume that the following four cases are under consideration.

Plan A Repair as failures occur

Plan B Repair as failures occur but after every second shift rebuild all equipment

Plan C Same as *B* but after every third shift

Plan D Same as *B* but after every fourth shift

For this example, the following conditions will be assumed to exist:

Cost of an unscheduled stoppage (failure) = \$250

Basic cost of maintenance per machine = \$50

A machine that fails will be repaired during the shift it fails and begin the next shift newly repaired. If a scheduled maintenance is to occur at the end of the same shift in which failure occurred, the cost of unscheduled stoppage (\$250) will be incurred. However, the basic maintenance cost will be applied to the scheduled program.

To evaluate plan A, refer to the steady-state conditions. Although the units may have started under the same conditions, after some time steady-state conditions will exist. Referring to X^*, an *average* of 2.74 units will have an unscheduled stoppage *every* period. Thus the average cost will be the cost of these repairs and additional costs:

$$\text{ATC (plan A)} = (250 + 50)\,2.74 = \$822 \text{ per shift}$$

In this case both the cost of maintenance and extra cost for an unscheduled stop are always incurred. Since the original cost of preparation is spread over many periods, it is considered insignificant.

To evaluate plan B, use the total-cost expression previously developed with slight modifications:

$$\text{ATC} = \frac{I}{n} + \frac{F(x_n)C}{n} \qquad (5\text{-}35)$$

where I = initial investment cost (basic cost of maintenance) = $\$50(10) = \$500$

n = planned service life for plan $B = 2$

$F(x_n)$ = expected number of failures during time n

C = cost of failure = $\$250 + \$50$

The terms $F(x_n)$ and C must be modified since if failure occurs during the nth period, only \$250 is charged against that cycle of service.

$$\text{ATC}_B = \frac{500}{2} + \tfrac{1}{2}[1(300) + 1.6(250)] = \$600 \text{ per shift}$$

where the first bracketed term is labeled "Number of failures during period 1" and the second "Number of failures during period 2."

Note that we have used the data on failures from X^1 and X^2 to determine the number of breakdowns.

To evaluate plan C, the same procedure is used except that $n = 3$, and thus the failures from X^1, X^2, and X^3 must be used.

$$\text{ATC}_C = \tfrac{500}{3} + \tfrac{1}{3}[(1 + 1.6)(300) + 1.81(250)]$$
$$= \$577.50 \text{ per shift}$$

Thus the cost is decreased by extending the planned service period.

Finally plan D must consider four periods with $n = 4$.

$$\text{ATC}_D = \tfrac{500}{4} + \tfrac{1}{4}[(1 + 1.6 + 1.81)(300) + 3.57(250)]$$
$$= \$678.87 \text{ per shift}$$

Since this is now increasing, there is no need to evaluate policies with larger values of n. Of all four plans, plan C with an ATC of \$577.50 and $n = 3$ gives the least cost of operation.

NOTES

1 Decision Rules for Optimal Replacement

To establish the existence of an optimum replacement interval n, the conditions which result in $\text{EAC}_{n-1} > \text{EAC}_n < \text{EAC}_{n+1}$ must be evaluated. If $\text{EAC}_n < \text{EAC}_{n+1}$, then $\text{EAC}_{n+1} - \text{EAC}_n$ must be positive, or greater than zero. The first decision rule is determined by using this relationship. As presented in the main body of the chapter, the equivalent annual cost when replacement occurs after n periods is given by

$$\text{EAC}_n = \left[I - \frac{T_n}{(1+i)^n} + \sum_{j=1}^{n} \frac{O_j + M_j}{(1+i)^j} \right] \frac{i(1+i)^n}{(1+i)^n - 1} \qquad (5\text{-}24)$$

For ease of algebraic manipulations, the following substitutions will be made. Let $V = 1 + i$ and $K_j = O_j + M_j$.

$$\text{EAC}_n = \left(I - \frac{T_n}{V^n} + \sum_{j=1}^{n} \frac{K_j}{V^j} \right) \frac{iV^n}{V^n - 1}$$

Rewrite the above equation in terms of $n + 1$.

$$\text{EAC}_{n+1} = \left(I - \frac{T_{n+1}}{V^{n+1}} + \sum_{j=1}^{n+1} \frac{K_j}{V^j} \right) \frac{iV^{n+1}}{V^{n+1} - 1}$$

This equation is rewritten to resemble the EAC_n equation:

$$\text{EAC}_{n+1} = \left[I - \frac{T_n}{V^n} + \frac{T_n}{V^n} - \frac{T_{n+1}}{V^{n+1}} + \left(\sum_{j=1}^{n} \frac{K_j}{V^j} \right) + \frac{K_{n+1}}{V^{n+1}} \right] \frac{iV^{n+1}}{V^{n+1} - 1}$$

$$= \left(I - \frac{T_n}{V^n} + \sum_{j=1}^{n} \frac{K_j}{V^j} \right) \frac{iV^{n+1}}{V^{n+1} - 1} + \left(\frac{T_n}{V^n} - \frac{T_{n+1}}{V^{n+1}} + \frac{K_{n+1}}{V^{n+1}} \right) \frac{iV^{n+1}}{V^{n+1} - 1}$$

Multiply the first group of terms by the factor

$$\frac{iV^n/V^n - 1}{iV^n/V^n - 1}$$

which is equal to 1 and regroup.

$$\underbrace{\mathrm{EAC}_{n+1} = \left(I - \frac{T_n}{V^n} + \sum_{j=1}^{n} \frac{K_j}{V^j}\right) \frac{iV^n}{V^n - 1} \frac{iV^{n+1}/(V^{n+1} - 1)}{iV^n/(V^n - 1)}}_{\text{Equal to } \mathrm{EAC}_n} + \left(\frac{T_n}{V^n} - \frac{T_{n+1}}{V^{n+1}} + \frac{K_{n+1}}{V^{n+1}}\right) \frac{iV^{n+1}}{V^{n+1} - 1}$$

Simplifying terms gives

$$\frac{iV^{n+1}/(V^{n+1} - 1)}{iV^n/(V^n - 1)} = \frac{V(V^n - 1)}{V^{n+1} - 1}$$

$$\mathrm{EAC}_{n+1} = \mathrm{EAC}_n \frac{V(V^n - 1)}{V^{n+1} - 1} + \left(\frac{T_n}{V^n} - \frac{T_{n+1}}{V^{n+1}} + \frac{K_{n+1}}{V^{n+1}}\right) \frac{iV^{n+1}}{V^{n+1} - 1}$$

$$= \mathrm{EAC}_n \frac{V(V^n - 1)}{V^{n+1} - 1} + \left(T_n - \frac{T_{n+1}}{V} + \frac{K_{n+1}}{V}\right) \frac{iV}{V^{n+1} - 1}$$

Subtracting the two equations, EAC_{n+1} and EAC_n, gives

$$\mathrm{EAC}_{n+1} - \mathrm{EAC}_n = \mathrm{EAC}_n \frac{V(V^n - 1)}{V^{n+1} - 1} - \mathrm{EAC}_n + \left(T_n - \frac{T_{n+1}}{V} + \frac{K_{n+1}}{V}\right) \frac{iV}{V^{n+1} - 1}$$

$$= \mathrm{EAC}_n \left[\frac{V(V^n - 1)}{V^{n+1} - 1} - 1\right] + \left(T_n - \frac{T_{n+1}}{V} + \frac{K_{n+1}}{V}\right) \frac{iV}{V^{n+1} - 1}$$

Since $\mathrm{EAC}_{n+1} > \mathrm{EAC}_n$, it must be true that $\mathrm{EAC}_{n+1} - \mathrm{EAC}_n > 0$.

$$0 < \mathrm{EAC}_n \left[\frac{V(V^n - 1)}{V^{n+1} - 1} - 1\right] + \left(T_n - \frac{T_{n+1}}{V} + \frac{K_{n+1}}{V}\right) \frac{iV}{V^{n+1} - 1}$$

Multiply both sides of the inequality by $V^{n+1} - 1$:

$$0 < \mathrm{EAC}_n[V(V^n - 1) - (V^{n+1} - 1)] + \left(T_n - \frac{T_{n+1}}{V} + \frac{K_{n+1}}{V}\right) iV$$

Simplify the bracketed term:

$$0 < \mathrm{EAC}_n(V^{n+1} - V - V^{n+1} + 1) + \left(T_n - \frac{T_{n+1}}{V} + \frac{K_{n+1}}{V}\right) iV$$

$$0 < \mathrm{EAC}_n(-V + 1) + \left(T_n - \frac{T_{n+1}}{V} + \frac{K_{n+1}}{V}\right) iV$$

Subtract $(T_n - T_{n+1}/V + K_{n+1}/V)iV$ from each side of the inequality:

$$-\left(T_n - \frac{T_{n+1}}{V} + \frac{K_{n+1}}{V}\right) iV < \mathrm{EAC}_{(n)} (-V + 1)$$

Solve for $\text{EAC}_{(n)}$ by dividing by $V - 1$ and multiplying both sides by -1.

$$\text{EAC}_{(n)} < \left(T_n - \frac{T_{n+1}}{V} + \frac{K_{n+1}}{V} \right) \frac{iV}{V-1}$$

But $V = 1 + i$; thus $V - 1 = 1 + i - 1 = i$.

$$\text{EAC}_n < \left(T_n - \frac{T_{n+1}}{V} + \frac{K_{n+1}}{V} \right) V$$

Substituting for V and K gives the final result

$$\text{EAC}_n < T_n(1 + i) - T_{n+1} + O_{n+1} + M_{n+1}$$

2   Average Total Cost of n Period of Service

The expression for average total cost of n periods of service ATC_n is

$$\text{ATC}_n = \frac{I + \sum\limits_{x=1}^{x=n}(C_o + C_m)x^k + \sum\limits_{x=1}^{x=n} C_o\left[1 - \left(\frac{1}{1+i}\right)^{x-1}\right]}{n}$$

The last summation term n can be reformulated by recognizing that one of the components is a geometric series:

$$\sum_{x=1}^{x=n} C_o\left[1 - \left(\frac{1}{1+i}\right)^{x-1}\right] = \sum_{x=1}^{x=n} C_o - \sum_{x=1}^{x=n} C_o\left(\frac{1}{1+i}\right)^{-}$$

$$= nC_o - C_o \sum_{x=1}^{x=n}\left(\frac{1}{1+i}\right)^{x-1}$$

$$= nC_o - C_o\left[1 + \frac{1}{1+i} + \left(\frac{1}{1+i}\right)^2 + \left(\frac{1}{1+i}\right)^3 + \cdots + \left(\frac{1}{1+i}\right)^{n-1}\right]$$

Although it is not necessary, it can be shown that this is a converging geometric series.   Since i is some positive value, $i > 0$, it must follow that $1 + i > 1$. As a result, $1/(1 + i) < 1$. If $1/(1 + i)$ is defined as r and C_o as a, this is the converging geometric series

$$a + ar + ar^2 + ar^3 + \cdots$$

The sum of n terms is known to be

$$S_n = \frac{a(1 - r^n)}{1 - r}$$

thus

$$\sum_{x=1}^{x=n} C_o\left(\frac{1}{1+i}\right)^{x-1} = \frac{C_o\{1 - [1/(1+i)]^n\}}{1 - 1/(1+i)}$$

Additional algebraic manipulations can be used to obtain a slightly simplified expression.

$$\frac{1 - [1/(1 + i)]^n}{1 - 1/(1 + i)} = \frac{1 - [1/(1 + i)]^n}{(1 + i)/(1 + i) - 1/(1 + i)}$$

$$= \frac{1 - [1/(1 + i)]^n}{i/(1 + i)}$$

$$= \frac{\{1 - [1/(1 + i)]^n\}(1 + i)}{i}$$

$$= \frac{1 + i - (1 + i)[1/(1 + i)]^n}{i}$$

$$= \frac{1 + i - [1/(1 + i)]^{n-1}}{i}$$

Substituting these expressions into the original equation for ATC_n gives

$$ATC_n = \frac{1}{n}\left(I + \sum_{x=1}^{x=n}(C_o + C_m)x^k + nC_o - C_o\frac{\{1 + i - [1/(1 + i)]^{n-1}\}}{i}\right)$$

$$= \frac{1}{n}\left[I + \sum_{x=1}^{x=n}(C_o + C_m)x^k + nC_o - C_o - \frac{C_o}{i} + \frac{C_o}{i}\left(\frac{1}{1 + i}\right)^{n-1}\right]$$

Writing this in terms of $n + 1$ instead of n, we have

$$ATC_{n+1} = \frac{1}{n+1}\left[I + \sum_{x=1}^{x=n+1}(C_o + C_m)x^k + (n + 1)C_o - C_o - \frac{C_o}{i} + \frac{C_o}{i}\left(\frac{1}{1 + i}\right)^n\right]$$

The next step will be to subtract $ATC_{n+1} - ATC_n$. To obtain maximum benefit from this step, first isolate the costs in the ATC_{n+1} expression that composed the ATC_n. Begin by regrouping the terms so that they will be of the same duration as n.

$$ATC_{n+1} = \frac{1}{n+1}\left[I + \sum_{x=1}^{x=n}(C_o + C_m)x^k + (C_o + C_m)(n + 1)^k + \underline{nC_o} + C_o - \underline{C_o} - \underline{\frac{C_o}{i}}\right.$$

$$\left. + \underline{\frac{C_o}{i}\left(\frac{1}{1 + i}\right)^{n-1}} - \frac{C_o}{i}\left(\frac{1}{1 + i}\right)^{n-1} + \frac{C_o}{i}\left(\frac{1}{1 + i}\right)^n\right]$$

The underlined terms, if divided by n, constitute the value, ATC_n:

$$ATC_{n+1} = \frac{1}{n+1}\left[I + \sum_{x=1}^{x=n}(C_o + C_m)x^k + nC_o - C_o - \frac{C_o}{i} + \frac{C_o}{i}\left(\frac{1}{1 + i}\right)^{n-1}\right]$$

$$+ \frac{1}{n+1}\left[(C_o + C_m)(n + 1)^k + C_o - \frac{C_o}{i}\left(\frac{1}{1 + i}\right)^{n-1} + \frac{C_o}{i}\left(\frac{1}{1 + i}\right)^n\right]$$

Multiply the first bracketed terms by n/n, and the resulting expression is

$$
\text{ATC}_{n+1} = \frac{n}{n+1}\left\{\frac{1}{n}\left[I + \sum_{x=1}^{x=n}(C_o + C_m)x^k + nC_o - C_o - \frac{C_o}{i} + \frac{C_o}{i}\left(\frac{1}{1+i}\right)^{n-1}\right]\right\}
$$

$$
+ \frac{1}{n+1}\left\{(C_o + C_m)(n+1)^k + C_o + \frac{C_o}{i}\left[\left(\frac{1}{1+i}\right)^n - \left(\frac{1}{1+i}\right)^{n-1}\right]\right\}
$$

$$
= \frac{n}{n+1}\text{ATC}_n + \frac{1}{n+1}\left\{(C_o + C_m)(n+1)^k + C_o + \frac{C_o}{i}\left[\left(\frac{1}{1+i}\right)^n - \left(\frac{1}{1+i}\right)^{n-1}\right]\right\}
$$

Note that the bracketed expression can be reduced as follows:

$$
\left(\frac{1}{1+i}\right)^n - \left(\frac{1}{1+i}\right)^{n-1} = \left(\frac{1}{1+i}\right)^{n-1}\left(\frac{1}{1+i} - 1\right)
$$

$$
= \left(\frac{1}{1+i}\right)^{n-1}\left(\frac{1-1-i}{1+i}\right)
$$

$$
= \left(\frac{1}{1+i}\right)^{n-1}\frac{-i}{1+i}
$$

$$
= -i\left(\frac{1}{1+i}\right)^n
$$

Substituting this expression and subtracting $\text{ATC}_{n+1} - \text{ATC}_n$ gives

$$
\text{ATC}_{n+1} - \text{ATC}_n = \frac{n}{n+1}\text{ATC}_n - \text{ATC}_n + \frac{1}{n+1}\left[(C_o + C_m)(n+1)^k + C_o - C_o\left(\frac{1}{1+i}\right)^n\right]
$$

$$
= \text{ATC}_n\frac{-1}{n+1} + \frac{1}{n+1}\left\{(C_o + C_m)(n+1)^k + C_o\left[1 - \left(\frac{i}{1+i}\right)^n\right]\right\}
$$

As long as $\text{ATC}_{n+1} > \text{ATC}_n$, the right-hand side of the equation will be greater than zero:

$$
0 < \frac{-\text{ATC}_n}{n+1} + \frac{1}{n+1}\left\{(C_o + C_m)(n+1)^k + C_o\left[1 - \left(\frac{1}{1+i}\right)^n\right]\right\}
$$

Multiply through by $n+1$.

$$
0 < -\text{ATC}_n + (C_o + C_m)(n+1)^k + C_o\left[1 - \left(\frac{1}{1+i}\right)^n\right]
$$

This says that at the optimal value of n, when ATC_n^* exists, the sum of the operation and maintenance cost plus obsolescence cost for next year will be in excess of the ATC_n^*. Therefore replacement should occur when the operation and maintenance cost plus the economic obsolescence for the next period exceed ATC_n.

Since $\text{ATC}_{n-1} > \text{ATC}_n^*$, a similar method of analysis will show that

$$
\text{ATC}_{n-1} > (C_o + C_m)n^k + C_o\left[1 - \left(\frac{1}{1+i}\right)^{n+1}\right]
$$

This may be interpreted as saying: Do not replace if the cost of operation, maintenance, and obsolescence is less than the present value of ATC.

REFERENCES

1 ACKOFF, RUSSELL L., and MAURICE W. SASIENI: "Fundamentals of Operations Research," chap. 8, John Wiley & Sons, Inc., New York, 1968.

2 BARISH, NORMAN N.: "Economic Analysis," McGraw-Hill Book Company, New York, 1962.

3 CHURCHMAN, C. WEST, RUSSELL L. ACKOFF, and E. LEONARD ARNOFF: "Introduction to Operations Research," chap. 17, John Wiley & Sons, Inc., New York, 1957.

4 FABRYCKY, W. J., and PAUL E. TORGERSEN: "Operations Economy," chap. 7, Prentice-Hall, Inc., Englewood Cliffs, N.J., 1966.

5 ROBERTS, N. H.: "Mathematical Methods in Reliability Engineering," McGraw-Hill Book Company, New York, 1964.

6 THUESEN, H. G., W. J. FABRYCKY, and G. J. THUESEN: "Engineering Economy," 4th ed., Prentice-Hall, Inc., Englewood Cliffs, N.J., 1971.

PROBLEMS

5-1 If a unit of equipment costs $5,000 as purchased and has the following schedule of costs and salvage value, find the least-cost service life using the tabular method. (Assume no interest rate is applicable.)

Year	Running cost	Salvage value
1	$2,500	$3,000
2	2,750	1,800
3	3,025	1,080
4	3,330	650
5	3,660	400
6	4,025	400
7	4,425	400
8	4,850	400

5-2 Repeat Prob. 5-1 considering an interest rate of 8 percent compounded annually.

5-3 New equipment for a data processing company will cost $50,000. Operation and maintenance cost for the first year are $10,000 and $5,000, respectively. This will increase with time by the factor n^k, where $n =$ life and $k = .10$. Technical advance of newer equipment would tend to reduce operating cost by 5 percent annually. If the time value of money were neglected, what should the minimum-cost life be?

5-4   The following data have been estimated for a piece of equipment that costs $6,000.

Time	Operation cost	Maintenance cost
1	$10,000	$1,000
2	10,100	1,100
3	10,200	1,300
4	10,300	1,700
5	10,400	2,200
6	10,500	2,800
7	10,600	3,500
8	10,700	4,700

(a) Neglecting the time value of money, when should it be replaced?

(b) If i is taken at 10 percent, when should it be replaced?

5-5   An individual is considering buying some mobile homes as an investment. These units cost $5,000 new. They depreciate so that at the end of each year they have a resale value equal to 80 percent of the previous year's value down to a minimum of $1,000. Maintenance costs amount to $50 the first year and increase by 30 percent each year. The first year the unit can be rented for $160 per month. Each year after that the rent will be 95 percent of the prior rate. Assume 100 percent use. When should the unit be replaced to maximize average yearly income? Neglect interest and use the tabular method.

5-6   A pumping unit cost $3,600 installed. The cost of the first year's operation was $800 plus $200 for maintenance. Experience with similar units indicates that the sum of these two costs will increase at a rate of approximately $125 per year. How long should this equipment be operated to minimize cost?

5-7   A numerical-control machine tool will cost $18,000. Although the operating and maintenance costs are not expected to increase significantly during its operating life, new improvements are expected. Thus later equipment would be capable of processing parts at a lower unit cost. The net result is that older equipment has an implied increase in operating cost. If the average rate of technical improvement is 3 percent per year and the present operating cost is $20,000 per year, what is the expected economic service life? Assume that the equipment has no trade-in value, and neglect the time value of money.

5-8   An automatic machine cost $10,000 and essentially has zero salvage value. The first year operating and maintenance costs were $8,000 and $2,000 respectively. The rate of increase in operation cost is expected to be $200 per year and for maintenance cost $50 per year. If interest is neglected, what is the least-cost life?

5-9   A unit cost $6,000 and after a normal operating life is expected to have a salvage value of $1,000. The cost of operation and maintenance was $800, and it is expected to increase in a non-linear manner as a function of life (n^k, where $k = .3$). What is the least-cost life, neglecting the time value of money?

5-10   The following average cost data on operation and maintenance were collected during a 10-year period. Since similar equipment has been planned for a new installation, it is assumed that these are valid estimates. It is desirable to approximate these points using the curve $(C_o + C_m)n^k$. Determine a value of k which provides a satisfactory fit.

(a)

n	$C_o + C_m$ for year n
1	1,000
2	2,200
3	3,500
4	5,000
5	6,400
6	7,800
7	9,400
8	11,000
9	12,500
10	14,100

(b)

n	$C_o + C_m$ for year n
1	1,000
2	1,400
3	1,650
4	1,850
5	2,050
6	2,250
7	2,400
8	2,550
9	2,700
10	2,820

Hint: When the cost increases at an increasing rate, k must be larger than 1. Try 1.10 as a first guess.

5-11 If the initial investment for the equipment in Prob. 5-10 was $20,000, compare the optimal service life for cases (a) and (b).

5-12 Using the results of Prob. 5-11, find the upper and lower values for a service life which will not result in an increased variable cost of more than 5 percent.

5-13 A trucking company has kept records on tire life. Although failure is a random process, it is a function of tire life. The following data taken from 1,000 failures have been summarized.

Thousands of miles	Number of failures
10	50
20	100
30	250
40	400
50	200

A scheduled tire change costs $350, including the tire. A failure results in loss of travel time and requires use of emergency tools which take even longer, resulting in a net loss of $500. In addition, this ruins the tire body, which is reusable and has a value of $100. What would be the least-cost practice for tire change?

5-14 Engines are used to power individual pump units in an irrigation project. Experience has shown that the probability of a breakdown due to a minor failure increases with time. This results in a cost of $200. Normal maintenance procedures developed to prevent this cost $50. Data relating failure to operating time are given below. What should be the approved policy for maintenance?

Operating time between maintenance* hundreds of hours	Number of times recorded
500	10
1,000	15
1,500	20
2,000	35
2,500	20†

* Present policy is to run to failure, then repair.
† No unit has ever run more than 2,500 hours without requiring maintenance.

5-15 Supply bins are located throughout a plant. When a bin is empty, the foreman calls the storeroom, and they refill it. There are 10 bins located over the plant. It has been suggested that it might be cheaper to routinely refill all bins instead of sending a man out to refill an individual bin as required. It is estimated that the time required to service a single bin costs $3, but that it would cost only $10 to service all bins in one trip. The probability of a bin's being empty is a function of time.

If it is recognized that an empty bin must be filled whenever this occurs, what is the best policy for supply?

Time since refill, shifts	Probability of becoming empty
1	.1
2	.2
3	.5
4	1.0

5-16 An automatic machine requires frequent adjustment to ensure quality output. Presently work is on a three-shift basis, and so the machine runs almost continuously. If it gets out of adjustment, approximately $150 of bad parts are made before it can be corrected. Adjustment cost $50 in labor and downtime. Since the probability of unsatisfactory operation is a function of running time, it would be possible to schedule maintenance before defects were made. Should they continue to run until defective parts are made? If not, when should the machine be readjusted?

Time since adjustment, hours	Probability of defective production
1	.0
2	.10
3	.20
4	.40
5	1.00

5-17 Ball bearings in a machine have an increased probability of failure with increased service life. This machine has two bearings. Bearings cost $15 each plus $50 per unit installation cost. A bearing failure results in an additional cost of $200. The possible maintenance procedures are:

(a) Replace as failures occur.

(b) Replace individual bearings on an optimum replacement life basis.

(c) Replace both bearings on an optimum replacement life basis (as a group).

Which will result in minimum cost?

Service life, thousands of hours	Number of times failure occurred
1	10
2	15
3	15
4	30
5*	20

* No bearing has ever run more than 5,000 hours.

6

INVENTORY MODELS AND SYSTEMS

Organizations maintain raw-materials and finished-goods inventories. Raw-materials inventories serve as inputs to the production process, and finished-goods inventories are used to satisfy customer demands. Since these inventories often amount to a considerable investment, decisions regarding the amounts of inventory are important. Inventory models and the mathematical description of inventory systems provide a basis for these decisions. In this chapter some basic inventory models and systems are presented.

INVENTORY MODELS

In this section four deterministic inventory models are developed. Because these models provide an order quantity which minimizes the total incremental costs, they are often referred to as *economic-order-quantity* (EOQ) models.

Model 6-1   Purchasing Model: No Shortages

This model is one of the simplest inventory models. It makes the following assumptions:

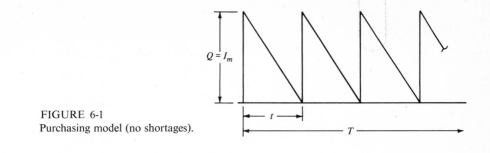

FIGURE 6-1
Purchasing model (no shortages).

1 Demand is at a constant rate.
2 Replacement is instantaneous (replacement rate is infinite).
3 All cost coefficients (C_1, C_2, C_3) are constants.

This model is illustrated schematically in Fig. 6-1.

In Fig. 6-1 the maximum inventory I_m and the purchase (order) quantity Q are shown equal. This is not always true. In fact, in most inventory models this condition ($Q = I_m$) is not true. The time t is the time between orders or the time of one period. The planning period T is taken as 1 year in the derivation of this model and the other inventory models in this chapter. This assumption is made because it simplifies the presentation, but it does not impose any limitations, as is shown in a later discussion.

The total cost for Model 6-1 is made up of three cost components:

$$\text{Total cost/Year} = \text{unit costs/year} + \text{purchasing cost/year} + \text{holding cost/year} \tag{6-1}$$

The total cost per year in this model and subsequent models is obtained by determining the total cost for one period C' and then multiplying this cost by the number of periods in a year:

$$\text{Total cost/year} = \text{total cost/period} \times \text{number of periods/year} \tag{6-2}$$

The unit cost per period is merely the cost of Q units, or

$$C_1 Q \tag{6-3}$$

where C_1 is the cost per unit.

Since only one purchase is made in a period, the purchasing cost is the cost of making one purchase, namely C_2.

The average inventory per period is $Q/2$. Therefore, the holding cost per period is

$$C_3 t \frac{Q}{2} \tag{6-4}$$

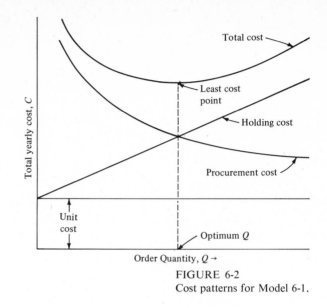

FIGURE 6-2
Cost patterns for Model 6-1.

where C_3 = cost of holding 1 unit in inventory 1 year, \$/unit-year

t = time of one period, years

The total cost per period C' is

$$C' = C_1 Q + C_2 + C_3 t \frac{Q}{2} \qquad (6\text{-}5)$$

The time of one period, expressed in years, is

$$t = \frac{Q}{D} \qquad (6\text{-}6)$$

The number of periods or orders per year N is the reciprocal of Eq. (6-6):

$$N = \frac{D}{Q} \qquad (6\text{-}7)$$

Substituting Eq. (6-6) into Eq. (6-5) and then multiplying the result by Eq. (6-7) gives

$$C = C_1 D + C_2 \frac{D}{Q} + C_3 \frac{Q}{2} \qquad (6\text{-}8)$$

If the cost components in Eq. (6-8) are plotted as shown in Fig. 6-2, an optimum point (least cost) results.

One way to determine the optimum Q is to assume various values for Q and substitute into Eq. (6-8) until the least-cost point is found.   An easier procedure is to take the derivative of Eq. (6-8) with respect to Q and set the derivative equal to zero. Since the term $C_1 D$ is a constant, the derivative of Eq. (6-8) is

$$\frac{dC}{dQ} = 0 = -\frac{C_2 D}{Q^2} + \frac{C_3}{2} \qquad (6\text{-}9)$$

Solving for Q gives

$$Q = \sqrt{\frac{2C_2 D}{C_3}} \qquad (6\text{-}10)$$

Equation (6-10) gives the order quantity which results in the least cost and is based on a balance between the two variable costs (holding costs and purchasing costs) included in the model. Any other order quantity will result in a higher cost.

EXAMPLE 6-1   The demand for a particular item is 18,000 units/year. The holding cost per unit is \$1.20 per year, and the cost of one procurement is \$400. No shortages are allowed, and the replacement rate is instantaneous. Determine:

(a) The optimum order quantity
(b) The total cost per year if the cost of 1 unit is \$1.
(c) The number of orders per year
(d) The time between orders

(a) The optimum order quantity is found using Eq. (6-10).

$$Q = \sqrt{\frac{2C_2 D}{C_3}} = \sqrt{\frac{2(400)(18,000)}{1.2}} = 3,465 \text{ units}$$

(b) The total cost is found using Eq. (6-8).

$$C = C_1 D + C_2 \frac{D}{Q} + C_3 \frac{Q}{2} = 1(18,000) + 400\frac{18,000}{3,465} + 1.2\frac{3,465}{2}$$

$$= 18,000 + 2,078 + 2,078 = \$22,156 \text{ per year}$$

(c) The number of orders per year is

$$N = \frac{D}{Q} = \frac{18,000}{3,465} = 5.2 \text{ orders/year}$$

(d) The time between orders is

$$t = \frac{1}{N} = \frac{Q}{D} = \frac{3,465}{18,000} = 0.1925 \text{ years} \qquad ////$$

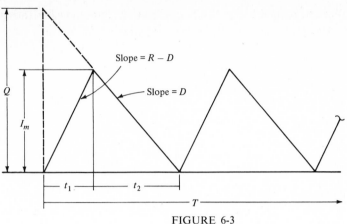

FIGURE 6-3
Manufacturing model (no shortages).

Model 6-2   Manufacturing Model: No Shortages

In this model the assumptions are the same as Model 6-1 except that the replacement rate (manufacturing rate) is finite and greater than the demand rate.   Schematically, this model is illustrated in Fig. 6-3.

The procedure used in this model to determine the optimum quantity to manufacture Q is basically the same as in Model 6-1.   Equation (6-1) is applicable; i.e., the same three cost components are involved as in Model 6-1, but in this model, a more meaningful term for purchasing cost is setup cost.

If the cost of one setup is C_2, the cost per period is

$$C' = C_1 Q + C_2 + C_3(t_1 + t_2)\frac{I_m}{2} \qquad (6\text{-}11)$$

where $I_m/2$ is the average inventory for a period.

It can be seen from Fig. 6-3 that the time between setups (time of one period), $t_1 + t_2$, is

$$t_1 + t_2 = \frac{Q}{D} \qquad (6\text{-}12)$$

With Eq. (6-12), it only remains to find an expression for I_m in terms of Q.

Since units are being used as they are made, the maximum inventory per period is the manufacturing time t_1 multiplied by the accumulation rate, where the accumulation rate is the manufacturing rate R minus the demand rate D; therefore,

$$I_m = t_1(R - D) \qquad (6\text{-}13)$$

The manufacturing time is the time required to make Q units or, in mathematical terms,

$$t_1 = \frac{Q}{R} \qquad (6\text{-}14)$$

Substituting Eq. (6-14) into Eq. (6-13) gives

$$I_m = \frac{Q}{R}(R - D) = Q\left(1 - \frac{D}{R}\right) \qquad (6\text{-}15)$$

With Eqs. (6-12) and (6-15), the total cost per period is

$$C' = C_1 Q + C_2 + C_3 \frac{Q}{D} \frac{Q}{2}\left(1 - \frac{D}{R}\right) \qquad (6\text{-}16)$$

When Eq. (6-16) is multiplied by the number of periods per year D/Q, the total annual cost is

$$C = C_1 D + C_2 \frac{D}{Q} + \frac{C_3 Q}{2}\left(1 - \frac{D}{R}\right) \qquad (6\text{-}17)$$

Taking the derivative of Eq. (6-17) gives

$$\frac{dC}{dQ} = 0 = -\frac{C_2 D}{Q^2} + \frac{C_3}{2}\left(1 - \frac{D}{R}\right) \qquad (6\text{-}18)$$

and solving for Q gives

$$Q = \sqrt{\frac{2C_2 D}{C_3(1 - D/R)}} \qquad (6\text{-}19)$$

Equation (6-19) is the optimum (least-cost) manufacturing quantity and is a balance between holding costs and setup costs.

EXAMPLE 6-2   The demand for an item in a company is 18,000 units/year, and the company can produce the item at a rate of 3,000 per month.   The cost of one setup is $500, and the holding cost of 1 unit/month is 15 cents.   Determine the optimum manufacturing quantity and the total cost per year assuming the cost of 1 unit is $2.00.

The optimum manufacturing quantity can be calculated using Eq. (6-19) and assuming 12 months/year.

$$Q = \sqrt{\frac{2(500)(18,000)}{.15(12)[1 - 18,000/3,000(12)]}} = 4,470 \text{ units}$$

The total annual cost is

$$C = 18,000(2) + 500 \frac{18,000}{4,470} + \frac{.15(12)(4470)}{2} \left[1 - \frac{18,000}{12(3,000)} \right]$$

$$= 36,000 + 2,013 + 2,013 = \$40,026$$

Certain other items may be of interest. For example, the maximum inventory is

$$I_m = Q\left(1 - \frac{D}{R}\right) = 4,470\left[1 - \frac{18,000}{12(3,000)} \right] = 2,235 \text{ units}$$

and the manufacturing time is

$$t_1 = \frac{Q}{R} = \frac{4,470}{12(3,000)} = .1241 \text{ years}$$

In addition, the total time between setups is found from the relation

$$t_1 + t_2 = \frac{Q}{R} + \frac{I_m}{D} = \frac{Q}{D}$$

$$= .1241 + .1241 = .2482 \text{ year} \qquad ////$$

Model 6-3 Purchasing Model with Shortages

This model has the same assumptions as Model 6-1 except that shortages are allowed. Consequently, a cost of shortage is incurred. This model is schematically illustrated in Fig. 6-4.

Figure 6-4 implies that back ordering is possible; i.e., once an order quantity is received, any shortages can be made up. Consequently, shortage costs are due to being short of stock for a period of time. They are not due to lost sales in this model.

Since shortage costs are included in this model, Eq. (6-1) must be modified to

$$C = \text{item cost/year} + \text{purchasing cost/year} + \text{holding cost/year}$$
$$+ \text{shortage cost/year} \tag{6-20}$$

Consequently, the cost per period is

$$C' = C_1 Q + C_2 + C_3 t_1 \frac{I_m}{2} + C_4 t_2 \frac{S}{2} \tag{6-21}$$

where $S/2$ = average number of units short per period
    C_4 = shortage cost for 1 unit/year

It now remains to find expressions for t_1, I_m, and t_2 in terms of Q and S, since these are the two basic variables in this model. This is accomplished by considering Fig. 6-4.

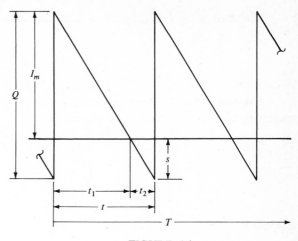

FIGURE 6-4
Purchasing model (with shortages).

The maximum inventory is

$$I_m = Q - S \qquad (6\text{-}22)$$

From similar triangle considerations, the following equations are obtained:

$$t_1 = \frac{tI_m}{Q} = \frac{t(Q - S)}{Q} \qquad (6\text{-}23)$$

$$t_2 = \frac{tS}{Q} \qquad (6\text{-}24)$$

Since the time of one period t is Q/D, Eq. (6-23) and (6-24) can be written

$$t_1 = \frac{Q - S}{Q}\frac{Q}{D} \qquad (6\text{-}25)$$

$$t_2 = \frac{S}{Q}\frac{Q}{D} \qquad (6\text{-}26)$$

Substituting Eq. (6-22), (6-23), and (6-26) into Eq. (6-21), gives

$$C' = C_1 Q + C_2 + C_3 \frac{Q - S}{Q}\frac{Q}{D}\frac{Q - S}{2} + C_4 \frac{S}{Q}\frac{Q}{D}\frac{S}{2} \qquad (6\text{-}27)$$

as the total cost per period.

Multiplying Eq. (6-27) by the number of periods per year, D/Q, gives

$$C = C_1 D + C_2 \frac{D}{Q} + \frac{C_3(Q - S)^2}{2Q} + \frac{C_4 S^2}{2Q} \qquad (6\text{-}28)$$

as the total cost per year.

Since there are two variables in Eq. (6-28) the partial derivatives are taken with respect to each variable and set equal to zero.

$$\frac{\partial C}{\partial Q} = 0 = -C_2 \frac{D}{Q^2} + \frac{C_3}{2} - \frac{C_3 S^2}{2Q^2} - \frac{C_4 S^2}{2Q^2} = -\frac{C_2 D}{Q^2} + \frac{C_3}{2} - \frac{S^2}{2Q^2}(C_3 + C_4) \qquad (6\text{-}29)$$

$$\frac{\partial C}{\partial S} = 0 = -C_3 + \frac{C_3 S}{Q} + \frac{C_4 S}{Q} \qquad (6\text{-}30)$$

Solving Eq. (6-30) for S gives

$$S = \frac{C_3}{C_3 + C_4} Q \qquad (6\text{-}31)$$

Substituting Eq. (6-31) into Eq. (6-29) gives

$$0 = -C_2 \frac{D}{Q^2} + \frac{C_3}{2} - \frac{C_3 + C_4}{2Q^2} \left(\frac{C_3}{C_3 + C_4} Q \right)^2 \qquad (6\text{-}32)$$

$$= -C_2 \frac{D}{Q^2} + \frac{C_3}{2} - \frac{C_3{}^2}{2(C_3 + C_4)} \qquad (6\text{-}33)$$

Solving Eq. (6-33) for Q gives

$$Q = \sqrt{\frac{2C_2 D}{C_3}} \sqrt{\frac{C_3 + C_4}{C_4}} \qquad (6\text{-}34)$$

which is the optimum purchase quantity for this model.

Another relationship can be obtained for the shortages by substituting Eq. (6-34) into Eq. (6-31), which results in

$$S = \sqrt{\frac{2C_2 D}{C_4}} \sqrt{\frac{C_3}{C_3 + C_4}} \qquad (6\text{-}35)$$

EXAMPLE 6-3 As an example of this model, Example 6-1 will be used with a cost of one shortage per year being $5/per unit-year.

(a) $Q = \sqrt{\dfrac{2(400)(18,000)}{1.2}} \sqrt{\dfrac{1.2 + 5}{5}}$

$= 3,465(1.114) = 3,860$ units

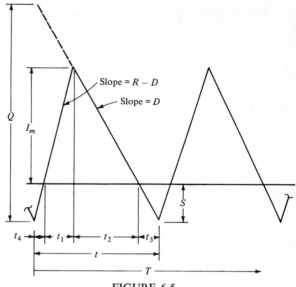

FIGURE 6-5
Manufacturing model (with shortages).

(b) In order to solve for the total cost, the number of shortages must be calculated.

$$S = \frac{C_3}{C_3 + C_4} Q = \frac{1.2}{1.2 + 5} \, 3,860 = 747 \text{ units}$$

Therefore

$$C = 18,000(1) + 400 \, \frac{18,000}{3,860} + \frac{1.2(3,860 - 747)^2}{2(3,860)} + \frac{5(747)^2}{2(3,860)}$$

$$= 18,000 + 1,865 + 1,507 + 361 = \$21,733 \text{ per year}$$

(c) The number of orders per year is $18,000/3,860 = 4.66$.

(d) The time between orders is $1/4.66 = .215$ year   ////

Model 6-4   Manufacturing Model with Shortages

In this model the assumptions are the same as model 6-2 except that shortages are allowed.   This model is illustrated schematically in Fig. 6-5.

The cost components in this model are the same as in Model 6-3, only, as before, the purchasing cost is more appropriately called setup cost.

The total cost per period is

$$C' = C_1 Q + C_2 + C_3(t_1 + t_2) \frac{I_m}{2} + C_4(t_3 + t_4) \frac{S}{2} \qquad (6\text{-}36)$$

The problem is to determine the values of t_1, t_2, t_3, t_4, and I_m in terms of Q and S. This is accomplished by considering Fig. 6-5, obtaining

$$I_m = t_1(R - D) \qquad (6\text{-}37)$$

$$I_m = t_2 D \qquad (6\text{-}38)$$

Therefore

$$t_1(R - D) = t_2 D \qquad (6\text{-}39)$$

$$S = t_4(R - D) \qquad (6\text{-}40)$$

$$S = t_3 D \qquad (6\text{-}41)$$

Therefore,

$$t_4(R - D) = t_3 D \qquad (6\text{-}42)$$

Adding Eq. (6-39) and (6-42) gives

$$(t_1 + t_4)(R - D) = (t_2 + t_3)D \qquad (6\text{-}43)$$

The manufacturing rate multiplied by the manufacturing time gives the manufactured quantity.

$$Q = (t_1 + t_4)R$$

Therefore

$$t_1 + t_4 = \frac{Q}{R} \qquad (6\text{-}44)$$

Now

$$I_m + S = (t_2 + t_3)D \qquad (6\text{-}45)$$

or using Eq. (6-43), Eq. (6-45) becomes

$$I_m + S = (t_1 + t_4)(R - D) \qquad (6\text{-}46)$$

Substituting Eq. (6-45) into Eq. (6-46) gives

$$I_m = \frac{Q}{R}(R - D) - S$$

$$= Q\left(1 - \frac{D}{R}\right) - S \qquad (6\text{-}47)$$

With Eq. (6-47), the term $t_1 + t_2$ is evaluated as

$$t_1 + t_2 = \frac{I_m}{R - D} + \frac{I_m}{D}$$

Substituting Eq. (6-47) into this result gives

$$t_1 + t_2 = \left[Q\left(1 - \frac{D}{R}\right) - S\right]\left(\frac{1}{R - D} + \frac{1}{D}\right) \quad (6\text{-}48)$$

In a similar manner, the term $t_3 + t_4$ is

$$t_3 + t_4 = S\left(\frac{1}{R - D} + \frac{1}{D}\right) \quad (6\text{-}49)$$

Substituting Eqs. (6-47) to (6-49) into Eq. (6-36) gives

$$C' = C_1 Q + C_2 + \frac{C_3}{2}\left[Q\left(1 - \frac{D}{R}\right) - S\right]^2 \left(\frac{1}{R - D} + \frac{1}{D}\right) + \frac{C_4 S^2}{2}\left(\frac{1}{R - D} + \frac{1}{D}\right) \quad (6\text{-}50)$$

Multiplying Eq. (6-50) by the number of periods per year and simplifying gives

$$C = C_1 D + C_2 \frac{D}{Q} + \frac{C_3}{2Q}\left[Q\left(1 - \frac{D}{R}\right) - S\right]^2 \left(\frac{1}{1 - D/R}\right) + \frac{C_4 S^2}{2Q}\left(\frac{1}{1 - D/R}\right) \quad (6\text{-}51)$$

To find the optimum quantity Q the partial derivatives are taken with respect to Q and S. In order to simplify this task, let

$$A = 1 - \frac{D}{R} \quad (6\text{-}52)$$

which is a constant. The partial derivatives are

$$\frac{\partial C}{\partial Q} = 0 = -C_2 \frac{D}{Q^2} + \frac{C_3 A}{2} - \frac{C_3 S^2}{2Q^2 A} - \frac{C_4 S^2}{2Q^2 A} \quad (6\text{-}53)$$

$$\frac{\partial C}{\partial S} = 0 = -C_3 + \frac{C_3 S}{AQ} + \frac{C_4 S}{AQ} \quad (6\text{-}54)$$

Solving Eq. (6-54) for S gives

$$S = \frac{C_3}{C_3 + C_4} QA = \frac{C_3}{C_3 + C_4} Q\left(1 - \frac{D}{R}\right) \quad (6\text{-}55)$$

and substituting this into Eq. (6-53) gives

$$0 = -C_2 \frac{D}{Q^2} + \frac{C_3 A}{2} - \frac{C_3}{2Q^2 A}\left(\frac{C_3}{C_3 + C_4}\right)^2 Q^2 A^2 - \frac{C_4}{2Q^2 A}\left(\frac{C_3}{C_3 + C_4}\right)^2 Q^2 A^2$$

$$= -2C_2 \frac{D}{Q^2} + C_3 A \frac{C_4}{C_3 + C_4} \quad (6\text{-}56)$$

Solving this for Q and substituting Eq. (6-52) gives

$$Q = \sqrt{\frac{2C_2 D}{C_3(1 - D/R)}} \sqrt{\frac{C_3 + C_4}{C_4}} \quad (6\text{-}57)$$

which is the optimum (least-cost) Q.

Substituting Eq. (6-57) into Eq. (6-55) results in

$$S = \sqrt{\frac{2C_2 D}{C_4}} \sqrt{1 - \frac{D}{R}} \sqrt{\frac{C_3}{C_3 + C_4}} \qquad (6\text{-}58)$$

EXAMPLE 6-4   The data for this example are the same as Example 6-2 except that the cost of 1 unit short is $20 per year.

$$Q = \sqrt{\frac{2C_2 D}{C_3(1 - D/R)}} \sqrt{\frac{C_3 + C_4}{C_4}} = \sqrt{\frac{2(500)(18,000)}{.15(12)[1 - 18,000/12(3,000)]}} \sqrt{\frac{.15(12) + 20}{20}}$$

$$= 4,470(1.045) = 4,670 \text{ units}$$

In order to calculate the annual cost, the number of shortages must be calculated.

$$S = \frac{C_3}{C_3 + C_4} Q\left(1 - \frac{D}{R}\right) = \frac{.15(12)}{.15(12) + 20} 4,670\left[1 - \frac{18,000}{12(3,000)}\right]$$

$$= \frac{1.8}{21.8} 4,670(.5) = 193 \text{ units}$$

Therefore

total Cost

$$TC = 18,000(2) + 500 \frac{18,000}{4,670} + \frac{.15(12)}{2(4,670)} \left\{4,670\left[1 - \frac{18,000}{12(3,000)}\right] - 193\right\}^2$$

$$\frac{1}{1 - 18,000/12(3,000)} + \frac{20(193)^2}{2(4,670)} \frac{1}{1 - 18,000/12(3,000)}$$

$$= 36,000 + 1,927 + 1,768 + 160 = \$39,855 \text{ per year}$$

The maximum inventory is

$$I_m = Q\left(1 - \frac{D}{R}\right) - S$$

$$= 4,670\left[1 - \frac{18,000}{12(3,000)}\right] - 193 = 2,142 \text{ units}$$

and the manufacturing time is

$$t_1 + t_4 = \frac{Q}{R} = \frac{4,670}{12(3,000)} = .1298 \text{ years}$$

In addition, the time between setups is

$$t_1 + t_2 + t_3 + t_4 = t = \frac{Q}{D} = \frac{4,670}{18,000} = .2595 \text{ years} \qquad ////$$

CHANGES IN TIME PERIODS

In the preceding inventory models, the derivation of optimum lot sizes was based on a planning period of 1 year.   This is not a necessary condition.   The important thing in regard to the time units is consistency; i.e., the time units must be the same for each quantity having a dimension of time.   For example, suppose the data of Example 6-1 are given per month instead of per year; then the following data are applicable (assuming 1 year = 12 months):

$$\text{Demand/month} = \frac{18{,}000}{12} = 1{,}500 \text{ units/month}$$

$$\text{Holding cost} = \frac{1.20}{12} = \$.10 \text{ per unit-month}$$

With these values, the optimum purchase quantity is

$$Q = \sqrt{\frac{2C_2 D}{C_3}} = \sqrt{\frac{2(400)(1{,}500)}{.10}} = 3{,}465 \text{ units}$$

which is the same answer as in Example 6-1.

The total cost per month can be calculated using Eq. (6-8) by adjusting the time units in the following manner:

$$\text{Total cost/month} = \frac{18{,}000}{12}(1) + 400 \frac{18{,}000/12}{3{,}465} + \frac{1.2}{12} \frac{3{,}465}{2}$$

$$= 1{,}500 + 173 + 173 = \$1{,}846 \text{ per month}$$

This value could also have been obtained by merely dividing the total cost per year by 12.

$$\text{Total cost/month} = \frac{C}{12} = \frac{22{,}156}{12} = \$1{,}846$$

UNIT COSTS

In the previous examples four costs (C_1, C_2, C_3, C_4) were used.   Questions often arise concerning what items should be included in the determination of these costs.

Item Cost C_1   In manufacturing, the cost of 1 unit consists of such items as direct and indirect labor, direct and indirect materials, and overhead.   When the unit is purchased, item cost is the purchase price of 1 unit.

Purchasing (setup) cost C_2 Purchasing unit costs consist of such items as clerical and administrative costs involved in processing a purchase order, expediting and follow-up costs of an order, and transportation costs. When a unit is manufactured, the unit setup cost includes the cost of labor and materials used in the setup and setup testing costs.

Inventory cost C_3 Some of the costs included in the unit holding cost are;

1 Money tied up in inventory
2 Storage-space costs
3 Handling cost
4 Taxes on inventories
5 Insurance costs
6 Obsolescence
7 Deterioration of quality
8 Cost of maintaining inventory records

Shortage costs C_4 The unit shortage cost used in the preceding inventory models is cost due to the delay in satisfying a demand; the demand is eventually satisfied (back-ordering) after a period of time, i.e., the shortage cost is not considered as the cost of lost sales. In this context, unit cost of shortage includes such items as:

1 Overtime requirements due to the shortage
2 Special clerical and administrative costs
3 Expediting
4 Loss of goodwill due to the delay
5 Special handling or packaging costs
6 Lost production time
7 Any other costs that can be attributed to the shortage of stock

Comments

There are, of course, many other inventory models besides the ones described in this chapter. One need only look at the literature of inventory control, production control, and operations research to find a large number of inventory models. Suggested references are listed at the end of this chapter.

In many texts, the inventory models presented here are derived on the basis of total variable cost and consequently do not include item costs $C_1 D$. This is a matter of preference. In determining the total inventory cost, the item cost should be included.

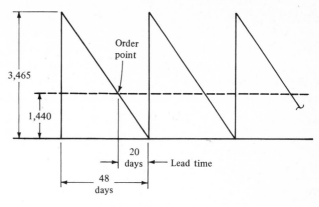

FIGURE 6-6
The Q system with deterministic quantities.

INVENTORY SYSTEMS

Two widely used inventory systems are the fixed-order-size system and the fixed-order-interval system. In this chapter the fixed-order-size system is designated as the Q system, and the fixed-order-interval system is designated as the P system. The basic difference between the two is that in the Q system a fixed quantity is ordered at varying time intervals and in the P system a variable quantity is ordered at fixed time intervals.

When the inventory system is deterministic and the demand rate is constant, there is actually little difference between the Q and P systems. This is demonstrated using the data of Example 6-1. Consider a Q system first. The following quantities are obtained (it is assumed 250 days = 1 year):

$$Q = 3,465 \text{ units}$$

$$t = \text{time between orders} = .1925 (250) = 48.1 = 48 \text{ days}$$

$$\text{Demand/day} = \frac{18,000}{250} = 72 \text{ units/day}$$

Now suppose the lead time L is 20 days; then the number of units that would be required over the lead time is

$$\text{Demand over lead time} = DL = 72(20) = 1,440 \text{ units}$$

A plot of these quantities shown in Fig. 6-6 indicates the following order rule: monitor the inventory level continuously, and when the inventory level reaches 1,440 units, order 3,465 units.

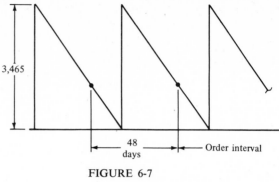

FIGURE 6-7
The P system for deterministic quantities.

This rule has the same total annual cost (\$22,156) as calculated in Example 6-1 and does not allow shortages.   If shortages are allowed, the order point is decreased. For example, if a lead time of 20 days is used in Example 6-3, the order point is

$$72(20) - 747 = 693 \text{ units}$$

If the lead time had been greater than 48 days, the order level (point) would have to be reworded.   For example, suppose the lead time in Example 6-1 is 60 days instead of 20 days.   This would indicate an order point of

$$60(72) = 4,320 \text{ units}$$

However, this is impossible since Fig. 6-6 indicates that the inventory level never exceeds 3,465 units.   The value 4,320 units implies that when the number of units in inventory (on hand) *and* the number of units on order but not received is 4,320 units, then an order for 3,465 units is placed.

Now consider a P system.   An order interval of 48 days would be used in Example 6-1, since this is the optimal interval indicated by a balance between the purchasing and inventory costs.   Any order interval of less than 48 days would result in greater purchasing costs, and any order interval greater than 48 days would result in shortages.   The P system for the data of Example 6-1 is shown in Fig. 6-7 and indicates the following order rule: determine the inventory level every 48 days and at that time order an amount equal to

Order amount = optimum Q + safety stock − on hand

− units on order + amount to last through lead time

In this case, the order quantity is equal to

$$3,465 + 0 - 1,440 - 0 + 72(20) = 3,465 \text{ units}$$

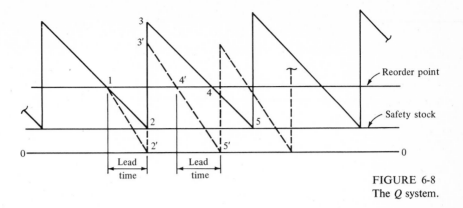

FIGURE 6-8
The Q system.

This order quantity would be the same at each order point since all the items in the order amount equation are constants because the system is deterministic and the demand rate is constant.   Also, the times between orders (48 days) for both systems are equal for the same reasons.   Consequently, the two systems give the same results *provided* the systems are deterministic and the demand rate is constant.

Differences between the two systems occur when demand, lead time, or both become probabilistic.   Probabilistic considerations are presented in the balance of this chapter.

One approach to handling probabilistic inventory systems is to superimpose an inventory model on a safety stock (buffer stock).   The safety stock serves as a cushion that absorbs variations in demand and lead time.   It also serves as a means of adjusting the number of shortages.   This approach provides a reasonable approximation to an optimum solution.   It is an approximation because it assumes that safety stock for the lead time and the order interval are independent.   This assumption, of course, is not true.

One of the major differences between the Q and P systems is the amount of safety stock required for each.   In general, the Q system requires less safety-stock than the P system because in the Q system the safety-stock requirement depends on fluctuations in demand during the lead time, while in the P system, the safety-stock amount depends on the sum of the lead time and order interval.   This point is illustrated in Figs. 6-8 and 6-9.

In Fig. 6-8 a schematic of the Q system is shown.   The solid lines (1-2-3-4-5) indicate a normal demand rate; the dotted lines (1-2'-3'-4'-5') indicate a maximum demand rate.   It should be noted that in this system with a maximum demand rate, the time between orders is less than if a normal demand rate is experienced; in other words, the number of orders increases.   Consequently, the inventory remaining at the order points needs only protect for maximum demand over the lead time.

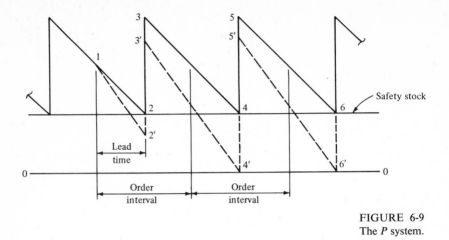

FIGURE 6-9
The P system.

In Fig. 6-9, the P system is shown. The solid lines indicate a normal demand rate, and the dotted lines indicate a maximum demand rate. In this model the number of orders is the same for both conditions of normal and maximum demand rates. Assume that the demand rate up to point 1 has been normal; then an order will be placed at this point that reflects a normal demand. If the demand rate becomes a maximum in the time period 1 to 4 (or 4'), this is equivalent to experiencing maximum demand over the lead time and the order interval. Remember that the order interval and the time period 2 to 4 are equal. The only order received in this period that reflects this maximum demand is the order received at point 4 (or 4'). Consequently, the safety stock must protect against maximum demand during the lead time and the order interval.

EXAMPLE 6-5   **The Q system (varying demand, constant lead time)**   A Q-type inventory system is desired based on the following data. The demand for a particular item has the distribution shown in Fig. 6-10, and the lead time L is 2 weeks. The cost of one purchase is \$160, and the cost of holding 1 unit is 10 cents per week.

The first step is to determine the order amount based on the average demand ($\bar{D}$):

$$Q = \sqrt{\frac{2C_2\bar{D}}{C_3}} = \sqrt{\frac{2(160)(200)}{.1}} = 800 \text{ units}$$

The average time between orders is

$$t = \frac{Q}{\bar{D}} = \frac{800}{200} = 4 \text{ weeks}$$

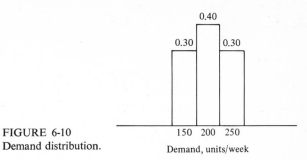

FIGURE 6-10
Demand distribution.

In order to specify the order point and safety stock, the various possible demands during the lead time must be generated.   The possible various demands during the lead time and their associated probabilities are shown in Table 6-1 and summarized in Table 6-2.   Plotting the values in Table 6-2 as a cumulative distribution gives Fig. 6-11.

Table 6-1   POSSIBLE DEMANDS AND PROBABILITIES

| Possible demand over lead time | Manner of occurrence | | Probability |
	First week	Second week	
300	150	150	.3(.3) = .09
350	150	200	.3(.4) = .12
	200	150	.4(.3) = .12
400	200	200	.4(.4) = .16
	150	250	.3(.3) = .09
	250	150	.3(.3) = .09
450	200	250	.4(.3) = .12
	250	200	.3(.4) = .12
500	250	250	.3(.3) = .09
			$\overline{1.00}$

Table 6-2   DEMAND OVER LEAD TIME

Demand over lead time	Probability
300	.09
350	.24
400	.34
450	.24
500	.09

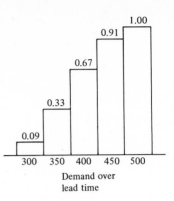

FIGURE 6-11
Cumulative distribution for demand over
lead time.

With Fig. 6-11, the safety stock and the order point can be determined for a specified risk of shortage. For example, if no shortages are allowed (zero risk of shortage), the total amount of stock remaining in inventory at the order point (level) should be 500 units. Therefore the safety stock (SS) in this case is

$$SS = D_m - \bar{D}L = 500 - 200(2) = 100 \text{ units}$$

where D_m is the demand at some specified risk of shortage. Additional risk levels and safety stocks are shown in Table 6-3.

In Fig. 6-12 different demand rates have been assumed to illustrate how a Q system will perform for the data in this example and a zero risk of shortage. This figure shows the different times between orders and indicates that the total inventory will vary between 800 and 1,000 units.

In general, the order quantity for both the Q and P inventory systems is given by

Order quantity = optimum Q + safety stock
                     − inventory on hand
                     − units on order
                     + average demand over lead time   (6-59)

Table 6-3 SAFETY STOCK FOR
VARIOUS RISKS OF
SHORTAGE

Demand over lead time	Safety stock	Risk of shortage, %
500	100	.0
450	50	9.0
400	0	33.0

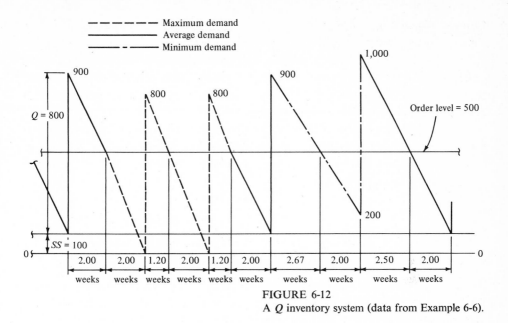

FIGURE 6-12

A Q inventory system (data from Example 6-6).

Since this is a Q system, all the items in Eq. (6-59) are constants.   The term $Q + SS$ is

$$Q + SS = 800 + 100 = 900 \text{ units}$$

Since the order level is specified as D_m, the inventory on hand is a constant of 500 units.   The units on order are zero for this example since the time between orders is less than the lead time.   The average demand over the lead time $\bar{D}L$, is a constant with a value of

$$\bar{D}L = 200(2) = 400 \text{ units}$$

Consequently, the order quantity is a constant value of

$$900 - 500 - 0 + 400 = 800 \text{ units}$$

Of course, by definition of the Q system, the order quantity is known ($Q = 800$) without the use of Eq. (6-59).   However, this is not the case for the P system, since the values of the inventory on hand and the units on order vary.

The data in this example and a zero risk of shortage indicate the following order rule: monitor the inventory level continuously, and whenever this level reaches 500 units, order 800 units.   ////

A modification of the Q system is the *two-bin system*, which divides the inventory into two parts and places it (physically or on paper) in two bins.   Using the results of

Example 6-6, 400 units are placed in first bin and 500 units in the second bin.   As demand occurs, units are withdrawn from the first bin until it is empty, at which time, an order for 800 units is placed.   Demand is then satisfied from the second bin until the order is received.   Upon receipt of the order, enough units are placed in the second bin to make the total number of units 500.   The remaining units are placed in the first bin.   This entire procedure is then repeated.

If the lead time is greater than the average time between orders, the procedure is basically the same.   For example, suppose the lead time is 6 weeks and a zero risk of shortage is specified.   Then the maximum demand for the 6-week period is $6(250) = 1,500$ units.   The safety stock is

$$\text{SS} = D_m - \bar{D}L$$

$$= 1,500 - 200(6)$$

$$= 1,500 - 1,200 = 300 \text{ units}$$

Therefore, the term $Q + \text{SS}$ is 1,100 units, and an order is placed for 800 units whenever the amount on hand plus the amount on order but not received becomes 1,500.   Actually, this is equivalent to ordering 800 units whenever the inventory level becomes 700 units $(1,500 - 800)$, since there will be 800 units on order at each order point.   As an example of the use of Eq. (6-59), the order quantity is

$$1,100 - 700 - 800 + 6(200) = 800 \text{ units}$$

Of course, this value is fully expected by definition of a Q system.

The total expected cost per year is the total cost of Model 6-1 plus the cost of holding the safety stock.   Assuming a unit cost of $2 per unit and 50 weeks/year, the total expected cost $\bar{C}$ per year is

$$\bar{C} = C_1\bar{D} + C_2\frac{\bar{D}}{Q} + C_3\frac{Q}{2} + C_3(\text{SS})$$

$$= 2(50)(200) + 160\frac{200(50)}{800} + .1(50)\frac{800}{2} + .1(50)(100)$$

$$= 20,000 + 2,000 + 2,000 + 500 = \$24,500 \text{ per year} \qquad (6\text{-}60)$$

If some risk level other than zero is desired, it would be necessary to generate the distribution of demand over a lead time of 6 weeks.   This is a very tedious task.   This point is discussed later in this chapter.

Demand Distribution over a Constant Lead Time

At this point, a digression is made in order to show a systematic method of generating the demand over a constant lead time.   This method does not reduce the amount of calculation, but it is a systematic procedure and if done correctly will give the desired results without concern for the possible combinations that give a particular demand.

The distribution of demand over a constant lead time is given by

$$(p_1 x^{d_1} + p_2 x^{d_2} + \cdots + p_n x^{d_n})^L \qquad (6\text{-}61)$$

where L = lead time

$p_1, p_2, \ldots$ = probability of demand $d_1, d_2, \ldots$

Applying Eq. (6-61) to the demand distribution and lead time of Example 6-5 gives

$$(.3x^{d_1} + .4x^{d_2} + .3x^{d_3})^2 \qquad (6\text{-}62)$$

where $d_1 = 150$, $d_2 = 200$, and $d_3 = 250$.

Expanding Eq. (6-62) gives

$$.09x^{2d_1} + .24x^{d_1+d_2} + .18x^{d_1+d_3} + .16x^{2d_2} + .24x^{d_2+d_3} + .09x^{2d_3}$$

and substituting in the values of d_n gives

$$.09x^{300} + .24x^{350} + .18x^{400} + .16x^{400} + .24x^{450} + .09x^{500}$$

Combining like terms results in

$$.09x^{300} + .24x^{350} + .34x^{400} + .24x^{450} + .09x^{500} \qquad (6\text{-}63)$$

In Eq. (6-63), the coefficients are the probabilities of the various demands shown as exponents. These probabilities and demands, of course, agree with the results shown in Table 6-2.

This method for generating the distribution of lead time during demand and the method used in Example 6-5 imply two assumptions: (1) the probability distributions for each week are the same, and (2) demands from one week to the next are independent. These two assumptions are made throughout the remainder of this chapter. Although the validity of these assumptions can be questioned, they are often made in practical inventory problems.

Technically, these methods are called the *convolution* of the original probability distribution with itself. The convolutions of many probability distributions are difficult to calculate. Fortunately, certain theoretical distributions used in many inventory problems offer computational advantages. These theoretical distributions are considered later in this chapter.

One final point in regard to convolutions is that the time units of the demand and lead time must be compatible; i.e., the time units of the lead time must be expressed as multiple integers of the time units used for the demand.

EXAMPLE 6-6   **The P system (varying demand, constant lead time)**   In this example the data in Example 6-5 are used with the modification that a P system is required.

The first step is to determine the order interval (OI) based on the average demand. This is accomplished by calculating Q in the same manner as in Example 6-5 ($Q = 800$

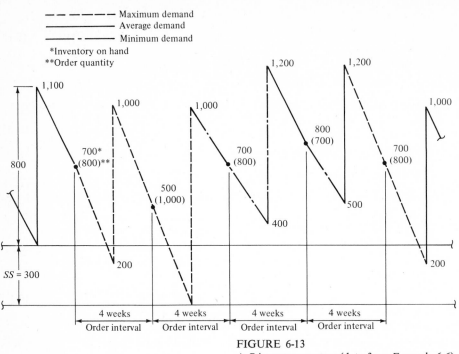

FIGURE 6-13

A P inventory system (data from Example 6-6).

units) and then determining the order interval by setting it equal to the average time between orders:

$$\text{OI} = \bar{t} = \frac{Q}{\bar{D}} = \frac{800}{200} = 4 \text{ weeks}$$

Since this is a P system, the safety stock is based on the lead time ($L = 2$ weeks) plus the order interval (OI $= 4$ weeks), a total of 6 weeks. At this point the demand distribution over 6 weeks can be generated by expanding the expression [Eq. (6-61)]

$$(.3x^{150} + .4x^{200} + .3x^{250})^6$$

Evaluation of this expression is not difficult, but it requires a considerable amount of work. To avoid it a zero risk of shortage will be assumed. This assumption implies that the maximum demand over a 6-week period (lead time plus order interval) is

$$D_m = 6(250) = 1,500 \text{ units}$$

Therefore, the safety stock is

$$\text{SS} = D_m - \bar{D}(L + \text{OI})$$
$$= 1,500 - 200(2 + 4) = 300 \text{ units}$$

The order quantity is given by Eq. (6-59). However, as previously mentioned, the order quantity is not a constant for the P system.

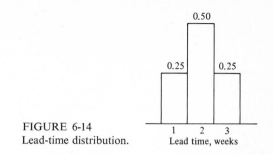

FIGURE 6-14
Lead-time distribution.

The order rule for this P inventory system is to determine the inventory on hand every 4 weeks and order the amount given by Eq. (6-59). Figure 6-13 illustrates how this system operates for various assumed demand rates.

The total expected cost for this system, using Eq. (6-60), is

$$\bar{C} = 20{,}000 + 2{,}000 + 2{,}000 + 1{,}500 = \$25{,}500 \text{ per year}$$

This cost points out a disadvantage of the P system. That is, because of the larger safety stock requirement, the P system is more expensive than a comparable Q system. However, the P system has the advantage of requiring only periodic review of the inventory level whereas the Q system requires continuous review of the inventory level. /////

EXAMPLE 6-7 **The Q system (constant demand, varying lead time)** In this example the data in Example 6-5 are used with the exceptions of demand and lead time. In this example demand is 200 units/week (a constant), and lead time has the distribution shown in Fig. 6-14. The problem is to design a Q system for these conditions.

The calculation of Q and t is the same in this example as in Example 6-5. These values are $Q = 800$ units and $t = 4$ weeks.

Table 6-4 gives the demands over the possible lead times. With these results, the safety stock can be determined from

$$\text{SS} = D_m - D\bar{L} \qquad (6\text{-}64)$$

Table 6-4 DEMAND OVER LEAD TIME FOR EXAMPLE 6-7

Lead time	Demand over lead time	Probability
1	200	.25
2	400	.50
3	600	.25

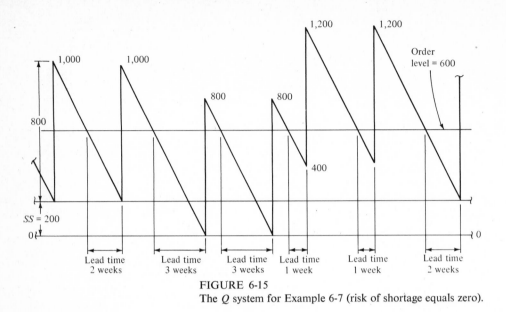

FIGURE 6-15
The Q system for Example 6-7 (risk of shortage equals zero).

where $\bar{L}$ is the average lead time. As an example, if the risk of shortage is taken as zero, the safety stock is

$$SS = 600 - 200(2) = 200 \text{ units}$$

The order rule for this case is to order 800 units whenever the inventory level drops to 600 units. The expected cost, calculated from Eq. (6-60), is $25,000 per year.

In Fig. 6-15, various lead times have been assumed to show how a Q system would perform for the conditions of this example. ////

EXAMPLE 6-8 **The P system (constant demand, varying lead time)** In this example a P system is designed using the data given in Example 6-7.

The values of Q and t are the same as in Example 6-7; namely $Q = 800$ and $t = 4$ weeks. Since this is a P system, the safety stock is based on the order interval (OI $= t$) plus the average lead time, which is equal to

$$OI + \bar{L} = 4 + 2 = 6 \text{ weeks}$$

The demands over the order interval plus the possible lead times are shown in Table 6-5.

The safety stock for a zero risk of shortage is

$$SS = D_m - D(\bar{L} + OI)$$
$$= 1,400 - 200(2 + 4) = 200 \text{ units}$$

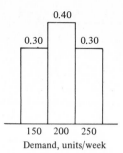

FIGURE 6-16
Demand distribution for Example 6-9.

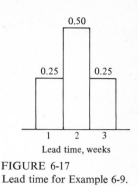

FIGURE 6-17
Lead time for Example 6-9.

and the order rule is to determine the inventory on hand every 4 weeks and order an amount equal to that given by Eq. (6-59). The expected cost for the conditions in this example is $25,000 per year, the same cost as in Example 6-7.

It should be noted that for the conditions of constant demand and varying lead time, the Q and P systems are basically the same. In this example, the net result is to order 800 units every time the inventory level becomes 600 units, which is the same result as in Example 6-7. This is because with a constant demand the amount of inventory on hand is a constant. Consequently, the order quantity given by Eq. (6-59) is a constant. This situation can also be seen in Fig. 6-15. That is, the time between order points is a constant of 4 weeks.

EXAMPLE 6-9   The Q system (varying demand, varying lead time)   In this example a Q system is required for the cost coefficients given in Example 6-5 and the distributions of demand and lead time shown in Fig. 6-16 and 6-17.

The first step is to calculate the value of Q based on the average demand. From Example 6-5 this value is 800 units. The next step is to generate the distribution of demand over lead time. This procedure is illustrated in Table 6-6 and sumarized in Table 6-7.

Table 6-5   **DISTRIBUTION OF LEAD TIME AND ORDER INTERVAL FOR EXAMPLE 6-8**

Lead time	Order interval plus lead time	Demand over lead time plus order interval	Probability
1	5	1,000	.25
2	6	1,200	.50
3	7	1,400	.25

Table 6-6 DEMAND OVER LEAD TIME FOR EXAMPLE 6-9

Lead time	Possible demands	Manner of occurrence			Probability
		First week	Second week	Third week	
1	150	150	—	—	.25(.3) = .07500
	200	200	—	—	.25(.4) = .10000
	250	250	—	—	.25(.3) = .07500
2	300	150	150	—	.50(.3)(.3) = .04500
	350	150	200	—	.50(.3)(.4) = .06000
		200	150	—	.50(.4)(.3) = .06000
	400	200	200	—	.50(.4)(.4) = .08000
		150	250	—	.50(.3)(.3) = .04500
		250	150	—	.50(.3)(.3) = .04500
	450	200	250	—	.50(.4)(.3) = .06000
		250	200	—	.50(.3)(.4) = .06000
	500	250	250	—	.50(.3)(.3) = .04500
3	450	150	150	150	.25(.3)(.3)(.3) = .00675
	500	150	150	200	.25(.3)(.3)(.4) = .00900
		150	200	150	.25(.3)(.4)(.3) = .00900
		200	150	150	.25(.4)(.3)(.3) = .00900
	550	200	200	150	.25(.4)(.4)(.3) = .01200
		200	150	200	.25(.4)(.3)(.4) = .01200
		150	200	200	.25(.3)(.4)(.4) = .01200
		150	150	250	.25(.3)(.3)(.3) = .00675
		150	250	150	.25(.3)(.3)(.3) = .00675
		250	150	150	.25(.3)(.3)(.3) = .00675
	600	200	200	200	.25(.4)(.4)(.4) = .01600
		150	200	250	.25(.4)(.4)(.3) = .00900
		150	250	200	.25(.3)(.3)(.4) = .00900
		250	150	200	.25(.3)(.3)(.4) = .00900
		200	150	250	.25(.4)(.3)(.3) = .00900
		200	250	150	.25(.4)(.3)(.3) = .00900
		250	200	150	.25(.3)(.4)(.3) = .00900
	650	200	200	250	.25(.4)(.4)(.3) = .01200
		200	250	200	.25(.4)(.3)(.4) = .01200
		250	200	200	.25(.3)(.4)(.4) = .01200
		250	250	150	.25(.3)(.3)(.3) = .00675
		250	150	250	.25(.3)(.3)(.3) = .00675
		150	250	250	.25(.3)(.3)(.3) = .00675
	700	250	250	200	.25(.3)(.3)(.4) = .00900
		250	200	250	.25(.3)(.4)(.3) = .00900
		200	250	250	.25(.4)(.3)(.3) = .00900
	750	250	250	250	.25(.3)(.3)(.3) = .00675

As an example, suppose the risk for shortage is specified as 3.375 percent. For this risk of shortage, Table 6-7 indicates $D_m = 650$. Therefore, the safety stock is

$$\text{SS} = D_m - \overline{DL} = 650 - 200(2) = 250 \text{ units}$$

Other safety stocks for different risks of shortages are shown in Table 6-8.

The order rule is to order 800 units whenever the inventory level becomes 650 units, and the expected cost [Eq. (5-60)] is $25,250 per year for a risk of shortage of 3.375 percent. For comparative purposes, the expected cost is $27,270 per year for a zero risk of shortage (SS = 350). This is the highest cost yet and is the penalty for uncertainty in both lead time and demand.

Table 6-7 SUMMARY OF DEMAND OVER LEAD TIME

Average = 400 units

Possible demand over lead time	Probability	Cumulative probability
150	.07500	.07500
200	.10000	.17500
250	.07500	.25000
300	.04500	.29500
350	.12000	.41500
400	.17000	.58500
450	.12675	.71175
500	.07200	.78375
550	.05625	.84000
600	.07000	.91000
650	.05625	.96625
700	.02700	.99325
750	.00675	1.00000

Table 6-8 SAFETY STOCKS FOR EXAMPLE 6-9

Demand over lead time	Safety stock	Risk of shortage, %
750	350	.000
700	300	.675
650	250	3.375
600	200	9.000
550	150	16.000
500	100	21.625

EXAMPLE 6-10   **The P system (varying demand, varying lead time)**   In this example a P system is designed using the data given in Example 6-9.   The first step is to determine the order interval.   This is accomplished by setting the order interval equal to the average time between orders:

$$\text{OI} = \bar{i} = \frac{Q}{\bar{D}} = \frac{800}{200} = 4 \text{ weeks}$$

The next step is to generate the various demands over the lead time plus the order interval.   The possible values of lead time plus order interval are 5, 6, and 7 weeks. These values are the possible lead times given in Fig. 6-17 plus the constant order interval of 4 weeks.   The procedure for generating the various demands is outlined in Table 6-9 and is basically the same as in Example 6-9.   However, the task of completing Table 6-9 is considerably larger than in Example 6-9 due to the length of time involved.   This is another example of why theoretical distributions and simulation are often used to determine the maximum inventory, safety stock, and order points for some types of inventory problems.

To proceed with this example and avoid having to complete Table 6-9, a zero risk of shortage is assumed.   Consequently, the safety stock is

$$\text{SS} = D_m - \bar{D}(\text{OI} + \bar{L})$$

$$= 1{,}750 - 200(4 + 2) = 550 \text{ units}$$

The order rule for this system is to determine the inventory level every 4 weeks and order an amount indicated by Eq. (6-59).

Table 6-9   OUTLINE FOR THE GENERATION OF DEMAND OVER LEAD TIME PLUS ORDER INTERVAL FOR EXAMPLE 6-10

Lead time plus order interval, (weeks)	Demand units	Manner of occurrence							Probability
		First week	Second week	Third week	Fourth week	Fifth week	Sixth week	Seventh week	
5	750	150	150	150	150	150	—	—	$.25(.3)^5$
$(p = .25)$	⋮	⋮	⋮	⋮	⋮	⋮			
	1,250	250	250	250	250	250	—	—	$.25(.3)^5$
6	900	150	150	150	150	150	150	—	$.50(.3)^6$
$(p = .50)$	⋮	⋮	⋮	⋮	⋮	⋮	⋮		⋮
	1,500	250	250	250	250	250	250	—	$.50(.3)^6$
7	1,050	150	150	150	150	150	150	150	$.25(.3)^7$
$(p = .25)$	⋮	⋮	⋮	⋮	⋮	⋮	⋮	⋮	⋮
	1,750	250	250	250	250	250	250	250	$.25(.3)^7$

The total expected cost for this system (SS = 550), using Eq. (6-60), is $26,750 per year.   This is the highest expected cost and is expected since this is a P system with variable lead time and demand.   ////

THEORETICAL DISTRIBUTIONS

In the preceding examples of the Q and P inventory systems, the demand and lead time were described by empirical distributions.   Some of these examples illustrated that computational difficulties can occur.   It was mentioned that computational advantages are possible if the empirical distributions are replaced with certain theoretical distributions, provided, of course, that the theoretical distribution adequately describes the variable in question.

These computational advantages are possible when the convolution of a theoretical distribution with itself is easily calculated.   The convolutions of many distributions are not easily calculated.   Fortunately, the distributions used in many inventory problems are well behaved, in particular, the normal and Poisson distributions. For example, if a normal distribution with mean μ and variance σ^2 is convoluted with itself n times, the final convolution is a normal distribution with a mean of $n\mu$ and a variance of $n\sigma^2$.   For the Poisson distribution, the final convolution is a Poisson distribution with a mean and variance of $n\mu$, since for the Poisson distribution, the mean and variance are equal.   When these results are used, certain assumptions are implied, namely that the distributions are the same and independent.

EXAMPLE 6-11   As an example of the use of a theoretical distribution consider the following problem.   A Q system is required for the data in Example 6-5 except that in this example the demand is distributed normally with a mean of 200 units/week and a standard deviation of 25 units/week.

Since the average demand in this example is the same as in Example 6-5, the optimum order quantity Q is the same, namely $Q = 800$ units.   The lead time specified in Example 6-5 is a constant of 2 weeks.   Therefore, the mean $\bar{D}_1$ and standard deviation σ_1 of the distribution of demand over lead time are

$$\bar{D}_1 = L\bar{D}$$
$$= 2(200) = 400 \text{ units} \qquad (6\text{-}65)$$
$$\sigma_1 = \sigma\sqrt{L}$$
$$= 25\sqrt{2} = 35.35 \text{ units} \qquad (6\text{-}66)$$

If a risk of shortage α is specified as .05 the order point D_m is calculated from

$$K_{1-\alpha} = \frac{D_m - \bar{D}_1}{\sigma_1} \qquad (6\text{-}67)$$

where $K_{1-\alpha}$ is the normal deviate and for this example is

$$K_{.95} = 1.645$$

Substituting into Eq. (6-67) gives the order point:

$$1.645 = \frac{D_m - 400}{35.35}$$

$$D_m = 400 + 1.645(35.35) = 458.15 = 458 \text{ units}$$

and the safety stock is

$$SS = D_m - \bar{D}_1 = 458 - 400 = 58 \text{ units}$$

Therefore the order rule for this example is to order 800 units whenever the inventory level is 458 units.

If a P system is required, Eq. (6-65) and (6-66) must be modified to include the order interval. Consequently, for a P system, the average demand and standard deviation over the lead time plus order interval are

$$\bar{D}_1 = (L + \text{OI})\bar{D} \qquad (6\text{-}68)$$

$$\sigma_1 = \sigma\sqrt{L + \text{OI}} \qquad (6\text{-}69)$$

From this point on, the analysis is the same as previously discussed.

When both demand and lead time are variable, the distribution of demand during lead time involves a considerable amount of calculation, as illustrated in Example 6-9. Also, using theoretical distributions for this case offers no computational advantage. A common approach is to use Monte Carlo simulation, discussed in Chap. 7. If simulation is used, either the entire inventory system can be analyzed, or just the demand over lead time (or lead time plus order interval for the P system) can be generated. Simulation of the entire system will show the net effect of the interaction between fluctuating demand and lead time and consequently provides a closer representation of the actual system. However, the analysis and computer time is greater than if only the demand over the lead time is simulated. Examples of the simulation of an inventory system and the demand over lead time are given in the Chap. 7.

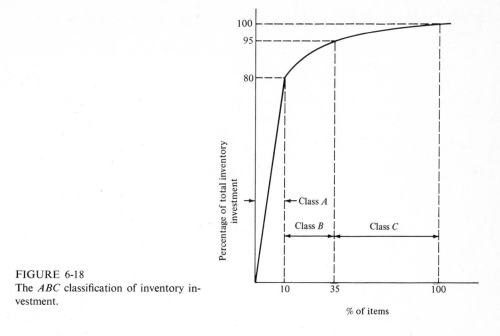

FIGURE 6-18
The *ABC* classification of inventory investment.

CONCLUDING COMMENTS

It is pointed out again that the methods used in Examples 6-5 to 6-10 give approximate solutions and not optimum solutions.   However, they do offer a good approximation to the *Q* system and at least a fair approximation to the *P* system.   For the true optimum to the *Q* system, a balance between ordering, holding, and shortage costs taking into account the interaction between the safety-stock requirement and the order period is required.   The optimum solution for the *P* system requires the consideration of the interaction between the amount ordered in any one period and following periods. A better approximation of the safety stock in a *P* system is possible by balancing the holding costs and shortage costs.   Because of the mathematical complexities of these considerations, they are not presented in this text.   For details, see the references.

Examples 6-5 to 6-10 used an instantaneous replacement rate.   However, in manufacturing models this is not the case.   If the replacement rate is considered constant (often the case or nearly so in the manufacture of established products), the procedure of superimposing Model 6-2 on a safety stock is applicable.   When the replacement rate is not constant, simulation can be used.

The inventory models and systems presented in this chapter are for a single item. Obviously, most companies have many items requiring some form of inventory control and analysis.   An important thing to remember when approaching inventory problems is that the degree of analysis of the inventory problem and sophistication of the control methods be commensurate with the total inventory investment of the item in question.   This idea leads to what is commonly referred to as the *ABC classification* of inventory investment.

In many companies, the major portion of the total inventory investment is due to a relatively few items, as shown in Fig. 6-18.   The objective is to classify the inventory investment into the three class shown in Fig. 6-18.   These classes indicate the degree of analysis and sophistication of control.   Obviously, those items resulting in the greatest inventory investment (class *A*) receive the greatest attention, and those items resulting in the least inventory investment (class *C*) receive only routine consideration.

REFERENCES

1 BUFFA, E. S.: "Production: Inventory Systems, Planning and Control," Richard D. Irwin, Inc., Homewood, Ill., 1968.
2 CHURCHMAN, C. W., R. L. ACKOFF, and E. L. ARNOFF: "Introduction to Operations Research," John Wiley & Sons, Inc., New York, 1957.
3 MAGEE, J. F., and D. M. BOODMAN: Production Planning and Inventory Control, 2nd ed., McGraw-Hill Book Company, New York, 1968.
4 NADDOR, E.: "Inventory Systems," John Wiley & Sons, Inc., New York, 1966.
5 STARR, M. K., and D. W. MILLER: "Inventory Control: Theory and Practice," pp. 121–122, Prentice-Hall, Inc., Englewood Cliffs, N.J., 1962.

PROBLEMS

6-1 A company purchases 12,000 items per year for use in its production process.   If the unit cost of $5 per unit, the holding cost for 1 unit is 80 cents per month, and the cost of making a purchase is $100, determine the following if no shortages are allowed:
(*a*) The optimum order quantity.
(*b*) The optimum total yearly cost.
(*c*) The number of orders per year.
(*d*) The time between orders.

6-2 Suppose the company in Prob. 6-1 can manufacture the items at a rate of 48,000 units/year.   If all costs are the same as in Prob. 6-1 (setup cost = procurement cost), determine:
(*a*) The optimum manufacture quantity.
(*b*) The optimum total yearly cost.

(c) The maximum inventory.

(d) The manufacturing time.

(e) The time between setups.

(f) The number of setups.

6-3   Suppose in Prob. 6-2 the manufacturing and demand rate are exactly equal.   What does this imply?

6-4   Considering your answers in Probs. 6-1 to 6-3, what general statements can be made regarding the alternatives between purchasing and manufacturing, assuming the costs are the same?

6-5   The demand for a purchased item is 1,000 units/month, and shortages are allowed. If the unit cost is $1.50 per unit, the cost of making one purchase is $600, the holding cost for 1 unit is $2 per year, and the cost of one shortage is $10 per year, determine:

(a) The optimum purchase quantity.

(b) The optimum number of shortages.

(c) The optimum total yearly cost.

(d) The number of orders per year.

(e) The time between orders.

(f) The time of the shortages.

(g) The maximum inventory.

6-6   Suppose in Prob. 6-5 the item can be manufactured at a rate of 4,000 units/month If all costs are the same as in Prob. 6-5, determine:

(a) The optimum quantity to manufacture.

(b) The optimum number of shortages.

(c) The optimum yearly cost.

(d) The number of setups.

(e) The time between setups.

(f) The time to manufacture the optimum quantity.

(g) The time of shortages.

(h) The maximum inventory.

6-7   A company purchases a certain chemical to use in its process.   No shortages are allowed.   The demand for the chemical is 1,000 lb/month; the cost of one purchase is $800; and the holding cost for 1 unit is $10 per month.   The unit cost depends upon the amount purchased as tabulated.   Determine the optimum purchase quantity. *Hint:* The optimum quantity implies least cost.

Amount, lb	Cost per pound
0–249	$8.00
250–449	7.50
450–649	7.00
650 and above	6.75

6-8   Using the cost data in Prob. 6-1 (assume 25 days = 1 month), the demand distribution shown below, and a constant lead time of 4 days, design a Q inventory system for a zero risk of shortage and determine the total expected annual cost.
Considering the figure shown and your results from above, determine:

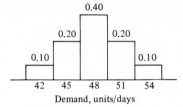

Demand, units/days

(a) How many days after the receipt of the order at point A will another order be placed assuming an average demand rate prior to point A and during the time from point A to point B?

(b) How many units would be ordered at point B?

(c) How many units would be in inventory at point C if a maximum demand rate is experienced during the time from B to C?

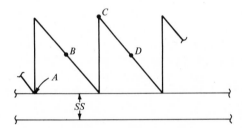

(d) How soon after the receipt of the order at point C would another order be placed?

(e) Suppose that after placing the order at point D, the demand rate becomes a minimum; how much time would elapse before the next order assuming minimum demand up to the order point?

6-9   Repeat Prob. 6-8 for a lead time of 15 days.

6-10   Using the data in Prob. 6-8, design a P inventory system for a zero risk of shortage and determine the total expected cost.   Consider the figure shown below and your results from above, and answer the following questions:

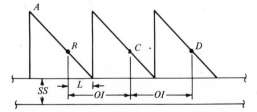

(a) Suppose it is time to place an order at point B and average demand has been experienced prior to this time; determine the order quantity assuming the amount of inventory at point A is $Q + $ SS.

(b) Suppose after placing the order at point B, maximum demand is experienced in the time interval from B to C. What is the order quantity at point C?

(c) Suppose after placing the order at point C, maximum demand is experienced in the time interval from C to D. What is the order quantity at point D?

6-11 Repeat Prob. 6-10 for a lead time of 15 days.

6-12 Suppose the demand for a particular unit is distributed as sketched. Determine the order point and safety stock for a Q system if the lead time is a constant of 2 months.

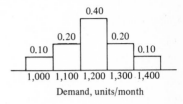

Demand, units/month

The risk of a stockout is specified as .01.

6-13 Suppose the demand for product is normally distributed with a mean of 1,000 units/ months and a standard deviation of 120 units/month. What is the order point and safety stock for a Q system if the lead time is 2 weeks (assume 4 weeks = 1 month) and the risk of shortage is specified as 5 percent. Assume monthly demand is independent but the same.

6-14 Using the distributions shown below, specify the order point and safety stock for a Q system and a risk of shortage of 4 percent.

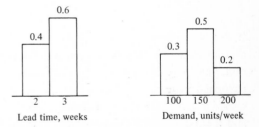

Lead time, weeks   Demand, units/week

6-15 With the data given below, design a Q system with a risk of shortage of 1.0 percent. Demand is normally distributed with a mean of 50 units/day and a standard deviation of 10 units/day. Lead time is 20 days (a constant). The setup cost is $500 per setup. The holding cost is $1.80 per unit-year. The manufacturing rate is 100 units/day (constant). Assume 360 days/year.

7

MONTE CARLO SIMULATION

In describing a system by a model, it is sometimes found that the system is too complex to describe or the model, once developed, is not amenable to an analytical solution. In these cases, simulation can be a valuable tool in obtaining an answer to a particular problem. There are several types of simulation; e.g., scale models of airplanes tested in wind tunnels, an electric circuit used to describe a hydraulic circuit, and the description of some system by a mathematical model. In this latter type of simulation a mathematical model of some real system is manipulated and the results observed. These manipulations and observations are then used to make inferences about the real system. If the model involves random sampling from a probability distribution, the procedure is called *Monte Carlo* simulation.

It will become obvious in this chapter that Monte Carlo simulation is computer-oriented, for without the speed of the computer, most Monte Carlo simulation models become impractical. A discussion of Monte Carlo simulation is best approached through the use of examples.

EXAMPLE 7-1 Suppose the demand per day for a particular item can be expressed by the distribution shown in Fig. 7-1 and it is desired to generate a demand pattern for 10 days.

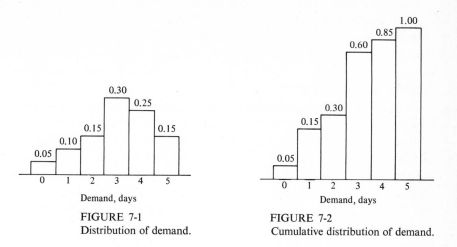

FIGURE 7-1
Distribution of demand.

FIGURE 7-2
Cumulative distribution of demand.

The first step is to establish the cumulative distribution function (CDF) shown in Fig. 7-2.   The next step is to set up the table shown in Table 7-1 and assign tag numbers.   The tag numbers are assigned in such a way as to reflect the probability of the various demands.   With the random numbers shown in Table 7-2 the demand pattern for the 10-day period shown in Table 7-3 is obtained.   ////

At this point, several comments and additional information are necessary. First, remember that this is a very simple example, showing only some of the rudiments of Monte Carlo simulation.

Table 7-1   TAG NUMBERS

Demand/day	Tag numbers
0	00–04
1	05–14
2	15–29
3	30–59
4	60–84
5	85–99

Table 7-2   RANDOM NUMBERS

14	74	24	87	07	45	26	66	26	94

One question that usually arises is: Where does one obtain the probability distribution (Fig. 7-1) for a variable?   It is usually obtained from historical data or from estimates.   If historical data are used, the assumption, of course, is that past data will adequately describe the future.   If this assumption is not considered correct, one must rely upon estimates.

In Example 7-1 the demand per day was shown as an integer value, starting at 0 and ending at 5, the intervening values being an arithmetic progression.   Neither of these two considerations is required for simulation purposes.   If physical considerations allow the use of noninteger values for a variable and these values are considered probable, they should be included in the distribution for the variable.   In establishing a distribution for a variable if it is believed that certain intervening values will not happen (the probability is 0), they should be omitted.   Another point that is obvious but sometimes overlooked is that when certain values of a variable are not included in the distribution, it implies that these values will not occur in the real system being simulated.

Table 7-3   DEMAND SCHEDULE

Day	Demand
1	1
2	4
3	2
4	5
5	1
6	3
7	2
8	4
9	2
10	5

Table 7-4   ANOTHER METHOD FOR ASSIGNING TAG NUMBERS

Demand/week	Tag numbers
0	01–05
1	06–15
2	16–30
3	31–60
4	61–85
5	86–00

In assigning the tag numbers in Table 7-1, the first tag number was 00 and the last was 99.   It is possible to begin with a tag number of 01 and end with a tag number of 00, as shown in Table 7-4.   This is a matter of personal preference.   The point to remember is that the tag numbers should reflect the probabilities of various values of the variable and that the sequence of tag numbers must be closed.

The number of digits used in the tag numbers should be the same as the number of decimal places used in the probabilities for various values of the variable.   The number of digits used in the random numbers should be the same as the number of digits used in the tag numbers.

In Example 7-1 the random numbers were obtained from a random-number table. When using a random-number table, one can start at any point in the table and proceed in any direction.   The important thing is not to "choose" the random numbers. Further discussion of random-number generation is given later in this chapter.

A question often raised in regard to Monte Carlo simulation is: If the relative frequencies (probability) of the values of a variable are known, why use random numbers to simulate it?   In other words, if 10,000 random numbers were used in Example 7-1, it would be expected that the number of occurrences for each demand level would be as shown in Table 7-5.   In addition, the mean and standard deviation can also be calculated for the distribution shown in Fig. 7-1.

The answer to this question is that although the probability for each demand level is known and consequently the frequency of each demand level, the *order* of occurrence is not known.   It is the order of occurrence which is assumed random and which is being simulated.

EXAMPLE 7-2   Consider another simple example.   Assume the effectiveness function for some system is represented by

$$w = 5x + 2y + z \qquad (7\text{-}1)$$

Table 7-5   EXPECTED NUMBER OF OCCURRENCES FOR THE VARIOUS DEMAND LEVELS OF EXAMPLE 7-1 IN 10,000 TRIALS

Demand/week	Frequency
0	500
1	1,000
2	1,500
3	3,000
4	2,500
5	1,500

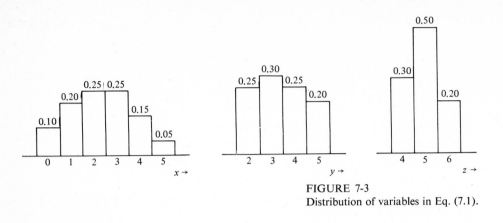

FIGURE 7-3
Distribution of variables in Eq. (7.1).

where the variables x, y, and z are described by the probability distributions shown in Fig. 7-3. The problem is to determine, by a simulation, the distribution of the effectiveness function. This is accomplished by proceeding as in Example 7-1.

Establishing the CDFs for each variable and assigning tag numbers results in Table 7-6.

Table 7-6 TAG NUMBERS FOR VARIABLES IN EQ. (7-1)

Values of x	Tag numbers	Values of y	Tag numbers	Values of z	Tag numbers
0	00–09	2	00–24	4	0–2
1	10–29	3	25–54	5	3–7
2	30–54	4	55–79	6	8–9
3	55–79	5	80–99		
4	80–94				
5	95–99				

Table 7-7 SIMULATION FOR EQ. (7-1)

Trial number	Random number for x	x	Random number for y	y	Random number for z	z	Value of w $w = 5x + 2y + z$
1	43	2	22	2	1	4	18
2	96	5	50	3	8	6	37
3	57	3	13	2	0	4	23
4	53	2	36	3	2	4	20
5	14	1	91	5	7	5	20
6	03	0	58	4	6	5	13
7	33	2	45	3	1	4	20
8	40	2	43	3	3	5	21
. . . . .	. . . . .	. . . . .	. . . . .	. . . . .	. . . . .	. . . . .	. . . . .
n							

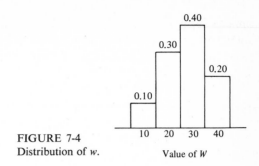

FIGURE 7-4
Distribution of w.

The next step is to set up Table 7-7, where a value w is calculated for each trial using the values of x, y, and z obtained by random sampling from Table 7-6.   This is done for n trials (the number of trials is discussed later).

After the values of w have been obtained, a probability distribution of w can be plotted and the mean and standard deviation for w calculated.   In addition, it is possible to make probability statements from the distribution of w.   For example, suppose, after many trials, a plot of the distribution of w gives the results shown in Fig. 7-4.   One can then make such statements as the probability that the value of w is 20 is 30 percent or the probability that the value of w is 20 or less is 40 percent. These probability statements often help in a decision-making process.   ////

Using the same set of random numbers for each variable is incorrect.   The assumption made in this example, and in many simulation problems, is that the variables are independent.   Consequently, if the same set of random numbers is used for each variable, a degree of correlation might result between the variables, contradicting the assumption of independence.   A discussion of dependency between variables is discussed later.

At this point, more practical problems are in order.

EXAMPLE 7-3   Suppose it is desired to simulate the demand over the lead time of Example 6-9.   Assigning tag numbers to the distributions of lead time and demand gives the results shown in Tables 7-8 and 7-9.

Next, the procedure is to generate a random number for the lead time.   Using this lead time, the demand for each week in the lead time is determined by generating different random numbers for each week.   An outline of this procedure is shown in Table 7-10.

The figures in the total-demand column are then summarized in a table similar to Table 6-7 and the relative frequencies computed.   If this particular problem is simulated, the relative frequency of each demand should agree closely with the probabilities given in Table 6-7. With these values, the order point and safety stock can be specified, as shown in Chap. 6. ////

Table 7-8 DEMAND TAG NUMBERS

Demand, units/week	Tag numbers
150	0–2
200	3–6
250	7–9

Table 7-9 LEAD-TIME TAG NUMBERS

Lead time, weeks	Tag numbers
1	00–24
2	25–74
3	75–99

Table 7-10 SIMULATION OF DEMAND OVER LEAD TIME

Trial	Lead-time Random number	Lead time	Demand							Total demand
			Random number	First week	Random number	Second week	Random number	Third week		
1	68	2	3	200	1	150	—	—		350
2	89	3	5	200	4	200	2	150		550
3	10	1	3	200	—	—	—	—		200
4	40	2	4	200	6	200	—	—		400
n										

EXAMPLE 7-4 One method used to evaluate the desirability of a capital investment is to determine the internal rate of return and compare it with a minimum attractive rate of return. The internal rate of return is defined as the interest rate, i, which makes

$$0 = \sum_{r=0}^{n} \frac{x_r}{(1+i)^r} \qquad (7\text{-}2)$$

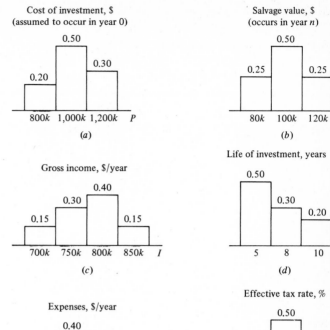

Cost of investment, $ (assumed to occur in year 0)

(a)

Salvage value, $ (occurs in year n)

(b)

Gross income, $/year

(c)

Life of investment, years

(d)

Expenses, $/year

(e)

Effective tax rate, %

(f)

FIGURE 7-5
Distributions for Example 7-4.

true, where n is the estimated life of the investment and x_r is the cash flow for the year r. More specifically, x_r can be expressed as

$$x_r = (I - C) - (I - C - D)t - P \qquad (7\text{-}3)$$

where I = gross income for year r
C = expenses for year r (out-of-pocket costs)
D = depreciation for year r
t = effective tax rate
P = capital expenditure for year r

It is often assumed that the variables in Eq. (7-3) are known with certainty, and based on these point estimates the cash flows for each year are calculated. In this

Table 7-11   SIMULATION OF CASH FLOW

End of year	Investment	Depreciation	Random number for I	Gross income I	Random number for C	Expenses C	Random number for t	Tax rate t, %	Taxable income	Tax	Cash flow
0	$1,000,000										−$1,000,000
1		$180,000	51	$800,000	7	$200,000	6	52	$420,000	$218,400	381,600
2		180,000	35	750,000	2	150,000	2	52	420,000	218,400	381,600
3		180,000	30	750,000	6	200,000	4	52	370,000	192,400	357,600
4		180,000	90	850,000	0	100,000	1	50	570,000	285,000	465,000
5		180,000	20	750,000	3	150,000	8	54	420,000	226,800	473,200*

* This value includes the $100,000 salvage value.

case, the rate of return is then calculated using Eq. (7-2).   However, if the variables can have more than one value, another approach, using Monte Carlo simulation, is possible if probability distributions are established for the variables in Eq. (7-3).   For example, suppose the distributions shown in Fig. 7-5 are established for each variable. With these data and the assumption of a straight-line depreciation model, a distribution of the internal rate of return can be generated.

The first step is to set up cumulative distributions for each variable and assign the tag numbers.   By now, these steps should be familiar, and they are left as an exercise.

The next step is to generate individual random numbers for the life of project, cost of the investment, and salvage value.   Say, for example, that these random numbers are 3, 5, and 48, respectively.   These random numbers indicate a life of 5 years, an investment cost of $1 million and a salvage value of $100,000.   With these values, a depreciation schedule for each year is established as

$$\text{Depreciation per year} = \frac{\$1,000,000 - 100,000}{5} = \$180,000$$

Table 7-11 can now be set up and the simulation continued as indicated.   Substituting the cash flows generated in Table 7-11 in Eq. (7-2) gives

$$0 = -1,000,000 + \frac{381,600}{1+i} + \frac{381,600}{(1+i)^2} + \frac{357,600}{(1+i)^3} + \frac{465,000}{(1+i)^4} + \frac{473,200}{(1+i)^5} \cdot$$

Equation (7-2) is solved for i ($i \simeq 28$ percent in this case).   These steps and calculations are repeated many times, and from these results a distribution of the internal rate of return is determined.   With this distribution, probability statements can be made regarding the rate of return similar to the probability statements mentioned in Example 7-2.

To anyone familiar with engineering-economy concepts, it is obvious that the procedure illustrated in this example can be extended to more complex cash-flow situations and be used to generate the distribution of net present value and payback period.   ////

DEPENDENCY BETWEEN VARIABLES

So far in our examples of Monte Carlo simulation, the assumption has been that the variables are independent.   Although this is a common assumption, it is not always correct.   For example, the variable gross income per year used in Example 7-4 can be considered to be given by

$$\text{Gross income/year} = \text{sales/year} \times \text{selling price/unit}$$

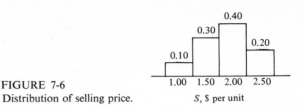

FIGURE 7-6
Distribution of selling price.

Obviously, sales and selling price are not independent; in fact, they are dependent. For, in general, as the selling price decreases, sales will increase. This dependency can be included in a simulation model by establishing a selling-price distribution like that shown in Fig. 7-6 and then establishing a demand distribution for each level of selling price, as shown in Fig. 7-7.

The procedure in the simulation process would be to generate a random number which would be used to determine the selling price. Once the selling price has been determined, it would dictate the distribution to be used in finding the sales quantity. Another random number would be generated and used to determine the sales. The two values obtained would then be multiplied to determine the gross income. For

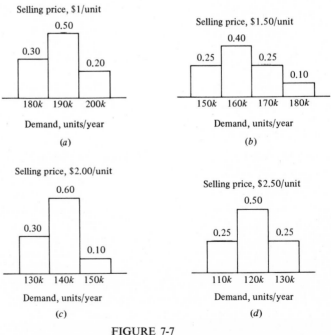

FIGURE 7-7
Demand distributions for various selling prices.

example, suppose the first random number is 22; this indicates a selling price of $1.50 using Fig. 7-6 and also indicates that Fig. 7-7*b* should be used to determine the sales. Suppose the second random number generated is 73. This indicates a sales of 170,000 units. Therefore the gross income for the year is

$$\text{Gross income per year} = 1.50(170,000) = \$255,000$$

This value would then be used in the simulation process and would be repeated each time a value was required for gross income. In Fig. 7-7 a certain amount of overlap has been included in the distributions. For a particular application this may or may not be appropriate. The correctness of this overlap depends on the particular problem being simulated.

Another approach to dependency is to use a mathematical function which exhibits the dependency between the variables. For example, in the case of selling price and sales per year, a mathematical function of the form

$$\text{Sales per year} = f(\text{selling price})$$

would be established. The procedure would be to generate a random number that would determine the selling price. The sales per year would then be calculated using the mathematical function and the determined selling price. With these two values, the gross income would be calculated.

Obviously, these procedures can be simplified. In Fig. 7-7 each of the demand distributions can be converted into gross-income distributions by multiplying the demand in a particular distribution by its respective selling price. In the case of a mathematical function, the function could be established in terms of selling price and gross income.

OTHER DISTRIBUTIONS

In the previous examples all the variables were described by discrete empirical distributions. This type of distribution is not a requirement in Monte Carlo simulation. Any variable can be represented by a theoretical distribution, provided, of course, that the distribution adequately describes the variable. In fact, it is possible to represent one variable by an empirical distribution and another by a theoretical distribution in the same simulation model. In this section three theoretical distributions are presented as examples.

The Poisson Distribution

The Poisson distribution is used in many queuing problems to describe the arrival rate. It is a discrete distribution. To use this distribution, one must know, estimate, or guess the average value of the distribution.   Suppose a variable x is to be represented by a Poisson distribution with a mean of 1.1; then Table 7-12 can be established using the values in Appendix A.

The Normal Distribution

To use the normal distribution to describe a variable, one must somehow obtain the mean and standard deviation.   If the variable x in a simulation problem can be considered continuous and normally distributed, Ref. 5 shows that x can be calculated from

$$x = \sigma_x \left(\frac{12}{K}\right)^{1/2} \left(\sum_{i=1}^{K} r_i - \frac{K}{2}\right) + \mu_x \qquad (7\text{-}4)$$

where σ_x = standard deviation of distribution
μ_x = mean of distribution
K = empirical constant

From experience $K = 10$ (Ref. 5).   Sometimes, it is taken as 12 because of the computational advantage, i.e., the term $(12/K)^{1/2}$ is equal to 1.

$$\sum_{i=1}^{K} r_i = \text{sum of } K \text{ random digits defined over interval 0 to 1}$$

For example, suppose $K = 12$, $\mu_x = 3$, $\sigma_x = 1.2$ and the 12 random numbers are 10, 37, 08, 99, 12, 66, 31, 85, 63, 73, 98, 11.   Then x is

$$x = 1.2 \left(\frac{12}{12}\right)^{1/2} \left(5.93 - \frac{12}{2}\right) + 3$$

$$x = 1.2(5.93 - 6) + 3 = 2.916$$

Table 7-12   TAG NUMBER FOR THE VARIABLE X (POISSON DISTRIBUTION)

Value of x	Cumulative probability	Tag numbers
0	.333	000–332
1	.699	333–698
2	.900	699–899
3	.974	900–973
4	.995	974–994
5	.999	995–998
6	1.000	999

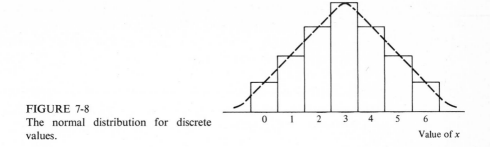

FIGURE 7-8
The normal distribution for discrete
values.

Value of x

The value 2.916 is then used as a value for x in the simulation.   When the next value of x is required, 12 new random numbers are generated and a new value of x calculated.

The Exponential Distribution

The exponential distribution is a continuous distribution widely used in simulation problems.   In order to use it, the mean must be known or estimated.   The cumulative distribution function is given by

$$F(x) = 1 - e^{-x/\theta} \qquad (7\text{-}5)$$

where θ is the mean.

If the variable x can be considered continuous, Ref. 3 indicates that x can be calculated from

$$X = -\theta \log r \qquad (7\text{-}6)$$

where r is a random number in the interval 0 to 1.

There are, of course, many other theoretical distributions used in simulation studies.   The references treat other distributions.

At times a variable can only have integer values, but it is still desired to describe the variable by a continuous distribution.   In these cases, the probability of a particular value is approximated by using the continuous distribution.   For example, a variable x has a mean of 3.00 and a standard deviation of 1.00 and it is assumed to be normally distributed.   However, for physical reasons, the values of x can only be integers.   This situation is illustrated in Fig. 7-8.   In approximating the probabilities of the various x values a cell interval must be chosen.   In Fig. 7-8 a cell interval of 1 is implied.   The cell interval will depend upon practical considerations and the degree of accuracy desired in the approximation.   For instance, if the mean were 300 instead of 3, a cell interval of 1 could still be used, but would result in a large number of cells and a large number of calculations.   A cell interval of 10 or even 50 might be adequate.

Returning to this example, the probabilities in the discrete case can be obtained by calculating the cumulative probabilities for each cell division using the normal distribution. Once the cumulative probabilities have been obtained, the tag numbers can be assigned. These steps are shown in Table 7-13.

EXAMPLE 7-5 In this example Monte Carlo simulation is used in a simple inventory problem. Theoretical distributions are used to approximate the distributions of demand and lead time. Suppose that the demand for a particular item is normally distributed with a mean of 200 units/week and a standard deviation of 50 units/week and the lead time is distributed exponentially with a mean of 1 week. The cost of making one order is $90 and the cost of holding 1 unit is 10 cents per week. The problem is to determine the order quantity and order point that results in a minimum total system cost.

Before beginning the simulation, a starting point must be selected and certain assumptions made. In the simulation that follows a constant order quantity of 600 units and an order point of 100 units or less are chosen, based on relationships developed in the inventory chapter. The relationships and calculations resulting in these choices are

$$Q = \sqrt{\frac{2C_1 \bar{D}}{C_2}} = \sqrt{\frac{2(90)(200)}{.1}} = 600 \text{ units}$$

$$\text{Order point} = \bar{D}\bar{L} = 200(1) = 200 \text{ units}$$

A decision must also be made regarding the initial inventory level. An initial inventory level of 600 units is used. This level is, of course, an arbitrary choice.

In this problem it is assumed that the demand rate within any 1-week period is constant. In addition, it is assumed that the inventory level is reviewed at the end of

Table 7-13   A NORMAL APPROXIMATION OF A DISCRETE CASE

Value of x	Lower cell boundary x' of x	Upper cell boundary x'' of x	Normal deviate $K_x = \dfrac{x'' - 3.0}{1.0}$	Cumulative probability α	Tag numbers
0	$-\infty$	0.5	-2.5	.006	000–005
1	0.5	1.5	-1.5	.067	006–066
2	1.5	2.5	-0.5	.309	067–308
3	2.5	3.5	0.5	.691	309–690
4	3.5	4.5	1.5	.933	691–932
5	4.5	5.5	2.5	.944	933–943
6	5.5	6.5	3.5	1.000	944–999
7	6.5	∞	∞	1.000	—

each week.   If at this time the inventory is greater than the order point, no order is placed.   However, if the inventory level is equal to or less than 200 units an order for 600 units is placed.

The next step is to assign the tag numbers for the demand and lead time.   A cell interval of 50 units is used for the demand, and a cell interval of 1 day is used for the lead time.   Of course, smaller or larger cell intervals can be used, but for illustrative purposes these cell intervals are believed to be sufficient.   The necessary calculations for assigning the tag numbers are shown in Tables 7-14 and 7-15.

After the tag numbers have been assigned, the actual simulation can be done. This is shown in Table 7-16 for a period of 16 weeks.   In an actual study, a longer period of time would be used.

A plot of the data in Table 7-16 is shown in Fig. 7-9.   With this figure an economic analysis of this particular simulation run is possible.   The expected variable cost VC is given by

$$VC = c_1(\text{number of orders}) + c_2 (\text{average inventory})$$

$$+ c_3 (\text{average shortages}) \tag{7-7}$$

Table 7-14   TAG NUMBERS FOR DEMAND (EXAMPLE 7-5)

Value of demand	Lower cell boundary x'	Upper cell boundary x''	Normal deviate $K_a = \dfrac{x'' - 200}{50}$	Cumulative probability	Tag numbers
50	$-\infty$	75	-2.5	.006	000–005
100	75	125	-1.5	.067	006–066
150	125	175	-0.5	.309	067–308
200	175	225	0.5	.692	309–691
250	225	275	1.5	.933	692–932
300	275	325	2.5	.994	933–993
350	325	375	3.5	1.000	994–999
400	375	∞	∞	1.000	—

Table 7-15   TAG NUMBERS FOR LEAD TIME (EXAMPLE 7-5)

Lead time x	Lower cell boundary x'	Upper cell boundary x''	Cumulative probability $F(x) = 1 - e^{-x''/1}$	Tag number
1	0	1.5	.78	00–77
2	1.5	2.5	.92	78–91
3	2.5	3.5	.97	92–96
4	3.5	4.5	.99	97–98
5	4.5	5.5	1.00	99

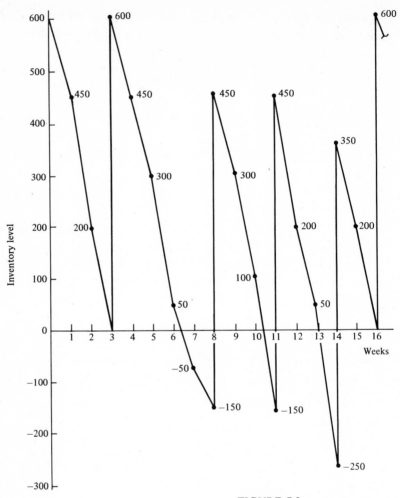

FIGURE 7-9
Simulation results of Example 7-5.

The number of orders shown in Fig. 7-9 is 5, and the average inventory is given by

$$\text{Average inventory} = \frac{\text{inventory area}}{\text{number of weeks}}$$

$$= \frac{3,461.7}{16} = 216.3 \text{ units} \qquad (7\text{-}8)$$

The shortage area in Fig. 7-9 is 261.5 unit-weeks; therefore

$$\text{Average shortage} = \frac{\text{shortage area}}{\text{number of weeks}}$$

$$= \frac{261.5}{16} = 16.3 \text{ units} \qquad (7\text{-}9)$$

With these values, the variable cost can be determined using Eq. (7-7). Assuming that the cost of one shortage is \$10 per week, Eq. (7-7) gives

$$VC = 90(5) + .1(216.3) + 10(16.3) = \$634.63 \text{ per week}$$

Additional combinations of order quantities and order points should be tried to see if the cost can be reduced. It should be remembered that simulation of a system provides an answer only for a particular set of circumstances. Consequently, the answer for one set of circumstances is not necessarily the best answer.   ////

Table 7-16 SIMULATION FOR EXAMPLE 7-5

End of week	Random number for demand	Demand	Inventory level	Random number for lead time	Lead time	Comment
0			600			Starting point
1	201	150	450			
2	765	250	200	52	1	Order 600 units
			$-200 + 200 + 600$			
3	648	200	$= 600$			Receive 600 units
4	196	150	450			
5	093	150	300			
6	705	250	50	82	2	Order 600 units
7	010	100	-50			
			$-50 - 100 + 600$			
8	020	100	$= 450$			Receive 600 units
9	149	150	300			
10	398	200	100	35	1	Order 600 units
			$100 - 250 + 600$			
11	865	250	$= 450$			Receive 600 units
12	875	250	200	79	2	Order 600 units
13	174	150	50			
			$50 - 300 + 600$			
14	975	300	$= 350$			Receive 600 units
15	269	150	200	43	1	Order 600 units
			$200 - 200 + 600$			
16	361	200	$= 600$			Receive 600 units

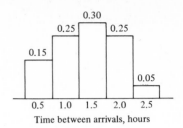

FIGURE 7-10
Distribution of time between arrivals.

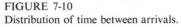

EXAMPLE 7-6. In probabilistic queuing problems Monte Carlo simulation has been used to evaluate various service policies. For example, suppose that the empirical distribution shown in Fig. 7-10 describes the time between arrivals at a single-channel service facility and that the service time is exponentially distributed. The problem is to determine the mean service time such that the total cost of the system is minimum, where the total cost of the system (TC) is given by

$$TC = \text{waiting-time cost} + \text{service-facility cost} \qquad (7\text{-}10)$$

The procedure in this problem would be to choose various mean service times and simulate the system for each chosen value. The total cost for each service time would be computed and evaluated.

In Fig. 7-10 the mean time between arrivals is 1.4 hours. This provides a starting point for a choice of the mean service time, since the mean service time must be equal to or less than the mean time between arrivals. Otherwise, the queue would grow without bounds. Therefore, a mean service time of 1.2 hours is used in this example, and the cost of the service facility is assumed to be $20 per hour.

From Fig. 7-10, it is possible to assign the tag numbers shown in Table 7-17. Since it is possible to consider the time of service as continuous, Eq. (7-6) is used in the simulation of the service times. For simplicity only one-digit random numbers were used for this part of the simulation, and the service times were rounded off to one decimal.

Table 7-17   TAG NUMBERS FOR
TIME BETWEEN
ARRIVALS FOR
EXAMPLE 7-6

Time between arrivals	Tag numbers
.5	00–14
1.0	15–39
1.5	40–69
2.0	70–94
2.5	95–99

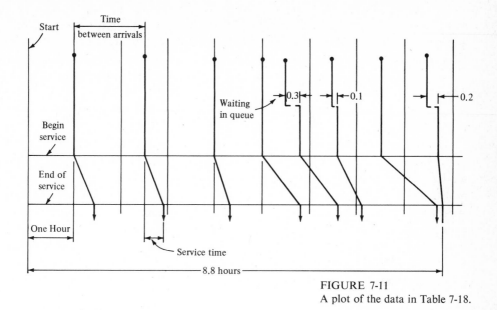

FIGURE 7-11
A plot of the data in Table 7-18.

Table 7-18 shows the results of the simulation of eight arrivals.   As a starting condition, it was assumed that the first arrival occurred after the service facility was opened (1 hour in this case).   With the data of Table 7-18, Fig. 7-11 can be plotted. At this point, the total cost is computed using Eq. (7-10).   The total waiting time is given by

$$\text{Total waiting time} = \text{waiting time in service facility} + \text{waiting time in queue} \qquad (7\text{-}11)$$
$$= 4.5 + 0.3 + 0.1 + 0.2 = 5.1 \text{ hours}$$

Table 7-18   SIMULATION FOR EXAMPLE 7-6

Arrival number	Random number for time between arrivals	Time between arrivals	Random number r for service time	Service time $x = -1.2 \log r$
1	34	1.0	5	.4
2	43	1.5	5	.4
3	40	1.5	6	.3
4	15	1.0	2	.8
5	05	0.5	2	.8
6	25	1.0	4	.5
7	83	2.0	1	1.2
8	33	1.0	9	.1
				4.5

The total time for processing the eight arrivals is 8.8 hours. Consequently, assuming that the cost of waiting for 1 unit is \$5 per hour, the total cost for 8.8 hours of operation is

$$TC = 5(5.1) + 20(8.8) = \$201.50$$

Then

$$\text{Average cost per hour} = \frac{201.50}{8.8} = \$22.90. \qquad ////$$

Obviously, in an actual case a much longer time would be used and various other service conditions would be tried. The preceding example is a very simple queuing problem. Obtaining a solution through Monte Carlo simulation is not the only approach. It may be possible to obtain a solution by analytical procedures. More complex examples and other applications of Monte Carlo simulation can be found in the literature. References 1, 3 to 5, 7, and 8 and most texts on operations research, production control, and inventory control provide additional applications and examples of Monte Carlo simulation.

RANDOM NUMBERS

Monte Carlo simulation requires random numbers to obtain random observations from a probability distribution. A random number is a number in a sequence of numbers whose probability of occurrence is the same as that of any other number in the sequence. Random numbers may be obtained manually, by tables, or by computer methods.

Manual methods are laborious and not very practical except for illustrative purposes in the classroom. They usually involve such devices as roulette wheels, card shuffling, beads in an urn, coin flipping, and dice rolling.

Tables of random numbers are available in the literature, e.g. Ref. 6. These random numbers were generated using some random physical process (electric current in the Rand case) and are considered to be "truly" random numbers. The problem with using tables of random numbers is making them available in a computer program. To use tables it would be necessary to record the random numbers on magnetic tapes or disks. This is a big job. In addition, calling for a random number when needed is a relatively slow computer process.

Perhaps the most common process for obtaining random numbers is to generate pseudo random numbers, usually through a computer program. A pseudo random sequence of numbers is not truly random because they are obtained using a completely deterministic mathematical process. However, numbers generated in this manner are treated as random since they pass a certain number of statistical tests for randomness. A sequence of pseudo random numbers will eventually cycle, i.e. repeat itself, but cycling presents no difficulties if the cycle is long enough.   Two procedures for generating pseudo random numbers are the midsquare and congruential techniques.

The midsquare technique starts with a number that consists of an even number of digits, squaring the number, and choosing the middle, n digits of this result as the random number.   The value of n is the number of digits in the original number.   The next random number is obtained by repeating this process using the previous random number as the beginning point.   For example, if the starting number is 56, squaring gives 3,136.   Therefore the random number is 13.   Squaring 13 gives 169, and the random number is 16.   If the procedure is repeated six times, the random-number sequence is 56, 13, 16, 25, 62, and 84.   This method of determining random numbers is not widely used because the length of the cycle depends on the starting number used.

Congruential techniques make use of some recursive formula.   For example, the multiplicative congruential method uses the formula

$$x_{n+1} = kx_n \quad \text{modulo } m \qquad (7\text{-}12)$$

where k and m are positive integers and k is less then m.   Equation (7-12) implies that the x_{n+1} random number is generated from the x_n random number and that these random numbers are the remainders when kx_n is divided by m.   For example, if $k = 8$, $m = 10$, and $x_0 = 2$, then Eq. (7-12) gives

$$x_1 = kx_0 \ (\text{mod } m) = 8(2)(\text{mod } 10) = \frac{10 + 6}{10} = 6$$

$$x_2 = 8(6)(\text{mod } 10) = \frac{40 + 8}{10} = 8$$

$$x_3 = 8(8)(\text{mod } 10) = \frac{60 + 4}{10} = 4$$

Therefore, the random-number sequence is 2, 6, 8, and 4.   If this example is continued for x_4 and x_5, it will be seen that the sequence cycles.   Consequently, care must be exercised in choosing k, m, and x_0.   For a binary computer, Ref. 4 suggests $m = 2^b$ (the computer word length), x_0 to be selected as any odd number, and k to be selected from the equation $8t + 3$ (t an integer).   Additional information on the generation of random numbers and statistical testing for randomness can be found in the reference.

SAMPLE SIZE ESTIMATES

Determining the sample size before running a particular simulation is an important decision.   However, it is a difficult one since much of the information required to specify a sample size correctly is not known until after the simulation has been done.   For this reason, some assumptions will be required, and one should consider the relationships presented here as only reasonable estimates.

In most simulations there are usually two (there may be, of course, others) parameters of particular interest, namely the mean and the standard deviation of the population.

Population Mean

Assuming that the sample mean is normally distributed and that a sufficiently large sample size will be taken, the sample size is given by

$$n = \frac{\sigma^2 (Z_{\alpha/2})^2}{d^2} \qquad (7\text{-}13)$$

where n = sample size

σ = known standard deviation of population

$Z_{\alpha/2}$ = normal deviate corresponding to a confidence level $1 - \alpha$ that the true mean will be between $\alpha/2$ and $1 - \alpha/2$.

d = difference between sample mean true mean

As an example, suppose one wants to know the sample size so that the difference between the sample mean and the true mean is ± 2 at a confidence level of 99 percent. Assuming that the standard deviation is known and has a value of 10, Eq. (7-13) gives

$$n = \frac{10^2 (2.575)^2}{2^2} = 165.75 \simeq 166$$

In Eq. (7-13) it was assumed that the standard deviation is known. In general this is not the case. When the standard deviation σ is not known, it can be estimated by the standard deviations of the sample s given by

$$s = \sqrt{\frac{\sum\limits_{i}^{n} (x - \bar{x})^2}{n - 1}} \qquad (7\text{-}14)$$

In addition, from a statistical consideration, $Z_{\alpha/2}$ should be replaced by $t_{\alpha/2;\, n-1}$ where t implies the t distribution and the term $n - 1$ is the degrees of freedom. The problem here is that in order to determine $t_{\alpha/2;\, n-1}$ the sample size, n, must be known and this is what needs to be found. Fortunately, by assuming a large sample size, the term $t_{\alpha/2;\, n-1}$ can be replaced with $Z_{\alpha/2}$. These considerations result in

$$n = \frac{s^2 (Z_{\alpha/2})^2}{d^2} \qquad (7\text{-}15)$$

Standard Deviation of the Population

An approximate sample size can be obtained from consideration of a prescribed confidence level and precision for the variance of the population. The usual approach is to base the determination of a sample size on the test statistic

$$\chi^2 = \frac{(n-1)s^2}{\sigma^2} \qquad (7\text{-}16)$$

which has a chi-squared distribution with $n-1$ degrees of freedom and assumes normality. The same problem exists here as in the preceding discussion, namely the sample size must be known beforehand. However, if the assumption of a large sample size and a normal distribution is made, Ref. 4 shows that an approximation to the sample size can be obtained from

$$Z_{\alpha/2} = \frac{d'(n-1)}{\sqrt{2(n-1)}} \qquad (7\text{-}17)$$

which can be put in the form

$$n_\alpha = \frac{2(Z_{\alpha/2})^2}{(d')^2} + 1 \qquad (7\text{-}18)$$

where the value d' expresses the symmetrical relative accuracy between the sample variance and true variance. For example, the sample size required for the sample variance to be within ± 10 percent of the true variance with a confidence level of 99 percent is

$$n = \frac{2(Z_{.995})^2}{(.10)^2} + 1$$

$$= \frac{2(2.575)^2}{.01} + 1 = 1{,}327.2 \simeq 1328$$

Obviously, the sample sizes given by Eq. (7-15) and (7-18) may be different for a particular simulation. When this is the case, one must make a balance between precision and such practical considerations as the cost of coumpter time.

There are, of course, other approaches to sample-size determination. One is simply to choose a large number for the sample size. Then, using the results of the simulation, establish the confidence levels. Another approach is to compute the average value after each trial until it approaches a limit, as shown in Fig. 7-12. When the distance between the high and low points is equal to or less than some stated amount, the simulation is stopped. This procedure can also be used for the standard deviation or variance.

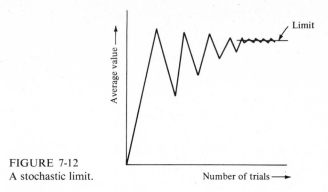

FIGURE 7-12
A stochastic limit.

Still another approach, but a more costly one, is to make several pilot runs to obtain an idea of the population mean and standard deviation. These initial estimates of the mean and standard deviation can then be used to approximate a sample size.

The sample-size methods discussed here are approximate. In the final analysis, as in most cases, a balance between the practical and the theoretical must be made.

SOME PRACTICAL CONSIDERATIONS

In many simulation studies the starting-point conditions of the system being simulated are an important consideration, e.g., in inventory and queuing systems. In systems of this type the simulation is not usually considered representative of the actual system until steady-state conditions exist. Consequently, data taken during the transient period should not be included in the analysis, unless, of course, the transient period is the period of interest.

Steady-state condition implies here that the state of the system is independent of the starting conditions, in other words, a steady-state condition exists when the limiting state distribution is independent of time. In practice it is difficult to determine the number of trials necessary before steady-state conditions are reached. Two approaches are usually taken to resolve this problem: (1) to make several pilot runs to determine when steady-state conditions are reached and (2) to load the system initially in order to make the starting conditions as close as possible to the steady-state conditions. Considerable computer time can be involved in the first approach, and some idea at least of steady-state conditions is required for the second.

In some simulation studies starting conditions are not a problem, e.g., the simulation model described earlier in this chapter to generate a distribution of the internal rate of return.

The purpose of many simulation studies is to determine which alternative decisions give the best measure of some effectiveness criterion, e.g., determination of a priority rule (alternatives) in a job-shop situation that minimizes machine idle time (effectiveness criterion).   In this type of study Hillier and Lieberman (Ref. 3) point out that the same starting conditions and random numbers should be used for each alternative.   The results of each alternative should then be used to make a decision.

In an earlier section consideration was given to the determination of a sample size.   However, few texts indicate the number of samples.   Hillier and Lieberman (Ref. 3, p. 464) indicate that between 10 and 15 samples is desirable.   Two approaches are possible here.

The first makes a completely separate series of runs and computes an average for each run, using this value as an observation.   Since each observation is independent and an average, the observations, according to the central-limit theorem, will approximate a normal distribution.   Therefore, a confidence level can be established for the total mean.   The disadvantage to this approach is that each run requires time to reach a steady-state condition.   This could result in a large amount of computer time.

The second approach is to make the runs consecutive, using the end condition of one run as the starting condition for the next run.   In this way only one initial run-in period is required.   The total overall simulation run is divided into a series of smaller equal runs, and the averages of these smaller runs are used as observations. The disadvantage in this method is that the smaller runs may not be independent. However, if each of these runs is made long enough, an assumption of independence might be valid for all practical purposes.

Hillier and Lieberman (Ref. 3) point out that in determining the probability distributions to use for a variable, it is better to use the theoretical distribution that best fits the variable than to use some frequency distribution based on historical data, their argument being that the theoretical distribution will be closer to predicting future performance than reproducing idiosyncracies of the past.

SIMULATION LANGUAGES

Since simulation studies are computer-oriented, it may appear, from the discussion in this chapter, that programming all the details (generation of random number, assignment of tag numbers, computations, proper data output, etc.) required in a simulation study would be very involved.   If a general purpose programming language such as FORTRAN were used, this would be true.   Fortunately, general simulation languages such as GPSS, SIMSCRIPT, SIMPAC, DYNAMO, and GASP are readily available.   These special languages relieve the programmer of many of the details required in a computer simulation model. References 4, 5, and 7 discuss the use and relative merits of these special languages and provide the information necessary to obtain user's manuals and compiler programs.

CONCLUSIONS

Simulation is a powerful tool that is particularly useful in analyzing systems which are too complex for mathematical analysis. However, it should be remembered that simulation does not necessarily provide an optimum answer. In addition, sensitivity analysis is expensive; for in order to find the effect of a change in a variable, a new simulation run is necessary.

REFERENCES

1 BONINI, C. P.: "Simulation of Information and Decision Systems in the Firm," Prentice-Hall, Inc., Englewood Cliffs, N.J., 1963.

2 HAHN, G. J., and S. S. SHAPIRO: "Statistical Models in Engineering," chap. 7, John Wiley & Sons, Inc., New York, 1967.

3 HILLIER, F. S., and G. J. LIEBERMAN: "Introduction to Operations Research," chap. 14, Holden-Day, Inc., Publisher, San Francisco, 1968.

4 MIZE, J. H., and J. G. COX: "Essentials of Simulation," Prentice-Hall, Inc., Englewood Cliffs, N.J., 1968.

5 NAYLOR, T. H., J. L. BALINTFY, D. S. BURDICK, and C. KONG: "Computer Simulation Techniques," John Wiley & Sons, Inc., New York, 1966.

6 RAND CORPORATION: "A Million Random Digits with 100,000 Normal Deviates," The Free Press, Glencoe, Ill., 1955.

7 SCHMIDT, J. W., and R. E. TAYLOR: "Simulation and Analysis of Industrial Systems," Richard D. Irwin, Inc., Homewood, Ill., 1970.

8 TOCHER, K. D.: "The Art of Simulation," The English University Press, Ltd., London, 1963.

PROBLEMS

7-1 Given the function $w = ab + x$ and the distributions for each variable shown below, determine the average value of w for a total of 15 trials. Use the random numbers specified for each variable.

Variable *a*

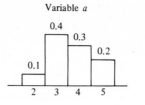

Random numbers for *a*
1, 2, 2, 4, 3, 7, 9, 9,
8, 9, 2, 6, 0, 1, 0.

Variable *b*

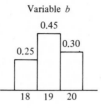

Random numbers for *b*
15, 46, 48, 93, 39, 06, 72, 91
14, 36, 69, 40, 93, 61, 97.

Variable *x*

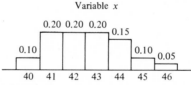

Random numbers for *x*
01, 25, 22, 06, 81, 11, 56, 05
63, 53, 88, 48, 52, 87, 71.

7-2   The value of an effectiveness function *z* is given by

$$z = \frac{x}{y} + 1.5w$$

where *x* is normally distributed with a mean of 90 and a standard deviation of 10 [assume that this variable is continuous; therefore, Eq. (7-4) is applicable]; *w* is Poisson distributed with a mean of 1.0; and *y* has the tabulated empirical distribution.

Value of *y*	20	30	40	50	60	70
Probability	.28	.20	.18	.15	.10	.09

Using the random numbers shown below, determine the value of *z* for 10 trials.

x	*w*	*y*
$\sum_{i=1}^{12} r_i = 4.4$	990	35
6.2	539	42
5.0	891	11
3.5	241	58
5.8	935	84
6.1	693	25
3.9	432	35
4.3	369	02
6.6	464	97
4.9	702	31

7-3 Determine the tag numbers for a discrete random variable with a mean of 90 and a standard deviation of 10 using a normal approximation and a cell interval of 10.

7-4 A simulation has been run for a particular effectiveness function. After 100 trials the following values are obtained:

$$\sum_{i=1}^{100} x_i = 4,500$$

$$\sum_{i=1}^{100} x_i^2 = 217,500$$

where x is the value of the effectiveness function.

(a) What is the absolute accuracy between the sample mean and true mean at a confidence level of 95 percent?

(b) What is the relative accuracy between the sample standard deviation and true standard deviation at a confidence level of 95 percent?

7-5 The sales of a particular item have been observed to be either 450, 475, or 500 items per week with probabilities of .25, .40, and .35, respectively. The lead times between placing and receipt of an order are 1, 2, and 3 weeks with probabilities of .75, .20, and .05, respectively. Using the data shown below, determine the stock on hand after 15 weeks of simulated operation.

Constant order quantity = 1,400 items

Order point = 500 units

Starting inventory level = 1,400 units

RANDOM NUMBERS

For demand				For lead time	
68	22	83	29	52	08
37	31	55	71	81	20
41	58	32	12	10	95
16	66	61		36	74

7-6 The demand and lead time for a particular item have the distributions shown below. Explain how the demand over the lead time could be generated using Monte Carlo simulation. Use the random numbers shown in your explanation.

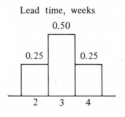

Lead time, weeks

Random numbers
38, 10, 41, 82

Demand, items/week

Random numbers
15, 51, 60, 30, 72, 09,
40, 50, 84, 76, 49, 32.

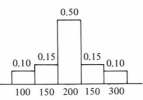

7-7 Using the distributions shown below and assuming straight-line depreciation, explain how a distribution of the interval rate can be generated using Monte Carlo simulation. For an initial example, use the following random numbers:

Initial investment	3
Life of project	1
Salvage value	25
Gross income	36, 65, 99, 48
Expense	48, 82, 87, 13
Effective tax rate	22, 35, 58, 11

Initial investment,$
(occurs in year 0)

Salvage value, $

Life of project, years

Gross income, $/year

Expenses, $/year

Effective tax rate, %

7-8 The volume of sales of a certain item depends upon the selling price of the item. The selling price of one item can be $800, $825, $850, $825, or $900 with probabilities of .15, .35, .25, .15, and .10, respectively. The volume of sales is assumed to be continuous and normally distributed. The means and standard deviations for each selling price are tabulated. Explain how the gross income for a period of 50 weeks can be generated using Monte Carlo simulation.

Selling price	Volume of sales units/week	
	Mean	Standard deviation
$800	280	30
825	250	25
850	230	20
875	200	15
900	150	15

7-9   Preventive maintenance is performed on plant vehicles.   All maintenance tasks can be done by one man, but sometimes the job can be done in less time by a two-man crew.   With one man, the times to perform the maintenance on one vehicle are 1.25, 1.50, 1.75, or 2.00 hours with probabilities of .15, .25, .40, and .20, respectively. A two-man crew requires .50, .75, 1.00, or 1.25 hours with probabilities of .25, .35, .30, and .10, respectively.   Each crew member is paid $4.50 per hour, and the overhead charge is $1 per hour per crew.   Using the random numbers shown below, determine whether a one- or two-man crew is more economical.

RANDOM NUMBERS

38	46	91
89	25	43
40	20	59
02	20	66
99	78	16
37	92	34
46	34	87

8

QUEUING OR WAITING-LINE THEORY

INTRODUCTION

Of all the concepts dealt with by basic operations research techniques, queuing theory appears to have the widest potential application and yet is perhaps the most difficult to apply. Businesses of all types, government, industry, schools, and hospitals, large and small—all have queuing problems. Many of these could benefit from an OR analysis to determine the minimum-cost (maximum-output) operating conditions. Unfortunately the assumptions required to provide relatively simple mathematics often make the model a poor fit to reality, but many of these difficulties can be overcome if a sound understanding of queuing theory is combined with imagination.

The classical example of a queue consists of two major elements, as depicted in Fig. 8-1. Customers arriving at the queuing system wait in line until service is provided, or if the system is empty, the arriving customer may be serviced immediately. Once service has been completed, the customer leaves the system.

The rate at which customers arrive to be serviced is called the *arrival rate* λ (lambda). As the name implies, this is a *rate* with units of customers per hour, customers per day, etc. The rate at which the service unit can provide customer service is called the *service rate* μ (mu). This is also a rate with the same units as λ

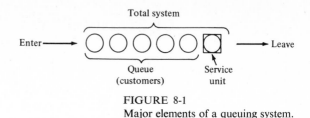

FIGURE 8-1
Major elements of a queuing system.

and reflects maximum service capacity assuming that the service unit is not idle. Normally it is assumed that these rates reflect an average of many possible values that can be described by a Poisson distribution.   Typically one must find an acceptable rate of arrivals of customers for a given service capacity or a desirable service rate to match a given arrival rate.   Several variations are possible.

Although it is contrary to common practice, this chapter will first present the equations required for analysis and use them to analyze typical problems.   Following that, the basic equations will be derived.   It is felt that the derivation can be followed more easily after the student is familiar with the terms and concepts.

DEFINITION OF TERMS

Queuing problems consist of properly matching the service rate of the process with the arrival rate of the work to be done.   Some basic terms will be defined.

Customer   The arriving unit that requires some service to be performed.   The customer may be people, machines, parts, etc.

Queue (*waiting line*)   The number of customers waiting to be serviced.   Normally, the queue does not include the customer being serviced.

Service channel   That process or system which is performing the service to the customer.   This may be single or multichannel.   The symbol k will indicate the number of service channels.

EXAMPLE 8-1   Fans waiting to buy tickets for a football game: the arriving fans are the customers, and the ticket agent is the service channel.   If there is more than one ticket agent, this is a multichannel problem.

Letters waiting to be typed: the letters are the customers, and the typist(s) are the service channel(s).

A parking lot: the cars to be parked are the customers, and the parking space is the service channel.   There are as many channels as there are parking spaces.   In this type of problem one computes the probability that all channels (spaces) are busy.

Credit-card bills waiting to be punched: the cards are the customers, and the keypunch is the service unit.

Arrival rate The *rate* (customers per time period) at which customers arrive to be serviced. The assumption regarding the distribution of this value has a great effect upon the mathematical model. A typical assumption, which will be used in this text, is that the arrival rate is randomly distributed according to the Poisson distribution. The mean value of the arrival rate is λ.

Service rate The *rate* (customers per time period) at which one service channel can perform the required customer service. Note that this is the rate which could be attained if the service channel were always busy, i.e., no idle time. The distribution of this value is equally important in the determination of the degree of mathematical complexity. Unless otherwise noted, this text will assume that the service rate is randomly distributed according to the Poisson process. The mean value of the service is μ.

Priority The method of deciding which customer will be serviced next. The most common assumption is first come, first served. This assumption also affects the derivation of the equations used for analysis.

Population size The size of the group that provides customers. If there are only a few potential customers, the population is finite. If there are a large number of potential customers, say over 30 to 50, the population is usually said to be infinite. As another rule of thumb, the assumption of an infinite population will generally be valid when the potential customer population is large enough to mean that the arrival of one customer does not significantly affect the probability of another arrival.

Distribution of arrival (service) rates The most common assumption is the Poisson distribution. This assumption requires that the events of service or arrival be completely independent. This is probably one of the more restrictive assumptions and will be discussed in more detail later. In all cases it must be remembered that the analysis gives results in terms of expected or average values. In addition, it is normally assumed that both the service rate and arrival rates are constant over time. Realistically, this may not be true since it is common practice occasionally to use overtime or extra effort when an excessive queue condition is present. This represents a temporary change in μ.

Expected number in queue L_q The expected number of customers waiting to be serviced.

Expected number in system L The expected number of customers either waiting in line and/or being serviced.

Expected time in queue W_q The expected time a customer spends waiting in line.

Expected system time W The expected time a customer spends waiting plus being serviced, $W_q + 1/\mu$.

Expected number in nonempty queue L_n The average or expected number of customers waiting in line *excluding* those times when the line is empty. For example, if one randomly took samples by counting the number of customers in line and averaged only nonzero values, it would be equivalent to L.

Expected waiting time for nonempty queue W_n   The expected time a customer waits in line *if* he has to wait at all.   That is, this value is the average of waiting times for all customers that enter the queue when the service channel is filled. Customers that arrive when the channel is empty have zero waiting time, and these values are not averaged in W_n.

Using these terms, the various queuing models can be broken into classes based on the types of problems that are modeled.   This should help in presenting a better overall view of the subject.

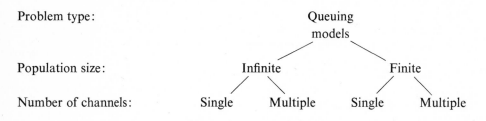

Problem type: Queuing
                                                                  models

Population size: Infinite   Finite

Number of channels: Single   Multiple   Single   Multiple

Actually the single-channel model is just a simple, special case of the multichannel model.   In addition to this simple breakdown, the distribution of the arrival times and/or service times may be varied to create an even larger tree.   Although this text is concerned only with the Poisson distribution, some other common types are the Erlang distribution and constant or fixed times.   Inclusion of these two would increase the set from four models to twelve models.   Consideration of different priority rules compound this even further.

ANALYSIS OF INFINITE-POPULATION QUEUING PROBLEMS

Perhaps the simplest queuing model to work with is that of a single-channel queue serving an infinite population.   For this reason, it is considered first.   There are seven basic equations that can be used to analyze problems of this type.
     The probability of a busy system or system utilization is

$$\rho = \frac{\lambda}{\mu}$$

where ρ = system utilization

   λ = arrival rate, units/time period

   μ = service rate, units/time period

The following equations are valid only when $\lambda/\mu < 1$.

The probability of an empty or idle system P_0 is

$$P_0 = 1 - \frac{\lambda}{\mu} \qquad (8\text{-}1)$$

The expected number in the queue L_q is

$$L_q = \frac{\lambda^2}{\mu(\mu - \lambda)} \qquad (8\text{-}2)$$

The expected number in the system (queue and service) L is

$$L = \frac{\lambda}{\mu - \lambda} \qquad (8\text{-}3)$$

The expected time in the queue W_q is

$$W_q = \frac{\lambda}{\mu(\mu - \lambda)} \qquad (8\text{-}4)$$

The expected time in the system W is

$$W = \frac{1}{\mu - \lambda} \qquad (8\text{-}5)$$

The expected number in the nonempty queue L_n is

$$L_n = \frac{\lambda}{\mu - \lambda} \qquad (8\text{-}6)$$

The expected time in the queue for nonempty queues W_n is

$$W_n = \frac{1}{\mu - \lambda} \qquad (8\text{-}7)$$

EXAMPLE 8-2   A duplicating machine maintained for office use is used and operated by people in the office who need to make copies, mostly secretaries.   Since the work to be copied varies in length (number of pages of the original) and copies required, the service rate is randomly distributed, but it does approximate a Poisson having a mean service rate of 10 jobs per hour.   Generally the requirements for use are random over the entire 8-hour workday but arrive at a rate of 5 per hour.   Several people have noted that a waiting line develops occasionally and have questioned the policy of maintaining only one unit.   If the time of a secretary is valued at $3.50 per hour, make an analysis to determine:

(a) equipment utilization
(b) The percent time that an arrival has to wait
(c) The average system time
(d) The average cost due to waiting and operating the machine

The arrival rate λ is 5 per hour, and the service rate μ is 10 per hour.
(a) The equipment utilization is ρ.

$$\rho = \frac{\lambda}{\mu} = \frac{5}{10} = .50$$

Thus the equipment is in use 50 percent of the time.

(b) The percent time an arrival has to wait is simply the percent time that it is busy, .50.

(c) The average system time W

$$W = \frac{1}{\mu - \lambda} = \frac{1}{10 - 5} = \frac{1}{5} = .20 \text{ hours}$$

The average arrival will spend .20 hour in waiting *and* processing the job.

(d) The average cost is

$$\text{Cost per day} = \text{number of jobs processed per day}$$
$$\times \text{ average cost per job}$$
$$\text{Average cost per job} = \text{average time per job} \times \text{\$/hour}$$
$$= W (\$3.50/\text{hour})$$
$$= .20(3.50)$$
$$\text{Cost per day} = 8(5)(.20)(3.50) = \$28 \text{ per day}$$

EXAMPLE 8-3   A refinery distributes its products by trucks, loaded at the loading dock.   Both company trucks and independent distributors' trucks are loaded.   The independent firms complained that sometimes they must wait in line and thus lose money paying for a truck and driver that is only waiting.   They have asked the refinery either to put in a second loading dock or discount prices equivalent to the waiting time.   The following data have been accumulated.

$$\text{Average arrival rate (all trucks)} = 2/\text{hour}$$
$$\text{Average service rate} = 3/\text{hour}$$

Thirty percent of all trucks are independent.   Assuming that these rates are random according to the Poisson distribution, determine:

(a) The probability that a truck has to wait
(b) The waiting time of a truck that waits
(c) The expected waiting time of independent trucks per day

(*a*) The probability that a truck has to wait for service is the utilization factor

$$\rho = \frac{\lambda}{\mu} = \frac{2}{3} = .66$$

(*b*) The waiting time of a truck that waits is

$$W_n = \frac{1}{\mu - \lambda} = \frac{1}{3 - 2} = 1 \text{ hour}$$

(*c*) The total expected waiting time of independent trucks per day is

Trucks per day $\times$ % independent $\times \rho W_n$

$$= (2 \times 8)(.30)(.67)(1) = 3.2 \text{ hours/day}$$

This could have been obtained in another way:

Expected time = trucks/day $\times$ % independent

$\times$ expected waiting time/truck

$$= (2 \times 8)(.3W_q) = 16(.3)\frac{\lambda}{\mu(\mu - \lambda)}$$

$$= 16(.3)\frac{2}{3(3 - 2)} = 3.2 \text{ hours/day}$$

EXAMPLE 8-4   An overhead crane moves jobs from one machine to another and must be used every time a machine requires loading or unloading. The demand for service is random.   Data taken by recording the elapsed time between service calls followed an exponential distribution having a mean of a call every 30 minutes.   In a similar manner, the actual service time of loading or unloading took an average of 10 minutes.   If the machine time is valued at $8.50 per hour, how much does the downtime cost per day?

First the data must be restructured to provide values for μ and λ.   These are both *rates*, i.e., units per time period, while the data are given in terms of time per unit.   If a call for service on the average occurs every 30 minutes, this is 2 calls per hour, a rate.   Thus the arrival rate λ is 2 per hour.   In a similar manner, if it takes 10 minutes to service an average customer, the service rate is 6 per hour.   Thus $\mu = 6$ units/hour.   It can also be shown that if the service *times* (or arrival times) are distributed exponentially, this is equivalent to a Poisson distribution based on the *rate* of service (or arrival).

The downtime per machine is the average system time W.

$$W = \frac{1}{\mu - \lambda} = \frac{1}{6 - 2} = \frac{1}{4} = .25 \text{ hour}$$

The daily demand for service, assuming an 8-hour day, is 8 times the demand per hour.

$$\text{Daily demand} = 8\lambda = 8(2) = 16 \text{ calls for service/day}$$

Since each call requires an average downtime of .25 hour,

$$\text{Total cost/day} = (\$8.50/\text{hour})(.25 \text{ hour/call}) (16 \text{ calls/day})$$
$$(16 \text{ calls/day}) = \$34/\text{day}$$

Similar expressions for system time, etc., can be developed for the *multichannel* queuing problem while still assuming an infinite population. Actually these are more general than those given previously since they can be reduced to the single-channel case by setting $k = 1$ and simplifying. The basic equations are presented below.

The probability of an empty system P_0 is

$$P_0 = \frac{1}{\left[\sum_{n=0}^{n=k-1} \frac{1}{n!}\left(\frac{\lambda}{\mu}\right)^n\right] + \frac{1}{k!}\left(\frac{\lambda}{\mu}\right)^k \frac{k\mu}{k\mu - \lambda}} \qquad (8\text{-}8)$$

where k = number of service channels

λ = arrival *rate* of customers

μ = service rate of single channel (this assumes all μ are equal)

The probability P_k that an arrival has to wait (the probability that there are k or more units in the system) is

$$P_k = \frac{1}{k!}\left(\frac{\lambda}{\mu}\right)^k \frac{k\mu}{k\mu - \lambda} P_0 \qquad (8\text{-}9)$$

The expected number L in the System is

$$L = \frac{\lambda\mu(\lambda/\mu)^k}{(k-1)!(k\mu - \lambda)^2} P_0 + \frac{\lambda}{\mu} \qquad (8\text{-}10)$$

The expected number L_q in the queue is

$$L_q = \frac{\lambda\mu(\lambda/\mu)^k P_0}{(k-1)!(k\mu - \lambda)^2} \qquad (8\text{-}11)$$

The expected time W_q in the queue is

$$W_q = \frac{\mu(\lambda/\mu)^k P_0}{(k-1)!(k\mu - \lambda)^2} \qquad (8\text{-}12)$$

The expected time W in the System is

$$W = \frac{\mu(\lambda/\mu)^k P_0}{(k-1)!(k\mu - \lambda)^2} + \frac{1}{\mu} \qquad (8\text{-}13)$$

EXAMPLE 8-5   The situation presented in Example 8-2 has been questioned as a result of the last analysis.   The possibility is being considered of installing two machines or renting one larger machine.   The data are summarized below.

	Service rate μ, per hour	Daily rental cost
Small (present) machine	10	$5
Large machine	15	10

The *total* cost per day is the rental cost plus lost time cost.   Thus the total cost of *one* small machine can be determined from previous calculations

$$TC(1 \text{ small}) = \$5 \text{ (rental)} + \$28 \text{ (time)} = \$33 \text{ per day}$$

The cost for one large machine is

$$W \text{ (large)} = \frac{1}{\mu - \lambda} = \frac{1}{15 - 5} = \frac{1}{10} = .10 \text{ hour}$$

$$TC \text{ (large)} = \$10 \text{ (rental)} + (8 \times 5)(.10)(3.50) = \$24 \text{ per day}$$

To compute the system time for two small machines, first compute P_0 using Eq. (7-8):

$$P_0 = \cfrac{1}{\left[\sum_{n=0}^{n=k-1} \frac{1}{n!}\left(\frac{\lambda}{\mu}\right)^n\right] + \frac{1}{k!}\left(\frac{\lambda}{\mu}\right)^k \frac{k\mu}{k\mu - \lambda}}$$

$$= \cfrac{1}{\left[\sum_{n=0}^{n=1} \frac{1}{n!}\left(\frac{5}{10}\right)^n\right] + \frac{1}{2!}\left(\frac{5}{10}\right)^2 \frac{2(10)}{2(10) - 5}}$$

$$= \cfrac{1}{\frac{1}{0!}.5^0 + \frac{1}{1}.5^1 + \frac{1}{2}.5^2 \frac{20}{15}}$$

$$= \frac{1}{1 + .5 + .167} = .600$$

The expected time W in the system is

$$W = \frac{\mu(\lambda/\mu)^k P_0}{(k - 1)!(k\mu - \lambda)^2} + \frac{1}{\mu}$$

$$= \frac{10(.5)^2(.600)}{(2 - 1)![(2)(10) - 5]^2} + \frac{1}{10}$$

$$= .107$$

Thus the total daily cost sums rental fee plus lost time

$$TC = 2(5) + (8 \times 5)(.107)(3.50) = \$24.98 \text{ per day}$$

This indicates that it would be slightly less expensive to use the one larger machine. If the advantage of locating the two machines in different places could cut down on travel time, it would probably be better to rent the two smaller machines.

EXAMPLE 8-6   Repeat Example 8-3 using two equal-sized channels.

(a) The probability that a truck has to wait is equal to the probability P_k that there are two or more trucks already in the system.

$$P_k = \frac{1}{k!} \left(\frac{\lambda}{\mu}\right)^k \frac{k\mu}{k\mu - \lambda} P_0$$

$$P_0 = \frac{1}{\left[\sum_{n=0}^{n=1} \frac{1}{n!} \left(\frac{2}{3}\right)^n\right] + \frac{1}{2!} \left(\frac{2}{3}\right)^2 \frac{2(3)}{2(3) - 2}}$$

$$P_0 = \frac{1}{1 + \frac{2}{3} + \frac{1}{2}(.67)^2 6/(6 - 2)} = .50$$

$$P_2 = \frac{1}{2!} \left(\frac{2}{3}\right)^2 \frac{2(3)}{2(3) - 2} .50 = .167$$

The probability that a truck must wait is .167.

(b) The waiting time of a truck that waits is

$$W_q = \frac{\mu(\lambda/\mu)^k P_0}{(k - 1)!(k\mu - \lambda)^2}$$

$$= \frac{3(\frac{2}{3})^2(.50)}{1[2(3) - 2]^2} = .042$$

Note that W_q is the expected waiting time of a truck.   This is not a conditional probability like W_n : thus it must be divided by the probability that a truck actually has to wait.

$$W_n = \frac{W_q}{P_k} = \frac{.042}{.167} = .252$$

(c) The total expected waiting time of independent trucks per day is

$$(2 \times 8)(.30)(.167)(.252) = .202 \text{ hours/day}$$

or

$$16(.3W_q) = 16(.3)(.042) = .202 \text{ hour/day}$$

EXAMPLE 8-7   A telephone company is planning to install telephone booths in a new airport.   It has established the policy that a person should not have to wait more than 10 percent of the times he tries to use a phone.   The demand for use is estimated to be Poisson with an average of 30 per hour.   The average phone call has an exponential distribution with a mean time of 5 minutes.   How many phone booths should be installed?

$$\lambda = 30/\text{hour}$$

$$\frac{1}{\mu} = \frac{5}{60} \text{ hour} \qquad \mu = 12/\text{hour}$$

When $k = 2$, $2\mu = 24$, they must have at least three just to meet demand for service.   Try $k = 5$.

$$P_0 = \cfrac{1}{\left[\displaystyle\sum_{n=0}^{n=5-1} \frac{1}{n!}\left(\frac{30}{12}\right)^n\right] + \frac{1}{5!}\left(\frac{30}{12}\right)^5 \frac{5(12)}{5(12) - 30}}$$

$$= \cfrac{1}{1 + 2.5 + \dfrac{2.5^2}{2!} + \dfrac{2.5^3}{3!} + \dfrac{2.5^4}{4!} + \dfrac{1}{5!}2.5^5\dfrac{60}{30}}$$

$$= .0801$$

$$P_5 = \frac{1}{5!}2.5^5 \frac{5(12)}{5(12) - 30}.0801 = .13$$

This gives a probability of .13 that a customer must wait.   Try $k = 6$.

$$P_0 = \cfrac{1}{1 + 2.5 + \dfrac{2.5^2}{2!} + \dfrac{2.5^3}{3!} + \dfrac{2.5^4}{4!} + \dfrac{2.5^5}{5!} + \dfrac{1}{6!}2.5^6\dfrac{72}{42}}$$

$$P_6 = \frac{1}{6!}2.5^6 \frac{72}{42}.08162 = .047$$

Thus an installation of six phones would give a probability of .047 that a customer would have to wait.   Since this is less than .10 it is the smallest number that will meet the company policy.

DERIVATION OF SINGLE-CHANNEL INFINITE-POPULATION MODEL

Before beginning the development of the basic equations it would be proper to discuss the assumption of independence.   When this is done, the distribution of the arrival rates can be shown to be Poisson (Ref. 1).   This is quite restrictive in some cases, for it requires that the arrivals or services be random and independent of all other conditions. For example, the mean does not vary over time and is not influenced by the number of units in queue, previously serviced, etc. This means that the probability of an arrival during any time period Δt is constant and equal to $\lambda \, \Delta t$. Correspondingly the conditional probability of a service completion is $\mu \, \Delta t$ *given* that there is a customer there to be serviced. Finally it will be assumed that the time period Δt is sufficiently small for $(\Delta t)^2 \to 0$, that is, it is not significant and may be ignored.

Actually there are many different ways of deriving these equations, using difference equations, Markov chains, etc. The method suggested in this text has been selected primarily because it is logical and easy to follow and not for its mathematical rigor.

First consider the basic steps to be used in the derivations. Let n be the number of units in the system and $P_n(t)$ be the probability of n units in the system at time t. Then

1 First find $P_n(t)$ in terms of λ and μ.

2 Using this expression, find the expected number of units in the system in terms of λ and μ.

3 Finally, using the results of step 2, find the other expressions for system time, etc.

The probability of n units in the system can be determined by summing the probabilities of all the ways this event could occur. List all the ways of ending up with n units at time $t + \Delta t$:

Case	No of units at time t	No. of arrivals	No. of services	No. of units at time $t + \Delta t$
1	n	0	0	n
2	$n + 1$	0	1	n
3	$n - 1$	1	0	n

Now compute each case, remembering that the probability of a service or arrival is $\mu \, \Delta t$ or $\lambda \, \Delta t$ *and* $(\Delta t)^2 \to 0$.

$$\text{Probability of case 1} = \frac{\text{Probability of}}{n \text{ at time } t} \times \frac{\text{Probability of}}{\text{no arrivals}} \times \frac{\text{Probability of}}{\text{no services}}$$

$$= [P_n(t)](1 - \lambda \, \Delta t)(1 - \mu \, \Delta t)$$

$$= P_n(t)[1 - \lambda \, \Delta t - \mu \, \Delta t + \lambda\mu(\Delta t)^2]$$

$$= P_n(t)(1 - \lambda \, \Delta t - \mu \, \Delta t)$$

Remember that $\Delta t^2 = 0$.

$$\text{Probability of case 2} = \frac{\text{Probability of}}{n+1 \text{ at time } t} \times \frac{\text{Probability of}}{\text{no arrivals}} \times \frac{\text{Probability of}}{1 \text{ service}}$$

$$= [P_{n+1}(t)][1 - \lambda\,\Delta t][\mu\,\Delta t]$$

$$= P_{n+1}(t)[\mu\,\Delta t - \mu\lambda(\Delta t)^2]$$

$$= P_{n+1}(t)(\mu\,\Delta t)$$

$$\text{Probability of case 3} = \frac{\text{Probability of}}{n-1 \text{ at time } t} \times \frac{\text{Probability of}}{1 \text{ arrival}} \times \frac{\text{Probability of}}{\text{no services}}$$

$$= [P_{n-1}(t)](\lambda\,\Delta t)(1 - \mu\,\Delta t)$$

$$= P_{n-1}(t)(\lambda\,\Delta t)$$

Note that other cases are not possible because of the small value of Δt that causes $(\Delta t)^2$ to approach 0. As an example, a possible combination is to have n units on hand at time t then have one arrival and one service completion during Δt. This can be formulated as follows:

$$P_n(t + \Delta t) = P_n(t)(\mu\,\Delta t)(\lambda\,\Delta t)$$

$$= P_n(t)[\mu\lambda(\Delta t)^2] = 0$$

The reader should check that all other combinations except the three cases listed will have this same result.

Now sum all three cases to find $P_n(t + \Delta t)$.

$$P_n(t + \Delta t) = \text{case 1 and case 2 and case 3}$$

$$= P_n(t)(1 - \lambda\,\Delta t - \mu\,\Delta t) + P_{n+1}(t)(\mu\,\Delta t) + P_{n-1}(t)(\lambda\,\Delta t)$$

This approaches what is desired in step 1, i.e., to find $P_n(t)$ in terms of λ and μ. However, it contains two separate points in time, t and $t + \Delta t$. Remember that the assumption of independence means that the services and arrivals are independent of time. This means that the probability of n units in the system at time t is the same as at time $t + \Delta t$. Thus $P_n(t) = P_n(t + \Delta t)$. Substitute this in the above equation:

$$P_n(t) = P_n(t)(1 - \lambda\,\Delta t - \mu\,\Delta t) + P_{n+1}(t)(\mu\,\Delta t) + P_{n-1}(t)(\lambda\,\Delta t)$$

Solve this for $P_{n+1}(t)$:

$$P_{n+1}(t)(\mu\,\Delta t) = P_n(t) - P_n(t) + P_n(t)\lambda\,\Delta t + P_n(t)\mu\,\Delta t - P_{n-1}(t)\lambda\,\Delta t$$

$$= P_n(t)\,\Delta t(\lambda + \mu) - P_{n-1}(t)\,\Delta t\,\lambda$$

$$P_{n+1}(t) = \frac{P_n(t)\,\Delta t(\lambda + \mu) - P_{n-1}(t)\,\Delta t\,\lambda}{\mu\,\Delta t}$$

$$= P_n(t)\,\frac{\lambda + \mu}{\mu} - P_{n-1}(t)\,\frac{\lambda}{\mu}$$

This expresses the probability of $n + 1$ units as a function of the last two stages (like dynamic programming) n and $n - 1$. However, the final requirement of step 1 has not yet been obtained; i.e., a general expression for $P_n(t)$ is still needed. To complete this step, first find an expression for $P_1(t)$ in terms of $P_0(t)$ and λ, μ. Then an expression for $P_n(t)$ in terms of $P_0(t)$ on λ, μ can be developed. Finally $P_0(t)$ can be expressed in terms of λ and μ to complete step 1.

First list all possible ways for $P_0(t + \Delta t)$ to occur.

CASE 1 None at time t, no arrivals, no service

$$P_0(t)(1 - \lambda\,\Delta t)(1)$$

Note that if no units were in the system, the probability of no service would be 1.

CASE 2 One at time t, no arrivals, one service

$$P_1(t)(1 - \lambda\,\Delta t)(\mu\,\Delta t)$$

$$P_0(t + \Delta t) = \text{case 1 and case 2}$$
$$= P_0(t)(1 - \lambda\,\Delta t)(1) + P_1(t)(1 - \lambda\,\Delta t)\mu\,\Delta t$$
$$= P_0(t) - P_0(t)\lambda\,\Delta t + P_1(t)\mu\,\Delta t$$

Remember that

$$P_0(t) = P_0(t + \Delta t)$$
$$P_0(t) = P_0(t) - P_0(t)\lambda\,\Delta t + P_1(t)\mu\,\Delta t$$

Solve for $P_1(t)$:

$$P_1(t)\mu\,\Delta t = P_0(t) - P_0(t) + P_0(t)\lambda\,\Delta t$$
$$P_1(t) = P_0(t)\,\frac{\lambda}{\mu}$$

Next, develop an expression for $P_n(t)$ in terms of P_0, λ, and μ. Note that since $P_0(t) = P_0$ (any time t) due to the independence assumption, the time notation will be omitted for simplicity.

$$P_0 = P_0$$
$$P_1 = P_0\left(\frac{\lambda}{\mu}\right)$$

(just developed)

$$P_2 = P_1\left(\frac{\lambda + \mu}{\mu}\right) - P_0\left(\frac{\lambda}{\mu}\right)$$

from

$$P_{n+1} = P_n\left(\frac{\lambda + \mu}{\mu}\right) - P_{n-1}\left(\frac{\lambda}{\mu}\right)$$

But

$$P_1 = P_0\left(\frac{\lambda}{\mu}\right)$$

$$P_2 = P_0\left(\frac{\lambda}{\mu}\right)\frac{\lambda + \mu}{\mu} - P_0\left(\frac{\lambda}{\mu}\right)$$

$$= P_0\left(\frac{\lambda}{\mu}\right)\left(\frac{\lambda + \mu}{\mu} - 1\right)$$

$$= P_0\left(\frac{\lambda}{\mu}\right)\left(\frac{\lambda + \mu}{\mu} - \frac{\mu}{\mu}\right)$$

$$= P_0\left(\frac{\lambda}{\mu}\right)\frac{\lambda}{\mu}$$

$$= P_0\left(\frac{\lambda}{\mu}\right)^2$$

In a similar manner, the following expressions can be developed.

$$P_3 = P_0\left(\frac{\lambda}{\mu}\right)^3 \qquad P_4 = P_0\left(\frac{\lambda}{\mu}\right)^4 \qquad P_5 = P_0\left(\frac{\lambda}{\mu}\right)^5$$

In general this is expressed

$$P_n = P_0\left(\frac{\lambda}{\mu}\right)^n \qquad\qquad (8\text{-}14)$$

This gives P_n in terms of P_0, λ, and μ.   Finally an expression for P_0 in terms of λ and μ must be obtained.   The easiest way to do this is to recognize that the probability that the channel is busy is the ratio of the arrival rate and service rate, λ/μ.   Thus P_0 is 1 minus this ratio.

$$P_0 = 1 - \frac{\lambda}{\mu} \qquad\qquad (8\text{-}15)$$

Since

$$P_n = P_0\left(\frac{\lambda}{\mu}\right)^n$$

and

$$P_0 = 1 - \frac{\lambda}{\mu}$$

we have

$$P_n = \left(1 - \frac{\lambda}{\mu}\right)\left(\frac{\lambda}{\mu}\right)^n \qquad (8\text{-}16)$$

This completes step 1.   Step 2 follows.

The expected number of units in the system L is obtained using the definition of an expected value.

$$E(x) = \sum_{i=0}^{i=\infty} x_i P(i) \qquad (8\text{-}17)$$

$$L = \sum_{n=0}^{n=\infty} n P_n \qquad (8\text{-}18)$$

$$L = \sum_{n=0}^{n=\infty} n\left(1 - \frac{\lambda}{\mu}\right)\left(\frac{\lambda}{\mu}\right)^n$$

$$= \left(1 - \frac{\lambda}{\mu}\right)\sum_{n=0}^{n=\infty} n\left(\frac{\lambda}{\mu}\right)^n$$

$$= \left(1 - \frac{\lambda}{\mu}\right)\left[0\left(\frac{\lambda}{\mu}\right)^0 + 1\left(\frac{\lambda}{\mu}\right)^1 + 2\left(\frac{\lambda}{\mu}\right)^2 + 3\left(\frac{\lambda}{\mu}\right)^3 + 4\left(\frac{\lambda}{\mu}\right)^4 + \cdots\right] \qquad (8\text{-}19)$$

This is an infinite series.   If it can be rearranged into a geometric series, it can be simply evaluated.   Thus first the series in brackets must be evaluated.   Let

$$y = 0 + \frac{\lambda}{\mu} + 2\left(\frac{\lambda}{\mu}\right)^2 + 3\left(\frac{\lambda}{\mu}\right)^3 + \cdots \qquad (8\text{-}20)$$

A geometric series has the form $1 + x + x^2 + x^3 + \cdots$ where $|x| < 1$.   Thus the expression for y must be manipulated to achieve an expression of geometric form.

Multiply both sides by λ/μ:

$$y\frac{\lambda}{\mu} = \left(\frac{\lambda}{\mu}\right)^2 + 2\left(\frac{\lambda}{\mu}\right)^3 + 3\left(\frac{\lambda}{\mu}\right)^4 + \cdots \qquad (8\text{-}21)$$

Subtract the two equations term by term.

$$y - y\frac{\lambda}{\mu} = \frac{\lambda}{\mu} + \left[2\left(\frac{\lambda}{\mu}\right)^2 - \left(\frac{\lambda}{\mu}\right)^2\right] + \left[3\left(\frac{\lambda}{\mu}\right)^3 - 2\left(\frac{\lambda}{\mu}\right)^3\right]$$

$$+ \left[4\left(\frac{\lambda}{\mu}\right)^4 - 3\left(\frac{\lambda}{\mu}\right)^4\right] + \cdots$$

$$= \frac{\lambda}{\mu} + \left(\frac{\lambda}{\mu}\right)^2 + \left(\frac{\lambda}{\mu}\right)^3 + \left(\frac{\lambda}{\mu}\right)^4 + \cdots \qquad (8\text{-}22)$$

Since $\lambda < \mu$, $|\lambda/\mu| < 1$, and this is almost like the geometric series. To complete the conversion, add 1 to each side.

$$y - y\frac{\lambda}{\mu} + 1 = 1 + \frac{\lambda}{\mu} + \left(\frac{\lambda}{\mu}\right)^2 + \left(\frac{\lambda}{\mu}\right)^3 + \left(\frac{\lambda}{\mu}\right)^4 + \cdots \qquad (8\text{-}23)$$

This series on the right is a converging, geometric series whose sum is $1/(1 - \lambda/\mu)$. Substitute this value and solve for y.

$$y\left(1 - \frac{\lambda}{\mu}\right) + 1 = \frac{1}{1 - \lambda/\mu} \qquad (8\text{-}24)$$

$$y\left(1 - \frac{\lambda}{\mu}\right) = \frac{1}{1 - \lambda/\mu} - 1$$

$$y = \frac{1}{(1 - \lambda/\mu)^2} - \frac{1}{1 - \lambda/\mu} = \frac{\lambda/\mu}{(1 - \lambda/\mu)^2} \qquad (8\text{-}25)$$

Now substitute the value for y in the equation for L [Eq. (8-18)]

$$L = \left(1 - \frac{\lambda}{\mu}\right)\left[0 + \frac{\lambda}{\mu} + 2\left(\frac{\lambda}{\mu}\right)^2 + 3\left(\frac{\lambda}{\mu}\right)^3 + \cdots\right] \qquad (8\text{-}26)$$

$$= \left(1 - \frac{\lambda}{\mu}\right)\frac{\lambda/\mu}{(1 - \lambda/\mu)^2} = \frac{\lambda/\mu}{1 - \lambda/\mu}$$

$$L = \frac{\lambda/\mu}{\mu/\mu - \lambda/\mu} = \frac{\lambda}{\mu - \lambda} \qquad (8\text{-}3)$$

Now step 3 requires that the other expressions L_q, W, W_q, L_n, and W_n be developed in terms of λ and μ.

The expected system time W is

$$W = \frac{\text{expected number in system}}{\text{arrival rate}}$$

$$= \frac{L}{\lambda}$$

$$W = \frac{\lambda}{\lambda(\mu - \lambda)} = \frac{1}{\mu - \lambda} \qquad (8\text{-}5)$$

Think about this one. If on the average there were 10 units always in the system and they arrived at a rate of 5 per hour, they must stay 10/5 or 2 hours to maintain the expected number in the system. Expressed another way,

Expected number in system = expected system time × arrival rate

$$\text{Expected system time} = \frac{\text{expected number in system}}{\text{arrival rate}}$$

The expected time W_q in the queue is

W_q = expected system time − time in service

$$= W - \frac{1}{\mu}$$

$$= \frac{1}{\mu - \lambda} - \frac{1}{\mu} = \frac{\mu}{\mu(\mu - \lambda)} - \frac{\mu - \lambda}{\mu(\mu - \lambda)} = \frac{\lambda}{\mu(\mu - \lambda)} \qquad (8\text{-}4)$$

The expected number L_q in the queue is

L_q = expected number in system − expected number in service

$$= \frac{\lambda}{\mu - \lambda} - \frac{\lambda}{\mu}$$

$$= \frac{\mu\lambda - \lambda(\mu - \lambda)}{\mu(\mu - \lambda)} = \frac{\mu\lambda - \lambda\mu + \lambda^2}{\mu(\mu - \lambda)}$$

$$= \frac{\lambda^2}{\mu(\mu - \lambda)} \qquad (8\text{-}2)$$

Note that the expected number in service is 1 times the probability that the service unit is busy, or $1\lambda/\mu$.

The expected number L_n in a nonempty queue is

$$L_n = \frac{\text{Expected number in queue}}{\text{Probability that queue is not empty}}$$

Probability of nonempty queue = $1 - P_0$

$$= 1 - \left(1 - \frac{\lambda}{\mu}\right)$$

$$= \frac{\lambda}{\mu}$$

$$L_n = \frac{\lambda^2}{\mu(\mu - \lambda)/(\lambda/\mu)} = \frac{\lambda^2}{\mu(\mu - \lambda)}\frac{\mu}{\lambda} = \frac{\lambda}{\mu - \lambda} \qquad (8\text{-}6)$$

The expected waiting time W_n for a nonempty queue is

$$W_n = \frac{\text{expected time in queue}}{\text{probability of waiting}}$$

$$= \frac{W_q}{\lambda/\mu} = \frac{\lambda}{\mu(\mu - \lambda)/(\lambda/\mu)} = \frac{\lambda}{\mu(\mu - \lambda)}\frac{\mu}{\lambda} = \frac{1}{\mu - \lambda} \qquad (8\text{-}7)$$

DERIVATION OF MULTIPLE-CHANNEL INFINITE-POPULATION MODEL

This derivation uses the same three steps as the derivation of the single-channel model. The major difference is that an arrival will not have to wait until there are at least k units in the system.   This requires that two cases be developed, one for a system number less than k and one for a system number of k or more.   Adding the variable k increases the complexity or messiness of the algebra somewhat but still does not change the procedure.   For this reason, the derivation is presented in condensed form in Note 1 at the end of the chapter.

ANALYSIS OF FINITE-POPULATION QUEUING PROBLEMS

In some cases, the number of potential customers is small.   If this value is so small that the arrival of a customer to be serviced or the completion of a single service will affect the probability of future arrivals, the assumption of an infinite population is not valid.   For example, if an operator tends three machines and his attention is required from each at random intervals, the machines (customers) come from a finite population.   Obviously the probability of a customer arrival changes with a change of only one arrival (customer leaving the population pool) or one completion (customer reentering the population pool).   As a rule of thumb, if the population is less than 30, the equations for a finite population should be used.

Although the concepts are the same as those in the infinite population, some of the terms are different and the equations required for analysis are different.   Computationally these are more time-consuming, but if a computer is available they do not require any significant computer time.   One term must be viewed in a somewhat different light.   The probability of an arrival must vary depending on the number of customers available to enter the system.   If M is defined as the total customer population and n is the number of customers already in the queuing system, any arrivals must come from the $M - n$ number that is not yet in the system.   Thus the probability of an arrival can be expressed if the probability of an individual unit arriving is known. If $1/\lambda$ is the mean time between service needs for any unit, i.e., mean time between arrival for a given customer, then λ is the probability that a customer will require service during the Δt time period.   Note again that this assumes that the probability is independent of the time period and thus is Poisson.   If λ is the probability of a specific unit requiring service and there are $M - n$ customers not in the queuing system, then the probability of a customer requiring service is $(M - n)\lambda$.   Note that it is still assuming that Δt is sufficiently small for the probability of two or more arrivals not to be significant.   The basic concepts required for the derivation of these equations are presented in Note 2.

SINGLE-CHANNEL QUEUE, FINITE POPULATION

The probability P_0 of an empty system is

$$P_o = \frac{1}{\sum_{n=0}^{n=M} \left[\frac{M!}{(M-n)!} \left(\frac{\lambda}{\mu}\right)^n \right]} \qquad (8\text{-}27)$$

where M is number of customers in the population. The probability P_n of n customers in the system is

$$P_n = \frac{M!}{(M-n)!} \left(\frac{\lambda}{\mu}\right)^n P_0 \qquad (8\text{-}28)$$

The expected number L of customers in the system is

$$L = \sum_{n=0}^{n=M} nP_n = M - \frac{\mu}{\lambda}(1 - P_0) \qquad (8\text{-}29)$$

and the expected number L_q of customers in the queue is

$$L_q = M - \frac{\lambda + \mu}{\lambda}(1 - P_0) \qquad (8\text{-}30)$$

MULTICHANNEL QUEUE, FINITE POPULATION

In this case, it is assumed that the number of channels k is more than 1, such that $1 < k \leq M$. The probability P_0 of an empty system is

$$P_0 = \frac{1}{\sum_{n=0}^{n=k-1} \left[\frac{M!}{(M-n)!n!} \left(\frac{\lambda}{\mu}\right)^n \right] + \sum_{n=k}^{n=M} \left[\frac{M!}{(M-n)!k!k^{n-k}} \left(\frac{\lambda}{\mu}\right)^n \right]} \qquad (8\text{-}31)$$

The probability P_n of n customers in the system is

$$P_n = P_0 \frac{M!}{(M-n)!n!} \left(\frac{\lambda}{\mu}\right)^n \qquad \text{where } 0 \leq n \leq k \qquad (8\text{-}32)$$

$$P_n = P_0 \frac{M!}{(M-n)!k!k^{n-k}} \left(\frac{\lambda}{\mu}\right)^n \qquad \text{where } k \leq n \leq M \qquad (8\text{-}33)$$

Note that n cannot be greater than M.   The expected number L of customers in the system is

$$L = \sum_{n=0}^{n=k-1} nP_n + \sum_{n=k}^{n=M} (n-k)P_n + k\left(1 - \sum_{n=0}^{n=k-1} P_n\right) \qquad (8\text{-}34)$$

The expected number of customers L_q in the queue is

$$L_q = \sum_{n=k}^{n=M} (n-k)P_n \qquad (8\text{-}35)$$

The application of these equations to queuing problems is similar to the infinite-population case.   A few problems require slightly different formulation since the question may be to determine an optimal population size instead of the service rate or number of channels.

EXAMPLE 8-8   A mechanic services four machines.   For each machine the mean time between service requirements is 10 hours and is assumed to be from an exponential distribution.   The repair time tends to follow the same distribution and has a mean time of 2 hours.   When a machine is down for repair, the time lost has a value of $20 per hour.   The mechanic costs $50 per day.

(a) What is the expected number of machines in operation?
(b) What is the expected cost of downtime per day?
(c) Would it be desirable to provide two mechanics, each to service only two machines?

(a) To find the expected number of machines in operation, first find λ and μ.

$$\frac{1}{\lambda} = 10 \qquad \lambda = .10$$

$$\frac{1}{\mu} = 2 \qquad \mu = .5$$

Now find P_0

$$P_0 = \frac{1}{\displaystyle\sum_{n=0}^{n=4} \left[\frac{4!}{(4-n)!}\left(\frac{.1}{.5}\right)^n\right]}$$

$$= \frac{1}{1 + 4(.2) + 4(3)(.2)^2 + 4(3)(2)(.2)^3 + 4(3)(2)(1)(.2)^4}$$

$$= .4$$

The expected number of machines in the system is

$$4 - \frac{.5}{.1}(1 - .4) = 4 - 3 = 1$$

the number not running.   The expected number of machines running is $4 - 1 = 3$.

(b) The expected cost of downtime per day is found as follows.   If an 8-hour day is assumed the total downtime is

$$8 \times \text{expected number down} = 8(1) = 8 \text{ hours/day}$$

$$\text{Cost} = (\$20/\text{hour})(8 \text{ hours/day}) = \$160/\text{day}$$

(c) Compare with two mechanics serving two machines each.   Now $M = 2$. Find P_0.

$$P_0 = \frac{1}{\displaystyle\sum_{n=0}^{n=2} \left[\frac{2!}{(2-n)!} \left(\frac{.1}{.5}\right)^n \right]}$$

$$= \frac{1}{1 + 2(.2) + 2(1)(.2)^2} = \frac{1}{1.48}$$

$$= .68$$

This assumes that each mechanic and his two machines constitute a separate system with no interplay.   The expected number of machines in the system (per mechanic) is

$$2 - \frac{.5}{.1}(1 - .68) = .4$$

The expected downtime per mechanic is

$$(8)(.4) = 3.2 \text{ hours/day}$$

$$\text{Total downtime/day} = 2(3.2) = 6.4 \text{ hours/day}$$

$$\text{Total cost} = 2(\$50/\text{man}) + (6.4 \text{ hours/day})(\$20/\text{day})$$

$$= 100 + 128 = \$228/\text{day}$$

Thus since $228 > 160 + 50$, the use of two men is not justified.

As an exercise, compare this with a similar system but having four customers (machines) and two channels (mechanics). $M = 4, k = 2.$

$$P_0 = \cfrac{1}{\sum\limits_{n=0}^{n=2-1}\left[\dfrac{4!}{(4-n)!\,n!}\left(\dfrac{.1}{.5}\right)^n\right] + \sum\limits_{n=2}^{n=4}\left[\dfrac{4!}{(4-n)!\,2!\,2^{n-2}}\left(\dfrac{.1}{.5}\right)^n\right]}$$

$$= \cfrac{1}{\dfrac{4!}{4!\,0!}\cdot2^0 + \dfrac{4!}{3!\,1!}\cdot2^1 + \dfrac{4!}{2!\,2!\,2^0}\cdot2^2 + \dfrac{4!}{1!\,2!\,2}\cdot2^3 + \dfrac{4!}{0!\,2!\,2^2}\cdot2^4}$$

$$= \frac{1}{2.09} = .48$$

Now find the expected number L of customers in the system.

$$L = \sum_{n=0}^{n=k-1} nP_n + \sum_{n=k}^{n=M} (n-k)P_n + k\left(1 - \sum_{n=0}^{n=k-1} P_n\right)$$

$$= \sum_{n=0}^{n=2-1} nP_n + \sum_{n=2}^{n=4} (n-2)P_n + 2\left(1 - \sum_{n=0}^{n=2-1} P_n\right)$$

$$= 0P_0 + 1P_1 + (2-2)P_2 + (3-2)P_3 + (4-2)P_4 + 2(1 - P_0 - P_1)$$

This means that P_1, P_2, P_3, and P_4 must be found.

Note that for P_1 and P_2, $n \le k$,

$$P_n = P_0 \frac{M!}{(M-n)!\,n!}\left(\frac{\lambda}{\mu}\right)^n$$

$$P_1 = .48\,\frac{4!}{3!\,1!}\cdot2^1 = .38$$

$$P_2 = .48\,\frac{4!}{2!\,2!}\cdot2^2 = .12$$

For P_3 and P_4, $k \le n \le M$,

$$P_n = P_0 \frac{M!}{(M-n)!\,k!\,k^{n-k}}\left(\frac{\lambda}{\mu}\right)^n$$

$$P_3 = .48\,\frac{4!}{1!\,2!\,2^1}\cdot2^3 = .02$$

$$P_4 = .48\,\frac{4!}{0!\,2!\,2^2}\cdot2^4 = .002 \qquad (\text{assume} = .00)$$

$$L = 0(.48) + 1(.38) + 0(.12) + 1(.02) + 2(0) + 2(1 - .48 - .38)$$
$$= 0 + .38 + 0 + .02 + 0 + .28 = .68$$

The downtime per 8-hour day is $8(.68) = 5.44$ hours.

$$\text{Total cost} = (2 \text{ men})(50) + (\$20/\text{hour})(5.44)$$
$$= 100 + 108.80 = \$208.80/\text{day}$$

This is the least expensive of all.   It would be expected to be superior to two separate systems of two machines per mechanic since the mechanics would be more fully utilized.

EXAMPLE 8-9   A company has decided to use substations located throughout the marketing region to service its delivery trucks.   The vice-president of marketing is quite anxious that service and maintenance requirements do not hamper the on-call delivery service.   Since the trucks operate on a 24-hour schedule, they may arrive for service at any time but generally will require service about every 8 hours.   Maintenance procedures require that a station be able to handle 10 trucks per 8-hour period. The time between arrivals approximates an exponential distribution, and the service rate is Poisson.   The vice-president has required that only one-half of the arriving trucks be forced to wait for service.   How many trucks should each station be responsible for?

Find M such that $P_0 > 0.50$.   Let $M = 4$.

$$P_0 = \frac{1}{\displaystyle\sum_{n=0}^{n=M} \frac{M!}{(M-n)!}\left(\frac{\lambda}{\mu}\right)^n}$$

$$= \frac{1}{\dfrac{4!}{(4-0)!}\left(\dfrac{1}{10}\right)^0 + \dfrac{4!}{3!}\left(\dfrac{1}{10}\right) + \dfrac{4!}{2!}\left(\dfrac{1}{10}\right)^2 + \dfrac{4!}{1!}\left(\dfrac{1}{10}\right)^3 + \dfrac{4!}{0!}\left(\dfrac{1}{10}\right)^4}$$

$$= 0.647$$

Let $M = 5$.

$$P_0 = \frac{1}{\dfrac{5!}{5!}.1^0 + \dfrac{5!}{4!}.1 + \dfrac{5!}{3!}.1^2 + \dfrac{5!}{2!}.1^3 + \dfrac{5!}{1!}.1^4 + \dfrac{5!}{0!}.1^5}$$

$$= 0.564$$

This is all right; try $M = 6$.

$$P_0 = \frac{1}{\dfrac{6!}{6!}.1^0 + \dfrac{6!}{5!}.1 + \dfrac{6!}{4!}.1^2 + \dfrac{6!}{3!}.1^3 + \dfrac{6!}{2!}.1^4 + \dfrac{6!}{1!}.1^5 + \dfrac{6!}{0!}.1^6}$$

$$= .485 \qquad \text{too small}$$

$M = 5$ gives the largest population size with $P_0 > .5$.

At this population ($M = 5$) find the total lost time for the trucks per 8-hour period per station.

At each station, $M = 5$; thus find the expected number of trucks in the system. This is the average number at any time. The total lost time in an 8-hour period would be $8L_s$.

$$L = M - \frac{\mu}{\lambda}(1 - P_0)$$

For $M = 5$, $P_0 = .564$ and

$$L = 5 - \tfrac{10}{1}(1 - .564) = 0.64$$

Average lost time per 8-hour period $= 8(.64) = 5.12$ hours.

EXAMPLE 8-10   A group of engineers has two terminals available to aid in their calculations. The average computing job requires 20 minutes of terminal time, and each engineer requires some computation about once every .5 hours, i.e., the mean time between a call for service is .5 hours. Assume these are distributed according to an exponential distribution. If there are six engineers in the group, find:

(*a*) The expected number of engineers waiting to use one of the terminals
(*b*) The total lost time per day

$M = 6$ and $k = 2$.   Let a unit of time be 1 hour.   Then $1/\lambda = .5$, and so $\lambda = 2$ and $1/\mu = .333$; therefore $\mu = 3$.
First find P_0.

$$P_0 = \frac{1}{\displaystyle\sum_{n=0}^{n=k-1}\left[\frac{M!}{(M-n)!n!}\left(\frac{\lambda}{\mu}\right)^n\right] + \sum_{n=k}^{n=M}\left[\frac{M!}{(M-n)!k!k^{n-k}}\left(\frac{\lambda}{\mu}\right)^n\right]}$$

$$P_0 = \frac{1}{\dfrac{6!}{6!0!}\left(\dfrac{2}{3}\right)^0 + \dfrac{6!}{5!1!}\left(\dfrac{2}{3}\right)^1 + \dfrac{6!}{4!2!2^0}\left(\dfrac{2}{3}\right)^2 + \dfrac{6!}{3!2!2^1}\left(\dfrac{2}{3}\right)^3 + \dfrac{6!}{2!2!2^2}\left(\dfrac{2}{3}\right)^4 + \dfrac{6!}{1!2!2^3}\left(\dfrac{2}{3}\right)^5 + \dfrac{6!}{0!2!2^4}\left(\dfrac{2}{3}\right)^6}$$

$$= \frac{1}{1 + 4 + \frac{20}{3} + \frac{80}{9} + \frac{80}{9} + \frac{160}{27} + \frac{160}{81}} = \frac{1}{37.346} = 0.0268$$

(*a*) $L_q = \displaystyle\sum_{n=k}^{n=M}(n-k)P_n$

$$P_n = P_0 \frac{M!}{(M-n)!k!k^{n-k}}\left(\frac{\lambda}{\mu}\right)^n \qquad k \le n \le M$$

Thus we must first find P_2, P_3, P_4, P_5, and P_6.

$$P_2 = .0268 \frac{6!}{4!\,2!\,2^0} \left(\frac{2}{3}\right)^2 = .18$$

$$P_3 = .0268 \frac{6!}{3!\,2!\,2^1} \left(\frac{2}{3}\right)^3 = .24$$

$$P_4 = .0268 \frac{6!}{2!\,2!\,2^2} \left(\frac{2}{3}\right)^4 = .24$$

$$P_5 = .0268 \frac{6!}{1!\,2!\,2^3} \left(\frac{2}{3}\right)^5 = .16$$

$$P_6 = .0268 \frac{6!}{0!\,2!\,2^4} \left(\frac{2}{3}\right)^6 = .05$$

$$L_q = P_2(2-2) + P_3(3-2) + P_4(4-2) + P_5(5-2) + P_6(6-2)$$
$$= 0 + .24 + .24(2) + .16(3) + .05(4)$$
$$= 1.40$$

(b) The total time lost per day is the expected number in the queue L_q multiplied by the number of hours in a day.

$$\text{Time lost per day} = 8(1.4) = 11.2 \text{ hours/day}$$

If many calculations are to be made without the use of a computer, it will be convenient to refer to the set of tables published by Peck and Hazelwood,[1] constructed for various values of $-1/u$, M and k. One can refer to the appropriate initial conditions and look up the computed value of P_0, for example. This greatly reduces the time required for hand computations. Other monographs have similar information in chart form instead of tables.[2] Charts are sometimes more convenient because they present the information in continuous form.

QUEUING PROBLEMS FORMULATED AS A MARKOV CHAIN

Although much work has been done to develop models to fit queuing situations, the assumptions required about distribution type, etc., often make it difficult to select an adequate model. In some cases it may be advantageous to model the queuing environment as a Markov chain. If a computer is available to perform the matrix calculations, this is even more likely to be beneficial. Markov chains were discussed

[1] Peck L. G. and R. N. Hazelwood, "Finite Queueing Tables," John Wiley & Sons, Inc., New York, 1968.
[2] A. M. Lee, "Applied Queueing Theory." The Macmillan Company, New York, 1966.

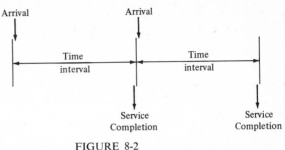

FIGURE 8-2
Time reference for a step in a Markov chain.

in Chap. 4.   This section presents a problem formulated as a Markov chain to serve as an example.   In particular, some adaptation is required to approximate the assumption of allowing an infinite queue length.

EXAMPLE 8-11   A repair station services incoming trucks on an as-arrived basis. Since these are large units, there is only space for two trucks to be stored before service; i.e., system capacity is three.   The following data on arrivals and services have been accumulated.

Number of trucks arriving in 1 hour	Probability of occurrence
0	.6
1	.3
2	.1

Data accumulated on service times indicate that the probability of a service completion during a 1-hour period is .60 given that a unit is there to be serviced.   Since all service times equal 1 hour or more, the probability of more than one service is 0.

To formulate this as a Markov chain, a state is defined as the number of trucks in the system.   Thus the transition matrix is a 4×4 matrix.

$$
P = \begin{array}{c} \\ 0 \\ 1 \\ 2 \\ 3 \end{array} \begin{array}{cccc} 0 & 1 & 2 & 3 \\ \left[\begin{array}{cccc} & & & \\ & & p_{ij} & \\ & & & \\ & & & \end{array} \right] \end{array}
$$

A step will be defined as a 1-hour period.   The time reference for a step is illustrated in Fig. 8.2.

As this sketch illustrates, it is assumed that arrivals occur at the beginning of each period. Thus an arrival can be serviced during that period if the queue was previously empty. A service is assumed to be completed at the end of a period. The next step will be to formulate the p_{ij} terms that make up the transition matrix.

p_{ij}	Ways event can occur	Probability
p_{00}	None there, no arrivals $= .6$	.60
	None there, one arrival, one service $= .3(.6)$	.18
		$p_{00} = .78$
p_{01}	None there, one arrival, no service $= .3(.4)$	.12
	None there, two arrivals, one service $= .1(.6)$	.06
		$p_{01} = .18$
p_{02}	None there, two arrivals, no service $= .1(.4)$	$p_{02} = .04$
p_{03}	Not possible	
	Check $\Sigma_j\, p_{ij} = 1 = .78 + .18 + .04 + 0 = 1.00$ OK	
p_{10}	One there, no arrivals, one service $= .6(.6)$	$p_{10} = .36$
p_{11}	One there, no arrivals, no service $= .6(.4)$	.24
	One there, one arrival, one service $= .3(.6)$	.18
		$p_{11} = .42$
p_{12}	One there, one arrival, no service $= .3(.4)$	.12
	One there, two arrivals, one service $= .1(.6)$	.06
		$p_{12} = .18$
p_{13}	One there, two arrivals, no service $= .1(.4)$	$p_{13} = .04$
p_{20}	Not possible	$p_{20} = 0$
p_{21}	Two there, no arrivals, one service $= .6(.6)$	$p_{21} = .36$
p_{22}	Two there, no arrivals, no service $= .6(.4)$	.24
	Two there, one or two* arrivals, one service $= .4(.6)$	.24
		$p_{22} = .48$
p_{23}	Two there, one or two* arrivals, no service $= .4(.4)$	$p_{23} = .16$
p_{30}	Not possible	$p_{30} = 0$
p_{31}	Not possible	$p_{31} = 0$
p_{32}	Three there, one service*	$p_{32} = .60$
p_{33}	Three there, no service*	$p_{33} = .40$

* Note that if more arrive than the system can hold, it fills up and others are turned away.

$$P = \begin{array}{c} \\ 0 \\ 1 \\ 2 \\ 3 \end{array} \begin{array}{cccc} 0 & 1 & 2 & 3 \\ \left[\begin{array}{cccc} .78 & .18 & .04 & 0 \\ .36 & .42 & .18 & .04 \\ 0 & .36 & .48 & .16 \\ 0 & 0 & .6 & .4 \end{array}\right] \end{array}$$

To answer questions regarding this system, first find steady-state conditions.

$$V^* = [.44 \quad .27 \quad .21 \quad .08]$$

This says that 44 percent of the time the system is empty; that is, $P_0 = .44$. The *expected number of units in the system is*

$$\Sigma n P_n = 0(.44) + 1(.27) + 2(.21) + 3(.08) = 0.93$$

The *expected number of units waiting is*

$$1(.21) + 2(.08) = 0.37$$

Note that .21 is the probability of two in the system or one in the queue.

As an example of the case with no limit on queue length, assume that this problem had an infinite number of spaces. To work this merely truncate the problem to a reasonable number of spaces. For example, since the probability of two in the system is .16, if one assumes that the maximum number of spaces is 5, there will not be a large error.

$$
\begin{array}{c}
 & \begin{array}{cccccc} 0 & \;\;1 & \;\;2 & \;\;3 & \;\;4 & \;\;5 \end{array} \\
\begin{array}{c} 0 \\ 1 \\ 2 \\ 3 \\ 4 \\ 5 \end{array}
&
\left[
\begin{array}{cccccc}
.78 & .18 & .04 & 0 & 0 & 0 \\
.36 & .42 & .18 & .04 & 0 & 0 \\
0 & .36 & .42 & .18 & .04 & 0 \\
0 & 0 & .36 & .42 & .18 & .04 \\
0 & 0 & 0 & .36 & .48 & .16 \\
0 & 0 & 0 & 0 & .6 & .4
\end{array}
\right]
\end{array}
$$

Solving this to find the steady-state vector V gives

$$V^* = [.35 \quad .22 \quad .17 \quad .13 \quad .10 \quad .03]$$

Since v_5 is small, the error in truncation is small; i.e., no *more* than 3 percent can be distributed to states 6 and larger. If v_n does not get small, the system is not stable.

NOTES

1 Derivation of Multichannel Infinite-Population Model

Let

n = number of customers in system

P_n = probability of n customers in system

k = number of channels

λ = arrival rate of customers

μ = service rate of individual channel

Make the following assumptions:

1 All service rates are equal
2 Both λ and μ are mean values from a Poisson distribution
3 Service is first come, first serve and taken from a single queue; i.e., any empty channel is filled by the next customer in line

First find $P_n(t)$ in terms of λ, μ, and k. This will have to be done for two cases, one where $n \le k$. As a simplification, first let $k = 2$.

List the ways that P_0 can occur at time $t + \Delta L$.

A Have customers at time t and no arrivals.
B Have one customer at time t, complete this service, and have no arrivals.[1]

$$A = P_0(t)(1 - \lambda \Delta t)$$
$$B = P_1(t)(1 - \lambda \Delta t)(\mu \Delta t)$$

Summing these gives

$$P_0(t + \Delta t) = P_0(t)(1 - \lambda \Delta t) + P_1(t)(1 - \lambda \Delta t)(\mu \Delta t)$$

Remember that if the system is independent of time, $P_0(t + \Delta t) = P_0(t)$; thus for simplicity the index t will be dropped.

$$P_0 = P_0(1 - \lambda \Delta t) + P_1(\mu \Delta t - \mu\lambda \Delta t^2)^{\nearrow 0}$$
$$= P_0 - P_0 \lambda \Delta t + P_1 \mu \Delta t$$
$$P_1 = P_0 \frac{\lambda}{\mu}$$

Now list the ways that P_1 can occur:

A Zero units at time t, one arrival, no service
B One unit at time t, no arrivals, no service
C Two units at time t, no arrivals, one service

Sum A, B, and C, omitting the t index:

$$P_1 = \underbrace{P_0(\lambda \Delta t)}_{A} + \underbrace{P_1(1 - \lambda \Delta t)(1 - \mu \Delta t)}_{B} + \underbrace{P_2(1 - y \Delta t)(2\mu \Delta t)}_{C} \qquad (8\text{-}37)$$

Note that if both channels are filled, the probability of one service is $\mu \Delta t + \mu \Delta t = 2\mu \Delta t$.

$$P_2(2\mu \Delta t - 2\mu\lambda \Delta t^2) = P_1 - P_1(1 - \lambda \Delta t - \mu \Delta t + \mu\lambda \Delta t^2) - P_0(\lambda \Delta t)$$
$$P_2(2\mu \Delta t) = P_1 - P_1 + P_1 \lambda \Delta t + P_1 \mu \Delta t - P_0 \lambda \Delta t$$
$$P_2 = P_1 \frac{(\lambda + \mu)}{2\mu} \frac{\Delta t}{\Delta t} - P_0 \frac{\lambda}{2\mu} \frac{\Delta t}{\Delta t}$$
$$= P_1 \frac{\lambda + \mu}{2\mu} - P_0 \frac{\lambda}{2\mu} \qquad (8\text{-}38)$$

---

[1] The situation described by two units in the system, zero arrivals, and two completions is not possible:

$$P_2(1 - \lambda \Delta t)(\mu \Delta t)(\mu \Delta t) = P_2(1 - \lambda \Delta t)(\mu \Delta t)^{2 \nearrow 0} \qquad (8\text{-}36)$$

These can be generalized for k channels.

$$P_1 = \frac{\lambda}{\mu} P_0 \qquad (8\text{-}39)$$

$$P_n = \frac{\lambda + (n-1)\mu}{n\mu} P_{n-1} - \frac{\lambda}{n\mu} P_{n-2} \qquad n = 2, 3, \ldots, k \qquad (8\text{-}40)$$

When $n > 2$, list the ways to have n units in the system at time $t + \Delta t$:

A n units at t, zero arrivals, zero services
B $n+1$ units at t, zero arrivals, one service
C $n-1$ units at t, one arrival, zero service

$$P_n(t) = A + B + C$$

$$P_n = \underbrace{P_n(1 - \lambda\,\Delta t)(1 - 2\mu\,\Delta t)}_{A} + \underbrace{P_{n+1}(1 - y\,\Delta t)(2\mu\,\Delta t)}_{B}$$

$$+ \underbrace{P_{n-1}(\lambda\,\Delta t)(1 - 2\mu\,\Delta t)}_{C} \qquad (8\text{-}41)$$

$$P_n = P_n(1 - \lambda\,\Delta t - 2\mu\,\Delta t + 2\mu\lambda\,\overset{0}{\cancel{\Delta t^2}}) + P_{n+1}(2\mu\,\Delta t - 2\mu\lambda\,\overset{0}{\cancel{\Delta t^2}})$$

$$+ P_{n-1}(\lambda\,\Delta t - 2\mu\lambda\,\overset{0}{\cancel{\Delta t^2}})$$

$$P_{n+1} = \frac{\lambda + 2\mu}{2\mu} P_n - \frac{\lambda}{2\mu} P_{n+1} \qquad n \ge 2 \qquad (8\text{-}42)$$

This can be generalized to k channels.

$$P_n = \frac{\lambda + k\mu}{k\mu} P_{n-1} - \frac{\lambda}{k\mu} P_{n-2} \qquad n \ge k+1 \qquad (8\text{-}43)$$

Next, these equations will be used to express P_n in terms of λ, μ, k, and P_0. The two cases $n < k$ and $n \ge k$ must still be considered separately. For $n < k$

$$P_1 = \frac{\lambda}{\mu} P_0$$

$$P_2 = \frac{\lambda + \mu}{2\mu} P_1 - \frac{\lambda}{2\mu} P_0 = \frac{\lambda + \mu}{2\mu} \frac{\lambda}{\mu} P_0 - \frac{\lambda}{2\mu} P_0$$

$$= \frac{P_0\,\lambda}{2\,\mu}\left(\frac{\lambda + \mu}{\mu} - 1\right) = \frac{P_0}{2}\left(\frac{\lambda}{\mu}\right)^2$$

$$P_3 = \frac{\lambda + 2\mu}{3\mu} P_2 - \frac{\lambda}{3\mu} P_1$$

$$= \frac{\lambda + 2\mu}{3\mu} \frac{P_0}{2}\left(\frac{\lambda}{\mu}\right)^2 - \frac{\lambda}{3\mu}\frac{\lambda}{\mu} P_0 = \frac{P_0}{3(2)}\left(\frac{\lambda}{\mu}\right)^3$$

Thus

$$P_n = \frac{P_0}{n!}\left(\frac{\lambda}{\mu}\right)^n \qquad n = 0, 1, 2, \ldots, k-1 \qquad (8\text{-}44)$$

Now express P_n in terms of λ, μ, k, and P_0 for $n \geq k$.

$$P_n = \frac{\lambda + k\mu}{k\mu} P_{n-1} - \frac{\lambda}{k\mu} P_{n-2} \qquad n \geq k+1 \qquad (8\text{-}45)$$

$$P_n = \frac{\lambda + (n-1)\mu}{n\mu} P_{n-1} - \frac{\lambda}{n\mu} P_{n-2} \qquad n = 2, 3, \ldots, k \qquad (8\text{-}46)$$

Let $n = k$.

$$
\begin{aligned}
P_k &= \frac{\lambda + (k-1)\mu}{k\mu} P_{k-1} - \frac{\lambda}{k\mu} P_{k-2} \\
&= \frac{\lambda + (k-1)\mu}{k\mu} \frac{1}{(k-1)!} \left(\frac{\lambda}{\mu}\right)^{k-1} P_0 - \frac{\lambda}{k\mu} \frac{1}{(k-2)!} \left(\frac{\lambda}{\mu}\right)^{k-2} P_0 \\
&= \frac{P_0}{k(k-2)!} \left(\frac{\lambda}{\mu}\right)^{k-1} \left[\frac{\lambda + (k-1)\mu}{\mu(k-1)} - 1\right] \\
&= \frac{P_0}{k(k-2)!} \left(\frac{\lambda}{\mu}\right)^{k-1} \frac{\lambda}{\mu(k-1)} = \frac{P_0}{k!}\left(\frac{\lambda}{\mu}\right)^k \qquad (8\text{-}47)
\end{aligned}
$$

Let $n = k+1$.

$$P_{k+1} = \frac{\lambda + k\mu}{k\mu} P_k - \frac{\lambda}{k\mu} P_{k-1}$$

$$
\begin{aligned}
&= \frac{\lambda + k\mu}{k\mu} \frac{P_0}{k!}\left(\frac{\lambda}{\mu}\right)^k - \frac{\lambda}{k\mu} \frac{1}{(k-1)!}\left(\frac{\lambda}{\mu}\right)^{k-1} P_0 \\
&= \frac{P_0}{k!}\left(\frac{\lambda}{\mu}\right)^k \left(\frac{\lambda + k\mu}{k\mu} - 1\right) \\
&= \frac{P_0}{k!}\left(\frac{\lambda}{\mu}\right)^k \frac{\lambda}{k\mu} \\
&= \frac{P_0}{k!\,k}\left(\frac{\lambda}{\mu}\right)^{k+1} \qquad (8\text{-}48)
\end{aligned}
$$

Let $n = k+2$.

$$P_{k+2} = \frac{\lambda + k\mu}{k\mu} P_{k+1} - \frac{\lambda}{k\mu} P_k$$

$$
\begin{aligned}
&= \frac{\lambda + k\mu}{k\mu} \frac{P_0}{k!\,k}\left(\frac{\lambda}{\mu}\right)^{k+1} - \frac{\lambda}{k\mu} \frac{P_0}{k!}\left(\frac{\lambda}{\mu}\right)^k \\
&= P_0 \left(\frac{\lambda}{\mu}\right)^{k+1} \frac{1}{k!\,k}\left(\frac{\lambda + k\mu}{k\mu} - 1\right) \\
&= P_0 \left(\frac{\lambda}{\mu}\right)^{k+1} \frac{1}{k!\,k} \frac{\lambda}{\mu}\frac{1}{k} = \frac{P_0}{k!\,k^2}\left(\frac{\lambda}{\mu}\right)^{k+2} \qquad (8\text{-}49)
\end{aligned}
$$

Thus

$$P_n = \frac{1}{k!k^{n-k}} \left(\frac{\lambda}{\mu}\right)^n P_0 \qquad n \geq k \qquad (8\text{-}50)$$

Now P_0 must be expressed in terms of k, μ, and λ.   Then the values for P_n and P_0 can be used to develop the other equations.

$$\sum_{n=0}^{n=\infty} P_n = 1 \qquad (8\text{-}51)$$

The sum of all possible probabilities must equal 1.   Remember that P_n is expressed in two cases, $n < k - 1$ and $n \geq k$.

$$\sum_{n=0}^{n=k-1} \left[\frac{1}{n!} \left(\frac{\lambda}{\mu}\right)^n P_0 \right] + \sum_{n=k}^{n=\infty} \left[\frac{P_0}{k!} \left(\frac{\lambda}{\mu}\right)^n \frac{1}{k^{n-k}} \right] = 1 \qquad (8\text{-}25)$$

$$P_0 \left\{ \sum_{n=0}^{n=k-1} \left[\frac{1}{n!} \left(\frac{\lambda}{\mu}\right)^n \right] + \frac{1}{k!} \sum_{n=k}^{n=\infty} \left[\left(\frac{\lambda}{\mu}\right)^n \frac{1}{k^{n-k}} \right] \right\} = 1 \qquad (8\text{-}53)$$

The second term within the brace is an infinite series.   This needs to be expressed as a limit.   For ease of notation let $x = \lambda/\mu$.

$$y = \sum_{n=k}^{n=\infty} x^n \frac{1}{k^{n-k}} \qquad (8\text{-}54)$$

$$= \frac{x^k}{k^0} + \frac{x^{k+1}}{k^1} + \frac{x^{k+2}}{k^2} + \cdots \qquad (8\text{-}55)$$

This has the general form of the converging geometric series $1 + x + x^2 + \cdots$.   Several manipulations will be required to obtain a series in this form.
Multiply both sides by $1/x^k$

$$\frac{y}{x^k} = 1 + \frac{x}{k} + \frac{x^2}{k^2} + \cdots$$

$$= 1 + \left(\frac{x}{k}\right) + \left(\frac{x}{k}\right)^2 + \left(\frac{x}{k}\right)^3 + \cdots \qquad (8\text{-}56)$$

Now, x/k is less than 1 since $x/k = \lambda/k\mu < 1$.   Thus this is a converging infinite series with a known limit.

$$\frac{y}{x^k} = \frac{1}{1 - x/k}$$

$$y = \frac{x^k}{1 - x/k} = \frac{x^k}{(k-x)/k} = \frac{kx^k}{k - x}$$

Substitute $x = \lambda/\mu$

$$y = \frac{k(\lambda/\mu)^k}{k - \lambda/\mu} = \frac{k(\lambda/\mu)^k}{(k\mu - \lambda)/\mu} = \frac{\mu k(\lambda/\mu)^k}{k\mu - \lambda} \qquad (8\text{-}57)$$

Substitute y in original equation and solve for P_0.

$$P_0 = \frac{1}{\left[\sum_{n=0}^{n=k-1} \frac{1}{n!} \left(\frac{\lambda}{\mu} \right)^n \right] + \left[\frac{1}{k!} \left(\frac{\lambda}{\mu} \right)^k \frac{k\mu}{k\mu - \lambda} \right]} \qquad (8\text{-}58)$$

Now the various equations required for analysis can be formulated and developed. The expected number in the system is

$$L = \sum_{n=0}^{n=\infty} nP_n$$

$$= \sum_{n=0}^{n=k-1} \frac{n}{n!} \frac{\lambda}{\mu} P_0 + \sum_{n=k}^{n=\infty} \frac{n}{k! k^{n-k}} \left(\frac{\lambda}{\mu} \right)^n P_0$$

$$= \sum_{n=0}^{n=\infty} \frac{n}{n!} \frac{\lambda}{\mu} P_0 - \sum_{n=k}^{n=\infty} \frac{n}{n!} \frac{\lambda}{\mu} P_0 + \sum_{n=k}^{n=\infty} \frac{n}{k! k^{n-k}} \left(\frac{\lambda}{\mu} \right)^n P_0 \qquad (8\text{-}59)$$

Using a similar method of evaluating an infinite series, this reduces to

$$L = \frac{\lambda\mu(\lambda/\mu)^k}{(k-1)!(k\mu - \lambda)^2} P_0 + \frac{\lambda}{\mu} \qquad (8\text{-}10)$$

The expected queue length L_q is

$$L_q = L - \text{mean number being serviced}$$

$$= L - k\frac{\lambda}{k\mu}$$

$$= L - \frac{\lambda}{\mu}$$

The expected time in the queue W_q is

$$W_q = L_q \frac{1}{\lambda} = \frac{\mu(\lambda/\mu)^k P_0}{(k-1)!(k\mu - \lambda)^2} \qquad (8\text{-}12)$$

The expected system time W is

$$W = \text{expected queue time} + \text{expected service time}$$

$$= W_q + \frac{1}{\mu}$$

$$= \frac{\mu(\lambda/\mu)^k P_0}{(k-1)!(k\mu - \lambda)^2} + \frac{1}{\mu} \qquad (8\text{-}13)$$

2   Derivation Concepts for the Single-Channel Finite-Population Model

The basic steps required are the same as those used in the other derivations. This note shows the development for the terms P_0 and P_n.

List the ways P_n can occur, $M > n$:

    A n units in system, no arrivals, no service
    B $n+1$ units in system, no arrivals, one service
    C $n-1$ units in system, one arrival, no service

$$P_n = \underbrace{P_n[1 - (M-n)\lambda\,\Delta t](1 - \mu\,\Delta t)}_{A} + \underbrace{P_{n+1}[1 - (M-n+1)\lambda\,\Delta t](\mu\,\Delta t)}_{B}$$

$$+ \underbrace{P_{n-1}[(M-n-1)\lambda\,\Delta t](1 - \mu\,\Delta t)}_{C} \tag{8-60}$$

$$P_n = P_n - P_n(M-n)\lambda\,\Delta t - P_n\mu\,\Delta t + P_{n+1}\mu\,\Delta t + P_{n-1}(M-n+1)\lambda\,\Delta t$$

$$P_{n+1} = P_n\left[\frac{(M-n)\lambda}{\mu} + 1\right] - P_{n-1}(M-n+1)\frac{\lambda}{\mu} \tag{8-61}$$

This is a general expression for P_{n+1} as a function of P_n and P_{n-1}. Now find an expression for P_n in terms of P_0, λ, μ, and M.

$$n = 0: P_0 = P_0$$

$$n = 1: P_1 = P_0 M\left(\frac{\lambda}{\mu}\right)$$

$$n = 2: P_2 = P_1\left[\frac{(M-1)\lambda}{\mu} + 1\right] - P_0(M-1+1)\frac{\lambda}{\mu}$$

But

$$P_1 = P_0 M\frac{\lambda}{\mu}$$

$$P_2 = P_0 M\frac{\lambda}{\mu}\left[\frac{(M-1)\lambda}{\mu} + 1\right] - P_0 M\frac{\lambda}{\mu}$$

$$= P_0\frac{\lambda}{\mu}M\left[\frac{(M-1)\lambda}{\mu} + 1 - 1\right]$$

$$= P_0\frac{\lambda}{\mu}M(M-1)\frac{\lambda}{\mu} = P_0 M(M-1)\left(\frac{\lambda}{\mu}\right)^2$$

And it can be shown that

$$P_n = P_0 M(M-1)(M-2)\cdots(M-n+1)\left(\frac{\lambda}{\mu}\right)^n$$

$$= P_0\frac{M!}{(M-n)!}\left(\frac{\lambda}{\mu}\right)^n \tag{8-28}$$

Now find P_0 in terms of M, λ, and μ.

$$\sum_{n=0}^{n=M} P_n = \sum_{n=0}^{n=M} P_0\frac{M!}{(M-n)!}\left(\frac{\lambda}{\mu}\right)^n = 1$$

Now solve for P_0

$$P_0 = \frac{1}{\sum\limits_{n=0}^{n=M} \dfrac{M!}{(M-n)!}\left(\dfrac{\lambda}{\mu}\right)^n} \qquad (8\text{-}27)$$

REFERENCES

1 FELLER, WILLIAM: "Introduction to Probability Theory and Its Applications," 3d ed., John Wiley & Sons, Inc., New York, 1968.

2 HILLIER, FREDERICK S., and GERALD J. LIEBERMAN: "Introduction to Operations Research," chaps. 10 and 11, Holden-Day, Inc., Publisher, San Francisco, 1967.

3 MORSE, PHILIP M.: "Queues, Inventories and Maintenance," John Wiley & Sons, Inc., New York, 1958.

4 SAATY, THOMAS L.: "Elements of Queueing Theory," McGraw-Hill Book Company, New York, 1961.

5 SAATY, THOMAS L.: "Mathematical Methods of Operations Research," chap. 11, McGraw-Hill Book Company, New York, 1959.

PROBLEMS

8-1 A drive-in bank window has a mean service time of 2 minutes, and customers arrive at a rate of 20 per hour. Assuming that these represent rates with a Poisson distribution:

(a) What percent of the time will the teller be idle?

(b) After driving up, how long will it take the average customer to wait in line and be served?

(c) What fraction of customers will have to wait in line?

8-2 A processing station can handle an average of 25 units/hour although the times vary due to the condition of the incoming material. The arrival rate and service rate can be approximated by a Poisson distribution. How many units per hour should be assigned to keep the mean system time no greater than 4 minutes?

8-3 A secretary types a letter in an average time of 8 minutes. This time actually varies and is distributed exponentially. If she needs 40 percent of her time for other activities, how many letters per day can she be expected to handle?

8-4 An airport can accommodate three airplanes in 2 minutes for either take-off or landing. If this rate is Poisson, what is the mean time between arrivals (for landing or departure) to ensure that the average waiting time is 5 minutes or less? (Assume an exponential distribution on the time between arrivals.)

8-5 Units arrive to be serviced at a rate of 10 per hour. Two types of service units may be purchased. Type *A* will handle 6 per hour (two would be needed); type *B* has a service rate of 12 per hour. Compare the expected system time and the expected number in the system for the two alternatives.

8-6   Trucks are unloaded by forklift.   The mean time between arrivals is 30 minutes distributed exponentially.   The rate of unloading is three trucks per hour.   Cost of an operator and fork truck is $7 per hour.   Idle-time cost for a truck and driver is $10 per hour.   How many forklift trucks should be used?

8-7   An office now has only one telephone extension line.   Presently calls are made (in or out) at a rate of 10 per hour.   The mean call takes 3 minutes.   What is the probability that when a call is to be made, the line is busy?   If this probability is to be .10 or less, how many extension lines are required?

8-8   A servicing unit has a mean rate of 10 items per hour.   These items arrive at a rate of 7 per hour.

(a) If both rates are approximated by a Poisson distribution, find the probability of 0, 1, 2, and 3 units in the system.

(b) If an arrival should not find more than three in the system with a probability of .2, what must the service rate be?

8-9   A mechanic-operator services three machines.   When a machine requires attention, he shuts them down and makes the necessary modifications.   This modification has a mean time of 10 minutes with an exponential distribution.   The mean time between service for any given machine is 2 hours.   What is the utilization of the equipment?

8-10   In a shop, the present practice is to accumulate defective assemblies until at least four require rework.   If an average of two defective assemblies per hour are found, what is the mean time between beginning rework?   Assume the accumulation rate is Poisson.

8-11   In an office, one typist handles the work from three persons.   An average typing job requires 30 minutes, and it varies according to an exponential distribution.   Each person generates a typing job about every 3 hours.   What is the expected waiting time before an entering job is begun?

8-12   Laborers carry concrete to be poured in wheelbarrows.   A cement man supervises the pouring and then makes sure it is well settled and smooth.   The cement man cost the company $8 per hour; the laborers cost $5 per hour.   For purposes of computation, assume that a given wheelbarrow is delivered about every 15 minutes with an exponential distribution of this time.   The cement man requires an average of 6 minutes to handle a load of cement.   If his time is also exponential in nature, how many laborers should be used?

8-13   A chemist runs tests on various products from different units in a refinery.   This time and equipment are worth $18 per hour.   He can run about three tests per hour, but this rate varies and can be described by a Poisson distribution.   An operating unit has a mean time between test requirements of 2 hours with an exponential distribution of times.   When the sample requires over 1 hour, it costs $100 for extra monitoring of equipment.   Six units are in continuous operation.   How many chemists should be used?

8-14   Credit-card payments are received at a rate of 800 per day with a variation approximately Poisson.   One person can process approximately 300 per 8-hour day.   Plot the mean time between arrival and completion as a function of the number of people used.

8-15   A gager in an oil field measures the amount of oil in an oil tank and then has it pumped into a pipeline. It takes about 30 minutes to perform the required work including travel time between tanks. Because of other duties, he has only 7 hours available for this work. As an approximation, assume that a tank battery has an interval of about 3 days between the time it is empty and then filled again requiring further service. The expected number waiting should approximately equal the average rate of service ($7/.5 = 14$ per day). How many tank batteries should be assigned to the gager?

8-16   A mobile repair truck and mechanic service field units. The average travel plus service time is 2 hours/unit. The mean time between service requirements is 4 days. When service is required, the field unit shuts down at a cost of $25 per hour. The mechanic and truck are costed at a rate of $8 per hour. How many field units should he be responsible for to minimize cost?

8-17   A study showed that the number of customers already in a filling station affect the probability of a new arrival. If one assumes that the possibilities of service is .6,

Number in station	Probability of next arrival
0	.4
1	.3
2	.2
3	.05
4	0

formulate this as a Markov chain stating all required assumptions. Find the expected number in the system and the system utilization.

8-18   One man handles incoming customers in a service station. The service time is exponentially distributed with a mean time of 6 minutes. Whenever more than one car is waiting for service, a mechanic comes out to help. If the arrival rate of customers is six per hour, what is the probability that the extra man will be required?

8-19   A recreation park on a lake has a boat ramp. It takes approximately 7 minutes to launch or take out a boat. This time may be assumed random and exponential in nature. During the busy periods, boats arrive to be launched or removed at a rate of five per hour (Poisson distribution). What is the expected system time? How many ramps would be needed to cut this to 20 minutes or less?

8-20   An office manager is trying to determine how many extension numbers he should have. The average call requires about 3 minutes and is Poisson. His first computations assumed an infinite population for customers, but he now has recognized that when one person is talking, the probability of another call is lessened. There are 10 people requiring phone service with a mean time between requirements of 1 hour. If the probability of all lines busy when a call is needed is to be .10 or less, how many extension numbers are needed?

9

SENSITIVITY ANALYSIS
OF CONTINUOUS FUNCTIONS

INTRODUCTION

Some of the techniques of sensitivity analysis can greatly increase the usefulness and applicability of many OR models. Sensitivity analysis helps in two ways: (1) by indicating the need for accuracy in data and the model being used and (2) by informing the manager how far he can deviate from the optimal solution before excessive costs may result. In actual practice, data for analysis are commonly scanty and often of questionable validity. As an example, cost data for the holding cost of inventory, future demand rates or arrival rates, operating costs for future time periods, and the like, are almost always combinations of estimates and averaged historical data. Sensitivity analysis allows the investigator to determine which data are most important and which should therefore be determined most accurately. If an estimate of the cost of improving the accuracy of the estimate of a variable can be made, sensitivity analysis can be used to determine the economic feasibility of the additional work.

In a practical sense it is usually impossible to completely quantify all the variables which contribute to the objective function. As a result, simplifying assumptions must be made to provide a practical and useful decision model. Sensitivity analysis can be used to determine whether these assumptions can be safely made or under what conditions they are applicable.

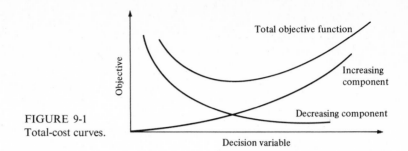

FIGURE 9-1
Total-cost curves.

From the manager's viewpoint, sensitivity analysis can be used to determine a managerial operating range. Most OR techniques provide management with an optimal solution. Sensitivity analysis indicates the cost of deviating from the indicated optimum. Establishing a range of values for the decision variable provides management with flexibility to manage and meet changing needs without continually updating or recomputing the decision variable. In effect, it can give a quick answer to the "what if" type question that concerns change of policy, prices, or other pertinent factors. Thus sensitivity analysis *may* provide management with more useful information than the original decision model itself.

This chapter presents some basic techniques of sensitivity analysis for continuous models, illustrating how these methods are applied and providing tools for application. Objective functions which are continuous, e.g., total variable cost for inventory lot-size determination, are treated in this chapter. The application of sensitivity analysis to linear-programming models provides similar information but requires a different method of analysis. This technique is developed in Chap. 12.

BASIC CONCEPTS

The objective function is a quantitative expression of the values to be optimized. It may be desirable to minimize (total cost, idle time, manpower) or maximize (profit or income, production, etc.) this function, usually by differentiation. Generally this objective function is a combination of increasing and decreasing terms, as illustrated in Fig. 9-1. For purposes of discussion, the inventory lot-size model will be used to illustrate the concepts of sensitivity analysis for continuous functions.

The EOQ model determines the value for lot size which results in the least total variable cost (TVC_o). Any other value for the decision variable (lot size) will cause an increase in the TVC. In this method of analysis the cost equation includes only those cost components which are a function of the decision variable. This means that the comparison is based only on costs which can be influenced by managerial decisions, i.e., choices in the decision variable.

For comparison, a measure of sensitivity is defined by the ratio TVC/TVC_o, where TVC is the total variable cost actually incurred and TVC_o is the minimum cost obtained at the optimal value of the decision variable, in this case Q_o. This ratio then defines the sensitivity ratio k.

$$k = \frac{TVC}{TVC_o} \qquad k \geq 1 \qquad (9\text{-}1)$$

An error term w is defined as the deviation of the decision variable from the optimal value. If Q_o is the optimal economic lot size, any other value Q can be expressed as the product of Q_o and an error term w.

$$Q = wQ_o, \qquad w \geq 0 \qquad (9\text{-}2)$$

Note that w is a nonnegative decimal fraction. When $w = 1$, the decision variable Q is exactly Q_o (optimal). If w is greater than 1, Q is larger than optimal; and if w is less than 1, Q is less than optimal. For example, if $w = 1.25$, this indicates a value of Q that is 25 percent larger than the optimal value; a value of $w = .60$ indicates that Q is only 60 percent of the optimal value.

EXAMPLE 9-1   If the minimum total variable cost (TVC_o) is \$5,000, what is the sensitivity ratio k for an actual TVC of \$5,250?

$$k = \frac{TVC}{TVC_o} = \frac{5,250}{5,000} = 1.05$$

If $k = 1.02$ and $TVC_o = \$6,000$, what would the actual TVC value be?

$$k = \frac{TVC}{TVC_o}$$

$$TVC = k(TVC_o) = 1.02(6,000) = \$6,120$$

If $Q_o = 600$, what is the value of the error term w for an actual lot size of 580?

$$Q = wQ_o, \qquad w = \frac{Q}{Q_o}$$

$$w = \frac{580}{600} = .97$$

If $w = 1.15$, what is the actual lot size?

$$Q = wQ_o = 1.15(600) = 690$$

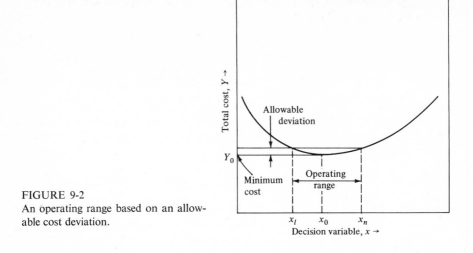

FIGURE 9-2
An operating range based on an allow-able cost deviation.

If the actual lot size must be within 10 percent of the optimal value, what range of values can Q have?

$$Q_{\text{upper}} = 1.10(600) = 660$$
$$Q_{\text{lower}} = 0.90(600) = 540 \qquad ////$$

A particularly useful concept for management is a managerial operating range (MOR) which interprets and presents the sensitivity of any model in a form easy to understand and use. This concept may be applied in several ways. Let management define an allowable or tolerable cost increase; then it is possible to determine the MOR. For example, an allowable cost increase in the TVC might be set at 1 percent; from this, an upper and lower limit on Q could be set. This is illustrated in Fig. 9-2. Thus any value of the decision variable with that MOR will result in a TVC which is within 1 percent of the minimum.

GENERAL FORMULATION, TVC $= ax + b/x$

The objective function which is to be optimized can be viewed as a collection of in-creasing and decreasing factors. For example, the TVC equation previously des-cribed is composed of an increasing cost function, e.g., the holding cost increases with lot size, and a decreasing cost function, e.g., procurement costs decrease with lot size. Thus the TVC is the sum of two cost curves, an increasing straight line and a decreasing hyperbola. This can be represented in the general form.

$$\text{TVC} = ax + \frac{b}{x} \qquad (9\text{-}3)$$

The optimal value x_o of x can be found by taking the derivative of TVC with respect to x and solving for x with the derivative set equal to zero.

$$\frac{d(\text{TVC})}{dx} = a - \frac{b}{x^2} \qquad (9\text{-}4)$$

$$a - \frac{b}{x^2} = 0$$

$$x_o = \sqrt{\frac{b}{a}} \qquad (9\text{-}5)$$

Substituting this value of x_o into the original equation of TVC yields the minimum value TVC_o of TVC:

$$\text{TVC}_o = a\sqrt{\frac{b}{a}} + \frac{b}{\sqrt{b/a}}$$

$$= \sqrt{\frac{a^2 b}{a}} + \sqrt{\frac{b^2 a}{b}}$$

$$= \sqrt{ab} + \sqrt{ab}$$

$$= 2\sqrt{ab}$$

If any other value of x is used, the TVC will have a higher value. Using the same technique as before, let $x = wx_o$, where w is a decimal fraction such that $w \geq 0$. This then is the deviation of x from x_o. The resulting TVC thus obtained is

$$\text{TVC} = ax + \frac{b}{x}$$

$$= a(wx_o) + \frac{b}{wx_o}$$

$$= aw\sqrt{\frac{b}{a}} + \frac{b}{w\sqrt{b/a}}$$

$$= w\sqrt{\frac{a^2 b}{a}} + \frac{1}{w}\sqrt{\frac{b^2 a}{b}}$$

$$= w\sqrt{ab} + \frac{1}{w}\sqrt{ab}$$

$$= \sqrt{ab}\left(w + \frac{1}{w}\right) \qquad (9\text{-}7)$$

Table 9-1   SENSITIVITY OF THE DECISION
VARIABLE x ON THE COST RATIO k
(TVC/TVC$_o$)

w	$\dfrac{x}{x_o}$	$\dfrac{\text{TVC}}{\text{TVC}_o} = k$	w	$\dfrac{x}{x_o}$	$\dfrac{\text{TVC}}{\text{TVC}_o} = k$
.5	.5	1.25	1.1	1.1	1.005
.6	.6	1.133	1.2	1.2	1.017
.7	.7	1.064	1.3	1.3	1.035
.8	.8	1.025	1.4	1.4	1.057
.9	.9	1.006	1.5	1.5	1.083
1.0	1.0	1.000	2.0	2.0	1.25

The effect of this deviation from TVC can be expressed by the sensitivity ratio, TVC/TVC$_o$, k.

$$\frac{\text{TVC}}{\text{TVC}_o} = k = \frac{\sqrt{ab}(w + 1/w)}{2\sqrt{ab}}$$

$$k = \frac{1}{2}\left(w + \frac{1}{w}\right) \tag{9-8}$$

This will be the result in all cases where the objective function is composed of an increasing linear term and a decreasing hyperbola term.   Since this approximates many situations analyzed by OR techniques, the procedure will have considerably wider application than inventory models.   Observing that the sum of two or more increasing linear terms is still an increasing linear term, it is not surprising that this same expression is obtained for most of the common inventory and simple-replacement models.

Using this equation for the sensitivity cost ratio k we compute Table 9-1 to illustrate the effect of an error or a deviation in the decision variable.

This may be interpreted by saying that if a value of x equal to $0.8x_o$ (20 percent below Q_o) is used, the TVC is increased by 2.5 percent.   Similarly, if an error of 30 percent on the high side is made in the decision variable, the added cost will be 3. 5 percent of the minimum TVC$_o$.

EXAMPLE 9-2   In the simple EOQ model (see Chap. 6).

$$\text{TVC} = \frac{C_h Q}{2} + \frac{C_p D}{Q}$$

This can be expressed in the general form by the following substitutions. Let

$$x = Q$$

$$a = \frac{C_h}{2}$$

$$b = C_p D$$

$$\text{TVC} = ax + \frac{b}{x}$$

If

$$C_p = \$50$$

$$D = 15{,}000 \text{ units/year}$$

$$C_h = \$1.50 \text{ per unit-year}$$

$$a = \frac{C_h}{2} = \frac{1.50}{2} = .75$$

$$b = C_p D = 50(15{,}000) = 750{,}000$$

$$x_o = \sqrt{\frac{b}{a}} = 1{,}000 \text{ units} = Q_o$$

$$\text{TVC}_o = 2\sqrt{ab} = 2\sqrt{.75\,(750{,}000)} = \$1{,}500 \text{ per year}$$

If a lot size of 1,500 is purchased, a yearly savings of $500 on the direct item cost can be obtained because of a special price reduction. This results in an increase in lot size of 50 percent above the optimal, or $w = Q'/Q = 1{,}500/1{,}000 = 1.5$. As indicated in Table 9-1 a w of 1.5 results in an increase in TVC of 8.5 percent or 1,500 (.085) = $127.50 per year. Obviously it is economically desirable to increase TVC by $127.50 to realize a savings of $500 per year on the direct item cost.

As another example using the same data, consider the case where the shipping and receiving personnel request an increase in lot size to 1,250 to allow monthly deliveries. They claim this will allow combining shipments with another item and result in increased handling efficiency as well as a reduction in time required by purchasing. The estimated savings are $250 per year in tangible items plus intangibles. This is an increase of 25 percent or a w of 1.25. Estimating from Table 9-1 shows an increase in TVC/TVC$_o$ of 2.6 percent for a total increase of 0.026 (1,500) = $39 per year. Again this is a justifiable variation.   ////

This leads to the development of the concept of the managerial operating range, (MOR). It is, or should be, of great importance to management to know how far they can move from the computed optimal value of the decision variable before a defined cost increase is incurred. For example, over what range can the decision variable Q or x vary without making the TVC increase above 1 percent of the minimum cost TVC_o? This was illustrated in Fig. 9-2. This MOR is developed as follows.

$$k = \frac{TVC}{TVC_o} = \frac{1}{2}\left(\frac{1}{w} + w\right) \qquad (9\text{-}9)$$

Solve this for w in terms of k.

$$2k = \frac{1}{w} + w$$

$$2kw = 1 + w^2$$

$$w^2 - 2kw + 1 = 0 \qquad (9\text{-}10)$$

This is a quadratic equation in terms of w and can be solved by the general expression

$$y = \frac{-b \pm \sqrt{b^2 - 4ac}}{2a} \qquad (9\text{-}11)$$

where

$$ay^2 + by + c = 0$$

From this, $a = 1$, $b = -2k$, and $c = 1$.

$$w = \frac{-(-2k) \pm \sqrt{4k^2 - 4(1)(1)}}{2(1)} = \frac{2k \pm \sqrt{4k^2 - 4}}{2}$$

$$= \frac{2k \pm 2\sqrt{k^2 - 1}}{2} = k \pm \sqrt{k^2 - 1} \qquad (9\text{-}12)$$

Since $w = x/x_o$, the allowable range on the decision variable can be expressed as a function of the optimal value.

$$w = \frac{x}{x_o} = k \pm \sqrt{k^2 - 1} \qquad (9\text{-}13)$$

$$x = x_o(k \pm \sqrt{k^2 - 1}) \qquad (9\text{-}14)$$

$$x_{\text{upper limit}} = x_o(k + \sqrt{k^2 - 1}) \qquad (9\text{-}15)$$

$$x_{\text{lower limit}} = x_o(k - \sqrt{k^2 - 1}) \qquad (9\text{-}16)$$

EXAMPLE 9-3   In the economic lot-size example, find the MOR for an allowable increase in TVC of 1 percent.

$$TVC = 1.01 TVC_o$$

$$\frac{TVC}{TVC_o} = 1.01 = k$$

From Example 9–2, $Q_o = 1,000$.

$$Q = Q_o(1.01 \pm \sqrt{1.01^2 - 1})$$

$$= 1,000(1.01 \pm .142)$$

$$Q_{\text{upper}} = 1,152$$

$$Q_{\text{lower}} = 868 \qquad\qquad ////$$

A similar method of analysis can be used to indicate the sensitivity of input data.   Since data used in OR are seldom determined with complete certainty, the effects of any error in estimating these input data are most important.   When questionable data are used, this method of analysis provides the opportunity of evaluating the probable degree of decision error.   Conversely, it provides a tool for determining the worth of more accurate data and thus indicates how much might be spent to achieve this accuracy.

It has been shown that the optimal value of the decision variable is a function of the data factors a and b.

$$x_o = \sqrt{\frac{b}{a}} \qquad (9\text{-}5)$$

If the values obtained for a and/or b were incorrect, the value computed for x_o would be incorrect and thus a TVC above the TVC_o would be incurred.   For this case, let

$$b' = \text{input data (estimated)}$$

$$b = \text{actual data, unknown}$$

$$a' = \text{input data (estimated)}$$

$$a = \text{actual data, unknown}$$

When these estimates are used, some nonoptimal value x is calculated

$$x = \sqrt{\frac{b'}{a'}} \qquad (9\text{-}17)$$

Table 9-2   EFFECT OF DATA ERROR ON COST

$\dfrac{b'}{b}$ *	w	$\dfrac{\text{TVC}}{\text{TVC}_o}$	$\dfrac{a'}{a}$ †	w	$\dfrac{\text{TVC}}{\text{TVC}_o}$
.5	.707	1.250	.5	.707	1.250
.8	.894	1.025	.8	.894	1.025
1.0	1.000	1.000	1.0	1.000	1.000
1.2	1.095	1.017	1.2	1.095	1.017
1.5	1.225	1.021	1.5	1.225	1.021
2.0	1.414	1.250	2.0	1.414	1.250

* Assume $a/a' = 1$.
† Assume $b'/b = 1$.

An error term w has already been defined as

$$w = \frac{x}{x_o} = \frac{\sqrt{b'/a'}}{\sqrt{b/a}} \qquad (9\text{-}18)$$

These terms can be rearranged in components of common ratios:

$$w = \sqrt{\frac{b'}{b}\frac{a'}{a}} \qquad (9\text{-}19)$$

These ratios b'/b and a/a' are indications of the deviation of the estimate from the true value.   For example, $b'/b = 1.2$ indicates that the estimate of b is 20 percent high. From this relationship and the relationship developed for k, Table 9-2 has been developed to illustrate the effect of an error in data estimation upon cost.

As Table 9-2 indicates, the effects of errors in estimating the input data for this model do not have a very significant effect on cost because an incorrect decision variable was used.

EXAMPLE 9-4   Since information is inadequate, the validity of the estimate of a is in question.   However, the researcher feels confident that his estimate is within 10 percent of the true value.   What effect might this error have on cost?
a/a' is between .90 and 1.10.   Since

$$w = \sqrt{\frac{a}{a'}}$$

or

$$= \sqrt{.9} = .949$$

$$w = \sqrt{1.1} = 1.049$$

Check these two values for TVC/TVC_o :

$$\frac{TVC}{TVC_o} = \frac{1}{2}\left(\frac{1}{.949} + .949\right) = 1.001$$

$$\frac{TVC}{TVC_o} = \frac{1}{2}\left(\frac{1}{1.1} + 1.1\right) = 1.005$$

Thus the maximum cost increase from the incorrect data would be .5 percent. If this cost is less than the cost of obtaining more accurate data, the present estimates should be used.   If not, more accurate data should be obtained.   ////

EXAMPLE 9-5   In the inventory example, how accurate should the estimate on holding cost be to ensure that the cost of an incorre ct lot size is no more than .2 percent of TVC_o ?

$$TVC = \frac{C_h Q}{2} + \frac{C_p D}{Q}$$

$$a = \frac{C_h}{2}$$

$$\frac{TVC}{TVC_o} = 1.002 = k$$

$$w = k \pm \sqrt{k^2 - 1}$$

$$= 1.002 \pm \sqrt{1.002^2 - 1}$$

$$= 1.065, .939$$

$$w = \sqrt{\frac{a}{a'}}$$

$$w^2 = \frac{a}{a'}$$

$$\frac{a}{a'} = 1.065^2 = 1.134$$

$$\frac{a}{a'} = .939^2 = .882$$

$$\frac{C_h}{2} = a$$

$$\frac{C_h/2}{C_h'/2} = \frac{a}{a'}$$

$$\frac{C_h}{C_h'} = \frac{a}{a'}$$

Thus the estimate of C_h should be within 13 percent on the high side and 12 percent on the low side to ensure that the cost increase is less than .2 percent of TVC_o.

GENERAL FORMULATION, $TVC = Ax^n + b/x^m$

A more general formulation of increasing and decreasing components can be presented by using the general TVC cost equation which allows other powers of x.

$$TVC = ax^n + \frac{b}{x^m}, \qquad \begin{matrix} n > 0 \\ m > 0 \end{matrix} \qquad (9\text{-}20)$$

First an optimal values of x is obtained by differentiation, etc.

$$\frac{d(TVC)}{dx} = anx^{n-1} - \frac{bm}{x^{m+1}} \qquad (9\text{-}21)$$

$$anx^{n-1} = \frac{bm}{x^{m+1}} = 0$$

$$an(x^{n-1})(x^{m+1}) - bm\frac{x^{m+1}}{x^{m+1}} = 0$$

$$anx^{m+n} = bm$$

$$x_o = \left(\frac{bm}{an}\right)^{1/(m+n)} \qquad (9\text{-}22)$$

Substituting x_o into the TVC equation (8-20) gives the optimal value TVC_o.

$$TVC_o = ax_o{}^n + \frac{b}{x_o{}^m} = a\left[\left(\frac{bm}{an}\right)^{1/(m+n)}\right]^n + b\frac{1}{[(bm/an)^{1/(m+n)}]^m}$$

$$= a\left(\frac{bm}{an}\right)^{n/(m+n)} + \frac{b}{(bm/an)^{m/(m+n)}} \qquad (9\text{-}23)$$

This can be manipulated algebraically to give

$$TVC_o = a^{\frac{m}{m+n}} b^{\frac{n}{m+n}} \frac{m/n + 1}{(m/n)^{m/(m+n)}} \qquad (9\text{-}24)$$

As previously defined, $x = wx_o$. Substituting this into the expression for TVC gives the TVC in terms of a, b, m, n and w.

$$TVC = a(wx_o)^n + \frac{b}{(wx_o)^m}$$

$$= a\left[w\left(\frac{bm}{an}\right)^{1/(m+n)}\right]^n + \frac{b}{[w(bm/an)^{1/(m+n)}]^m}$$

$$= a^{m/(m+n)}b^{n/(m+n)}\frac{(m/n)w^{m+n} + 1}{w^m(m/n)^{m/(m+n)}} \qquad (9\text{-}25)$$

Table 9-3   SUMMARY OF SENSITIVITY TERMS

Basic equation	Optimal decision value x_o	Minimum total variable cost Y_o'	Sensitivity term	Limits of w for $k = .02$	
				Upper	Lower
$Y = ax^2 + \dfrac{b}{x}$	$\left(\dfrac{b}{2a}\right)^{1/3}$	$\dfrac{3}{2^{2/3}} a^{1/3}b^{2/3}$	$\frac{1}{3}\left(w^2 + \dfrac{2}{w}\right)$	1.15	.87
$Y = a\sqrt{x} + \dfrac{b}{\sqrt{x}}$	$\dfrac{b}{a}$	$2\sqrt{ab}$	$\dfrac{\sqrt{w}}{2} + \dfrac{1}{2\sqrt{w}}$	1.49	.67
$Y = a\sqrt{x} + \dfrac{b}{x}$	$\left(\dfrac{2b}{a}\right)^{2/3}$	$\dfrac{3}{2^{2/3}} a^{2/3}b^{1/3}$	$\frac{2}{3}\left(\sqrt{w} + \dfrac{1}{2w}\right)$	1.34	.76
$Y = ax + \dfrac{b}{x}$	$\left(\dfrac{b}{a}\right)^{1/2}$	$2(ab)^{1/2}$	$\frac{1}{2}\left(w + \dfrac{1}{w}\right)$	1.22	.82
$Y = ax^3 + \dfrac{b}{x}$	$\left(\dfrac{b}{3a}\right)^{1/4}$	$1.741(ab^3)^{1/4}$	$\frac{1}{4}\left(w^3 + \dfrac{3}{w}\right)$	1.12	.88
$Y = ax^3 + \dfrac{b}{x^3}$	$\left(\dfrac{b}{a}\right)^{1/6}$	$2\sqrt{ab}$	$\frac{1}{6}\left(3w^3 + \dfrac{3}{w^3}\right)$	1.07	.94
$Y = ax + \dfrac{b}{x^2}$	$\left(\dfrac{2b}{a}\right)^{1/3}$	$\dfrac{3}{2^{2/3}}(a^2b)^{1/3}$	$\frac{1}{3}\left(2w + \dfrac{1}{w^2}\right)$	1.16	.87
$Y = ax^n + \dfrac{b}{x^m}$	$\left(\dfrac{mb}{na}\right)^{1/(m+n)}$	$a^{\frac{m}{m+n}} b^{\frac{n}{m+n}} \dfrac{m/n+1}{(m/n)^{m/(m+n)}}$	$\dfrac{1}{m+n}\left(mw^n + \dfrac{n}{w^m}\right)$		

Using these two expressions for TVC and TVC_o, the sensitivity term k can be evaluated and simplified

$$k = \frac{\text{TVC}}{\text{TVC}_o} = \frac{1}{m+n}\left(mw^n + \frac{n}{w^m}\right) \qquad (9\text{-}26)$$

Both m and n must be defined before this term can be evaluated.

     Using these results, TVC equations composed of other forms can be evaluated. Some of these results are summarized in Table 9-3. As expected, the equations involving higher powers of x are more sensitive. Of the equations presented in Table 9-3, the model $\text{TVC} = ax^3 + b/x^3$ has the smallest MOR and $\text{TVC} = a\sqrt{x} + b/\sqrt{x}$ has the largest MOR.   ////

EXAMPLE 9-6   Suppose that a company operates equipment requiring an initial investment of \$30,000 and having a negligible salvage value. Past data indicate that the operating and maintenance cost will follow the data presented in Table 9-4.

Table 9-4   OPERATING AND COST DATA

Years of operation, x	Average cost per year
1	$1,000
2	2,300
3	3,740
4	5,270
5	6,910
6	8,600
7	10,350

Regression analysis indicates that these data can be approximated by the function $1,000x^{1.2}$, where x is the number of years of operation. The average-total-variable-cost equation is then

$$\text{ATVC} = 1,000x^{1.2} + \frac{30,000}{x}$$

Referring to Table 9-3, this can be represented as a general equation of the form

$$Y' = ax^n + \frac{b}{x^m}$$

where $a = 1,000$

$\qquad b = 30,000$

$\qquad n = 1.2$

$\qquad m = 1$

From this the optimal decision value x_o and the minimum cost Y_o can be determined.

$$x_o = \left(\frac{mb}{na}\right)^{1/(m+n)}$$

$$= \left[\frac{30,000}{(1.2)(1,000)}\right]^{1/1+1.2)} = 4.31$$

$$Y_o = a^{m/(m+n)}b^{n(m+n)}\left[\frac{m/n+1}{(m/n)^{m/(m+n)}}\right]$$

$$= 1,000^{1/2.2}30,000^{1.2/2.2}\left[\frac{1/1.2+1}{(1/1.2)^{1/2.2}}\right]$$

$$= \$12,677$$

Table 9-5 COST INCREASE IN TERMS OF w

Deviation w from optimal x_o	Increased cost k	Deviation w from optimal x_o	Increased cost k
.60	.1550	1.10	.0108
.70	.0756	1.20	.0202
.80	.0291	1.30	.0422
.83	.0208	1.40	.0700
.90	.0065	1.50	.1027
1.00	0		

If an allowable deviation from the minimum cost is set at 2 percent, the operating range can be determined from the sensitivity ratio.

$$\frac{Y'_w}{Y'_o} = \frac{1}{m+n}\left(mw^n + \frac{n}{w^m}\right)$$

$$= \frac{1}{2.2}\left(w^{1.2} + \frac{1.2}{w}\right)$$

Table 9-5 presents some evaluations of this term.

If a 2 percent increase in average total variable cost is allowed, the management range is from an error value of $w_1 = .83$ to $w_u = 1.12$, from Table 9-5. Since $x_o = 4.31$, this means that any replacement interval between 3.57 to 5.17 will result in an average total variable cost within 2 percent of the minimum.   ////

REFERENCES

1 ABOUEL-NOUR, ABDEL-RAZEK A., and JAMES E. SHAMBLIN: Sensitivity Anal. of Continuous Functions, *AIIE Trans.*, March 1971, pp. 1–6.

2 DISNEY, R. L.: Some Comments of the Control of Inventories, *Eng. Econ.*, vol. 7, no. 3 (1962).

3 NADDOR, E.: "Inventory Systems," John Wiley & Sons, Inc., New York, 1966.

4 RUTENBERG, Y. H.: Calculation of Economic Order Quantities Using Ranges of Set-up Cost, *J. Ind. Eng.*, January–February 1964.

5 SOLOMON, M. J.: The Use of an Economic Lot Range in Scheduling Production, *Manage. Sci.*, July 1959.

6 WITHYCOMBE, R.: Deviation from the Economic Order Quantity, *J. Ind. Eng.*, January–February 1963.

PROBLEMS

9-1   A cost equation for one phase of operation was found to be

$$\text{TVC} = C_1\sqrt{x} + \frac{C_2}{\sqrt{x}}$$

where $x =$ decision variable
$C_1 =$ cost factor $1 = 10$
$C_2 =$ cost factor $2 = 3{,}500$

(*a*) What is x^* for a minimum cost?
(*b*) Plot the added cost (percent increase) as a function of x for the range of $x = x^* \pm$ $.50x^*$.   (Use the sensitivity term.)

9-2   If the cost equation in Prob. 9-1 is valid, find the range of x which will not increase the minimum TVC by more than 5 percent.

9-3   A company has planned to use the simple EOQ model for planning lot-size purchases.

$$Q = \sqrt{\frac{2C_2 D}{C_3}}$$

where $C_2 =$ cost of making one purchase $= \$15$
$D =$ demand, 500 units/year
$C_3 =$ cost of holding 1 unit in inventory 1 year, 1 \$/unit-year

Find the largest and smallest lot sizes which would not increase the TVC by more than 1 percent (the MOR).

9-4   In Prob. 9-3, it is difficult to estimate the value of the demand D correctly.
(*a*) If this estimate had been 10 percent high, how much might this have increased the total TVC?
(*b*) How much in error may the estimate of demand be without increasing the TVC by more than 1 percent?
(*c*) Revised accounting procedures and a new analysis would allow a better estimate of C_3.   Presently this value may be in error by as much as 25 percent.   The new study would reduce the possibility of error to 5 percent but would cost \$300 and be valid for 2 years.   Should it be done?

9-5   The output of a machine varies directly with its operating speed, but maintenance costs also increase as the operating speed goes up.   Labor costs for the operator are constant at \$6 per hour.   At the standard output of 10 units/hour, the operating and maintenance costs are \$1 per hour.   As production increases, the maintenance and operating costs increase as the square of the production rate.
(*a*) What is the production rate which minimizes the TVC in terms of the dollar per unit cost?
(*b*) What would this value be if wage costs went up 10 percent?
(*c*) What is the maximum production rate which will not increase the TVC by more than 5 percent?

9-6   A computer facility has studied the cost of owning and operating periphery equipment. As time passes, the direct operating and maintenance cost increase somewhat and the equipment becomes economically less desirable because newer, more efficient models are introduced. The average cost including depreciation is approximately

$$\text{Average cost} = \frac{I}{n} + C\sqrt{n}$$

where $I = $ investment cost $= \$10,000$
 $C = $ first-year operating and maintenance cost $= \$3,000$

(a) What is the least-cost operating life?
(b) At this time it seems desirable to stretch equipment life to reduce capital expenditures. How much can the operating life be extended before increasing the average cost by more than 2 percent?

9-7 The cost of yield in dollars per pound from a process is primarily related to the operating temperature. At low temperatures the reaction rate is so slow that the output is very low, while at high temperatures undesirable by-products reduce the amount of usable output. This relationship has been established by experimental testing and is approximately

$$\text{Cost} = \frac{PT^{.013}}{150} + \frac{k}{T^2}$$

where $T = $ temperature, °F
 $P = $ pressure, lb/in²
 $k = $ an emperical constant $= 60$

The pressure must be maintained at 35 lb/in² for satisfactory operation of other equipment.

(a) What is the optimal temperature for minimum cost?
(b) At present, the controlling equipment maintains a temperature of $T \pm 5°$. Better equipment can be used to reduce the variation to ± 2 degrees of the desired temperature. If the yearly production rate is 300,000 lb and the equipment would be used for 3 years, how much can they afford to pay to obtain better control?
(c) Since the constant k was determined by limited experimental testing, its accuracy is not firmly established. Additional tests may be run to completely verify this if needed. At this time, they are sure that k is not in error by more than 10 percent. What would this do to the cost of the yield?

9-8 A police department keeps records on the cost of maintaining and operating police vehicles. The cost data for a typical unit are presented in the table.

Time, years	Average annual operating and maintenance cost	Average investment cost (considering salvage value)
1	$3,200	$3,500
2	4,000	2,500
3	4,600	2,000
4	5,050	1,750
5	5,450	1,600
6	5,800	1,430

(*a*) Fit these data to a curve of the form $y = ax^n + b/x^m$.

(*b*) Find the minimum cost life using this curve and compare it to a plot of the data.

(*c*) If the minimum life is extended 50 percent, what will the increase in cost be? Show this graphically.

9-9 Referring to the equation

$$Y = ax^n + \frac{b}{x^m}$$

discuss what properties will make it more important to estimate *a* and *b* correctly.

9-10 Set $a = 1$ and $b = 100$ and plot the equation in Prob. 9-9 for various values of $n = 1, 2, 3$ with $m = 1$ and repeat with $m = 1, 2, 3$ for $n = 1$. Discuss the effect of the value of *m* and/or *n* upon the sensitivity. Which has the greatest effect upon the left (or right) side of the curve? In general, if you were to guess incorrectly in establishing a "best" value for *x*, would it be best to guess on the high side or low side?

10

LINEAR PROGRAMMING

INTRODUCTION

Linear programming is a mathematical means of assigning a fixed amount of resources to satisfy a number of demands in such a way that some objective is optimized and other defined conditions are still satisfied. Perhaps this is best illustrated by means of a very simple example. Suppose a small manufacturing company makes two products, 1 and 2, and that they are fortunate enough to sell all they can produce at present. Each product requires manufacturing time in the three manufacturing departments as indicated in Table 10-1. At this time, each department has a fixed amount of man-hours available per week, as indicated in Table 10-2. The problem is to decide how many of each product to manufacture in order to make best use of the limited production facilities. If the profit per unit was known, this might be done to maximize profit. Assume that the profit for each unit of product 1 is $1 and for product 2 is $1.50. In effect, then, management must assign the fixed resources (manufacturing time of each department) so as to optimize some objective (maximize profit) and still satisfy some other defined conditions (not exceeding the departmental capacities for work).

It is possible to express both the objective and the restrictions mathematically. As the name of this technique suggests, these relationships must *all* be linear. Actually linear programming is simply the application of matrix algebra to solving these equations using some special rules to ensure that the solution satisfies all necessary conditions and still gives the best results with respect to the objective. Many problems in the business world can be treated by linear programming. Even some problems which do not have strictly linear functions yield valuable answers when care is taken in approximation. Usually recognizing and formulating the problem in a form which can be worked and also yield a desirable objective to optimize is perhaps the most difficult task. This requires imagination and understanding of both the problem and the solution technique. It is important to understand both how linear programming works and why it works since some assumptions are almost always required; without this understanding these assumptions cannot be properly made.

In applying linear programming, the first step should be to quantify the objective. Once this is done, many of the conditions become more apparent, at least with respect to form. Problem formulation itself is discussed in more detail later in this chapter. In Example 10-1 it was decided to maximize profit as an objective. Thus it is necessary to quantify the problem in terms of profit. In this case, total profit will simply be the sum of the profit made per product. Let x_1 be the decision variable representing the number of units of product 1 to be made and x_2 similarly represent the number of units of product 2. Since the unit profit for 1 is \$1 and for 2 is \$1.50, the profit equation is

$$\text{Profit} = 1x_1 + 1.50x_2 \qquad (10\text{-}1)$$

This is the linear objective function to be maximized.

Table 10-1 MANUFACTURING-TIME REQUIREMENTS TO PRODUCE 1 UNIT OF PRODUCT PER DEPARTMENT

Product	Manufacturing time, hours		
	Dept. A	Dept. B	Dept. C
1	2	1	4
2	2	2	2

Table 10-2 MANUFACTURING-CAPACITY LIMITS

Department	Man-hours/week available
A	160
B	120
C	280

The conditions for this problem which must be satisfied are to avoid exceeding the available manufacturing time for each department.   Note that the time required in department A depends upon the number of units of both product 1 and product 2 to be made. Thus

> Manufacturing time
> required in department A = time required per unit of 1
> $\times$ no. of units of 1 made
> + time required per unit of 2
> $\times$ no. of units of 2 made
> $= 2x_1 + 2x_2$ (10-2)

It is required that this not exceed the capacity of department A:

> Manufacturing time required in $A \leq$ Capacity of A
> $2x_1 + 2x_2 \leq 160$ (10-3)

Similar analysis for departments B and C yields

> $x_1 + 2x_2 \leq 120$ department B (10-4)
> $4x_1 + 2x_2 \leq 280$ department C (10-5)

In addition, since it is not possible to manufacture a negative number of product 1 or 2, these values must be greater than or equal to zero.

$$x_1 \geq 0$$
$$x_2 \geq 0$$

Collecting these relationships, we can represent the problem mathematically as follows.   Maximize

$$\text{Profit} = x_1 + 1.5x_2$$

subject to the restrictions

$$2x_1 + 2x_2 \leq 160$$
$$x_1 + 2x_2 \leq 120$$
$$4x_1 + 2x_2 \leq 280$$
$$x_1 \geq 0$$
$$x_2 \geq 0$$

These last two restrictions of nonnegative values for the decision variables are *always* implied and thus not expressed formally.

This problem can be expressed in more general terms for mathematical treatment. Let

$$x_j = \text{decision variable for } j\text{th variable}$$
$$c_j = \text{profit (or cost) coefficient for } j\text{th variable}$$
$$z = \text{function to be maximized (or minimized)}$$

Thus, for n decision variables, the objective becomes to maximize

$$z = c_1 x_1 + c_2 x_2 + \cdots + c_j x_j + \cdots + c_n x_n \qquad \text{for } n \text{ variables} \qquad (10\text{-}6)$$

The restrictions require definition of two general terms.

$$a_{ij} = \text{coefficient for the } j\text{th variable in } i\text{th constraint}$$
$$b_i = \text{capacity limitation of } i\text{th constraint}$$

Thus the restrictions may be expressed in general form.

$$a_{11}x_1 + a_{12}x_2 + \cdots + a_{1j}x_j + \cdots + a_{1n}x_n \le b_1$$
$$a_{21}x_1 + a_{22}x_2 + \cdots + a_{2j}x_j + \cdots + a_{2n}x_n \le b_2$$
$$\dots\dots\dots\dots\dots\dots\dots\dots\dots\dots\dots\dots\dots\dots\dots\dots$$
$$a_{i1}x_1 + a_{i2}x_2 + \cdots + a_{ij}x_j + \cdots + a_{in}x_n \le b_i$$
$$\dots\dots\dots\dots\dots\dots\dots\dots\dots\dots\dots\dots\dots\dots\dots\dots$$
$$a_{m1}x_1 + a_{m2}x_2 + \cdots + a_{mj}x_j + \cdots + a_{mn}x_n \le b_m$$

Typically the same linear-programming problem can be expressed in a more condensed version of the general form using summations or even matrix notation.   Maximize

$$z = \sum_{j=1}^{n} c_j x_j$$

subject to

$$\sum_{j=1}^{n} a_{ij} x_j \le b_i \qquad \text{for all } i = 1, 2, \ldots, m$$

or maximize

$$z = \tilde{c}\tilde{x}$$

subject to

$$A\tilde{x} \le \tilde{b}$$

where $\tilde{c}$ is a row vector and $\tilde{x}$ and $\tilde{b}$ are column vectors. A represents an $m \times n$ matrix.   The reader should expand a simple case expressed by this notation to verify this method of notation.

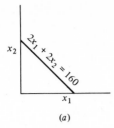

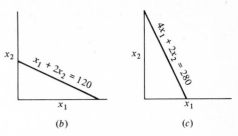

(a)   (b)   (c)

FIGURE 10-1
Graphical representation of three constraints.

EXAMPLE 10-1 Let $n = 2$ and $m = 3$.

$$\sum_{j=1}^{n} c_j x_j = c_1 x_1 + c_2 x_2$$

$$\sum_{j=1}^{n} a_{ij} x_j \leq b_i \quad \text{for } i = 1, 2, 3$$

$$a_{11} x_1 + a_{12} x_2 \leq b_1$$

$$a_{21} x_1 + a_{22} x_2 \leq b_2$$

$$a_{31} x_1 + a_{32} x_2 \leq b_3$$

or

$$[c_1 \quad c_2] \begin{bmatrix} x_1 \\ x_2 \end{bmatrix} = c_1 x_1 + c_2 x_2$$

$$\begin{bmatrix} a_{11} & a_{12} \\ a_{21} & a_{22} \\ a_{31} & a_{32} \end{bmatrix} \begin{bmatrix} x_1 \\ x_2 \end{bmatrix} \leq \begin{bmatrix} b_1 \\ b_2 \\ b_3 \end{bmatrix}$$

$$\begin{bmatrix} a_{11} x_1 + a_{12} x_2 \\ a_{21} x_1 + a_{22} x_2 \\ a_{31} x_1 + a_{32} x_2 \end{bmatrix} \leq \begin{bmatrix} b_1 \\ b_2 \\ b_3 \end{bmatrix} \qquad ////$$

GRAPHICAL INTERPRETATION

As long as the problem is restricted to only two variables, it is possible to portray (and solve) the problem graphically. This provides greater insight into the problem and makes the interpretation of some of the steps and results easier. Actually each constraint defines an area containing an infinite number of points, represented by an area, which do not exceed the constraining inequation. Figure 10-1a to c illustrates the

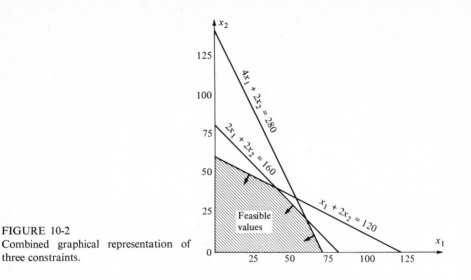

FIGURE 10-2
Combined graphical representation of three constraints.

three constraints used in the example problem. Combining these three into one figure (Fig. 10-2) defines the acceptable or feasible area for an answer. Any nonnegative values of x_1 and x_2 which lie within the area bounded by these three constraints are said to be feasible. The problem then becomes one of selecting the point which is feasible and which at the same time maximizes the objective function.

If some arbitrary value is assigned to the objective function, it can also be plotted (see Fig. 10-3). Since this is a linear function, the slopes of all lines are equal for all values of z, merely translated in position. Overlaying Figs. 10-2 and 10-3 makes it

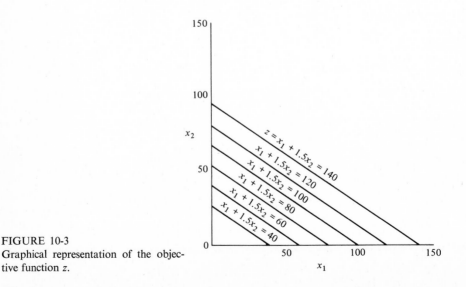

FIGURE 10-3
Graphical representation of the objective function z.

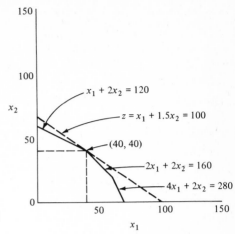

FIGURE 10-4
Graphical solution of the maximization
problem.

possible to determine that maximum value of z which still lies on the furthermost
edge of the feasible area.   This then is the solution giving the values of x_1 and x_2 which
provide a maximum value of the objective function z while not exceeding any of the
constraining inequations.

From Fig. 10-4, the solution values are

$$x_1 = 40$$
$$x_2 = 40$$

and
$$z = x_1 + 1.5x_2 = 40 + 1.5(40) = 100$$

a maximum feasible solution.   It is also of interest to check the constraints,

(1) $2x_1 + 2x_2 \leq 160$

$2(40) + 2(40) = 160$ OK

(2) $x_1 + 2x_2 \leq 120$

$40 + 2(40) = 120$ OK

(3) $4x_1 + 2x_2 \leq 280$

$4(40) + 2(40) = 240 \leq 280$ OK

Thus the solution lies at the intersection of the first and second constraints, as indicated
in Fig. 10-4 graphically and by the fact that both constraints are equal to their limits
of 160 and 120, respectively.   Only in the third constraint (representing department C)
is there unused or slack capacity.

It is important to realize that as long as both the constraints and objective
functions are linear, the optimal feasible answer will be at a corner represented by the

intersection of two or more constraints (or one of the boundaries represented by the axis). Only if the objective function is parallel to a constraint is it possible for the optimal feasible answer to occur at any other location, and even then the answer represented at the appropriate corner would also be feasible and optimum. If three variables were used, this could be represented in a three-dimensional plot with the constraints and objective functions represented by plane surfaces. In more than three dimensions (more than three variables) it is not possible to portray the problem graphically, yet the analogy is still valid and the constraints and objective function are said to be linear hyperplanes in n-dimensional space. It is important to realize that in all cases, the optimal feasible solution will be at the intersection of two or more constraints (or axes) and of the objective function represented as lines or planes.

EXAMPLE 10-2 Find the graphical solution to the following maximization problem. Maximize

$$z = 3x_1 + 2x_2$$

subject to the constraints

$$x_1 + x_2 \leq 20$$
$$x_1 \leq 15$$
$$x_1 + 3x_2 \leq 45$$
$$-3x_1 + 5x_2 \leq 60$$

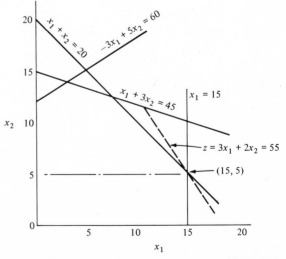

Ex. 10-2

SOLUTION

$$x_1 = 15 \qquad x_2 = 5 \qquad z = 55 \qquad ////$$

ALGEBRAIC SOLUTION

The importance of the last concept developed in the previous section is that the inter-section of two lines is a point and can be solved by algebraic means. Similarly the intersection of three planes is a point which can also be solved by simultaneous equations. Since the constraints, as expressed, are not equations but inequalities, it is first necessary to modify them so that they can be expressed as equations. This is done by introducing an additional term to each constraint called a *slack variable*. Typically the slack variable is represented by the term u_i, the subscript referring to the ith constraint since a different slack variable is used for each constraint.

In the first inequality used in the sample problem

$$2x_1 + 2x_2 \leq 160 \qquad (10\text{-}3)$$

there exists some nonnegative value u_1 which if added to the left side of the inequality would make an equality out of the expression. For example, let

$$x_1 = 50 \qquad x_2 = 20$$
$$2x_1 + 2x_2 = 2(50) + 2(20) = 140$$
$$140 \leq 160 \text{ is still true}$$

Add u_1 to the left side and make the expression an equality.

$$140 + u_1 = 160$$

Thus, in this case

$$u_1 = 20$$

Thus the slack variable represents the nonnegative value that is required to make an equality exist. By this means, the three constraints represented as inequalities are converted into equalities.

$$(1) \qquad 2x_1 + 2x_2 \leq 160$$
$$(2) \qquad x_1 + 2x_2 \leq 120$$
$$(3) \qquad 4x_1 + 2x_2 \leq 280$$

$$(1) \qquad 2x_1 + 2x_2 + u_1 = 160$$
$$(2) \qquad x_1 + 2x_2 + u_2 = 120$$
$$(3) \qquad 4x_1 + 2x_2 + u_3 = 280$$

This forms a system of simultaneous linear equations which can be treated by ordinary algebraic methods. At this point, however, there are an infinite number of solutions since there are now a total of five $(m + n)$ unknowns and only three (m) equations. At least two of the variables must be equal to zero for the unique solution to exist. In the graphical solution presented previously, this was indeed the case. The optimal answer was at the intersection of the first and second constraints, and at these values of x_1 and x_2 both relationships were equalities, that is, u_1 and u_2 were zero. In this case, the value of u_3 can be determined to be

$$4x_1 + 2x_2 + u_3 = 280$$
$$4(40) + 2(40) + u_3 = 280$$
$$u_3 = 40$$

This positive value of u_3 represents an unused capacity in department C, 40 man-hours to be exact. Typically this is referred to as 40 units of slack.

If sufficient insight had been possible, the solution occurring at the intersection of constraints (1) and (2) could have been obtained by algebra.

EXAMPLE 10-3   Assume $u_1 = u_2 = 0$ [no slack in (1) and (2)]. The three equations then reduce to

$$2x_1 + 2x_2 = 160$$
$$x_1 + 2x_2 = 120$$
$$4x_1 + 2x_2 + u_3 = 280$$

Solving for x_1, x_2, u_3 by elimination using row operations.

STEP 1   Divide row 1 by 2 to obtain a coefficient of 1 for x_1.

$$1x_1 + 1x_2 + 0u_3 = 80$$
$$1x_1 + 2x_2 + 0u_3 = 120$$
$$4x_1 + 2x_2 + 1u_3 = 280$$

STEP 2   Subtract row 1 from row 2 *and* multiply row 1 by -4 and add to row 3.

$$1x_1 + 1x_2 + 0u_3 = 80$$
$$0x_1 + 1x_2 + 0u_3 = 40$$
$$0x_1 - 2x_2 + 1u_3 = -40$$

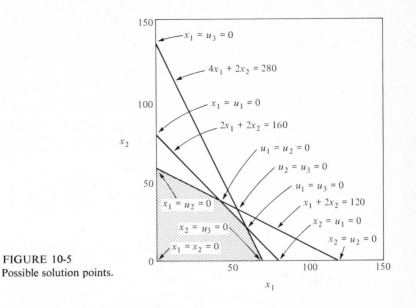

$$x_1 = u_3 = 0$$

$$4x_1 + 2x_2 = 280$$

$$x_1 = u_1 = 0$$

$$2x_1 + 2x_2 = 160$$

$$u_1 = u_2 = 0$$

$$u_2 = u_3 = 0$$

$$u_1 = u_3 = 0$$

$$x_1 = u_2 = 0$$

$$x_1 + 2x_2 = 120$$

$$x_2 = u_1 = 0$$

$$x_2 = u_3 = 0$$

$$x_2 = u_2 = 0$$

$$x_1 = x_2 = 0$$

FIGURE 10-5
Possible solution points.

STEP 3   Subtract row 2 from row 1 *and* multiply row 2 by 2 and add to row 3.

$$1x_1 + 0x_2 + 0u_3 = 40$$

$$0x_1 + 1x_2 + 0u_3 = 40$$

$$0x_1 + 0x_2 + 1u_3 = 40$$

or

$$x_1 = 40$$

$$x_2 = 40$$

$$u_3 = 40$$

If any two of the five variables in the three equations were assumed to be zero, there would be 10 different unique solutions. These are illustrated in Fig. 10-5. However, only those points which border on the shaded area are feasible. All others exceed the restrictions of at least one other constraint. Thus the feasible intersections (solutions) are, in this case, reduced to five, as indicated in Fig. 10-6. In this simple problem it is possible to solve for the variables at all five intersections and then use the one giving the largest value of the objective function. This has been done and the results summarized.

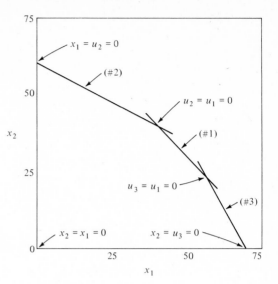

FIGURE 10-6
Feasible intersection points.

POINT a $x_1 = x_2 = 0$:

$$u_1 = 160$$
$$u_2 = 120$$
$$u_3 = 280$$
$$z = 0$$

POINT b $x_1 = u_2 = 0$:

$$x_2 = 60$$
$$u_1 = 40$$
$$u_3 = 160$$
$$z = 1(0) + 60(1.5) = 90$$

POINT c $u_1 = u_2 = 0$:

$$x_1 = 40$$
$$x_2 = 40$$
$$u_3 = 40$$
$$z = 1(40) + 1.5(40) = 100 \qquad \text{maximum}$$

POINT d $u_3 = u_1 = 0$:

$$x_1 = 60$$
$$x_2 = 20$$
$$u_2 = 20$$
$$z = 1(60) + 1.5(20) = 90$$

POINT e $x_2 = u_3 = 0$:

$$x_1 = 70$$
$$u_1 = 20$$
$$u_2 = 50$$
$$z = 1(70) + 1.5(0) = 70 \qquad ////$$

All these cases represent the simultaneous solution of three linear equations and as such could also have been solved by matrix methods. For an example, consider point c again. The three equations were obtained by setting $u_1 = u_2 = 0$.

$$2x_1 + 2x_2 = 160$$
$$x_1 + 2x_2 = 120$$
$$4x_1 + 2x_2 + u_3 = 280$$

In matrix form, this becomes

$$\begin{bmatrix} 2 & 2 & 0 \\ 1 & 2 & 0 \\ 4 & 2 & 1 \end{bmatrix} \begin{bmatrix} x_1 \\ x_2 \\ u_3 \end{bmatrix} = \begin{bmatrix} 160 \\ 120 \\ 280 \end{bmatrix}$$

or

$$A\tilde{x} = \tilde{b}$$

In matrix notation, the solution is

$$A^{-1}A\tilde{x} = A^{-1}\tilde{b}$$
$$I\tilde{x} = A^{-1}\tilde{b}$$
$$\tilde{x} = A^{-1}\tilde{b}$$

Thus A^{-1} must be obtained. This is done as indicated.

$$\begin{bmatrix} 2 & 2 & 0 \\ 1 & 2 & 0 \\ 4 & 2 & 1 \end{bmatrix} \quad \begin{bmatrix} 1 & 0 & 0 \\ 0 & 1 & 0 \\ 0 & 0 & 1 \end{bmatrix}$$

STEP 1 Obtain a 1 in position (1,1) in the left matrix by dividing row 1 by 2.

$$\begin{bmatrix} 1 & 1 & 0 \\ 1 & 2 & 0 \\ 4 & 2 & 1 \end{bmatrix} \qquad \begin{bmatrix} \frac{1}{2} & 0 & 0 \\ 0 & 1 & 0 \\ 0 & 0 & 1 \end{bmatrix}$$

STEP 2 Obtain zeros in rows 2 and 3 of column 1 by subtracting row 1 from row 2 *and* multiplying row 1 by -4 and adding to row 3.

$$\begin{bmatrix} 1 & 1 & 0 \\ 0 & 1 & 0 \\ 0 & -2 & 1 \end{bmatrix} \qquad \begin{bmatrix} \frac{1}{2} & 0 & 0 \\ -\frac{1}{2} & 1 & 0 \\ -2 & 0 & 1 \end{bmatrix}$$

STEP 3 Since position (2,2) in the left matrix is already a 1, obtain zeros elsewhere in column 2 by subtracting row 2 from row 1 *and* multiplying row 2 by 2 and adding to row 3.

$$\begin{bmatrix} 1 & 0 & 0 \\ 0 & 1 & 0 \\ 0 & 0 & 1 \end{bmatrix} \qquad \begin{bmatrix} 1 & -1 & 0 \\ -\frac{1}{2} & 1 & 0 \\ -3 & 2 & 1 \end{bmatrix}$$

This produces an identity matrix on the left and A^{-1} on the right. Using A^{-1}, the vector $\tilde{x}$ can now be determined.

$$\tilde{x} = A^{-1}\tilde{b}$$

$$\begin{bmatrix} x_1 \\ x_2 \\ u_3 \end{bmatrix} = \begin{bmatrix} 1 & -1 & 0 \\ -\frac{1}{2} & 1 & 0 \\ -3 & 2 & 1 \end{bmatrix} \begin{bmatrix} 160 \\ 120 \\ 280 \end{bmatrix}$$

$$= \begin{bmatrix} 40 \\ 40 \\ 40 \end{bmatrix}$$

or

$$x_1 = 40$$
$$x_2 = 40$$
$$u_3 = 40$$

Thus a linear-programming problem can be treated with simple mathematical techniques. The only problem lies in deciding which intersection will not only be feasible but also provide the optimal value of the objective function. As will be shown, the simplex method of solution is simply a combination of matrix algebra with some basic rules to guide the computation to an optimal answer without exceeding any restrictions.

EXAMPLE 10-4   Maximize the following linear-programming problem by solving the equations for all intersection points.

$$z = 3x_1 + 2x_2$$

subject to the constraints

$$x_1 + x_2 \leq 20$$
$$x_1 \leq 15$$
$$x_1 + 3x_2 \leq 45$$
$$-3x_1 + 5x_2 \leq 60$$

First convert to equalities by adding slack variables

$$x_1 + x_2 + u_1 = 20$$
$$x_1 + u_2 = 15$$
$$x_1 + 3x_2 + u_3 = 45$$
$$-3x_1 + 5x_2 + u_4 = 60$$

Now there are six variables, x_1, x_2, u_1, u_2, u_3, and u_4.

Since there are only four equations, at least 6-4 (number of variables less the number of constraints) must be zero.   This gives 15 (6!/4!2!), possible combinations, some of which will not be feasible.   For purposes of illustration, all are tabulated here.

CASE 1   Assume $x_1 = x_2 = 0$.

SOLUTION

$$u_1 = 20 \qquad u_2 = 15 \qquad u_3 = 45 \qquad u_4 = 60$$
$$z = 3(0) + 2(0) = 0$$

CASE 2   Assume $x_1 = u_1 = 0$.

SOLUTION

$$x_2 = 20 \qquad u_2 = 15 \qquad u_3 = -15 \qquad u_4 = -40$$

Not feasible if any values are negative.

CASE 3   Assume $x_1 = u_2 = 0$.   This is not feasible because of the second constraint. $x_1 + u_2 = 15$ if both $= 0$; this is not possible.

CASE 4   Assume $x_1 = u_3 = 0$.

SOLUTION

$$x_2 = 15 \qquad u_1 = 5 \qquad u_2 = 15 \qquad u_4 = -15 \qquad \text{not feasible}$$

CASE 5 $x_1 = u_4 = 0.$

SOLUTION

$$x_2 = 12 \qquad u_1 = 8 \qquad u_2 = 15 \qquad u_3 = 9$$
$$z = 0 + 2(12) = 24$$

CASE 6 $x_2 = u_1 = 0.$

SOLUTION

$$x_1 = 20 \qquad u_2 = -5 \qquad u_3 = 25 \qquad u_4 = 120 \qquad \text{not feasible}$$

CASE 7 $x_2 = u_2 = 0$

SOLUTION

$$x_1 = 15 \qquad u_1 = 5 \qquad u_3 = 30 \qquad u_4 = 105$$
$$z = 3(15) + 2(0) = 45$$

CASE 8 $x_2 = u_3 = 0.$

SOLUTION

$$x_1 = 45 \qquad u_1 = -25 \qquad u_2 = -30 \qquad u_4 = 195 \qquad \text{not feasible}$$

CASE 9 $x_2 = u_4 = 0.$

SOLUTION

$$x_1 = -20 \qquad u_1 = 40 \qquad u_2 = 35 \qquad u_3 = 65 \qquad \text{not feasible}$$

CASE 10 $u_1 = u_2 = 0.$

SOLUTION

$$x_1 = 15 \qquad x_2 = 5 \qquad u_3 = 15 \qquad u_4 = 80$$
$$z = 3(15) + 2(5) = 55 \qquad \text{maximum value of } z$$

CASE 11 $u_1 = u_3 = 0.$

SOLUTION

$$x_1 = 7.5 \qquad x_2 = 12.5 \qquad u_2 = 7.5 \qquad u_4 = 20$$
$$z = 3(7.5) + 2(12.5) = 47.5$$

CASE 12 $u_1 = u_4 = 0.$

SOLUTION

$$x_1 = 5 \qquad x_2 = 15 \qquad u_2 = 10 \qquad u_3 = -5 \qquad \text{not feasible}$$

CASE 13 $u_2 = u_3 = 0.$

SOLUTION

$$x_1 = 15 \qquad x_2 = 10 \qquad u_1 = -5 \qquad u_4 = 55 \qquad \text{not feasible}$$

CASE 14 $u_2 = u_4 = 0.$

SOLUTION

$$x_1 = 15 \qquad x_2 = 21 \qquad u_1 = -16 \qquad u_3 = -33 \qquad \text{not feasible}$$

CASE 15 $u_3 = u_4 = 0.$

SOLUTION

$$x_1 = 3\tfrac{3}{14} \qquad x_2 = 13\tfrac{13}{14} \qquad u_1 = 2\tfrac{12}{14} \qquad u_2 = 11\tfrac{11}{14}$$
$$z = 3(3\tfrac{3}{14}) + 2(13\tfrac{13}{14}) = 37.5$$

The maximum feasible solution of $x_1 = 15$, $x_2 = 5$, $z = 55$ may be verified by the graphical solution given in Fig. 10-4.   ////

SIMPLEX COMPUTATION (MAXIMIZATION)

The simplex method of linear programming uses the basic concepts of matrix algebra to solve for the intersection of two or more lines or planes.   It begins at some feasible solution, one which satisfies all restrictions, and successively obtains solutions at intersections which offer better values in the objective function.   Finally this method of solution provides an indicator which determines when an optimum solution has been reached.

A matrix is used to present the data for calculation.   Although several forms are presented in the literature (Refs. 2 and 5), the one used in this book has been selected for its close relationship to the normal matrix methods.   Within the matrix, one column is provided for each real variable (x's) and one for each slack variable

(u's). One row is provided for each constraint. Using the three equations in the example problems that were obtained by the introduction of slack variables,

$$(1) \qquad 2x_1 + 2x_2 + u_1 = 160$$

$$(2) \qquad x_1 + 2x_2 + u_2 = 120$$

$$(3) \qquad 4x_1 + 2x_2 + u_3 = 280$$

gives the matrix

Matrix 1a

$$
\begin{array}{ccccc}
x_1 & x_2 & u_1 & u_2 & u_3 & & b
\end{array}
$$

$$
\left[
\begin{array}{ccccc|c}
2 & 2 & 1 & 0 & 0 & 160 \\
1 & 2 & 0 & 1 & 0 & 120 \\
4 & 2 & 0 & 0 & 1 & 280 \\
\hline
\end{array}
\right]
$$

As can be observed, these values were simply inserted from the three constraint equations (1) to (3). The vertical separation between the last variable column (u_3) and the constant column (b) can be considered to represent an equality sign. Thus, within the interior of the matrix, any row may be read as an equation. For example, row 2 may be read

$$x_1 + 2x_2 + u_2 = 120$$

As previously indicated, when there are n variables [in this case five (x_1, x_2, u_1, u_2, and u_3)] and only m equations [here three (row 1, row 2 and row 3)], it is necessary to assume that $n - m$ ($5 - 3 = 2$) of the variables are equal to zero in order to reach a solution point. For a starting point that satisfies all three constraints, assume[1] $x_1 = x_2 = 0$. This is the first feasible solution. In this case, from matrix 1a, the equations represented by rows become

$$1u_1 = 160$$

$$1u_2 = 120$$

$$1u_3 = 280$$

Notice that these three variables in the matrix make up an identity matrix. The variables represented by the columns which compose this identity matrix are said to be

---

[1] A later section of this chapter will discuss means of obtaining a feasible solution when the zero point is not satisfactory.

in solution while all others are zero.   The variables in solution are also often called *basic variables* while those not in solution, i.e., equal to zero, are called *nonbasic* variables.

The simplex procedure next solves for another intersection of the constraint lines (planes) which provides a better value for the objective function; in this case it would increase the objective function.   In terms of matrix algebra, this is done by assuming one of the basic (nonzero) variables to be zero and solving the new set of equations for the intersection that set of equations represents.   To do this in a systematic manner which always improves the value of the objective function requires the addition of one more row to the matrix.   This row (the bottom row) is simply the coefficients of the objective function itself, as indicated in matrix 1*b*.

$$\textit{Matrix 1b}$$

$$
\begin{array}{c}
\begin{array}{cccccc} x_1 & x_2 & u_1 & u_2 & u_3 & b \end{array} \\
\begin{array}{c}(1)\\(2)\\(3)\\{}\\{}\end{array}
\left[
\begin{array}{ccccc|c}
2 & 2 & 1 & 0 & 0 & 160 \\
1 & 2 & 0 & 1 & 0 & 120 \\
4 & 2 & 0 & 0 & 1 & 280 \\
\hline
1 & 1.5 & 0 & 0 & 0 & 0
\end{array}
\right]
\end{array}
$$

If the objective function were written to include all five variables, it would be

$$z = 1x_1 + 1.5x_2 + 0u_1 + 0u_2 + 0u_3 = 0 \qquad (10\text{-}7)$$

as indicated in matrix 1*b*.   Note that for the assumed values of $x_1 = 0$ and $x_2 = 0$ z is equal to zero.

Actually, in a linear equation, these coefficients are the partial derivatives of the function z.

$$\frac{\partial z}{\partial x_1} = 1 \qquad \frac{\partial z}{\partial u_1} = 0 \qquad \frac{\partial z}{\partial u_3} = 0$$

$$\frac{\partial z}{\partial x_2} = 1.5 \qquad \frac{\partial z}{\partial u_2} = 0$$

Thus these coefficients represent the slope of the objective function with respect to each of the variables.   A positive slope indicates an increasing value of the function z with an increase in the variable, as in any calculus problem.

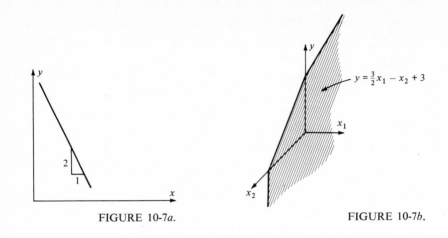

FIGURE 10-7a.   FIGURE 10-7b.

EXAMPLE 10-5   Figure 10-7a shows

$$y = 5 - 2x$$

graphically.

Differentiating with respect to x gives

$$\frac{dy}{dx} = -2$$

This indicates that the value of y will *decrease* 2 units in value for each unit increase in x. Graphically, it says that the slope of the line is -2 with respect to x.

Consider the three-variable function

$$y = \tfrac{3}{2}x_1 - x_2 + 3$$

This is displayed in Fig. 10-7b. Taking partial-differentials with respect to x_1 and x_2 gives

$$\frac{\partial y}{\partial x_1} = \frac{3}{2} \qquad \frac{\partial y}{\partial x_2} = -1$$

This indicates that a unit increase in x_1 will increase the value of y by $\tfrac{3}{2}$ units while a unit increase in x_2 will decrease the value of y by -1 unit (negative slope).   ////

In this example, the coefficients in the z row of matrix $1b$ indicate that an increase in x_2 of 1 unit will increase z by 1.5 units. Similarly, increasing $u_1, u_2,$ or u_3 will cause no increase in z because their respective partial differentials are zero. This is as expected since they have no value in the objective function. Thus it appears most profitable to increase the value of x_2, that is, assume $x_2 \neq 0$. The next decision is which of the present variables now in solution (basic variables) should be assumed equal to 0 to allow x_2 to have a nonzero value.

This step requires understanding exactly what the slack variables and the constants (b column) represent. The b column was first obtained from the capacity limits for each department. Thus it represents the total resources available for assignment. This capacity cannot reach a negative value; i.e., interpreted physically, one cannot assign more resources (capacity) than are available. The slack variables represent the difference between what has been assigned and what remains to be assigned, hence the term slack variable. When a slack variable is zero, all the resource originally defined by that constraint has been assigned. Graphically this is interpreted by saying that the solution is somewhere on the boundary line.

In this problem, the constraints represent departmental capacity. Thus department 1 has 160 units of capacity, department 2 has 120 units of capacity, and department 3 has 280 units of capacity. Since the first feasible solution is at $x_1 = x_2 = 0$, no production at all, obviously the slack is equal to the maximum capacity.

Since x_2 has been selected as the variable to increase, the question is how far to increase it. It can be increased until the ability to produce is exceeded in one department, i.e., all the slack is gone in one department. Referring to the original problem, note that each unit of x_2 requires 2 man-hours in departments 1, 2, and 3. This can also be seen from the constraint equations represented in matrix 1b.

$$(1) \qquad 2x_1 + 2x_2 + u_1 = 160$$

$$(2) \qquad x_1 + 2x_2 + u_2 = 120$$

$$(3) \qquad 4x_1 + 2x_2 + u_3 = 280$$

In department 1, represented by row 1, x_2 can be increased to a maximum of $160/a_{12} = 80$ units. Algebraically, this is obtained from the equation in row 1.

$$2x_1 + 2x_2 + u_1 = 160$$

$$x_1 = 0 \qquad \text{assumed}$$

If u_1 is decreased to its minimum value (zero), how large can x_2 be?

$$2(0) + 2(x_2) + 0 = 160$$

$$x_2 = 160/2 = 80 \text{ units} \qquad \text{maximum for row 1}$$

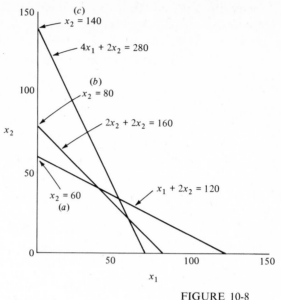

FIGURE 10-8
Limiting constraints.

Similarly for (2) and (3)

$$(2) \qquad x_1 + 2x_2 + u_2 = 120$$

$$0 + 2x_2 + \quad 0 = 120 \qquad \text{if } u_2 = 0 \text{ and } x_1 = 0$$

$$x_2 = \tfrac{120}{2} = 60 \text{ units} \qquad \text{maximum for row 2}$$

$$(3) \qquad 4x_1 + 2x_2 + u_3 = 280$$

$$4(0) + 2x_2 + \quad 0 = 280 \qquad \text{if } u_3 = 0 \text{ and } x_1 = 0$$

$$x_2 = \tfrac{280}{2} = 140 \text{ units} \qquad \text{maximum for row 3}$$

Once the maximum for any row (department) is reached, x_2 cannot be increased further without becoming infeasible. Thus the first maximum to be reached defines the limiting value for x_2; here from (2) $x_2 = 60$ is the limit. At this point u_2 is now zero because all slack is gone.

This effect can also be shown graphically. Figure 10-8 indicates the three values just computed. Points a, b, and c indicate the maximum allowable values for x_2 due to the respective capacities of the three departments. Note that any value of x_2 above 60 will exceed the boundary line indicated by the restriction $x_1 + 2x_2 = 120$.

The final step in this iteration calculates the values for the intersection where $x_1 = u_2 = 0$. Once this is done, the matrix will be changed with x_2, u_1, and u_3 composing the identity matrix, i.e., being in solution. Computation can be done by performing row operations on the matrix to make the x_2 column a member of the identity matrix, with a 1 in the row represented by the limiting constraint (2).

Begin by multiplying row 2 by $\frac{1}{2}$ to make a 1 entry in the *key* row (the limiting constraint) and the *key* column (the new variable $\neq 0$, x_2).

Matrix 2a

x_1	x_2	u_1	u_2	u_3	b
2	2	1	0	0	160
$\frac{1}{2}$	1	0	$\frac{1}{2}$	0	60
4	1	0	0	1	280
1	1.5	0	0	0	0

Perform row operations to make *all* other entries in the key column (x_2) zero. Multiply row 2 by -2 and add to row 1.

Matrix 2b

x_1	x_2	u_1	u_2	u_3	b
1	0	1	-1	0	40
$\frac{1}{2}$	1	0	$\frac{1}{2}$	0	60
4	2	0	0	1	280
1	1.5	0	0	0	0

Multiply row 2 by -2 and add to row 3.

Matrix 2c

x_1	x_2	u_1	u_2	u_3	b
1	0	1	-1	0	40
$\frac{1}{2}$	1	0	$\frac{1}{2}$	0	60
3	0	0	-1	1	160
1	1.5	0	0	0	0

Multiply row 2 by -1.5 and add to the z row, completing this iteration.

Matrix 2d

x_1	x_2	u_1	u_2	u_3	b
1	0	1	-1	0	40
$\frac{1}{2}$	1	0	$\frac{1}{2}$	0	60
3	0	0	-1	1	160
$\frac{1}{4}$	0	0	$-\frac{3}{4}$	0	-90

Note in matrix 2*d*, that if columns x_2 and u_2 were interchanged, the identity maxtrix would still exist.   This is not normally done.   In the process just completed, matrix-inversion manipulations were used to solve for a new nonzero variable x_2. The results obtained are the same as would have be achieved by basic matrix inversion used to solve simultaneous linear equations.   Matrix 2*d* still consists of equations represented by rows with basic (nonzero) variables and nonbasic (zero) variables.   It is read as follows: nonbasic variables (zero-valued):

$$x_1 = 0$$
$$u_2 = 0$$
not represented in the identity matrix

Basic variables (non-zero-valued):

$$u_1 = 40 \qquad \text{from } 1\overset{0}{\cancel{x_1}} + 0x_2 + u_1 - 1\overset{0}{\cancel{u_2}} + 0u_3 = 40$$

$$x_2 = 60 \qquad \text{from } \tfrac{1}{2}\overset{0}{\cancel{x_1}} + x_2 + 0u_1 + \tfrac{1}{2}\overset{0}{\cancel{u_2}} + 0u_3 = 60$$

$$u_3 = 160 \qquad \text{from } 3\overset{0}{\cancel{x_1}} + 0x_2 + 0u_1 - 1\overset{0}{\cancel{u_2}} + u_3 = 160$$

It can easily be shown that the previous procedure provides the same answer as that obtained by a basic matrix solution.

If $x_1 = u_2 = 0$, then

$$u_1 + 2x_2 + 0u_3 = 160$$
$$0u_1 + 2x_2 + 0u_3 = 120$$
$$0u_1 + 2x_2 + u_3 = 280$$

Set up for matrix inversion, this becomes

$$\begin{bmatrix} 1 & 2 & 0 \\ 0 & 2 & 0 \\ 0 & 2 & 1 \end{bmatrix} \quad \begin{bmatrix} 1 & 0 & 0 \\ 0 & 1 & 0 \\ 0 & 0 & 1 \end{bmatrix}$$

Multiply row 2 by $\tfrac{1}{2}$:

$$\begin{bmatrix} 1 & 2 & 0 \\ 0 & 1 & 0 \\ 0 & 2 & 1 \end{bmatrix} \quad \begin{bmatrix} 1 & 0 & 0 \\ 0 & \tfrac{1}{2} & 0 \\ 0 & 0 & 1 \end{bmatrix}$$

Multiply row 2 by -2 and add to row 1 and row 3:

$$\begin{bmatrix} 1 & 0 & 0 \\ 0 & 1 & 0 \\ 0 & 0 & 1 \end{bmatrix} \quad \begin{bmatrix} 1 & -1 & 0 \\ 0 & \tfrac{1}{2} & 0 \\ 0 & -1 & 1 \end{bmatrix}$$

Solve for the values of u_1, x_2 and u_3:

$$\tilde{x} = A^{-1}\tilde{b}$$

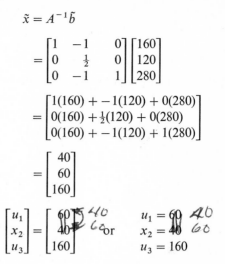

$$= \begin{bmatrix} 1 & -1 & 0 \\ 0 & \frac{1}{2} & 0 \\ 0 & -1 & 1 \end{bmatrix} \begin{bmatrix} 160 \\ 120 \\ 280 \end{bmatrix}$$

$$= \begin{bmatrix} 1(160) + -1(120) + 0(280) \\ 0(160) + \frac{1}{2}(120) + 0(280) \\ 0(160) + -1(120) + 1(280) \end{bmatrix}$$

$$= \begin{bmatrix} 40 \\ 60 \\ 160 \end{bmatrix}$$

$$\begin{bmatrix} u_1 \\ x_2 \\ u_3 \end{bmatrix} = \begin{bmatrix} 60 \\ 40 \\ 160 \end{bmatrix} \quad \text{or} \quad \begin{array}{l} u_1 = 60 \\ x_2 = 40 \\ u_3 = 160 \end{array}$$

Note that the inverse A^{-1} is the same as columns u_1, u_2, and u_3 (the original identity matrix) in matrix 2d.

Now refer to the last row, the z row, and the values below the interior of the matrix. The coefficients still represent the slopes of the objective function with respect to the variables. Below x_1 is the value $\frac{1}{4}$ indicating a slope of $\frac{1}{4}$; that is, an increase in x_1 of 1 unit will increase the function z by $\frac{1}{4}$ unit. Below u_2 the coefficient is $-\frac{3}{4}$, indicating that a unit increase in that variable will decrease z by $\frac{3}{4}$ units. This is logical since slack in department B, as represented by u_2, could be obtained only by decreasing x_2 and thus the production of a profitable product. All other coefficients on the left side are zero, indicating that no gain can be obtained by increasing these variables, i.e., that their limit has been reached. Thus it is profitable to increase x_1 since it is the only variable which will cause an increase in z. Column x_1 then becomes the key column in the next iteration. The -90 in the b column represents the value of z for the present solution. Actually in this case the sign must be reversed for maximization problems. This can be verified by substituting the present solution values into the objective function.

$$z = 1x_1 + 1.5x_2 + 0u_1 + 0u_2 + 0u_3$$

$$= 1(0) + 1.5(60) + 0(40) + 0 + 0(160)$$

$$= 90$$

What this really means is that z has a negative cost of 90 units, thus a profit of 90.

Graphically this solution is represented in Fig. 10-9. This iteration has moved from the first feasible solution of $x_1 = x_2 = 0$ to an improved solution of $x_1 = 0$,

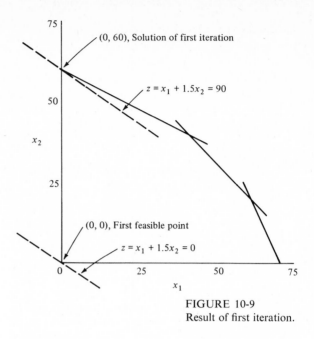

FIGURE 10-9
Result of first iteration.

$x_2 = 60$.   Note that the solution has moved from one intersection, the x_1 and x_2 axis, to the next feasible intersection, $x_1 = 0$ and $x_1 + 2x_2 = 120$.

It has already been determined that increasing x_1 will increase z since only x_1 has a positive slope, as indicated in the bottom row of matrix $2d$.   Column x_1 is then the key column.   Next determine how much x_1 can be increased before reaching a constraint.

Reading the rows as equations and letting all other variables go to zero, we get

$$(1) \quad 1x_1 + 0\overset{0}{x_2} + 1\overset{0}{\mu_1} - 1\overset{0}{\mu_2} + 0\overset{0}{\mu_3} = 40$$

$$(2) \quad \tfrac{1}{2}x_1 + 1\overset{0}{x_2} + 0\overset{0}{\mu_1} + \tfrac{1}{2}\overset{0}{\mu_2} + 0\overset{0}{\mu_3} = 60$$

$$(3) \quad 3x_1 + 0\overset{0}{x_2} + 0\overset{0}{\mu_1} - 1\overset{0}{\mu_2} + 1\overset{0}{\mu_3} = 160$$

Thus the present limits of x_1 for each constraint become

$$(1) \quad x_1 = \tfrac{40}{1} = 40$$

$$(2) \quad x_1 = \frac{60}{\tfrac{1}{2}} = 120$$

$$(3) \quad x_1 = \tfrac{160}{3} = 53\tfrac{1}{3}$$

Of these, row 1 has the smallest value of x_1 allowable.   Thus x_1 can be increased to a maximum of 40, and row 1 becomes the new key row.

Using the same procedure as before, begin by dividing row 1 by the coefficient of x_1 in the key row, in this case a 1.   Here there is no change in the matrix.

Matrix 3a

x_1	x_2	u_1	u_2	u_3	b
1	0	1	-1	0	40
$\frac{1}{2}$	1	0	$\frac{1}{2}$	0	60
3	0	0	-1	1	160
$\frac{1}{4}$	0	0	$-\frac{3}{4}$	0	-90

Next, multiply row 1, the key row, by $-\frac{1}{2}$ and add to row 2 to obtain a zero in the next position in the key column.

Matrix 3b

x_1	x_2	u_1	u_2	u_3	b
1	0	1	-1	0	40
0	1	$-\frac{1}{2}$	1	0	40
3	0	0	-1	1	160
$\frac{1}{4}$	0	0	$-\frac{3}{4}$	0	-90

Multiply row 1 by -3 and add to row 3.

Matrix 3c

x_1	x_2	u_1	u_2	u_3	b
1	0	1	-1	0	40
0	1	$-\frac{1}{2}$	1	0	40
0	0	-3	2	1	40
$\frac{1}{4}$	0	0	$-\frac{3}{4}$	0	-90

Finally, multiply row 1 by $-\frac{1}{4}$ and add to the z row to obtain all zeros in the key column except for the 1 in the key row.

Matrix 3d

x_1	x_2	u_1	u_2	u_3	b
1	0	1	-1	0	40
0	1	$-\frac{1}{2}$	1	0	40
0	0	-3	2	1	40
0	0	$-\frac{1}{4}$	$-\frac{1}{2}$	0	-100

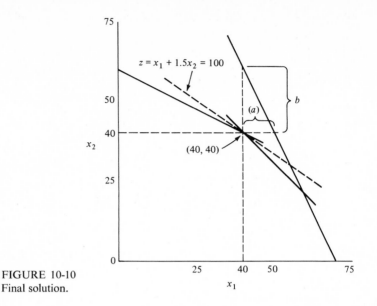

FIGURE 10-10
Final solution.

Matrix 3*d* indicates that an optimal solution has been reached because the objective function cannot be further increased by increasing any of the five variables. The z row indicates that neither x_1, x_2, nor u_3 can be increased (all zero coefficients), and increasing u_1 or u_2 will cause a decrease in z due to the negative slopes.   In this solution, $x_1 = 40$ and $x_2 = 40$.   The final value of the objective function is

$$z = x_1 + 1.5x_2 = 40 + 1.5(40) = 100$$

This is illustrated in Fig. 10-10.

Inspection of this figure shows that no other feasible solution will provide as large a value for the objective function z.   The final value of $u_3 = 40$ indicates that there are 40 units of capacity (man-hours) in department C that are not completely used. This is illustrated in Fig. 10-10 by the fact that the solution point is inside the constraint line representing the maximum capacity of department C.   Note in Fig. 10-10 that 10 more units of x_1 could be made before the constraint line for department C would be reached, distance a.   Since it takes 4 hours of time in department C to make 1 unit of x_1, this represents 4×10 or 40 unused man-hours.   Similarly, the solution point is 20 units of x_2 below the department C constraint line.   As before, this also represents $2 \times 20 = 40$ man-hours of unused production capacity.

The same answer could have been obtained using standard matrix algebra solution methods.   Since this solution is at the intersection of the first two constraints, both u_1 and u_2 are zero.   Thus the solution is obtained from the three constraint equations:

$$2x_1 + 2x_2 + 0u_3 = 160$$
$$x_1 + 2x_2 + 0u_3 = 120$$
$$4x_1 + 2x_2 + u_3 = 280$$

In matrix form these are

$$\begin{bmatrix} 2 & 2 & 0 \\ 1 & 2 & 0 \\ 4 & 2 & 1 \end{bmatrix} \begin{bmatrix} x_1 \\ x_2 \\ u_3 \end{bmatrix} = \begin{bmatrix} 160 \\ 120 \\ 280 \end{bmatrix}$$

or
$$A\tilde{x} = \tilde{b}$$

The inverse, A^{-1}, must now be found.

$$\begin{bmatrix} 2 & 2 & 0 \\ 1 & 2 & 0 \\ 4 & 2 & 1 \end{bmatrix} \qquad \begin{bmatrix} 1 & 0 & 0 \\ 0 & 1 & 0 \\ 0 & 0 & 1 \end{bmatrix}$$

Multiply row 1 by $\frac{1}{2}$.

$$\begin{bmatrix} 1 & 1 & 0 \\ 1 & 2 & 0 \\ 4 & 2 & 1 \end{bmatrix} \qquad \begin{bmatrix} \frac{1}{2} & 0 & 0 \\ 0 & 1 & 0 \\ 0 & 0 & 1 \end{bmatrix}$$

Combining some steps, next subtract row 1 from row 2 and then multiply row 1 by -4 and add to row 3.

$$\begin{bmatrix} 1 & 1 & 0 \\ 0 & 1 & 0 \\ 0 & -2 & 1 \end{bmatrix} \qquad \begin{bmatrix} \frac{1}{2} & 0 & 0 \\ -\frac{1}{2} & 1 & 0 \\ -2 & 0 & 1 \end{bmatrix}$$

Subtract row 2 from row 1, then multiply row 2 by 2 and add to row 3.

$$\begin{bmatrix} 1 & 0 & 0 \\ 0 & 1 & 0 \\ 0 & 0 & 1 \end{bmatrix} \qquad \begin{bmatrix} 1 & -1 & 0 \\ -\frac{1}{2} & 1 & 0 \\ -3 & 2 & 1 \end{bmatrix}$$

Thus

$$A^{-1} = \begin{bmatrix} 1 & -1 & 0 \\ -\frac{1}{2} & 1 & 0 \\ -3 & 2 & 1 \end{bmatrix}$$

Note that this is the same matrix as that expressed in the final solution matrix 3d under columns u_1, u_2, and u_3. Solving for x_1, x_2 and u_3 gives

$$\tilde{x} = \begin{bmatrix} 1 & -1 & 0 \\ -\frac{1}{2} & 1 & 0 \\ -3 & 2 & 1 \end{bmatrix} \begin{bmatrix} 160 \\ 120 \\ 280 \end{bmatrix}$$

$$= \begin{bmatrix} 160(1) + 120(-1) + 280(0) \\ 160(-\frac{1}{2}) + 120(1) + 280(0) \\ 160(-3) + 120(2) + 280(1) \end{bmatrix}$$

$$\begin{bmatrix} x_1 \\ x_2 \\ u_3 \end{bmatrix} = \begin{bmatrix} 40 \\ 40 \\ 40 \end{bmatrix} \qquad \text{the } b \text{ column in matrix } 3d$$

The steps required to simplex can be summarized into a procedural format once the reasoning is understood. This is done in the following paragraphs and illustrated by working another rather simple linear-programming maximization problem.

STEP 1   Define the objective to be maximized in terms of the decision variables

$$z = 3x_1 + 2x_2 + 6x_3$$

STEP 2   Define the problem limitations in terms of constraint inequalities using the decision variables.

$$6x_1 + 3x_2 - 4x_3 \leq 60$$
$$2x_1 - 4x_2 + 4x_3 \leq 40$$
$$3x_1 + 3x_2 + 3x_3 \leq 60$$

STEP 3   Convert the inequalities to equalities by adding slack variables.

$$6x_1 + 3x_2 - 4x_3 + u_1 = 60$$
$$2x_1 - 4x_2 + 4x_3 + u_2 = 40$$
$$3x_1 + 3x_2 + 3x_3 + u_3 = 60$$

STEP 4   Put the constraint equations and objective function in matrix form.

x_1	x_2	x_3	u_1	u_2	u_3	b
6	3	-4	1	0	0	60
2	-4	4	0	1	0	40
3	3	3	0	0	1	60
3	2	6	0	0	0	0

STEP 5   Select the key column, the largest positive value (slope) in the z row; the x_3 column has a value of 6.

STEP 6   Select the key row, i.e., the constraint limit reached first.

$$(1) \qquad -4x_3 = 60$$

$$x_3 = -\tfrac{60}{4}$$

No constraint at all; x_3 is limited only on the negative side, and negative values are not allowed.

$$(2) \qquad 4x_3 = 40$$

$$x_3 = \tfrac{40}{4} = 10$$

$$(3) \qquad 3x_3 = 60$$

$$x_3 = \tfrac{60}{3} = 20$$

Thus the first constraint limit reached by increasing x_3 is 10, as it hits the constraint represented in row 2.

STEP 7   Iterate using row manipulations to make column x_3 a part of the identity matrix with the 1 in the key row, row 2.   Divide the key row by the coefficient in the key row, here a 4.

	x_1	x_2	x_3	u_1	u_2	u_3	b	
	6	3	-4	1	0	0	60	
	$\frac{1}{2}$	-1	1	0	$\frac{1}{4}$	0	10	key row
	3	3	3	0	0	1	60	
	3	2	6	0	0	0	0	

key column

Perform row operations using the key row (2) to make all other entries in the key column zero.

	x_1	x_2	x_3	u_1	u_2	u_3	b
	8	-1	0	1	1	0	100
	$\frac{1}{2}$	-1	1	0	$\frac{1}{4}$	0	10
	$\frac{3}{2}$	6	0	0	$-\frac{3}{4}$	1	30
	0	8	0	0	$-\frac{3}{2}$	0	-60

STEP 8   Repeat step 7 until all values in the z row are nonpositive (no positive slopes)

$$\text{Key column} = x_2$$

$$\text{Key row} = 3$$

since row 1 and row 2 have negative values in the key column.   Divide the key row by 6.

$$
\begin{array}{c c c c c c c}
x_1 & x_2 & x_3 & u_1 & u_2 & u_3 & b \\
\end{array}
$$

$$
\begin{bmatrix}
8 & -1 & 0 & 1 & 1 & 0 & 100 \\
\frac{1}{2} & -1 & 1 & 0 & \frac{1}{4} & 0 & 10 \\
\frac{1}{4} & 1 & 0 & 0 & -\frac{1}{8} & \frac{1}{6} & 5 \\
\hline
0 & 8 & 0 & 0 & -\frac{3}{2} & 0 & -60 \\
\end{bmatrix}
$$

Perform row operations until all other rows have zero value in the key column.

$$
\begin{array}{c c c c c c c}
x_1 & x_2 & x_3 & u_1 & u_2 & u_3 & b \\
\end{array}
$$

$$
\begin{bmatrix}
8\frac{1}{4} & 0 & 0 & 1 & \frac{7}{8} & \frac{1}{6} & 105 \\
\frac{3}{4} & 0 & 1 & 0 & \frac{1}{8} & \frac{1}{6} & 15 \\
\frac{1}{4} & 1 & 0 & 0 & -\frac{1}{8} & \frac{1}{6} & 5 \\
\hline
-2 & 0 & 0 & 0 & -\frac{1}{2} & -\frac{4}{3} & -100 \\
\end{bmatrix}
\quad
\begin{array}{l}
\text{value of } u_1 \\
\text{value of } x_3 \\
\text{value of } x_2 \\
\end{array}
$$

At this point, all values in the z row are nonpositive; thus increasing any value will decrease or at least not improve the objective function z since all the slopes are zero or negative.   Thus the objective function has been maximized subject to the three constraints.

SOLUTION

$$x_1 = 0 \quad x_2 = 5 \quad x_3 = 15 \quad u_1 = 105 \quad u_2 = 0 \quad u_3 = 0$$

Since only x_2, x_3, and u_1 are columns in the identity matrix, all other variables are zero.   Thus the three values of x_2, x_3, and u_1 can be read straight from the matrix as indicated.   ////

OTHER CONSTRAINT FORMS

The restrictions of a problem are not always of the less-than-or-equal form.   Often it is necessary to stipulate that certain conditions must be greater than some assigned value.   For example, suppose that in the basic example used in this chapter a prior sales commitment had required a product 2 production rate of at least 45 units/week. Then the best solution would be to determine the proper product mix of 1 and 2 when at least 45 units/week of product 2 are made.   This new constraint can be expressed algebraically and added to the other constraints previously defined:

$$x_2 \geq 45 \qquad (10\text{-}8)$$

This new constraint is presented graphically in Fig. 10-11.

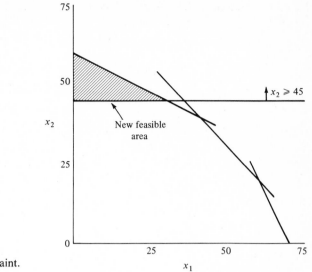

FIGURE 10-11
The effect of a greater-than constraint.

The addition of this new constraint has two major effects: (1) it reduces the size of the feasible or acceptable field as depicted in Fig. 10-10; this is not a major problem in itself as long as any feasible solution exists at all; (2) it requires a modification of the basic method of solution.   The new constraint has cut off the (0,0) point in Fig. 10-11. Thus the initial solution previously used, i.e., all decision variables are zero, is not feasible.   Since the simplex algorithm proceeds from one feasible (acceptable) solution to an improved solution, a new initial starting place must be obtained.   In terms of matrix algebra, an identity matrix must always exist in each matrix.   There are several procedures for handling this problem.

One procedure uses an additional variable called an *artificial variable*.   If the previous procedure is used to convert the inequality to an equality, the slack variable must be added on the other side of the inequality.

$$x_2 = 45 + u_4$$

$$x_2 - u_4 = 45$$

This gives

Matrix 4a

x_1	x_2	u_1	u_2	u_3	u_4	b
2	2	1	0	0	0	160
1	2	0	1	0	0	120
4	2	0	0	1	0	280
0	1	0	0	0	-1	45
1	1.5	0	0	0	0	0

In this case, the square matrix composed of the columns u_1, u_2, u_3, and u_4 is not an identity matrix since the u_4 column has a -1 instead of a 1. This problem is simply solved by adding an additional variable to the new constraint:

$$x_2 - u_4 + a_1 = 45 \qquad (10\text{-}9)$$

This new variable a_1 is the artificial variable. It is not defined in terms of slack but is simply a temporary variable which will be used to arrive at a feasible solution. Once there, it can be discarded and the regular simplex algorithm used. When the modified constraint is inserted, the new matrix is

Matrix 4b

x_1	x_2	u_1	u_2	u_3	u_4	a_1	b
2	2	1	0	0	0	0	160
1	2	0	1	0	0	0	120
4	2	0	0	1	0	0	280
0	1	0	0	0	-1	1	45
1	1.5	0	0	0	0	0	0

Now an identity matrix exists in terms of columns u_1, u_2, u_3, and a_1. The values of the variables these columns represent can be read as before.

$$u_1 = 160 \qquad u_2 = 120 \qquad u_3 = 280 \qquad a_1 = 45$$

All other variables have zero value at this time.

Since a_1 is simply an additional variable which has no physical meaning in this problem, it is not really wanted. Thus if a solution can be obtained which satisfies all the constraints and in which $a_1 = 0$, this variable can be discarded and the regular simplex algorithm used.

If the simplex algorithm can be used to maximize an objective function, obviously it can be used (with only a slight modification) to minimize some objective function. This will be the logic used to find a feasible solution where a_1 also equals 0. An objective function a_1 will be defined and minimized. When this function is minimized to the point where $a_1 = 0$, a feasible solution will have been obtained with a_1 also zero. Thus this variable can be discarded.

The fourth constraint has been previously defined by

$$x_2 - u_4 + a_1 = 45 \qquad (10\text{-}10)$$

Solving this for a_1 gives

$$a_1 = -x_2 + u_4 + 45 \qquad (10\text{-}11)$$

This then is the objective function a_1 to be minimized just as function z was maximized in previous examples. This function is added to the matrix as an additional row, remembering that the vertical line between the b column and the other columns represents an equals sign.

Matrix 4c

	x_1	x_2	u_1	u_2	u_3	u_4	a_1	b
1	2	2	1	0	0	0	0	160
2	1	2	0	1	0	0	0	120
3	4	2	0	0	1	0	0	280
4	0	1	0	0	0	-1	1	45
z	1	1.5	0	0	0	0	0	0
a_1	0	-1	0	0	0	1	0	-45

Note that in the last row of matrix 4c the coefficient of x_2 is -1 and of u_4 is 1; in the b column the value is -45. Since a_1 was found to be

$$a_1 = -x_2 + u_4 + 45 \qquad (10\text{-}11)$$

the sign on the constant was changed as it was registered on the other side of the equality line in the matrix. The fact that a_1 has a zero coefficient in the last row is correct since it does not appear in the function to be minimized; it *is* the value to be maximized in the previous examples.

The procedure to be used now is almost the same as that used previously. Only details will differ: (1) We want to minimize the function represented by the last row rather than the z row so that the former can be used as a basis for selecting the key column. Later this will be discarded and we shall proceed as before, but until $a_1 = 0$, the a_1 row will govern the key-column selection. (2) Since it is desired to *minimize* instead of maximize at this point, the logic must be slightly altered. The coefficients in the a_1 row still represent slopes or rates of change of a_1 for a unit change in the variable. Now a column representing a variable which *decreases* the function should be selected. Thus, the most negative value in the last row would indicate the greatest decrease in a_1 for a unit increase in a variable. Once all values are zero or positive, this stage is completed since it is no longer possible to decrease a_1 by increasing the values of the variables. In this case, the most negative value in the a_1 row is -1 in the x_2 column. Select this column for the key column and proceed as before.

If x_2 is the key column, the key row is that one which limits the increase of x_2.

$$(1) \qquad x_2 = \tfrac{160}{2} = 80$$

$$(2) \qquad x_2 = \tfrac{120}{2} = 60$$

$$(3) \qquad x_2 = \tfrac{280}{2} = 140$$

$$(4) \qquad x_2 = \tfrac{45}{1} = 45$$

This is the limiting positive value of x_2. Thus row 4 is the key row. Now perform row operations to obtain a 1 in row 4, column x_2 and zeros in *all* other rows of column x_2.

Matrix 4d   First Solution

	x_1	x_2	u_1	u_2	u_3	u_4	a_1	b	
(1)	2	0	1	0	0	$+2$	-2	70	Multiply row 4 by -2 and add to row 1
(2)	1	0	0	1	0	2	-2	30	Multiply row 4 by -2 and add to row 2
(3)	4	0	0	0	1	2	-2	190	Multiply row 4 by -2 and add to row 3
(4)	0	1	0	0	0	-1	1	45	x_2 value already 1
z	1	0	0	0	0	1.5	-1.5	-67.5	Multiply row 4 by -1.5 and add to z row
(a_1)	0	0	0	0	0	0	1	0	Add 4 to a_1 row

Inspect the a_1 row to find the most negative value. Since there are none, the function a_1 has been minimized. As an additional check, the value of a_1 indicated in the b column should be zero, indicating that a_1 now has a zero value. At this point a feasible solution has been found where $a_1 = 0$. If some negative values had been found in the a_1 row, the problem would have been iterated again until all negative values were gone. Since a feasible solution has been obtained where $a_1 = 0$, this part of the problem is of no use and should be discarded; i.e., discard column a_1 and row a_1 to form

Matrix 4e

	x_1	x_2	u_1	u_2	u_3	u_4	b
1	2	0	1	0	0	2	70
2	1	0	0	1	0	2	30
3	4	0	0	0	1	2	190
4	0	1	0	0	0	-1	45
z	1	0	0	0	0	1.5	-67.5

In this case, the new feasible solution is

$$x_1 = u_4 = 0 \qquad x_2 = 45$$
$$u_1 = 70 \qquad u_2 = 30 \qquad u_3 = 190$$

and the value of z is 67.5. This solution is represented graphically in Fig. 10-12. The reader should insert these values in the original equations to verify that the solutions

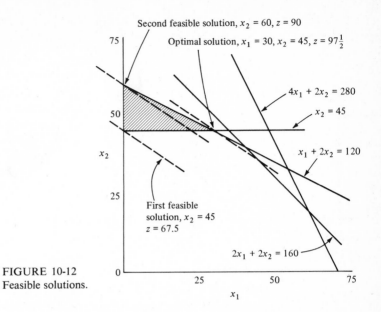

FIGURE 10-12
Feasible solutions.

are feasible and that $z = 67.5$. Now proceed in the normal manner to maximize z. Since this has been done before, the process is only indicated by the progressive matrices generated.

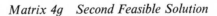

Matrix 4f   *First Feasible Solution*

	x_1	x_2	u_1	u_2	u_3	u_4	b	
	2	0	1	0	0	2	70	$\frac{70}{2} = 35$
	1	0	0	1	0	2	30	$\frac{30}{2} = 15$ key row (smallest positive limit)
	4	0	0	0	1	2	190	$\frac{190}{2} = 95$
	0	1	0	0	0	-1	45	$45/-1 = -45$
	1	0	0	0	0	1.5	-67.5	

key column (most positive value)

Matrix 4g   *Second Feasible Solution*

	x_1	x_2	u_1	u_2	u_3	u_4	b	
	1	0	1	-1	0	0	40	$\frac{40}{1} = 40$
	$\frac{1}{2}$	0	0	$\frac{1}{2}$	0	1	15	$15/\frac{1}{2} = 30$ key row (smallest positive limit)
	3	0	0	-1	1	0	160	$\frac{160}{3} = 53\frac{1}{3}$
	$\frac{1}{2}$	1	0	$\frac{1}{2}$	0	0	60	$60/\frac{1}{2} = 120$
	$\frac{1}{4}$	0	0	$-\frac{3}{4}$	0	0	-90	

key column (most positive value)

Matrix 4h   Optimal Solution

	x_1	x_2	u_1	u_2	u_3	u_4	b
	0	0	1	−2	0	−2	10
	1	0	0	1	0	2	30
	0	0	0	−4	1	−6	70
	0	1	0	0	0	−1	45
	0	0	0	−1	0	$-\frac{1}{2}$	$-97\frac{1}{2}$

Thus the final optimal solution is

$$x_1 = 30 \qquad x_2 = 45 \qquad u_1 = 10 \qquad u_2 = 0 \qquad u_3 = 70 \qquad u_4 = 0$$

The final value of the profit is $97\frac{1}{2}$. This has been reduced from the previous optimum of \$100 because the original solution of $x_1 = 40$, $x_2 = 40$ is not feasible with the added restriction that x_2 must be at least 45 units. Figure 10-12 graphically portrays the stepwise progress from the initial stage to the final solution.

The other type of constraint which may occur is the equality. Although less common, it is important in some types of optimization problems. Suppose that product 1 is made only for one customer and requires an output of exactly 25 units/week and that stockpiling excess capacity is not desirable. Thus it is necessary to determine the most profitable product mix which contains an output of product 1 of exactly 25 units. Mathematically this is expressed as $x_1 = 25$. Since this is an equality, no slack can exist; thus a slack variable cannot be used. However, if this is added as a constraint in the matrix, there will be no initial feasible solution; i.e., no identity matrix is present. As before, this is handled by adding another artificial variable a_2.

$$x_1 + a_2 = 25$$

From this point on it is treated like the previous example; i.e., define a function composed of the artificial variables, minimize this function until the variables are zero, discard these variables, and continue with the convention simplex. The first matrix with the new constraint added is

Matrix 5a

	x_1	x_2	u_1	u_2	u_3	u_4	a_1	a_2	b
	2	2	1	0	0	0	0	0	160
	1	2	0	1	0	0	0	0	120
	4	2	0	0	1	0	0	0	280
	0	1	0	0	0	−1	1	0	45
	1	0	0	0	0	0	0	1	25
	1	1.5	0	0	0	0	0	0	0

In this case there are two artificial variables (a_1 and a_2) that are not wanted in the final solution. Thus the function to be minimized first is the sum of a_1 and a_2. From the fourth and fifth constraints (rows of the matrix)

$$x_2 - u_4 + a_1 = 45 \qquad (10\text{-}10)$$
$$x_1 + a_2 = 25 \qquad (10\text{-}12)$$

Solving for a_1 and a_2 gives

$$a_1 = 45 - x_2 + u_4 \qquad (10\text{-}11)$$
$$a_2 = 25 - x_1$$

Sum these equations to get the function $a_1 + a_2$.

$$a_1 + a_2 = 70 - x_1 - x_2 + u_4 \qquad (10\text{-}13)$$

This, then, is the artificial function to be minimized first to obtain a feasible solution for the conventional simplex. The initial matrix now becomes

Matrix 5b

	x_1	x_2	u_1	u_2	u_3	u_4	a_1	a_2	b
	2	2	1	0	0	0	0	0	160
	1	2	0	1	0	0	0	0	120
	4	2	0	0	1	0	0	0	280
	0	1	0	0	0	−1	1	0	45
	1	0	0	0	0	0	0	1	25
z	1	1.5	0	0	0	0	0	0	0
$a_1 + a_2$	−1	−1	0	0	0	1	0	0	−70

To minimize, select the variable which will cause the greastest decrease in the $a_1 + a_2$ function (the one with the most negative slope). In this case both x_1 and x_2 will cause the same decrease (-1), and here x_1 is chosen arbitrarily as the key column. To select the key row, the limiting constraints are evaluated as before.

$$(1) \qquad \tfrac{160}{2} = 80$$
$$(2) \qquad \tfrac{120}{1} = 120$$
$$(3) \qquad \tfrac{280}{4} = 70$$
$$(4) \qquad \tfrac{45}{0} = \infty$$
$$(5) \qquad \tfrac{25}{1} = 25$$

This is the smallest *positive* limit and thus the first limiting value, i.e., the key row. Perform row operations to obtain a 1 in the key row and key column and zeros in *all* other positions in the key column.

Matrix 5c   First Solution

	x_1	x_2	u_1	u_2	u_3	u_4	a_1	a_2	b
	0	2	1	0	0	0	0	-2	110
	0	2	0	1	0	0	0	-1	95
	0	2	0	0	1	0	0	-4	180
	0	1	0	0	0	-1	1	0	45
	1	0	0	0	0	0	0	1	25
	0	1.5	0	0	0	0	0	-1	-25
$a_1 + a_2$	0	-1	0	0	0	1	0	1	-45

In this matrix, $a_1 + a_2$ can be decreased only by increasing x_2; thus it is automatically selected as the key column. The key row is next selected.

(1) $\frac{110}{2} = 55$

(2) $\frac{95}{2} = 47\frac{1}{2}$

(3) $\frac{180}{2} = 90$

(4) $\frac{45}{1} = 45$ smallest *positive*, the key row

(5) $\frac{25}{0} = \infty$

Perform row operations to obtain a 1 in the key column x_2 and key row 4 and zeros in all other positions in the key column.

Matrix 5d   Second Solution

	x_1	x_2	u_1	u_2	u_3	u_4	a_1	a_2	b
	0	0	1	0	0	2	-2	-2	20
	0	0	0	1	0	2	-2	-1	5
	0	0	0	0	1	2	-2	-4	90
	0	1	0	0	0	-1	1	0	45
	1	0	0	0	0	0	0	1	25
z	0	0	0	0	0	1.5	-1.5	-1	-92.5
$a_1 + a_2$	0	0	0	0	0	0	1	1	0

Examining the $a_1 + a_2$ row reveals no negative values; thus the function $a_1 + a_2$ has been minimized. Again this can be verified by the value of zero in the b column for

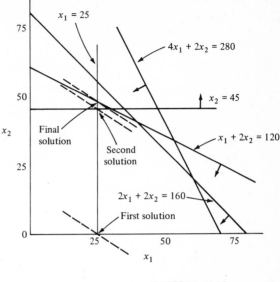

FIGURE 10-13
Steps in iterative solutions.

this function.   The artificial variables are no longer needed and may be discarded. These two steps are displayed graphically in Fig. 10-13 as the solution moves from $x_1 = x_2 = 0$ (not feasible) to $x_1 = 25$, $x_2 = 0$ (still not feasible), to the first feasible answer of $x_1 = 25$, $x_2 = 45$.   Discarding the a_1 and a_2 columns and the $a_1 + a_2$ row gives the reduced second solution.

Matrix 5e   First Feasible Solution

	x_1	x_2	u_1	u_2	u_3	u_4	b
	0	0	1	0	0	2	20
	0	0	0	1	0	2	5
	0	0	0	0	1	2	90
	0	1	0	0	0	−1	45
	1	0	0	0	0	0	25
z	0	0	0	0	0	1.5	−92.5

Since the z function (profit) is to be maximized, inspecting this row indicates that z will be increased 1.5 units for every increase in u_4.   Thus u_4 is selected as the key column for the next iteration.   The key row is selected from the limiting *positive* constraint.

(1) $\quad \frac{20}{2} = 10$

(2) $\quad \frac{5}{2} = 2\frac{1}{2}$ smallest positive limit, key row

(3) $\quad \frac{90}{2} = 45$

(4) $\quad 45/-1 = -45$ no positive limit

(5) $\quad \frac{25}{0} = \infty$

Now iterate to obtain the third solution, which in this case turns out to be the final optimal solution.

Matrix 5f   Optimal Solution

	x_1	x_2	u_1	u_2	u_3	u_4	b
	0	0	1	-1	0	0	15
	0	0	0	$\frac{1}{2}$	0	1	$2\frac{1}{2}$
	0	0	0	-1	1	0	85
	0	1	0	$\frac{1}{2}$	0	0	$47\frac{1}{2}$
	1	0	0	0	0	0	25
z	0	0	0	$-\frac{3}{4}$	0	0	$-96\frac{1}{4}$

Thus the final solution, as indicated above and in Fig. 10-13, is at $x_1 = 25$, $x_2 = 47\frac{1}{2}$ with a profit of $96\frac{1}{4}$.   As expected, this is somewhat less than in the previous example because the new constraint moves the solution further from the optimal.

Methods handling all three possible constraint forms ($\leq$, $\geq$, $=$) have now been discussed.   In addition, the concept and technique for minimization in linear programming has been developed.   The only variation required in maximizing or minimizing is the method of selecting the key column.   For maximization choose the variable with the most positive slope, as it will offer the greatest increase in the objective function for a unit increase in the variable.   Conversely for minimization, select the variable with the most negative slope, as it will reduce the objective function by the greatest amount for a unit increase in a variable.   The final solution is indicated when increasing a variable no longer improves (increases or decreases as desired) the objective function.   The steps for handling all three constraint forms are summarized in a procedural format in the following paragraphs and illustrated by working another simple linear-programming maximization problem.

STEP 1   Define the objective function to be maximized (or minimized) in terms of the decision variables.

$$z = 2x_1 + 2x_2 \qquad \text{maximize}$$

STEP 2   Define the problem limitations in terms of constraint inequalities or equations using the decision variables.

$$(1) \qquad x_1 + x_2 \le 10$$
$$(2) \qquad x_1 + 2x_2 \ge 8$$
$$(3) \qquad -x_1 + x_2 = 2$$

STEP 3   Convert the inequalities to equalities by adding or subtracting slack variables.

$$(1) \qquad x_1 + x_2 + u_1 = 10$$
$$(2) \qquad x_1 + 2x_2 - u_2 = 8$$
$$(3) \qquad -x_1 + x_2 = 2$$

STEP 4   Add artificial variables as needed to obtain an identity matrix.

$$(1) \qquad x_1 + x_2 \qquad + u_1 \qquad\qquad = 10$$
$$x_1 + 2x_2 - u_2 \qquad\qquad + a_1 \qquad = 8$$
$$-x_1 + x_2 \qquad\qquad\qquad\qquad + a_2 = 2$$

$$\underbrace{\qquad\qquad\qquad\qquad}_{\text{Identity matrix}}$$

STEP 5   Determine the artificial function to be minimized by solving each pertinent constraint equation for its artificial variable

$$a_1 = 8 - x_1 - 2x_2 + u_2$$
$$a_2 = 2 + x_1 - x_2$$

and summing all artificial variables

$$a_1 + a_2 = 10 - 3x_2 + u_2$$

STEP 6   Form the initial matrix, inserting the objective row z and the artificial-function row $a_1 + a_2$.

	x_1	x_2	u_1	u_2	a_1	a_2	b
(1)	1	1	1	0	0	0	10
(2)	1	2	0	-1	1	0	8
(3)	-1	1	0	0	0	1	2
z	2	2	0	0	0	0	0
$a_1 + a_2$	0	-3	0	1	0	0	-10

STEP 7   Select the key column using the $a_1 + a_2$ row; to minimize select the most negative value.   The x_2 column has a -3 value in the $a_1 + a_2$ row.

STEP 8 Select the key row by finding the limiting constraint as before.

(1) $\frac{10}{1} = 10$

(2) $\frac{8}{2} = 4$

(3) $\frac{2}{1} = 2$ smallest positive value, key row

STEP 9 Iterate using row manipulations.

First Solution

	x_1	x_2	u_1	u_2	a_1	a_2	b
(1)	2	0	1	0	0	-1	8
(2)	3	0	0	-1	1	-2	4
(3)	-1	1	0	0	0	1	2
z	4	0	0	0	0	-2	-4
$a_1 + a_2$	-3	0	0	1	0	3	-4

STEP 10 Repeat steps 8 and 9 until the $a_1 + a_2$ row has no negative values and the b value is zero.

Second Solution (x_1 Key Column; Second Row, Key Row)

	x_1	x_2	u_1	u_2	a_1	a_2	b
(1)	0	0	1	$\frac{2}{3}$	$-\frac{2}{3}$	$\frac{1}{3}$	$\frac{16}{3}$
(2)	1	0	0	$-\frac{1}{3}$	$\frac{1}{3}$	$-\frac{2}{3}$	$\frac{4}{3}$
(3)	0	1	0	$-\frac{1}{3}$	$\frac{1}{3}$	$\frac{1}{3}$	$\frac{10}{3}$
z	0	0	0	$\frac{4}{3}$	$-\frac{4}{3}$	$\frac{2}{3}$	$-\frac{28}{3}$
$a_1 + a_2$	0	0	0	0	1	1	0

At this point there are no more negative values in the $a_1 + a_2$ row; this indicates that the artificial function has been minimized. As a check, the value in the b column has also been reduced to zero. This means that a feasible solution has been reached.

STEP 11 Discard all entries pertaining to the artificial variables and make a new matrix.

	x_1	x_2	u_1	u_2	b
(1)	0	0	1	$\frac{2}{3}$	$\frac{16}{3}$
(2)	1	0	0	$-\frac{1}{3}$	$\frac{4}{3}$
(3)	0	1	0	$-\frac{1}{3}$	$\frac{10}{3}$
z	0	0	0	$\frac{4}{3}$	$-\frac{28}{3}$

STEP 12 Select a key column to maximize (or minimize) the objective function. Select the most positive value in the z row to maximize or the most negative value to minimize.[1] Key column is u_2 with a value of $\frac{4}{3}$.

STEP 13 Select a key row as before by finding the smallest positive limit.

$$(1) \qquad \frac{\frac{16}{3}}{\frac{2}{3}} = 8 \qquad \text{key row, smallest } \textit{positive } \text{limit}$$

$$(2) \qquad \frac{\frac{4}{3}}{-\frac{1}{3}} = -4 \qquad \text{negative limit}$$

$$(3) \qquad \frac{\frac{10}{3}}{-\frac{1}{3}} = -10 \qquad \text{negative limit}$$

STEP 14 Iterate using row operations as before; continue, repeating steps 12 to 14 until optimized.

$$
\begin{array}{c}
\begin{array}{ccccc} x_1 & x_2 & u_1 & u_2 & b \end{array} \\
\left[\begin{array}{cccc|c}
0 & 0 & \frac{3}{2} & 1 & 8 \\
1 & 0 & \frac{1}{2} & 0 & 4 \\
0 & 1 & \frac{1}{2} & 0 & 6 \\
\hline
z \quad 0 & 0 & -2 & 0 & -20
\end{array}\right]
\end{array}
$$

At this point the problem is maximized since there are no more positive values in the objective row z. Increasing u_1 would decrease the objective function as indicated by the -2 in the z row. The final solution is read from the matrix:

$$x_1 = 4 \qquad x_2 = 6 \qquad u_1 = 0 \qquad u_2 = 8 \qquad z = -(-20) = 20$$

For maximizing problems the objective value must be multiplied by (-1). Check:

$$2x_1 + 2x_2 = 2(4) + 2(6) = 20$$

PROBLEM FORMULATION

Almost every application of an OR tool is a unique exercise in formulation, model development, and data acquisition. The practitioner must match the mathematics available to the information and objectives of the problem. Even defining a desirable and applicable objective may be a difficult problem. This section presents two problem situations and discusses alternative problem formulations.

---

[1] In this problem, the present solution is already a minimum since there are no negative values in the objective row z.

A Blending Problem

This general problem is applicable to several industries and shares some common points. In general, the problem is one of mixing several ingredients to obtain an output product which meets some arbitrarily imposed conditions.   At the same time, some objective such as profit, production, facility use, etc., is optimized.   Some typical problems are mixing feed for livestock to maximize a weight-gain-vs.-food-cost relationship, blending refinery stocks to obtain a most profitable product output, blending input materials (ores, scrap, etc.) to obtain a metal meeting specifications at a minimum cost, or blending ingredients for fertilizer to meet content requirements at a lowest cost.

As an example, a blending problem to find the appropriate input to a furnace for a foundry will be discussed.   This problem will be simplified in the interest of space and ease of discussion, but the methods of formulation remain valid.   An electric furnace is used to melt iron to make gray-iron castings, and a charge of 2 tons (4,000 lb) is required.

A variety of materials give an end product that meets specifications.   The problem is to select the input which meet specifications at a minimum cost.   The product must meet the following material specifications:

	Min.	Max.
Carbon, %	3.25	3.40
Silicon, %	2.05	2.25

The materials available to make this product are:

Material	Carbon, %	Silicon, %	Cost
Steel scrap *A*	.45	.10	$60/ton
Steel scrap *B*	.40	.15	63/ton
Cast-iron scrap	3.50	2.30	68/ton
Foundry remelt	3.30	2.20	40/ton
Carbon briquettes	100	0	.30/lb
Silicon briquettes	0	100	.50/lb

The decision variables which can be controlled by management are the amounts of each of the six materials to be charged into the furnace.   These are represented mathematically as x_1 (steel scrap A), x_2 (steel scrap B), x_3 (cast-iron scrap), x_4 (foundry remelt), x_5 (carbon briquettes), and x_6 (silicon briquettes).   Each x_i represents the weight in pounds of that material used in the charging load.   Assume that the objective is to minimize the material input cost; therefore the objective function is the sum of the cost of each material being used.

$$z = \text{sum of material costs} = \sum_j c_j x_j$$

$$= c_1 x_1 + c_2 x_2 + c_3 x_3 + c_4 x_4 + c_5 x_5 + c_6 x_6$$

where c_j is the cost of the jth item in dollars per pound.

$$z = \frac{60}{2,000}x_1 + \frac{63}{2,000}x_2 + \frac{68}{2,000}x_3 + \frac{40}{2,000}x_4 + .30x_5 + .50x_6$$

$$= .030x_1 + .0315x_2 + .034x_3 + .020x_4 + .300x_5 + .500x_6$$

These materials must also be selected so that the material specifications are met. For example, the carbon content must not exceed .034.

$$\text{Carbon content} \leq .034$$

This can be more easily expressed in pounds by multiplying this value by the required charge weight. In this example, the carbon-weight loss during melting is neglected. Since this is typically a fairly constant amount for a given furnace, it would not be difficult to correct for.

$$\text{Carbon weight} = 4,000(.034)$$

$$= 136 \text{ lb}$$

The carbon weight will be the sum of the amount of carbon in each of the materials used. Thus the amount of carbon added by steel scrap A is $.0045x_1$, etc. Thus this restriction on maximum carbon content can be expressed by the inequality

$$.0045x_1 + .004x_2 + .035x_3 + .033x_4 + x_5 + 0x_6 \leq 136$$

The minimum carbon content requirement is described by a greater-than inequality:

$$\text{Minimum carbon weight} = .0325(4,000)$$

$$= 130 \text{ lb}$$

$$.0045x_1 + .004x_2 + .035x_3 + .033x_4 + x_5 + 0x_6 \geq 130$$

In a similar manner, the specifications on silicon are expressed by a set of inequalities.

$$.001x_1 + .0015x_2 + .023x_3 + .022x_4 + 0x_5 + x_6 \leq 90$$

$$.001x_1 + .0015x_2 + .023x_3 + .022x_4 + 0x_5 + x_6 \geq 82$$

Finally, the materials added must make up the full charge weight. Again, all weight loss in melting is neglected in this problem. Thus the sum of the weight added must equal 4,000 lb.

$$x_1 + x_2 + x_3 + x_4 + x_5 + x_6 = 4,000$$

This gives a total of five constraints which will satisfy all specification requirements and which can be combined with the objective function to compute a blend of charging ingredients at minimum cost.   Table 10-3 presents the summary of results for this problem.

If other restrictions are imposed on this problem, they are represented by additional constraints.   For example, even though remelt scrap from the foundry is the cheapest ingredient, there obviously will not be enough to use for all charges.   Experience has shown that only 20 percent of a charge can be expected to be available. This is represented by another inequality:

$$x_4 \leq .20(4,000)$$

$$\leq 800$$

Table 10-4 shows the effect of this constraint upon the solution.   Note the reduction in x_4 and the increase in total cost.

Table 10-3   SUMMARY OF RESULTS FOR FURNACE-CHARGING PROBLEM

Charging material	Amount to be charged, lb
Steel scrap A	0
Steel scrap B	0
Cast-iron scrap	0
Foundry remelt	4,000.0
Carbon	0
Silicon	0

Cost = $80

Table 10-4   SUMMARY OF RESULTS FOR MODIFIED FURNACE-CHARGING PROBLEM

Charging material	Amount to be charged, lb
Steel scrap A	275.41
Steel scrap B	0
Cast-iron scrap	2924.59
Foundry remelt	800
Carbon	0
Silicon	0

Cost = $123.70

As an added example, consider a situation of scarcity, as in wartime or during a labor dispute, when cost is secondary to output. In this case, the objective might switch from minimizing cost to maximizing output. For this situation assume that the total available materials are:

Material	Maximum availability, tons
Steel scrap A	100
Steel scrap B	30
Cast-iron scrap	120
Foundry remelt	60
Carbon briquettes	No limit
Silicon briquettes	4

In this case the objective becomes to maximize the total number of pounds of material blended.

$$z = x_1 + x_2 + x_3 + x_4 + x_5 + x_6 \qquad \text{maximize}$$

In addition to the constraints required for specification requirements, it is not possible to use more material than is available. Thus the following inequalities must be added.

$$x_1 \le 200{,}000 \qquad x_2 \le 60{,}000 \qquad x_3 \le 240{,}000$$
$$x_4 \le 120{,}000 \qquad x_6 \le 8{,}000$$

Since the total amount of material used is not fixed, the specification constraints must be reformulated. The total weight of carbon added will be the sum of the carbon added by each material, but the maximum allowable is no longer a constant.

$$.0045x_1 + .004x_2 + .035x_3 + .033x_4 + x_5 = \text{pounds of carbon added}$$

The pounds of carbon added must be equal to or less than 3.4 percent of the total weight used. Thus the first constraint becomes

$$\underbrace{.0045x_1 + .004x_2 + .035x_3 + .033x_4 + x_5}_{\text{Pounds of carbon}} \le \underbrace{.034(x_1 + x_2 + x_3 + x_4 + x_5 + x_6)}_{\text{Maximum allowable pounds of carbon}}$$

This inequality is modified to put all variables on the left-hand side.

$$-.0295x_1 - .030x_2 + .001x_3 - .001x_4 + .966x_5 - .034x_6 \le 0$$

The lower carbon limit is formulated in a similar manner.

$$.0045x_1 + .004x_2 + .035x_3 + .033x_4 + x_5 \ge (.0325)(x_1 + x_2 + x_3 + x_4 + x_5 + x_6)$$
$$-.028x_1 - .0285x_2 + .0025x_3 + .0005x_4 + .9675x_5 - .0325x_6 \ge 0$$

Similar analysis provides the two constraints for the silicon specifications:

$$-.0215x_1 - .021x_2 + .0005x_3 - .0005x_4 - x_5 + .9775x_6 \leq 0$$
$$-.0195x_1 - .0190x_2 + .0025x_3 + .0015x_4 - x_5 + .9795x_6 \geq 0$$

Thus the final problem is to maximize $z = x_1 + x_2 + x_3 + x_4 + x_5 + x_6$ subject to

$$-.0295x_1 - .030x_2 + .001x_3 - .001x_4 + .966x_5 - .034x_6 \leq 0$$
$$-.028x_1 - .0285x_2 + .0025x_3 + .0005x_4 + .9675x_5 - .0325x_6 \geq 0$$
$$-.0215x_1 - .021x_2 + .0005x_3 - .0005x_4 - .0225x_5 + .9775x_6 \leq 0$$
$$-.0195x_1 - .019x_2 + .0025x_3 + .0015x_4 - .0205x_5 + .9795x_6 \geq 0$$

$$x_1 \leq 200{,}000 \qquad x_2 \leq 60{,}000 \qquad x_3 \leq 240{,}000$$
$$x_4 \leq 120{,}000 \qquad x_6 \leq 8{,}000$$

A Shelf-Stocking Problem

Every grocery store potentially has more items to display and sell than space permits. Thus the problem facing any store manager is one of deciding which items to stock and how much space to allot to each item.   This is a scarce-resource-allocation problem that lends itself to a linear-programming formulation.   In this example, the actual number of items and space available have been restricted for simplicity, but for more realistic amounts the formulation and solution method would remain unchanged.

The following data have been accumulated:

Item no.	Demand*	Profit/unit, cents	Space/unit, in²
1	50	2	10
2	35	2	7
3	25	3	9
4	20	4	11
5	45	4	11
6	50	6	12
7	45	5	14
8	40	5	14
9	30	6	10
10	50	4	8
11	35	2	14
12	50	6	8
13	20	5	11
14	25	3	12
15	30	4	9
16	20	2	7
17	60	2	10
18	35	1	16
19	25	5	11
20	45	4	15

* Demand is expressed as an expected value during a time interval between restocking.

If all items were stocked to their expected demand levels, it would require approximately 8,105 in² of shelf area.   The manager only has 40 ft² of space to allocate to these items, and so the problem is one of allocating space to optimize some objective.

Usually the objective would be one of maximizing profit subject to the space plus other restrictions.   The profit is simply the sum of sales per item times the profit per item.

$$z = c_j x_j \qquad \text{maximize}$$
$$c_j = \text{profit for } j\text{th item}$$
$$x_j = \text{numbr of item } j \text{ stocked on shelf}$$

This objective function assumes that during a time period, the sales of any item will be equal to the number of items stocked and that the number stocked on a shelf will not exceed the demand.   In this case,

$$z = 2x_1 + 2x_2 + 3x_3 + 4x_4 + 4x_5 + 6x_6 + 5x_7 + 5x_8 + 6x_9 + 4x_{10} + 2x_{11}$$
$$+ 6x_{12} + 5x_{13} + 3x_{14} + 4x_{15} + 2x_{16} + 2x_{17} + 1x_{18} + 5x_{19} + 4x_{20}$$

The major restriction is obviously one of space.   The combined space used cannot exceed the 40 ft² = 5,760 in².   The space used is the sum of the product (number of items stocked times space required per item).

$$\sum_{j=1}^{20} s_j x_j \le 5{,}760$$

where s_j is the space required per unit in square inches.

$$10x_1 + 7x_2 + 9x_3 + 11x_4 + 11x_5 + 12x_6 + 14x_7 + 14x_8 + 10x_9 + 8x_{10} + 14x_{11}$$
$$+ 8x_{12} + 11x_{13} + 12x_{14} + 9x_{15} + 7x_{16} + 10x_{17} + 16x_{18} + 11x_{19} + 15x_{20} \le 5{,}760$$

In addition the number of items stocked should not exceed the demand.   This results in another series of constraint inequalities.

$$x_j \le d_j \qquad \text{for all } j$$

where d_j is the demand for the jth item.

$$x_1 \le 50 \qquad x_2 \le 35 \qquad x_3 \le 25 \qquad x_4 \le 20 \qquad x_5 \le 45$$
$$x_6 \le 50 \qquad x_7 \le 45 \qquad x_8 \le 40 \qquad x_9 \le 30 \qquad x_{10} \le 50$$
$$x_{11} \le 35 \qquad x_{12} \le 50 \qquad x_{13} \le 20 \qquad x_{14} \le 25 \qquad x_{15} \le 30$$
$$x_{16} \le 20 \qquad x_{17} \le 60 \qquad x_{18} \le 35 \qquad x_{19} \le 25 \qquad x_{20} \le 45$$

In this case the manager may also want to impose some arbitrary restrictions because of customer relations, prior commitments, etc.   Consider that he requires the following minimums for display of four items.

$$x_1 \ge 10 \qquad x_{12} \ge 10 \qquad x_{16} \ge 10 \qquad x_{17} \ge 10$$

The number 10 has been chosen as a minimum because the manager believes that to display fewer is totally ineffective.   Combining all these restrictions gives another

Table 10-5   SUMMARY OF RESULTS FOR
SHELF-STOCKING PROBLEM

Item no.	Number to be stocked	Item no.	Number to be stocked
1	10	11	0
2	35	12	50
3	25	13	20
4	20	14	0
5	45	15	30
6	50	16	20
7	45	17	10
8	40	18	0
9	30	19	25
10	50	20	38*

* Actual value was 38.667, rounded off to 38.   Profit =
$2,389.67.

application of linear programming.   Table 10-5 presents the final results for this problem.

COMPUTER SOLUTIONS

It is the computer that has made linear programming a practical computational technique.   Not only would the time for manual computations be excessive, even with calculators, but simple arithmetic mistakes would make a correct solution almost impossible.   Today a problem having 50 variables and 100 constraints is considered routine.   Almost any computer center will have an operational linear-programming software package.   When the package is used repeatedly for the same type of problem, the input-output formats will have been revised to match the information on an as-gathered and as-needed basis.   Since this text is devoted to the development and explanation of the concepts of various OR techniques, specific software packages are not covered in detail.

The student should gain some insight into problem solution by using a computer. A simple code is presented in the Note to this chapter.   The input requirements are described in enough detail for a student with some familiarity with computers to use this program for medium-sized problems.   Someone familiar with the operating system must provide the necessary information to input the required job cards to make the system work.   Sufficient details are provided to allow the DIMENSION statement to be rewritten to handle larger problems.   As written, the program will handle 20 constraints and *approximately* 20 real variables.   The total number of real variables plus slack and artificial variables must be 50 or less.   The program is written in FORTRAN IV for an IBM 360/65, but minor revisions should make it usable on any computer using FORTRAN IV.   It has been the authors' experience that undergraduates can successfully use this program even if they are unable to program the computer themselves as long as some care is taken in presenting a step-by-step review of the necessary job cards and the material presented in the Note. The Note also provides a useful instructional tool by allowing the instructor to assign larger, i.e., more realistic problems.

NOTE

Computer Programming Code and Its Use

General This program has been modified[1] to run on an IBM 360/65 using FORTRAN IV on the WATFIV compiler. As dimensioned, it requires 5,112 bytes for the object code and 4,560 bytes for the array area. The present dimensions allow a maximum of 20 constraints and 50 variables (including the real variables, slacks, and artificials). Since this code is presented for use by students, it has been dimensioned for a relatively small problem so that it can be used in smaller computers.

If a larger problem is to be run, the DIMENSION statement must be changed from the present form

DIMENSION D(20, 51), P(50), IBV(20), SC(50)

Assume that the number of constraints required is I and the *total* number of variables (real, artificial, and slack) is J. The new statement should be

DIMENSION D(I, J + 1), P(J), IBV(I), SC(J)

This program uses the big M method of handling artificial variables. Each artificial variable is assigned a c_j value of -999 in the original objective function. In addition, this program maximizes the objective function. To minimize, multiply the objective function by -1.

Data preparation Preparation of the input data for this program is best demonstrated by an example. Maximize $1.5x_1 + x_2$ subject to

$$2x_1 + x_2 \leq 8$$
$$x_2 = 4$$
$$2x_1 + 3x_2 \geq 7$$

STEP 1 Arrange the constraints in the following order:

Greater thans
Equals
Less thans

$$2x_1 + 3x_2 \geq 7$$
$$x_2 = 4$$
$$2x_1 + x_2 \leq 8$$

[1] Claude McMillan and Richard F. Gonzalez, "Systems Analysis," Richard D. Irwin, Inc., Homewood, Ill., 1968.

STEP 2   Add slacks and artificial variables as required.

$$2x_1 + 3x_2 \quad - x_3 \quad + x_4 \qquad\qquad\qquad = 7$$
$$x_2 \qquad\qquad\qquad + x_5 \qquad\qquad = 4$$
$$2x_1 + \quad x_2 \underbrace{\qquad\qquad} \underbrace{\qquad\qquad} \underbrace{+ x_6} = 8$$

Negative   Artificial   Slack
slack   variables   variable
variable

STEP 3   Prepare data card 1.   This card has the following code names as input:

READ(5, 104) IW, IZ, IY, IA, NEQ
  IW $=$ number of constraints (3)
  IZ $=$ number of columns in matrix, including the b column.   This is the
      sum of real variables $+$ 2X (number of greater thans) $+$ number of
      equalities $+$ number of less thans $+$ 1.   Or count all the columns
      in step 2 *including* the b column:

  $2 + 2(1) + 1 + 1 + 1 = 7$

  IY $=$ number of real variables $+$ 1 ($2 + 1 = 3$)
  IA $=$ number of greater thans (1)
  NEQ $=$ number of equals (1)

The format is

104 FORMAT(5I2).

1 2	3 4	5 6	7 8	9 10
0 3	0 7	0 3	0 1	0 1
IW	IZ	IY	IA	NEQ

Be sure to punch the value in each pair of columns as far to the right as possible.   For example, if IW was punched with a 3 in column 1 instead of column 2, the computer would read this as a 30 instead of a 3.

STEP 4   Prepare data card 2, ITAB.   This indicates whether or not you want the matrix printed after each iteration.   If this is desired, punch a 1 in column 1.   For only the original matrix and the final solution matrix, simply insert a blank card. In either case, a card must be used; do not omit this step.

STEP 5   Prepare data card(s) for the objective function c_j.   This card inputs the coefficients of the objective function for the real variables.   The program itself generates those required for the slacks and artificial variables.

READ(5, 102) (P(N), N $= 1$, I)
102 FORMAT(8F10.4)

This format spaces eight values on each card.   Use as many cards as required.   For example, 19 variables would require three cards, 8 each on the first two cards and 3 on the last card.   Ten columns are used for each coefficient.   This format will allow as many as four decimal places, with a decimal point punched in each column ending in a 6 (6, 16, 26, 36, ...). *Be sure to punch the decimal* and a negative sign if required.

1	2	3	4	5	6	7	8	9	10	11	12	13	14	15	16	17	18	19	20
				1	.	5								1	.	0			

$$\underbrace{\hspace{3cm}}_{\substack{\text{coefficient for}\\ x_1}} \qquad \underbrace{\hspace{3cm}}_{\substack{\text{coefficient for}\\ x_2}}$$

STEP 6 Prepare data cards for the original matrix a_{ij}. This inputs the coefficients of the real variables in the constraints a_{ij}. The coefficients for the slacks and artificial variables are generated by the program itself.

The program reads the coefficients, one constraint at a time, and does not mix them. When one constraint is complete, it *always* begins on a *new* data card, even if the last data card was not full. The spacing is the same as in step 5.

DO112 M = 1, IW
112 READ(5, 102) (D(M,N), N = 1,I)
102 FORMAT(8F10.4)

Card	Columns 1 2 3 4 5 6 7 8 9 10 11 12 13 14 15 16 17 18 19 20	Constraint
4	2 . 0 3 . 0	1
5	0 . 0 1 . 0	2
6	2 . 0 1 . 0	3

STEP 7 Insert data b_i for b column. The last input is for the b column. There will be as many input values as there are constraints. The spacing is the same as in steps 5 and 6. Be sure to begin on a new card and list the values according to the way the constraints were arranged. As before, you can put as many as eight values on a card.

READ(5,102) (D(M,IZ), M = 1, IW)
102 FORMAT(8F10.4)

$$\overbrace{\hspace{3cm}}^{\text{Constraint 1}} \quad \overbrace{\hspace{3cm}}^{\text{Constraint 2}} \quad \overbrace{\hspace{3cm}}^{\text{Constraint 3}}$$

1	2	3	4	5	6	7	8	9	10	11	12	13	14	15	16	17	18	19	20	21	22	23	24	25	26	27	28	29	30
		7	.	0										4	.	0								8	.	0			

The complete data deck will be as follows:

Card	Input information
1	IW, IZ, IY, IA, NEQ
2	ITAB = 1 (print all tables),
	ITAB = 0 only original and solution
3(+)	c_j values
?	a_{ij} values
?	b_i values

The program is listed next, followed by data cards for this problem, and finally the output when ITAB = 1.

```
      $JOB WATFIV   ****************,REGION=30K            JIM SHAMBLIN
1           DIMENSION D(20,51),P(50),IBV(20),SC(50)
2       101 FORMAT(I1)
3       102 FORMAT(8F10.4)
4       104 FORMAT(5I2)
5       105 FORMAT(1H1)
6       106 FORMAT(1H0,26HTABLEAU AFTER PIVOT NUMBER  ,I4)
7       108 FORMAT(1H0,8HSOLUTION)
8       109 FORMAT(1H0,8HVARIABLE,4X,5HVALUE)
9       110 FORMAT(1H ,I5,F12.2)
10      111 FORMAT(1H0,25HALL OTHER VARIABLES=ZERO.   )
      C  ARRANGE ROWS CONTAINING GREATER THANS FIRST, THEN EQUALITIES, THEN LESS THANS
      C  IW = NO OF CONSTRAINTS, IZ = NO OF COL IN MATRIX INCLUDING B COL
      C  IY = NO OF VAR(REAL) +1, IA = NO OF ROWS WITH NEG SLACK
      C  NEQ = NO OF EQUALITIES
      C  ITAB = 1, PRINT ALL ITERATIONS, =0, DO NOT
      C  P(N) = COEF OF REAL VAR IN OBJ FUNCT; DOES NOT INCLUDE SLACKS OR ART. VAR.
      CC D(M,N) = COEF OF CONST   NOTE MAY INCLUDE B COL
11          NN=0
12          READ(5,104) IW,IZ,IY,IA,NEQ
13          IX=IZ-1
14          I=IY-1
15          IR=I
16          READ(5,101)ITAB
17          READ(5,102) (P(N),N=1,I)
18          DO697 JIM=IY,IX
19      697 P(JIM)=0.0
20          IK=IA+NEQ
21          IF(IK.EQ.0) GO TO 69
22          NEG=IY+IA
23          NEF=NEG+IA-1+NEQ
24          DO 68 KKK=NEG,NEF
25       68 P(KKK)=-999.0
26       69 CONTINUE
27          DO 103 N=1,IX
28      103 SC(N)=P(N)
29          DO 112 M=1,IW
30      112 READ(5,102)(D(M,N),N=1,I)
31          READ(5,102) (D(M,IZ),M=1,IW)
32          DO 113 I=1,IW
33          DO 113 J = IY,IX
34      113 D(I,J) = 0.0
35          DO 114 I = 1,IW
36          J = I+IY+IA-1
37      114 D(I,J) = 1.0
38          IF(IA.EQ.0.0) GO TO 118
39          DO 115 I = 1,IA
40          J = I+IY-1
41      115 D(I,J) = -1.0
42      118 CONTINUE
43          DO 20 N=IY,IX
44          DO 30 L=1,IW
45          IF(D(L,N)-1.0) 30,40,30
46       30 CONTINUE
47          GO TO 20
48       40 IBV(L)=N
49       20 CONTINUE
50          NOPIV=0
51          WRITE(6,200) IF
52      200 FORMAT(1H1,20X,'X1 THRU X',I2,' ARE REAL VARIABLES')
53          IF(IA.EQ.0) GO TO 203
54          IX1 = IR+IA+1
55          IX2=IX1+IA -1   +NEQ
56          WRITE(6,202) IX1,IX2
57      202 FORMAT(1H0,20X,'X',I2,' THRU X',I2,' ARE ARTIFICAL VARIABLES')
58      203 CONTINUE
59          GO TO 100
60       13 SCMAX=0.0
61          NN=1
62          DO 31 N=1,IX
```

```
63              DO 32 I=1,IW
64              IF(-IBV(I)) 32,31,32
65           32 CONTINUE
66              SUM=0.0
67              DO 33 I=1,IW
68              J=IBV(I)
69           33 SUM=SUM+P(J)*D(I,N)
70              SC(N)=P(N)-SUM
71              IF(SC(N)-SCMAX) 31,31,310
72          310 SCMAX=SC(N)
73              IPIVC=N
74           31 CONTINUE
75              IF(SCMAX) 14,14,140
76          140 SMVAL=99999999.
77              IF(ITAB.EQ.1) GO TO 100
78           19 CONTINUE
79              DO 4 M=1,IW
80              IF(D(M,IPIVC)) 4,4,5
81            5 QUONT=D(M,IZ)/D(M,IPIVC)
82              IF(SMVAL-QUONT) 4,4,6
83            6 IPIVR=M
84              SMVAL=QUONT
85            4 CONTINUE
86              IBV(IPIVR)=IPIVC
87              DIV=D(IPIVR,IPIVC)
88              DO7 N=1,IZ
89            7 D(IPIVR,N)=D(IPIVR,N)/DIV
90              NOPIV=NOPIV+1
91              IF(ITAB-1) 12,120,12
92          120 WRITE(6,106) NOPIV
93           12 DO 10 M=1,IW
94              IF(M-IPIVR)9,10,9
95            9 CM = -D(M,IPIVC)
96              DO11 N=1,IZ
97              TM=D(IPIVR,N)*CM
98           11 D(M,N)=D(M,N)+TM
99           10 CONTINUE
100             GO TO 13
101         100 CONTINUE
102             GO TO 221
103          14 WRITE(6,108)
104             WRITE(6,109)
105             DO 21 M=1,IW
106          21 WRITE(6,110) IBV(M),D(M,IZ)
107             WRITE(6,111)
108         221 CONTINUE
109             A=IZ
110             IR=IZ/13
111             A=A/13.
112             IF(A.GT.IR) IR=IR+1
113             K1=1
114             DO 210 K=1,IR
115             K2=K1+12
116              K3=K2
117             IF(K2.GE.IZ) K3=IZ
118             IF(K2.GE.IZ) K2=IZ-1
119             WRITE(6,211) (KI,KI=K1,K2)
120         211 FORMAT(1H0,//,13(7X,'X',I2))
121             DO 212 M=1,IW
122         212 WRITE(6,213) (D(M,N),N=K1,K3)
123         213 FORMAT(1H ,2X,13(F9.3,1X))
124             WRITE(6,214) (SC(N),N=K1,K2)
125         214 FORMAT(1H0,2X,13(F9.3,1X))
126         210 K1=K2+1
127             IF(NN.EQ.0) GO TO 13
128             IF(SCMAX.GT.0) GO TO 19
129             WRITE(6,105)
130             STOP
131             END

        $ENTRY
```

X1 THRU X 2 ARE REAL VARIABLES

X 4 THRU X 5 ARE ARTIFICAL VARIABLES

X 1	X 2	X 3	X 4	X 5	X 6	X
2.000	3.000	-1.000	1.000	0.000	0.000	7.000
0.000	1.000	0.000	0.000	1.000	0.000	4.000
2.000	1.000	0.000	0.000	0.000	1.000	8.000
1.500	1.000	0.000	-999.000	-999.000	0.000	

X 1	X 2	X 3	X 4	X 5	X 6	X
2.000	3.000	-1.000	1.000	0.000	0.000	7.000
0.000	1.000	0.000	0.000	1.000	0.000	4.000
2.000	1.000	0.000	0.000	0.000	1.000	8.000
1999.500	3997.000	-999.000	0.000	0.000	0.000	

TABLEAU AFTER PIVOT NUMBER   1

X 1	X 2	X 3	X 4	X 5	X 6	X
0.667	1.000	-0.333	0.333	0.000	0.000	2.333
-0.667	0.000	0.333	-0.333	1.000	0.000	1.667
1.333	0.000	0.333	-0.333	0.000	1.000	5.667
-665.166	0.000	333.333	-1332.333	0.000	0.000	

TABLEAU AFTER PIVOT NUMBER   2

X 1	X 2	X 3	X 4	X 5	X 6	X
0.000	1.000	0.000	0.000	1.000	0.000	4.000
-2.000	0.000	1.000	-1.000	3.000	0.000	5.000
2.000	0.000	0.000	0.000	-1.000	1.000	4.000
1.500	0.000	0.000	-999.000	-1000.000	0.000	

TABLEAU AFTER PIVOT NUMBER   3

SOLUTION

VARIABLE	VALUE
2	4.00
3	9.00
1	2.00

ALL OTHER VARIABLES=ZERO.

X 1	X 2	X 3	X 4	X 5	X 6	X
0.000	1.000	0.000	0.000	1.000	0.000	4.000
0.000	0.000	1.000	-1.000	2.000	1.000	9.000
1.000	0.000	0.000	0.000	-0.500	0.500	2.000
0.000	0.000	0.000	-999.000	-999.250	-0.750	

REFERENCES

1 DANTZIG, GEORGE B.: "Linear Programming and Extensions," Princeton University Press, Princeton, N.J., 1963.

2 GARVIN, WALTER W.: "Introduction to Linear Programming," McGraw-Hill Book Company, New York, 1960.

3 GASS, SAUL I., "Linear Programming," 2d ed., McGraw-Hill Book Company, New York, 1964.

4 HADLEY, G.: "Linear Programming," Addison-Wesley Publishing Company, Inc., Reading, Mass., 1962.

5 LEVIN, RICHARD I., and RUDOLPH P. LAMONE: Linear Programming for Management Decisions," Richard D. Irwin, Inc., Homewood, Ill., 1969.

PROBLEMS

10-1 Graph and solve. Maximize $z = 3x_1 + 7x_2$ subject to

$$x_1 + 4x_2 \leq 20 \qquad 2x_1 + x_2 \leq 30 \qquad x_1 + x_2 \leq 8$$

10-2 Solve graphically for the following objective functions, given the restrictions.

$$-x + 2y \leq 16 \qquad x + y \leq 24 \qquad x + 3y \leq 44 \qquad -4x + 10y \geq 20$$

(*a*) Maximize $z = 2x + 2y - 4$.
(*b*) Minimize $z = 6x - 2y + 120$.
(*c*) Maximize $z = 4x + 4y$.

10-3 Maximize $z = 4x_1 - 2x_2 + 2x_3 + 0x_4$ subject to

$$
\begin{aligned}
2x_1 + 2x_2 + 2x_3 + 2x_4 &\leq 16 \\
4x_2 - 2x_3 &\leq 8 \\
4x_1 - 2x_2 \qquad - x_4 &\leq 4
\end{aligned}
$$

10-4 Minimize $z = .5x_1 + 1.5x_2 - .5x_3$ subject to

$$
\begin{aligned}
-.5x_1 - .5x_2 + x_3 &\leq 2.5 \\
x_1 - .5x_2 + .5x_3 &\leq 3 \\
.5x_1 - 1.5x_2 + 2.5x_3 &\geq 10
\end{aligned}
$$

10-5 Minimize $z = 6x_1 + 4x_2 + 2x_3$ subject to

$$
\begin{aligned}
6x_1 + 2x_2 + 6x_3 &\geq 6 \\
6x_1 + 4x_2 &= 12 \\
2x_1 - 2x_2 &\leq 2
\end{aligned}
$$

10-6 A hardware dealer plans to sell packages of mixed nuts and bolts. Each package is to weigh at least 2 lb. Three sizes of nuts and bolts are to make up the package and are bought in 200-lb lots. Sizes 1, 2, and 3 cost $20, $8, and $12, respectively. Also:

(a) The combined weight of sizes 1 and 3 must be at least one-half the total package weight.

(b) The weight of sizes 1 and 2 must not be more than 1.6 lb.

(c) Any size bolt must be at least 10 per cent of the total package.

What package composition will minimize cost?

10-7   An aviation fuel manufacturer sells two types of fuel, A and B. Type A fuel is 25 percent grade 1 gasoline, 25 percent grade 2 gasoline, and 50 percent grade 3 gasoline. Type B fuel is 50 percent grade 2 gasoline and 50 percent grade 3 gasoline. Available for production are 500 gal/hour of grade 1 and 200 gal/hour of grades 2 and 3. Costs are 30 cents per gallon for grade 1, 60 cents per gallon for grade 2, and 50 cents per gallon for grade 3. Type A can be sold for 75 per gallon, while type B brings 90/gal. How much of each fuel should be made?

10-8   The owner of the Little Dixie Ranch is trying to determine the correct blend of two types of feed. Both contain various percentages of four essential ingredients. What is the least-cost blend?

	% per pound of feed		Minimum requirement,
Ingredient	Feed 1	Feed 2	lb/50 lb sack
1	40	20	4
2	10	30	2
3	20	40	3
4	30	10	6
Cost, $/lb	$.50	$.30	

10-9   The Peer Company produces four products, 1 to 4. Raw-material requirements, storage space needed, production rates, and profits are given in the table below. The total amount of raw material available per day for all four products is 180 lb. Total space available for storage is 230 ft², and 7 hours/day is used for production.

	1	2	3	4
Raw materials, lb/piece	2	2	1.5	4
Space, ft²/piece	2	2.5	2	1.5
Production rate, pieces/hour	15	30	10	15
Profit, $/piece	$5	$6.50	$5	$5.50

How many units of each product should be produced to maximize total profit?

10-10   A company has three types of processing machines, each having a different speed and accuracy. Type 1 can process 20 pieces/hour with 99 percent accuracy; type 2 15 pieces/hour with 95 percent accuracy; and type 3 10 pieces/hour with 100 percent accuracy. Type 1 costs $2 per hour to operate, type 2 costs $1.75 per hour to operate, and type 3 costs $1.50 per hour to operate. At least 3,500 pieces must be processed each day (8 hours), but 8 type 1 machines, 10 type 2 machines, and 20 type 3 machines are available. Each error costs the company $1. How many machines of each type should be used to minimize cost?

10-11   The Johnson Company manufactures four products, *A*, *B*, *C*, and *D*. Is the present mix optimal? If not, what should it be?

MINIMUM WEEKLY SALES REQUIREMENTS

Product	Units
A	12
B	15
C	15
D	12

PRESENT WEEKLY PRODUCT MIX

Product	Units
A	750
B	15
C	15
D	12

PRODUCTION TIME AND REQUIREMENTS

Department	A	B	C	D	Time available
1	.125	.1	.075	.125	200
2	.15	.20	.25	.15	500
3	.125	.15	.125	.15	250
4	.125	.125	.125	.125	250
Profit, $/unit	$5.25	$4.50	$4.00	$5.00	

10-12   The MidWest Trucking Company owns 10 trucks with a 40,000-lb capacity and 5 trucks with a 30,000-lb capacity. The larger trucks have operating costs of 30 cents per mile, and the smaller trucks have costs of 25 cents per mile. Next week the firm must transport 400,000 lb of beer 800 miles. The possibility of other business means that for every two small trucks held in reserve there must be at least one of the large trucks. What is the optimum number of each of the two types of trucks to use to move the beer? (Ignore the fact that the answer should be in integer form.)

10-13   The Warehouse Company has $1.5 million for allocation to one of its warehouses. Three products, 1, 2, and 3, require 30, 3, and 15 ft^3 of space per unit, respectively, and 300,000 ft^3 of space is available. Product 1 costs $12, product 2 costs $4.50, and product 3 costs $15. How much of each product should be purchased if the sales prices of 1, 2, and 3 are $15, $6, and $21, respectively?

10-14   A salesman handles two products. He does not expect to sell more than 10 units/month of product 1 or 39 units/month of product 2. To avoid a penalty he must sell at least 24 units of product 2. He receives a commission of 10 percent on all sales, and he must pay his own costs, which are estimated at $1.50 per hour spent on making calls. He works only part time and therefore is willing to work a maximum of 80 hours/month. Product 1 sells for $150 per unit and requires an average of 1.5 hours on every call; the probability of making a sale is .5. Product 2 sells for $70 per unit and requires an average of 30 minutes on every call; the probability of making a sale is .6. How many calls per month should he make on customers for each product?

11

TRANSPORTATION AND ASSIGNMENT PROBLEMS

Two special types of linear-programming problem, transportation and assignment problems, are often referred to as *distribution models*. Because the solution of these two problems by the simplex solution is not efficient, special algorithms have been developed for their solution. These algorithms are presented in this chapter.

THE TRANSPORTATION PROBLEM

The transportation problem requires the allocation of units located at a number of origins to a number of destinations in such a way that the allocation is an optimum (least cost or maximum profit). Mathematically, the problem is defined in the following manner. The objective equation is

$$\sum_{i=1}^{m} \sum_{j=1}^{n} c_{ij} x_{ij} \qquad (11\text{-}1)$$

which is subject to the restrictions

$$\sum_{j=1}^{n} x_{ij} = a_i \qquad i = 1, 2, \ldots, m \qquad (11\text{-}2)$$

$$\sum_{i=1}^{m} x_{ij} = b_j \qquad j = 1, 2, \ldots, n \qquad (11\text{-}3)$$

$$\sum_{i=1}^{m} a_i = \sum_{j=1}^{n} b_j \qquad (11\text{-}4)$$

$$x_{ij} \geq 0 \qquad \text{for all } i \text{ and } j \qquad (11\text{-}5)$$

where x_{ij} is the amount allocated from origin i to destination j and c_{ij} is the cost or profit of allocating 1 unit from origin i to destination j.   The a_i values are the amounts available at each origin, and the b_j values are the amounts required at each destination.   These values are often referred to as *rim requirements*.   Equation (11-4) shows that the sums of the a_i and b_j values must be equal.   This restriction does not impose any serious limitations on the problem.   All that is required is the introduction of a dummy origin or destination to satisfy Eq. (11-4).   This point will be illustrated in subsequent examples.

Table 11-1 will help explain Eq. (11-1) to (11-5).

The most common methods of obtaining a solution to the transportation problem are the *northwest-corner method* and *Vogel's approximation method*, presented in the following examples.

Table 11-1   TABULAR FORM OF THE TRANSPORTATION PROBLEM

Origin	Destinations					Supply
	1	2	.	j	n	
1	c_{11} / x_{11}	c_{12} / x_{12}	.	c_{1j} / x_{1j}	c_{1n} / x_{1n}	a_1
2	c_{21} / x_{21}	c_{22} / x_{22}	.	c_{2j} / x_{2j}	c_{2n} / x_{2n}	a_2
.	. / .	. / .	.	. / .	. / .	.
i	c_{i1} / x_{i1}	c_{i2} / x_{i2}	.	c_{ij} / x_{ij}	. / .	a_i
.	. / .	. / .	.	. / .	. / .	.
m	c_{m1} / x_{m1}	c_{m2} / x_{m2}	.	. / .	c_{mn} / x_{mn}	a_m
Requirements	b_1	b_2	.	b_j	b_n	

EXAMPLE 11-1 **Northwest-corner method: a minimization case** Four gaso-
line dealers A, B, C, and D require 50,000, 40,000, 60,000 and 40,000 gal of gasoline,
respectively. It is possible to supply these demands from locations 1, 2, and 3, which
have 80,000, 100,000, and 50,000 gal, respectively. The costs for shipping 1,000 gal
of gasoline in Table 11-2, show that it costs $70 per 1,000 gal to ship gasoline from
location 1 to dealer A, $80 per 1,000 gal from location 2 to dealer B, etc.

The problem is to determine the amounts of gasoline to be shipped from each
location to each dealer so that all the dealers' requirements are satisfied and the total
shipping costs are a minimum

The first step in obtaining a solution to this problem is to set up the problem
and make the initial allocation, as shown in Table 11-3. The supply and requirement
values have been multiplied by 10^{-4} to make the computations easier.

In this example a dummy column is necessary because the supply is greater
than the demand. If the demand is greater than the supply, a dummy row is necessary.
By adding a dummy row or column, Eq. (11-4) is satisfied.

The initial allocation shown in Table 11-3 is accomplished by the northwest-
corner method. This method requires starting at the northwest corner (row 1 column

Table 11-2 COST OF SHIPPING 1,000
GAL OF GASOLINE
(EXAMPLE 11-1)

	A	B	C	D
1	70	60	60	60
2	50	80	60	70
3	80	50	80	60

Table 11-3 INITIAL ALLOCATION FOR EXAMPLE 11-1

Location	Dealer					Supply
	A	B	C	D	Dummy	
1	70 5	60 3	60	60	0	8
2	50	80 1	60 6	70 3	0	10
3	80	50	80	60 1	0 4	5
Required	5	4	6	4	4	23

1) and making an allocation large enough to ensure that either the origin capacity of the first row is exhausted or the destination requirement of the first column is satisfied or both. In this problem the amount allocated to x_{1A} is 5 since this is the amount required by dealer A. This results in 3 remaining at location 1. The northwest-corner method requires that this be allocated to x_{1B}. Since the allocation of 3 to x_{1B} completes the amount available at location 1, the next step is to consider row 2. A total of 4 is required by dealer B; since 3 has already been allocated, 1 more is allocated to dealer B from location 2. This allocation completes the requirements of dealer B. Consequently, allocations along row 2 are made until the amount available (supply) has been used without allocating more than is required. Continuing in this manner, the origin capacities are exhausted and the destination requirements are satisfied. This results in a movement toward the southeast corner.

The allocation shown in Table 11-3 indicates the following:

Ship 50,000 gal from location 1 to dealer A.
Ship 30,000 gal from location 1 to dealer B.
Ship 10,000 gal from location 2 to dealer B.
Ship 60,000 gal from location 2 to dealer C.
Ship 30,000 gal from location 2 to dealer D.
Ship 10,000 gal from location 3 to dealer D.
40,000 gal at location 3 is not shipped.

The total cost (TC) for this allocation is

$$TC = 50(70) + 30(60) + 10(80) + 60(60) + 30(70) + 10(60) + 40(0)$$
$$= \$12,400 \qquad\qquad ////$$

Degeneracy and Optimality Tests

After each allocation, tests for degeneracy and optimality must be made. When the number of cells having allocations is less than $m + n - 1$, where m is the number of rows and n is number of columns, the solution is said to be degenerate. In Example 11-1, $m + n - 1$ is equal to 7, and the number of cells with allocations in Table 11-3 is also 7. Therefore this solution is not degenerate. If the number of cells having allocations were 6 or less, the solution would be degenerate. Degeneracy is treated later in this chapter.

A test to determine whether a particular solution is optimal is summarized in the following steps.

STEP 1 Set up a matrix containing the costs associated with the cells for which allocations have been made.

STEP 2 Using this matrix, establish a set of numbers v_j and another set of numbers u_i such that their sum equals the costs obtained in step 1. Mathematically, this is expressed by

$$c_{ij} = u_i + v_j \qquad (11\text{-}6)$$

Steps 1 and 2 are shown in Table 11-4.

STEP 3 Place the value of $u_i + v_j$ in the cells which do not have allocations. This step is shown in Table 11-5.

STEP 4 Subtract the values in Table 11-5 from the respective cost coefficients in the original matrix (Table 11-3). Mathematically, this step is expressed by the equation

$$c_{ij} - (u_i + v_j) \qquad (11\text{-}7)$$

The results of this step are shown in Table 11-6. If any of the values in Table 11-6 are negative, the solution is not optimal. Obviously, Tables 11-4 to 11-6 can be combined if desired.

Table 11-4 u_i AND v_j VALUES

u_i	v_j				
	0	−10	−30	−20	−80
70	70	60	—	—	—
90	—	80	60	70	—
80	—	—	—	60	0

Table 11-5 $u_i + v_j$ VALUES

—	—	40	50	−10
90	—	—	—	10
80	70	50	—	—

Table 11-6 $c_{ij} - (u_i + v_j)$ VALUES

—	—	20	10	10
−40	—	—	—	−10
0	−20	30	—	—

Moving toward an Optimal Solution

Since the allocation in Table 11-3 is not optimal, it is necessary to make another allocation. A systematic approach to finding an optimal solution is described by the following steps.

STEP 1 Identify the cell in Table 11-6 that has the smallest value. In this case this is cell (2,1) (row 2, column 1), which has a value of -40. If there is a tie, an arbitrary choice must be made.

STEP 2 Trace a plus-minus path in the transportation matrix. This path must begin and end in the cell identified in step 1. In addition, this cell is a plus. The remaining

Table 11-7 PLUS-MINUS PATH FOR FIRST ITERATION (EXAMPLE 11-1)

| Location | Dealer | | | | | Supply |
	A	B	C	D	Dummy	
1	5 · 70 ⊖----	3 · 60 ·⊕	60	60	0	8
2	50 ⊕----·⊖	80 · 1	60 · 6	70 · 3	0	10
3	80	50	80	60 · 1	0 · 4	5
Required	5	4	6	4	4	23

Table 11-8 ALLOCATIONS FOR FIRST ITERATION AND PLUS-MINUS PATH FOR SECOND ITERATION (EXAMPLE 11-1)

| Location | Dealer | | | | | Supply |
	A	B	C	D	Dummy	
1	4 · 70 ⊖----	4 · 60	60	60	0 ·⊕	8
2	1 · 50 ⊕----	80	6 · 60	3 · 70 ·⊖	0	10
3	80	50	80	60 ⊕---- · 1	0 ·⊖ · 4	5
Required	5	4	6	4	4	23

corners of the path (where the path changes direction) are designated alternately minus and plus. Also, all corners must have an existing allocation except the cell identified in step 1. This path need not be rectangular. The appropriate plus-minus path is shown in Table 11-7.

STEP 3 Choose the smallest amount in the negative corners and make a new allocation by adding this amount to or subtracting it from the plus or minus corners, respectively. As a check, be sure that the rim requirements are not violated. This step is shown in Table 11-8.

Table 11-9 OPTIMALITY TEST FOR THE ALLOCATION SHOWN IN TABLE 11-8

u_i	v_j				
	0	-10	10	20	-40
70	70 —	60 —	60 -20	60 -30	0 -30
50	50 —	80 40	60 —	70 —	0 -10
40	80 40	50 20	80 30	60 —	0 —

Table 11-10 ALLOCATIONS FOR SECOND ITERATION AND PLUS-MINUS PATH FOR THIRD ITERATION (EXAMPLE 11-1)

Location	Dealer					Supply
	A	B	C	D	Dummy	
1	1 70 ⊖------	4 60 ---------	60 --⊕	60	0 3	8
2	50 ⊕------	80 ---------	60 --⊖ 6	70	0	10
	4					
3	80	50	80	60 4	0 1	5
Required	5	4	6	4	4	23

After each iteration a test for optimality and degeneracy must be made.   Table 11-9 is the optimality test presented in a more concise form.   Since there are negative values in Table 11-9, the allocations in Table 11-8 are not optimum.   Consequently, another iteration is necessary.   Using the plus-minus path shown in Table 11-8 results in the allocations shown in Table 11-10.

Tables 11-11 to 11-17 are iterations toward an optimal solution and their respective optimality tests.   The reader should verify these tables to make sure he understands the iterative procedure.

Table 11-11   OPTIMALITY TEST FOR THE ALLOCATION IN TABLE 11-10

u_i	v_j				
	0	−10	10	−10	−70
70	70 —	60 —	60 −20	60 0	0 —
50	50 —	80 40	60 —	70 30	0 20
70	80 10	50 −10	80 0	60 —	0 —

Table 11-12   ALLOCATIONS FOR THIRD ITERATION AND PLUS-MINUS PATH FOR FOURTH ITERATION (EXAMPLE 11-1)

Location	Dealer					Supply
	A	B	C	D	Dummy	
1	70	4 | 60 ⊖	1 | 60	60	3 | 0 ⊕	8
2	50 5	80	60 5	70	0	10
3	80 ⊕	50	80	4 | 60	0 | 1 ⊖	5
Required	5	4	6	4	4	23

Table 11-13 OPTIMALITY TEST FOR THE ALLOCATION IN TABLE 11-12

u_i	v_j = -10	0	0	0	-60
60	70 / 20	60 / —	60 / —	60 / 0	0 / —
60	50 / —	80 / 20	60 / —	70 / 10	0 / 0
60	80 / 30	50 / -10	80 / 20	60 / —	0 / —

Table 11-14 ALLOCATION FOR THE FOURTH ITERATION AND PLUS-MINUS PATH FOR THE FIFTH ITERATION (EXAMPLE 11-1)

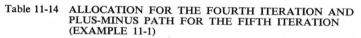

Location	Dealer					Supply
	A	B	C	D	Dummy	
1	70	3 | 60 ⊖	1 | 60	60 ⊕	0 / 4	8
2	50 / 5	80	60 / 5	70	0	10
3	80	50 ⊕ / 1	80	60 ⊖ / 4	0	5
Required	5	4	6	4	4	23

Table 11-15 OPTIMALITY TEST FOR THE ALLOCATION IN TABLE 11-14

u_i	v_j = -10	0	0	10	-60
60	70 / 20	60 / —	60 / —	60 / -10	0 / —
60	50 / —	80 / 20	60 / —	70 / 0	0 / 0
50	80 / 40	50 / —	80 / 30	60 / —	0 / 10

Since all the values in Table 11-17 are non-negative, the allocations in Table 11-16 are optimum. Therefore, the solution is:

From location 1 send 10,000 gal to dealer C.
From location 1 send 30,000 gal to dealer D.
40,000 gal remains at location 1.
From location 2 send 50,000 gal to dealer A.
From location 2 send 50,000 gal to dealer C.
From location 3 send 40,000 gal to dealer B.
From location 3 send 10,000 gal to dealer D.

The total cost of this solution is

$$TC = 10(60) + 30(60) + 40(0) + 50(50) + 50(60) + 40(50) + 10(60)$$
$$= \$10,500$$

Table 11-16 ALLOCATION FOR THE FIFTH ITERATION (EXAMPLE 11-1)

| Location | Dealer | | | | | Supply |
	A	B	C	D	Dummy	
1	70	60	60 1	60 3	0 4	8
2	50 5	80	60 5	70	0	10
3	80	50 4	80	60 1	0	5
Required	5	4	6	4	4	23

Table 11-17 OPTIMALITY TEST FOR THE ALLOCATION IN TABLE 11-16

| u_i | v_j | | | | |
	-10	-10	0	0	-60
60	70 20	60 10	60 —	60 —	0 —
60	50 —	80 30	60 —	70 10	0 0
60	80 30	50 —	80 20	60 —	0 0

If a zero occurs in the final $c_{ij} - (u_i + v_j)$ table, as it does in this case, this indicates that another allocation exists which gives the same optimal total cost. For example, if the following allocations are made,

From location 1 send 40,000 gal to dealer C.
From location 1 send 30,000 gal to dealer D.
10,000 gal at location 1 is not shipped.
From location 2 send 50,000 gal to dealer A.
From location 2 send 20,000 gal to dealer C.
30,000 gal at location 2 is not shipped.
From location 3 send 40,000 gal to dealer B.
From location 3 send 10,000 gal to dealer D.

then the total cost is

$$\text{TC} = 40(60) + 30(60) + 10(0) + 50(50) + 20(60) + 30(0) + 40(50) + 10(60)$$
$$= \$10,500$$

This is the same total cost as the previous allocation.

EXAMPLE 11-2   **Northwest-corner method: maximization case**   The procedure just described can also be used for maximization if a slight modification is made. Since minimizing the negative of a function is equivalent to maximizing the function, the modification required is to make all the profit coefficients negative. After this modification, the procedure is the same as that used in minimization. For example, consider the problem in Example 11-1 but with profits realized from the shipment of 1,000 gal as shown in Table 11-18.

The first steps are to set up the data in tabular form, multiply all the profit coefficients by -1, and make an initial allocation by the northwest-corner method. The result of these steps is shown in Table 11-19. From this point on, the steps are identical to those previously described.

The complete solution to this example is given in Tables 11-19 to 11-22.

Table 11-18   PROFIT PER 1,000
GAL (EXAMPLE 11-2)

	A	B	C	D
1	80	70	60	60
2	50	70	80	70
3	70	50	80	60

Table 11-19 INITIAL ALLOCATION AND PLUS-MINUS PATH FOR FIRST ITERATION (EXAMPLE 11-2)

Location	Dealer					Supply
	A	B	C	D	Dummy	
1	−80 5	−70 3	−60	−60	0	8
2	−50	−70 1	6 −80 ⊖- - - - -	3 −70 ⊕	0	10
3	−70	−50	−80 ⊕- - - - -	−60 1 ·⊖	0 4	5
Required	5	4	6	4	4	23

Table 11-20 OPTIMALITY TEST FOR ALLOCATION IN TABLE 11-19

u_i	v_j				
	0	10	0	10	70
−80	−80 —	−70 —	−60 20	−60 10	0 10
−80	−50 30	−70 —	−80 —	−70 —	0 10
−70	−70 0	−50 10	−80 −10	−60 —	0 —

Table 11-21 FIRST AND FINAL ITERATION (EXAMPLE 11-2)

Location	Dealer					Supply
	A	B	C	D	Dummy	
1	−80 5	−70 3	−60	−60	0	8
2	−50	−70 1	−80 5	−70 4	0	10
3	−70	−50	−80 1	−60	0 4	5
Required	5	4	6	4	4	23

Table 11-22 OPTIMALITY TEST FOR ALLOCATION IN TABLE 11-21

u_i	v_j = 0	10	0	10	80
−80	−80 —	−70 —	−60 20	−60 10	0 0
−80	−50 30	−70 —	−80 —	−70 —	0 0
−80	−70 10	−50 20	−80 —	−60 10	0 —

The final allocation (Table 11-21) indicates that the optimal solution is

From location 1 send 50,000 gal to dealer A.
From location 1 send 30,000 gal to dealer B.
From location 2 send 10,000 gal to dealer B.
From location 2 send 50,000 gal to dealer C.
From location 2 send 40,000 gal to dealer D.
From location 3 send 10,000 gal to dealer C.
40,000 gal at location 3 is not shipped.

The total profit for this solution is

$$TP = 50(80) + 30(70) + 10(70) + 50(80) + 40(70) + 10(80) + 49(0)$$
$$= \$14,400 \qquad\qquad ////$$

EXAMPLE 11-3 **Vogel's approximation method (VAM):** *a minimization case* In making the initial allocations using the northwest-corner method the magnitudes of the cost (or profit) coefficients c_{ij} were not considered. If the magnitudes of the cost coefficients are considered, there may be fewer iterations. Vogel's approxi-

Table 11-23 COST COEFFICIENTS FOR EXAMPLE 11-3

	1	2	3	4
A	420	395	400	435
B	460	305	380	345
C	300	375	455	405

mation method bases its initial allocation upon a comparison of the cost coefficients. Three origins A, B, and C have available 90, 110, and 50 units, respectively. Four destinations 1, 2, 3, and 4 require 60, 50, 85, and 45 units, respectively. The cost matrix is shown in Table 11-23. The problem is to determine the allocation which results in an optimum solution (least cost in this example) using the VAM method.

The VAM method is outlined in the following steps.

STEP 1 Set up the initial matrix, as shown in Table 11-24. Since the total demand (240) is less than the total amount available (250), the addition of a dummy column is required.

STEP 2 Determine the difference of the two smallest cost coefficients (next smallest and smallest) for each row and each column. These are the values shown in Table 11-24 to the right and bottom of the matrix. For example, the difference for row 1 is obtained from $395 - 0 = 395$; for column 1, $420 - 300 = 120$; for column 2, $375 - 305 = 70$, etc.

STEP 3. Find the row or column with the largest value determined in step 2 (it is 395 in row 1 in this case). Allocate to the cell having the smallest cost coefficient in this row (or column) the maximum amount allowed by the rim requirements (demand or supply). In case of a tie, make an arbitrary choice. In this particular

Table 11-24 VAM METHOD: MINIMIZATION CASE (EXAMPLE 11-3)

Origin	Destination 1	2	3	4	Dummy	Supply	
A	420 10	395	400 70	435	0 10	90	**395** 5 5 20 20
B	460	305 50	380 15	345 45	0	110	305 40 40 35 **80**
C	300 50	375	455	405	0	50	300 75 — — —
Demands	60	50	85	45	10	250	
	120	70	20	60	0		
	120	70	20	60	—		
	40	**90**	20	90	—		
	40	—	20	**90**	—		
	40	—	20	—	—		

problem, the smallest coefficient is zero, which appears in cell A-Dummy. The maximum amount that can be allocated is 10 units since that is all that is required (demand for the dummy is 10 units).

STEP 4 Allocate zero to the remaining cells in the row (or column) where the supply or demand is exhausted. In this problem, this is the dummy column. This step eliminates either a row or column (depending on which rim requirement is satisfied) from all further steps in making the initial allocation.

STEP 5 Repeat steps 2 to 4 until a complete solution is obtained. When only one cell remains in a row or column, allocate to that cell an amount that does not violate the rim requirements.

STEP 6 Test the solution for optimality using the test described in the discussion of the northwest-corner rule. If the solution is not optimal, iterate toward an optimal solution by tracing a plus-minus path as described for the northwest-corner rule. The test for optimality is shown in Table 11-25. This test indicates an optimal solution. Therefore the solution is

From origin A send 10 units to destination 1.
From origin A send 70 units to destination 3.
10 units remain at A.
From origin B send 50 units to destination 2.
From origin B send 15 units to destination 3.
From origin B send 45 units to destination 4.
From origin C send 50 units to destination 1.

$$TC = 10(420) + 70(400) + 10(0) + 50(305) + 15(380) + 45(345) + 50(300)$$
$$= \$83,675 \qquad ////$$

Table 11-25 OPTIMALITY TEST FOR ALLOCATION IN TABLE 11-24

u_i	v_j				
	0	−95	−20	−55	−420
420	420	395	400	365	0
	—	70	—	0	—
400	460	305	380	345	0
	60	—	—	—	20
300	300	375	455	405	0
	—	170	175	160	120

EXAMPLE 11-4   **Vogel's approximation method: a maximization case**   The VAM method presented in Example 11-3 can be used in a maximization problem by making a slight modification.   The required modification is to multiply all the c_{ij} values by -1, making use of the concept, mentioned in Example 11-2, that minimizing the negative of a function maximizes the original function.

As an example, the data in Example 11-3 are used except that the cost coefficients given in Table 11-23 are considered to be profit coefficients.   The solution to this example is shown in Tables 11-26 and 11-27.   The solution is

From origin A send 45 units to destination 2.
From origin A send 45 units to destination 4.
From origin B send 60 units to destination 1.
From origin B send 5 units to destination 2.
From origin B send 35 units to destination 3.
10 units at origin B are not sent.
From origin C send 50 units to destination 3.

The total profit (TP) for this solution is

$$TP = 395(45) + 435(45) + 60(460) + 5(305) + 35(380) + 110(0) + 50(455)$$
$$= \$102,525 \qquad\qquad ////$$

Table 11-26   VAM METHOD: MAXIMIZATION CASE (EXAMPLE 11-4)

Origin	Destination					Supply	
	1	2	3	4	Dummy		
A	-420	-395 45	-400	-435 45	0	90	15 35 35 5 —
B	-460 60	-305 5	-380 35	-345	0 10	110	**80** 35 35 75 **75**
C	-300	-375	-455 50	-405	0	50	50 50 — — —
Demand	60	50	85	45	10	250	
	40	20	55	30	0		
	—	20	**55**	30	0		
	—	90	20	**90**	0		
	—	**90**	20	—	0		
	—	70	20	—	0		

Table 11-27 OPTIMALITY TEST FOR ALLOCATION IN TABLE 11-26

u_i	v_j 0	155	80	115	460
−550	−420 130	−395 —	−400 70	−435 —	0 90
−460	−460 —	−305 —	−380 —	−345 0	0 —
−535	−300 235	−375 5	−455 —	−405 15	0 75

EXAMPLE 11-5 **The treatment of degeneracy** Degeneracy occurs when the number of cells having allocations is less than the quantity $m + n - 1$. Degeneracy can be resolved at any stage in the solution by placing an infinitesimally small allocation ε in an appropriate cell. The allocation of ε is made by inspection and does not affect the row or column totals since it is a very small amount. The treatment of the allocation of ε to a cell is the same as any other allocation. When the optimal solution is obtained, ε is set equal to zero. The actual details of treating a degenerate problem are best illustrated by a numerical example.

Table 11-28 A DEGENERATE PROBLEM (EXAMPLE 11-5)

Origins	Destinations 1	2	3	4	5	Supply
A	10 7	16	12	10	14	7
B	16 5	10 3	12	10	12	8
C	14	12	16 2	16 6	12	8
D	12	10	12	16	14 4	4
Dummy	0	0	0	0	0 5	5
Demand	12	3	2	6	9	32

Consider the initial solution of Table 11-28 obtained by the northwest-corner rule. Assume that this is a minimization problem. This solution has allocations in 7 cells., while $m + n - 1$ is 9. Therefore, this is a degenerate solution. In fact, the solution shown in Table 11-28 indicates that it is necessary to add more than one ε.

The reason that a solution is degenerate when less than $m + n - 1$ cells have allocations lies in the test for optimality. In the test for optimality, a unique set of u_i and v_j values is established once an initial value for one of the u_i or v_j values is chosen. If the number of occupied cells is less than $m + n - 1$, a unique set cannot be determined.

In order to test the allocation shown in Table 11-28 for optimality, two εs must be added. When more than one ε is required, one ε must arbitrarily be chosen as the larger. In this example, it is assumed that $\varepsilon < \varepsilon'$. The allocation of ε and ε' is shown in Table 11-29. It should be remembered that the εs must be put in cells that allow for a unique assignment of u_i and v_j values. For example, the allocation of ε to either cell $A2$, cell $D3$, or cell $D4$ and the allocation of ε' to cell $C5$ would not have provided a unique set of u_i and v_j values after the initial choice of either a u_i or v_j value.

The optimality test for the solution given Table 11-29 is given in Table 11-30. Since some of the $c_{ij} - (u_i + v_j)$ values are negative, the solution is not optimal. The

Table 11-29 ASSIGNMENT OF ε AND ε' TO TABLE 10-28 AND PLUS-MINUS PATH FOR FIRST ITERATION (EXAMPLE 11-5)

Origins	Destinations					Supply
	1	2	3	4	5	
A	10 / 7	16	12	10	14	7
B	16 / 5	10 / 3	12	10	12	8
C	14 / ε	12	16 / 2	16	12	8
D	12	10	12	16	14 / 4	4
Dummy	0	0	0	0	0 / 5	5
Demand	12	3	2	6	9	32

Table 11-30   OPTIMALITY TEST FOR THE ALLOCATION IN TABLE 11-29

u_i	v_j 0	-6	2	2	-2
10	10 —	16 12	12 0	10 -2	14 6
16	16 —	10 —	12 -6	10 -8	12 -2
14	14 —	12 4	16 —	16 —	12 —
16	12 -4	10 0	12 -6	16 -2	14 —
2	0 -2	0 4	0 -4	0 -4	0 —

Table 11-31   FIRST ITERATION AND PLUS-MINUS PATH FOR SECOND ITERATION (EXAMPLE 11-5)

Origins	Destinations 1	2	3	4	5	Supply
A	10 7	16	12	10	14	7
B	16	10 3	12	10 5	12	8
C	14 $5+\varepsilon$	12	16 2	16 1	12 ε'	8
D	12	10	12	16	14 4	4
Dummy	0	0	0	0	0 5	5
Demand	12	3	2	6	9	32

cell having the largest negative value is $B4$. Therefore an allocation should be made to this cell. This is accomplished by tracing the plus-minus path shown in Table 11-29. The results are shown in Table 11-31. At this point, it is possible to drop the ε from the calculations because with ε' there are nine cells having allocations. Therefore, the allocation in cell C1 is 5 instead of $5 + \varepsilon$. The test for optimality is shown in Table 11-32. This test indicates a nonoptimal solution, and the largest negative value is located in cell $D2$. Tracing the plus-minus path shown in Table 11-31 results in the allocations shown in Table 11-33. This plus-minus path demonstrates, again, that a plus-minus path does not have to be rectangular. The test for optimality of the allocations in Table 11-33 is shown in Table 11-34 and indicates a nonoptimal solution. At this point the ε' is eliminated because there are now nine cells with allocations and the problem is no longer degenerate. From this point on, moving toward an optimal solution is the same as before and is left as an exercise.

One optimal solution (there may be more than one) is

From origin A send 7 units to destination 1.
From origin B send 2 units to destination 2.
From origin B send 6 units to destination 4.
From origin C send 8 units to destination 5.
From origin D send 1 unit to destination 1.
From origin D send 1 unit to destination 2.
From origin D send 2 units to destination 3.

Table 11-32 OPTIMALITY TEST FOR THE
ALLOCATION IN TABLE 11-31

u_i \ v_j	0	2	2	2	−2
10	10 —	16 4	12 0	10 −2	14 6
8	16 8	10 —	12 2	10 —	12 6
14	14 —	12 −4	16 —	16 —	12 —
16	12 −4	10 −8	12 −6	16 −2	14 —
2	0 −2	0 −4	0 −4	0 −4	0 —

Table 11-33 SECOND ITERATION AND PLUS-MINUS PATH FOR THIRD ITERATION (EXAMPLE 11-5)

Origins	Destinations 1	2	3	4	5	Supply
A	10 7	16	12	10	14	7
B	16	10 2	12	10 6	12	8
C	14 5	12	2 │ 16 ⊖	16	12 ⊕ 1	8
D	12	10 1	12 ⊕	16	14 ⊖ 3	4
Dummy	0	0	0	0	0 5	5
Demand	12	3	2	6	9	32

Table 11-34 OPTIMALITY TEST FOR THE ALLOCATION IN TABLE 11-33

u_i	v_j = 0	−6	2	−6	−2
10	10 —	16 12	12 0	10 6	14 6
16	16 0	10 —	12 −6	10 —	12 −2
14	14 —	12 4	16 —	16 8	12 —
16	12 −4	10 —	12 −6	16 6	14 —
2	0 −2	0 4	0 −4	0 4	0 —

Since the demand is greater than the supply in this example, the solution indicates that destination 1 will be 4 units short and destination 5 will be 1 unit short.

The total cost for this optimum allocation is

$$TC = 7(10) + 2(10) + 6(10) + 8(12) + 1(12) + 1(10) + 2(12) + 4(0) + 1(0)$$
$$= \$292$$

////

THE ASSIGNMENT PROBLEM

Another type of distribution model is the assignment model. Specifically, the assignment model is concerned with assigning a number of origins to the same number of destinations in order to optimize some effectiveness function (usually cost *of* profit). Mathematically, the assignment model is defined as the optimization (maximization or minimization) of the function

$$\sum_{i=1}^{n} \sum_{j=1}^{n} c_{ij} x_{ij} \qquad (11\text{-}8)$$

where c_{ij} are the cost (profit) coefficients, subject to the restrictions

$$\sum_{i=1}^{n} x_{ij} = 1.0 \qquad j = 1, 2, 3, \ldots, n \qquad (11\text{-}9)$$

$$\sum_{j=1}^{n} x_{ij} = 1.0 \qquad i = 1, 2, 3, \ldots, n \qquad (11\text{-}10)$$

$$x_{ij} = 0 \text{ or } 1 \qquad \text{for all } x_{ij} \qquad (11\text{-}11)$$

The problem expressed by Eqs. (11-8) to (11-11) can be solved by one of the methods described in the discussion of the transportation problem, but because only one allocation is allowed in each row and column [Eqs. (11-9) and (11-10)] this is a degenerate transportation problem. Consequently a special method is available, as explained in the following examples.

EXAMPLE 11-6   **The assignment method: a minimization case**   Four different buildings *A*, *B*, *C*, and *D* are to be constructed on a college campus by four different contractors 1, 2, 3, and 4. Because all contractors contribute heavily to the alumni fund, each is to build one building. Each contractor has submitted bids for the four buildings. The bids are shown in Table 11-35.

Table 11-35   **BIDS FOR BUILDINGS**
(EXAMPLE 11-6)
(0000 omitted)

Building	Contractor			
	1	2	3	4
A	48	48	50	44
B	56	60	60	68
C	96	94	90	85
D	42	44	54	46

The problem is to determine which building is to be awarded to each contractor to keep the cost of procuring the four buildings at a minimum.

STEP 1   Subtract the smallest element in each row from the rest of the elements in the same row.   The results from this step are shown in Table 11-36.

STEP 2   Subtract the smallest element in each column from the rest of the elements in the same column.   The results of this step are shown in Table 11-37.

STEP 3   Test for optimality by drawing the *minimum* number of lines that will pass through all the zeros in Table 11-37.   This step is shown in Table 11-38.   This step sometimes causes difficulties, as often there are many ways to draw these lines.   This makes no difference provided the number of lines is a minimum and the lines are drawn horizontally or vertically.   Diagonal lines are not permitted.

Table 11-36   STEP 1: THE SMALLEST IN THE ROW (EXAMPLE 11-6)

Building	Contractor			
	1	2	3	4
A	4	4	6	0
B	0	4	4	12
C	11	9	5	0
D	0	2	12	4

Table 11-37   STEP 2: THE SMALLEST IN THE COLUMN (EXAMPLE 11-6)

Building	Contractor			
	1	2	3	4
A	4	2	2	0
B	0	2	0	12
C	11	7	1	0
D	0	0	8	4

Table 11-38   TEST FOR OPTIMALITY (EXAMPLE 11-6)

Building	Contractor			
	1	2	3	4
A	4	2	2	0
B	0	2	0	12
C	11	7	1	0
D	0	0	8	4

STEP 4   After the minimum number of lines have been drawn, the test for optimality is made.   If the number of lines is equal to n (the number of rows or columns), an optimal assignment can be made.   If the number of lines is less than n, iteration toward an optimal solution is required.

In Table 11-38 the minimum number of lines is 3.   Since $n = 4$, an iteration toward an optimal solution must be performed.   This can be accomplished by selecting the smallest element that does not have a line through it (this is 1 in this iteration) and subtracting it from all elements that do not have a line through them. Add this amount to all elements at the intersection of lines.   All other elements remain unchanged.   The result of this iteration procedure is shown in Table 11-39.

STEP 5   Test for optimality again.   This test is shown in Table 11-40 and indicates that an optimal assignment is possible.   If the number of lines had been less than 4, another iteration would be made.

STEP 6   Make the optimal assignment.   This is accomplished by finding where the zeros are located in the final table (minimum number of lines $= n$) and remembering

Table 11-39   ITERATION TOWARD AN OPTIMAL SOLUTION (EXAMPLE 11-6)

Building	Contractor			
	1	2	3	4
A	3	1	1	0
B	0	2	0	13
C	10	6	0	0
D	0	0	8	5

Table 11-40   FINAL OPTIMALITY TEST (EXAMPLE 11-6)

Building	Contractor			
	1	2	3	4
A	3	1	1	0
B	0	2	0	13
C	10	6	0	0
D	0	0	8	5

the constraints imposed by Eqs. (11-9) and (11-10).   The optimal assignment for this problem is

Contractor 4 builds building *A*.
Contractor 1 builds building *B*.
Contractor 3 builds building *C*.
Contractor 2 builds building *D*.

The total cost is

$$44 + 56 + 90 + 44 = 234 = \$2,340,000 \qquad ////$$

In some problems it is often possible to make more than one optimal assignment.   Also, the assignment problem, by definition, requires an $n \times n$ matrix.   However, for cases that do not have an $n \times n$ matrix, it is possible to modify the matrix to meet this requirement, provided, of course, that it meets the other requirements of an assignment problem.   These two points are illustrated in the following example.

EXAMPLE 11-7   A moving company has five trucks available for use located in cities *A*, *B*, *C*, *D*, and *E*.   One truck is required in cities 1, 2, 3, 4, 5, and 6.   The mileage between cities is shown in Table 11-41.   The problem is to determine the assignment of trucks that will minimize the mileage traveled by all trucks.

Since Table 11-41 is not a $n \times n$ matrix, it must be modified before the assignment method can be used.   This is accomplished by adding a dummy row, where the elements in the dummy row are zero since no mileage is associated with not moving a vehicle.   This step is shown in Table 11-42 and is the equivalent of saying that one city will not receive a truck.   Had the opposite situation been the case, i.e., more trucks available than are required, a dummy column would have been added.   It should also be pointed out that it is possible to add as many dummy rows or columns as required in order to make the initial matrix an $n \times n$ matrix.   The solution and the tests for optimality for the problem shown in Table 11-42 are given in Tables 11-43 to

Table 11-41   MILEAGE FOR EXAMPLE 11-7

From cities	To cities					
	1	2	3	4	5	6
A	20	15	26	40	32	12
B	15	32	46	26	28	20
C	18	15	2	12	6	14
D	8	24	12	22	22	20
E	12	20	18	10	22	15

Table 11-42   ADDITION OF DUMMY ROW (EXAMPLE 11-7)

	To cities					
From cities	1	2	3	4	5	6
A	20	15	26	40	32	12
B	15	32	46	26	28	20
C	18	15	2	12	6	14
D	8	24	12	22	22	20
E	12	20	18	10	22	15
Dummy	0	0	0	0	0	0

Table 11-43   STEPS 1 AND 2 AND OPTIMALITY TEST (EXAMPLE 11-7)

	To cities					
From cities	1	2	3	4	5	6
A	8	3	14	28	20	0
B	0	17	31	11	13	5
C	16	13	0	10	4	12
D	0	16	4	14	14	12
E	2	10	8	0	12	5
Dummy	0	0	0	0	0	0

Table 11-44   FIRST ITERATION AND OPTIMALITY TEST (EXAMPLE 11-7)

	To cities					
From cities	1	2	3	4	5	6
A	8	0	14	28	17	0
B	0	14	31	11	10	5
C	16	10	0	10	1	12
D	0	13	4	14	11	12
E	2	7	8	0	9	5
Dummy	3	0	3	3	0	3

11-46.   The final assignment (Table 11-46) indicates two assignments.   Assignment 1 is

From city A send a truck to city 6.
From city B send a truck to city 1.
From city C send a truck to city 5.
From city D send a truck to city 3.
From city E send a truck to city 4.
City 2 does not receive a truck.

The total mileage for this assignment is

$$12 + 15 + 6 + 12 + 10 + 0 = 55 \text{ miles}$$

Table 11-45   SECOND ITERATION AND OPTIMALITY TEST (EXAMPLE 11-7)

From cities	To cities					
	1	2	3	4	5	6
A	0	0	15	29	17	0
B	0	13	31	11	9	4
C	16	9	0	10	0	11
D	0	12	4	14	10	11
E	2	6	8	0	8	4
Dummy	4	0	4	4	0	3

Table 11-46   THIRD ITERATION AND OPTIMALITY TEST (EXAMPLE 11-7)

From cities	To cities					
	1	2	3	4	5	6
A	13	0	15	29	17	0
B	0	9	27	7	5	0
C	20	9	0	10	0	11
D	0	8	0	10	6	7
E	6	6	8	0	8	4
Dummy	8	0	4	4	0	3

Assignment 2 is

From city A send a truck to city 2.
From city B send a truck to city 6.
From city C send a truck to city 3.
From city D send a truck to city 1.
From city E send a truck to city 4.
City 5 does not receive a truck.

The total mileage for this assignment is

$$15 + 20 + 2 + 8 + 10 + 0 = 55 \text{ miles} \qquad ////$$

If an assignment problem is expressed in terms of profit or some other criterion that requires maximization, the same assignment method can be used after multiplying all elements in the initial matrix by -1.

REFERENCES

1 HADLEY, G.: "Linear Programming," Addison-Wesley Publishing Company, Inc., Reading, Mass., 1963.
2 LEVIN, R. I., and C. A. KIRKPATRICK: "Quantitative Approaches to Management," 2d ed., McGraw-Hill Book Company, New York, New York, 1971.
3 LLEWELLYN, R. W.: "Linear Programming," Holt, Rinehart and Winston, Inc., New York, 1964.
4 LOOMBA, N. P.: "Linear Programming," McGraw-Hill Book Company, New York, 1964.

PROBLEMS

11-1 Using the data in Example 11-1, expand Eqs. (11-1) to (11-3).

11-2 Complete the iterations toward an optimal solution omitted in Example 11-5.

11-3 Rework Example 11-5 using the VAM method.

11-4 A petroleum company has three major oil fields and five regional refineries. The shipping costs from the fields to the refineries, the capacities of the refineries, and

REFINERY CAPACITY		PRODUCTION	
Refinery	Barrels/day	Field	Barrels/day
A	10,000	1	20,000
B	12,000	2	25,000
C	14,000	3	30,000
D	16,000		
E	18,000		

the production from the three fields are all tabulated. Determine the optimum shipping scheme using the northwest-corner method.

COST PER 1,000 BARRELS/DAY

Field	Refinery				
	A	B	C	D	E
1	$42	$32	$33	$39	$36
2	34	36	37	32	34
3	38	31	40	35	35

11-5 A corporation has three manufacturing plants, 1, 2, and 3, which can produce one or all of four different products A, B, C, and D. Different variable costs at each plant mean that the profit for each product varies as tabulated.

Plant	Profit per unit				Capacity, units/week
	A	B	C	D	
1	$22	$26	$20	$21	450
2	21	24	20	21	300
3	18	20	19	20	250

The demand for the different products is:

Product	Units/week
A	200
B	340
C	150
D	270

Determine the amounts of products that should be made at each plant so that profits are maximized. Use the northwest-corner method.

11-6 A job shop makes three products A, B, and C, and the demand for these products is 90, 210, and 120 units/week, respectively. The products can be manufactured by any one of three methods, 1, 2, and 3. The capacity of each method and the

Method	Units/week
1	160
2	120
3	140

Product	Profit/unit		
	1	2	3
A	$139	$140	$137
B	209	207	210
C	254	255	255

profits associated with each product and each manufacturing method are tabulated. Determine the optimum method of manufacturing these products using the northwest-corner method.

11-7   Repeat Prob. 11-4 using the VAM method.

11-8   Solve Prob. 11-5 using the VAM method.

11-9   Assuming that this is a minimization problem, determine the optimum solution using the northwest-corner method.   Use the table provided.

Origin	Destination				Supply
	A	B	C	D	
1	10	9	12	9	28
2	12	15	15	12	15
3	13	14	13	13	35
4	10	12	14	10	80
Required	43	35	60	20	158

11-10   Work Prob. 11-9 using the VAM method.

11-11   A company has three major distributors which supply five retailers.   Distances from the distributors to the retailers, requirements of the retailers, and the distributors capacities are tabulated. Determine which distributors should supply the retailers to minimize the total distance traveled.   Use the VAM method.

Retailer	Distributor			Number required
	A	B	C	
1	6	7	8	12
2	4	6	7	15
3	5	7	6	21
4	4	4	9	24
5	8	3	5	24
Number available	15	48	33	

11-12   Three warehouses supply five stores.   The table indicates the cost of shipment per unit between warehouses and stores, warehouse capacities, and requirements of the stores. However, a major bridge has been damaged, preventing deliveries from warehouse *A* to store 5, from warehouse *B* to store 2, and from warehouse *C* to store 4.   Within these limitations, determine the optimum delivery scheme using the VAM method.

COST OF SHIPMENT, $/UNIT

| Store | Warehouse | | | Number required |
	A	B	C	
1	$2	$4	$6	75
2	3	8	7	345
3	4	3	8	180
4	4	6	3	90
5	2	6	5	210
Capacity	850	300	450	

11-13   Rework Prob. 11-12 assuming that the cost of shipment is profit of shipment.

11-14   Using the data in Example 11-6 expand Eqs. (11-8) to (11-10).

11-15   Four locations A, B, C, and D require a certain spare part. The four spare parts are stored in four different warehouses. If the mileages between warehouses and locations are as shown in the table, determine the least-mileage shipping schedule.

MILEAGE

| Warehouse | Location | | | |
	A	B	C	D
1	230	200	210	240
2	190	210	200	200
3	200	180	240	220
4	220	180	210	230

11-16   A construction company has five bulldozers at different locations, and one bulldozer is required at three different construction sites. If the transportation costs are as shown, determine the optimum shipping schedule.

SHIPPING COSTS
(000 omitted)

| Location | Construction site | | |
	A	B	C
1	$2	$3	$4
2	7	6	4
3	3	5	8
4	4	6	5
5	4	6	3

11-17   A manager has the problem of assigning four new methods to three production facilities. The assignment of the new methods will increase profits by the amounts shown. If only one method can be assigned to a production facility, determine the optimal assignment.

PROFITS
(000 omitted)

Method	Production facility		
	1	2	3
A	12	9	13.5
B	10	11	12.5
C	11.5	10	10
D	13	12	10.5

11-18 Suppose in Prob. 11-15 it is not possible to make a shipment from warehouse 3 to location A. What would be the optimum shipping schedule taking this limitation into account?

12

SENSITIVITY ANALYSIS FOR LINEAR PROGRAMMING

INTRODUCTION

The use of sensitivity analysis in linear-programming models is simply a knowledgeable interpretation of the results already obtained. Once the meaning of the matrix elements is understood, the analysis becomes logical and straightforward. In many cases, the information provided by an application of sensitivity analysis may be more important and much more informative than the single result obtained in the optimal solution. In a sense, sensitivity analysis makes the static linear-programming solution a dynamic tool that evaluates changing conditions. Thus, it becomes more useful as a managerial tool since business and industry are subject to continuous change and subsequent reevaluation. This topic will be presented with the stress on interpretation, using examples to illustrate these interpretations. Topics will be offered without formal proof by appealing to a basic understanding of the mathematics and their application. More rigorous proofs may be found in several of the references.

INTERPRETATION OF THE MATRIX

The interpretation of the elements of the linear-programming matrix is most easily followed by means of an example.   For convenience, the hypothetical manufacturing-plant problem already used in Chap. 10 will be used again.   The data are summarized in Tables 12-1 and 12-2.

      The reader will recall that these data can be formulated into the following equations and inequalities.   Maximize

$$1x_1 + 1.5x_2$$

subject to the constraints

$$2x_1 + 2x_2 \le 160$$

$$x_1 + 2x_2 \le 120$$

$$4x_1 + 2x_2 \le 280$$

$$x_1, x_2 \ge 0$$

Table 12-1   MANUFACTURING-TIME REQUIREMENTS PER DEPARTMENT TO PRODUCE 1 UNIT OF PRODUCT

Product	Manufacturing time, hours		
	Dept. A	Dept. B	Dept. C
1	2	1	4
2	2	2	2

Table 12-2   MANUFACTURING-CAPACITY LIMITS

Department	Man-hours/week available
A	160
B	120
C	280

Table 12-3   PROFIT PER UNIT OF PRODUCT

Product	Profit
1	$1.00
2	1.50

Adding slack variables allows the problem to be expressed by equations instead of inequalities. Maximize

$$1x_1 + 1.5x_2$$

subject to the constraints

(1) $\quad 2x_1 + 2x_2 + u_1 = 160$

(2) $\quad x_1 + 2x_2 + u_2 = 120$

(3) $\quad 4x_1 + 2x_2 + u_3 = 280$

plus nonnegativity requirements.

Putting this into linear-programming matrix form gives

Matrix 1   Initial Matrix

$$
\begin{array}{c c c c c c | c}
 & x_1 & x_2 & u_1 & u_2 & u_3 & b \\
A & 2 & 2 & 1 & 0 & 0 & 160 \\
B & 1 & 2 & 0 & 1 & 0 & 120 \\
C & 4 & 2 & 0 & 0 & 1 & 280 \\
\hline
z & 1 & 1.5 & 0 & 0 & 0 & 0
\end{array}
$$

In this matrix, row 1 represents the restriction placed on the problem as a result of the maximum available capacity in department A. It is the same as constraint (1) previously set up. It says

(Time/unit, product 1)(no. of units, product 1) + (time/unit, product 2)
$\quad \times$ (no. of units, product 2) + idle time = maximum available time

In general notation, this equation is

$$a_{11}x_1 + a_{12}x_2 + a_{13}u_1 = b_1 \qquad (12\text{-}1)$$

where a_{11} = time to produce 1 unit of x_1 in department A, hours/unit

x_1 = number of units of x_1 produced, units/week

a_{12} = time to produce 1 unit of x_2 in department A, hours/unit

x_2 = number of units of x_2 produced, units/week

a_{13} = time required for 1 unit of idle time in department A, hours/unit

u_1 = number of idle units available in department A, units/week

b_1 = total resource available (manufacturing time) available in department A, hours/week

Up to this point, u_1 has been called idle time or simply slack. Actually u_1 is the number of units of slack, idle time, or unused resource, and the coefficient tells how large that unit of slack is. Since the coefficient is 1, the number of units of u_1 has the same numerical value as the amount of unused resource, in this case, idle hours.

Dimensionally this equation becomes

$$\frac{\text{Hours units}}{\text{Unit week}} + \frac{\text{hours units}}{\text{unit week}} + \frac{\text{hours units}}{\text{unit week}} = \frac{\text{hours}}{\text{week}}$$

In a similar manner, the second row represents the second restriction equation, the third row represents the third restriction equation, etc. Actually the complete equation for row 1 includes values for all variables.

$$a_{11}x_1 + a_{12}x_2 + a_{13}u_1 + a_{14}u_2 + a_{15}u_3 = b_1 \qquad (12\text{-}2)$$

Referring to matrix 1, it can be observed that a_{14} and a_{15} are both zero and have no effect upon the equation represented. In a completely general form, no distinction is made between the real variables (x's) and the slack variables (u's).

$$a_{11}x_1 + a_{12} + x_2 + a_{13}x_3 + a_{14}x_4 + a_{15}x_5 = b_1 \qquad (12\text{-}3)$$

where
$$x_3 = u_1 \qquad x_4 = u_2 \qquad x_5 = u_3$$

In a similar manner, the second row in the matrix represents the second restriction equation, etc. Thus, the information provided by any row always relates to a specific restriction, in this example, the availability of manpower in departments A, B, and C.

The bottom row, or the z row, represents the objective function being optimized; in this example it is the profit equation.

$$1x_1 + 1.5x_2 + 0u_1 + 0u_2 + 0u_3 = \text{profit} \qquad (12\text{-}4)$$

Since the slack or idle units (u's) do not contribute to the profit, they have coefficients of zero. The coefficients in this equation are referred to as cost coefficients.

As in Chap. 10, only the variables in the identity matrix have positive values (are in solution). Thus in matrix 1, x_1 and x_2 are both zero since they are not in solution. These variables are referred to as nonbasic; those in solution are called basic variables. At the initial stage, if $x_1 = x_2 = 0$, the profit is also zero, as indicated in matrix 1.

The optimal solution is shown in matrix 2 after the simplex has been completed. This matrix can be similarly interpreted. The algebraic values in parentheses are included for easy reference. In this chapter, these coefficients will be referred to as *input values*.

Matrix 2   Optimal Matrix

	x_1	x_2	u_1	u_2	u_3	b
A	$1(a_{11})$	$0(a_{12})$	$1(a_{13})$	$-1(a_{14})$	$0(a_{15})$	$40(b_1)$
B	$0(a_{21})$	$1(a_{22})$	$-\frac{1}{2}(a_{23})$	$1(a_{24})$	$0(a_{25})$	$40(b_2)$
C	$0(a_{31})$	$0(a_{32})$	$-3(a_{33})$	$2(a_{34})$	$1(a_{35})$	$40(b_3)$
z	$0(c_1)$	$0(c_2)$	$-\frac{1}{4}(c_3)$	$-\frac{1}{2}(c_4)$	$0(c_5)$	$-100(z)$

As previously discussed, only the variables (columns) represented in the identity matrix have positive values; all others have a value of zero. Thus, both u_1 and u_2 have a value of zero.   Row 1 is read

$$1x_1 + 0x_2 + 1u_1 - 1u_2 + 0u_3 = 40 \qquad (12\text{-}5)$$

where
$$u_1 = u_2 = 0$$

Substituting the values for u_1 and u_2 gives
$$x_1 + 0x_2 + 0u_3 = 40 \qquad (12\text{-}6)$$

or
$$x_1 = 40$$

The remaining rows indicate that $x_2 = 40$ and $u_3 = 40$.   The reader should verify this result.

The coefficients of the nonbasic variables have meaning even if the values of the variables are presently zero.   Remembering that the value of the left-hand side of the equation must always equal 40 (b_1), it is apparent that if u_1 is increased to a positive value, the value assigned to x_1 must be decreased.

$$1x_1 + 1u_1 = 40$$

If u_1 is increased from 0 to 2 units, x_2 must be decreased to maintain a total sum of 40.

$$(1) \qquad (40 - 2) + 1(0 + 2) = 40$$

A similar method of reasoning shows that if u_2 is made positive, x_1 must be increased in value.

$$1x_1 - 1u_2 = 40$$

Thus the coefficients of the nonbasic variables indicate the effect of increasing their value upon the basic variable (in solution) in that row.

EXAMPLE 12-1   What is the effect of increasing u_1 by 1 unit, i.e., from 0 to 1?

$$\begin{aligned}
(1) \qquad & 1x_1 + 1u_1 = 40 \\
& 1x_1 + 1(0 + 1) = 40 \\
& x_1 = 40 - 1 = 39 \\
(2) \qquad & 1x_2 - \tfrac{1}{2}u_1 = 40 \\
& x_2 - \tfrac{1}{2}(0 + 1) = 40 \\
& x_2 = 40\tfrac{1}{2} \\
(3) \qquad & -3u_1 + 1u_3 = 40 \\
& -3(0 + 1) + u_3 = 40 \\
& u_3 = 43
\end{aligned}$$

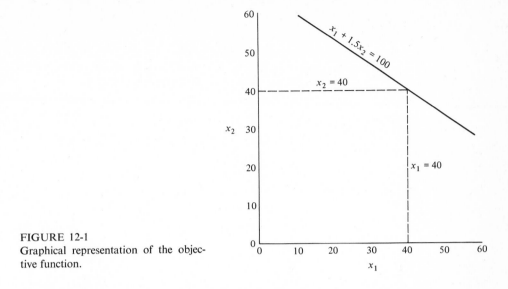

FIGURE 12-1
Graphical representation of the objective function.

In any matrix except the initial matrix, the bottom, or z, row no longer represents the original objective function; it now represents the effect upon the profit of any change in the indicated values.

$$0x_1 + 0x_2 - \tfrac{1}{4}u_1 - \tfrac{1}{2}u_2 + 0u_3 = 100 = \text{profit} \qquad (12\text{-}7)$$

In this case, the basic variables (x_1, x_2, and u_3) cannot be increased without exceeding some restriction, as indicated by the zero coefficients in the z row. The $-\tfrac{1}{4}u_1$ means that if u_1 is increased by 1 unit, the profit will be decreased by $\tfrac{1}{4}$ unit. Since the profit is not fixed but variable, any change in a variable may increase or decrease the z value accordingly.   ////

EFFECTS OF CHANGES IN COST COEFFICIENTS

The cost coefficients are those coefficient values in the objective-function, or z, row. Interpreted graphically, these coefficients determine the slope of the objective function which may be a line (two variables), a plane (three variables), or a hyperplane (four or more variables). In this example, the objective function is plotted as a line since there are only two decision variables (x_1 and x_2). The optimal solution yields a value of 100 from 40 units of x_1 and 40 units of x_2. This may be represented as a point on the line $x_1 + 1.5x_2 = 100$, as illustrated in Fig. 12-1. Changing the coefficient of either x_1 or x_2 would give a line with a different slope.

The values of $x_1 = 40$ and $x_2 = 40$ represent an optimal solution considering both the constraints and the objective. In addition, the point (40,40) is at the intersection of two constraint lines. It has already been shown that the solution to any

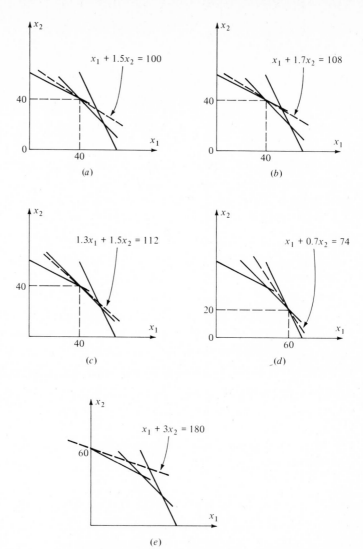

FIGURE 12-2
The effect of the cost coefficients in the objective function.

linear-programming problem will lie at an intersection (see Chap. 10). The optimal solution will remain there until for some reason it shifts to an entirely different intersection. This shift could be caused by changing the slope of the objective function.

Figure 12-2 presents the graphical solution of the example using several different objective functions but maintaining the same set of constraints. Referring to Fig. 12-2b, note that increasing the coefficient of the x_2 variable from 1.5 to 1.7 did not move the optimal solution from the intersection $x_1 = 40$, $x_2 = 40$, although the objec-

tive value has increased to 108.   In a similar manner, Fig. 12-2c illustrates the effect
of a small change in the coefficient of the x_1 variable.   When a large change in the
cost coefficient occurs, the slope of the objective function shifts enough to move the
optimal solution to a new intersection.   In Fig. 12-2d, if the cost coefficient of x_2 is
decreased to .7, the optimal solution shifts to the intersection $x_1 = 60$, $x_2 = 20$, an
entirely different product mix and objective value.   If the cost coefficient of x_2 is
increased from 1.5 to 3, the solution shifts to the intersection $x_1 = 0$, $x_2 = 60$.   Sensitivity analysis answers the question of how far these coefficients can be varied before
this shift takes place, i.e., before a new optimal solution must be obtained.   For those
variables in solution (basic variables) this can be referred to as an optimal range for
the basic cost coefficients.   When the coefficients, which represent price, profit, time,
etc., individually take on any value within this range, the same solution is still optimal.

OPTIMAL RANGE OF COST COEFFICIENTS

Basic Variables

Over what values of profit for x_2 will the present solution, $x_1 = 40$, $x_2 = 40$, still be
optimal?   This is illustrated in Fig. 12-3.

An analytical solution to this question is approached by determining the point
at which some other variable enters the solution.   From a practical standpoint it

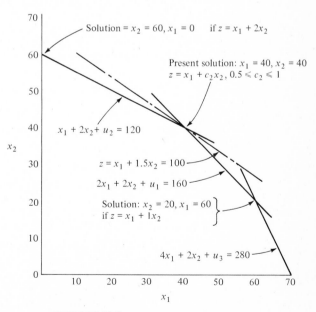

FIGURE 12-3
Graphical solution for sensitivity of cost coefficient c_2.

may be said that for each intersection, a unique set of variables is in solution (have nonzero values), some of which may be decision variables (x's) and some are slack variables (u's). This is not true only when some limiting constraint has the same slope as the objective functions. Thus, even if the same decision variables (x_1 and x_2) are in solution, the slack variables that are in solution may change. Referring to Fig. 12-3, if the cost coefficient of x_2 decreases to a value less than 1, then $u_3 = 0$ and u_2 will have a positive value and become a basic variable. If the cost coefficient of x_2 increases to a value greater than 2, then $x_1 = 0$ and u_1 will have a positive value and become a basic variable.

To find this range of values analytically, all nonbasic variables must be evaluated to determine the value of the x_2 cost coefficient which would cause each of the non-basic variables to become basic. The optimal range of a cost coefficient is thus defined by the set of values most closely bounding the present cost-coefficient value. This evaluation is made using the information presented in both the initial and final matrix. In a two-decision-variable problem the case is somewhat simplified but serves to illustrate the logic process. As previously indicated, the matrix coefficients of the nonbasic variables indicate a substitution rate. For example, if 1 unit of u_1 is to be provided without changing any constraints, it requires a reduction in output of 1 unit of x_1, of $-\frac{1}{2}$ unit of x_2, and of -3 units of u_3. A reduction of $-\frac{1}{2}$ represents an actual increase of $\frac{1}{2}$ in net production; u_1 is eligible for "production," or in solution, if the profit added as a result of the substitution is equal to the profit lost due to the reduction of the variables in solution; thus set these factors equal.

Profit added by 1 unit of $u_1 =$ profit lost by reduction of basic variables. Referring to the original objective function, the profit per unit for each of the variables is represented by their original cost coefficients.

Variable	Cost efficient
x_1	1
x_2	1.5
u_1	0
u_2	0
u_3	0

These values are used to write the equation representing the change in profit from the addition of 1 unit of u.

$$0\Delta u_1 = 1(1) + (-\tfrac{1}{2})(1.5) + (-3)(0) \qquad (12\text{-}8)$$

Since the problem is to find the value of the x_2 cost coefficient which allows u_1 to enter solution, $\bar{c}_2$ is substituted for the coefficient 1.5 and the equation solved for $\bar{c}_2$, where $\bar{c}_2$ represents some change in c_2.

$$0(1) = 1(1) + (-\tfrac{1}{2})(\bar{c}_2) + (-3)(0) \qquad (12\text{-}9)$$
$$\bar{c}_2 = 2$$

If c_2 should be larger than 2, u_1 will become a basic variable and the present product mix will not be optimal.   The other nonbasic variable is checked in a similar manner.

$$0\Delta u_2 = (-1)(1) + 1(1.5) + 2(0) \qquad (12\text{-}10)$$

$$0(1) = (-1) + c_2 + 0$$

$$\bar{c}_2 = 1$$

The variable u_2 will enter solution if c_2 becomes less than 1.   Thus the optimal range for the cost coefficient of x_2 is

$$1 \le c_2 \le 2$$

In this case c_2 was bracketed by a single limit.   If several values had been computed, the limiting values would be those closest to the original c_i value.

EXAMPLE 12-2   What is the optimal range for c_1?   Check u_1:

$$0\Delta u_1 = 1(1) + (-\tfrac{1}{2})(1.5) + (-3)(0)$$

$$0 = \bar{c}_1 - \tfrac{3}{4} + 0$$

$$\bar{c}_1 = \tfrac{3}{4}$$

Check u_2:

$$0\Delta u_1 = (-1)(1) + 1(1.5) + 2(0)$$

$$0 = -\bar{c}_1 + 1.5 + 0$$

$$\bar{c}_1 = 1.5$$

Optimal range for c_1 is $\tfrac{3}{4} \le c_1 \le 1.5$ ////

EXAMPLE 12-3   The initial and optimal matrix are shown for a maximization problem.

Initial Matrix

x_1	x_2	x_3	u_1	u_2	b
1	1	1	1	0	20
2	1	3	0	1	30
2	3	4	0	0	0

Optimal Matrix

x_1	x_2	x_3	u_1	u_2	b
$\tfrac{1}{2}$	1	0	$\tfrac{3}{2}$	$-\tfrac{1}{2}$	15
$\tfrac{1}{2}$	0	1	$-\tfrac{1}{2}$	$\tfrac{1}{2}$	5
$-\tfrac{3}{2}$	0	0	$-\tfrac{5}{2}$	$-\tfrac{1}{2}$	-65

Find the optimal range of the cost coefficient for x_2.
    Check x_1:

$$2x_1 = \tfrac{1}{2}(3) + \tfrac{1}{2}(4)$$

$$2(1) = \tfrac{1}{2}\bar{c}_2 + 2$$

$$\bar{c}_2 = 0$$

Check u_1:

$$0u_1 = \tfrac{3}{2}(3) + (-\tfrac{1}{2})(4)$$
$$0 = \tfrac{3}{2}\bar{c}_2 - 2$$
$$\bar{c}_2 = \tfrac{4}{3}$$

Check u_2:

$$0u_2 = (-\tfrac{1}{2})(3) + (\tfrac{1}{2})(4)$$
$$0 = -\tfrac{1}{2}\bar{c}_2 + 2$$
$$\bar{c}_2 = 4$$

The values for $\bar{c}_2$ are 0, $\tfrac{4}{3}$, and 4. The present or original cost coefficient is 3. Note that $0 \le \tfrac{4}{3} \le 3 \le 4$; thus the optimal range for c_2 is $\tfrac{4}{3} \le c_2 \le 4$.

Find the optimal range of the cost coefficient for x_3. Check x_1:

$$2x_1 = \tfrac{1}{2}(3) + \tfrac{1}{2}(4)$$
$$2(1) = \tfrac{3}{2} + \tfrac{1}{2}\bar{c}_3$$
$$\bar{c}_3 = 1$$

Check u_1:

$$0(1) = \tfrac{3}{2}(3) + (-\tfrac{1}{2}\bar{c}_3)$$
$$\bar{c}_3 = 9$$

Check u_2:

$$0(1) = (-\tfrac{1}{2})(3) + \tfrac{1}{2}\bar{c}_3$$
$$\bar{c}_3 = 3$$

The values are $1 < 3 < \bar{c}_3 < 9$. The optimal range for c_3 is $3 \le c_3 \le 9$.   ////

Nonbasic Variables

From a practical standpoint, the question to be answered by this analysis is how large (or small) the cost coefficient of a nonbasic variable must be before the variable enters the solution with a positive value. This analysis may treat decision variables which were not included in the original matrix or decision variables which were evaluated but for some reason or another did not enter the final solution.

In the example of the hypothetical manufacturing company, making products x_1 and x_2, suppose that a new product x_3 has been developed. If it is not possible to increase the present production facilities immediately, it is natural to question whether it is profitable to produce this product at all.

Obviously this can be done only by decreasing the production of x_1 and/or x_2 unless the plant capacity is increased. For this example, assume that the following estimates have been made regarding a new product x_3.

Manufacturing Time Requirements

Department	Hours/unit
A	1
B	3
C	3

The estimated profit per unit is $1.25.

Since product x_3 can be produced only by reducing the production of products x_1 and/or x_2, there will be a drop in total profit added by products x_1 and x_2. Essentially, before x_3 can be made, slack time must be obtained in departments A, B, and C; then this slack time can be applied to the production of x_3. From the estimates, to produce 1 unit of x_3 will require 1 hour in A, 3 hours in B, and 3 hours in C. From matrix 2, the revised cost coefficients for slack time in these departments are respectively $-\frac{1}{4}$, $-\frac{1}{2}$, and 0. This means that there will be a change in profit of $-\frac{1}{4}$ for each hour taken from productive work done in A, of $-\frac{1}{2}$ for each hour taken from B, and none in C because idle time already exists. Thus the change in profit due to manufacturing 1 unit of x_3 will be

$$\text{Profit} = 1(-\tfrac{1}{4}) + 3(-\tfrac{1}{2}) + 3(0) \tag{12-11}$$

$$= -\tfrac{7}{4} \text{ or } -\$1.75 \text{ per unit of } x_3$$

Since x_3 has an estimated profit from itself of only $1.25 per unit, it does not appear profitable to produce under these conditions. In addition, since product x_3 will not be profitable until its profit is equal to or greater than $1.75 per unit, the optimality range for x_3 becomes

$$c_3 \geq 1.75$$

EXAMPLE 12-4   Refer to the Example 12-3.

Initial Matrix

$$
\begin{array}{cccccc}
x_1 & x_2 & x_3 & u_1 & u_2 & b \\
\end{array}
$$
$$
\left[
\begin{array}{ccccc|c}
1 & 1 & 1 & 1 & 0 & 20 \\
2 & 1 & 3 & 0 & 1 & 30 \\
\hline
2 & 3 & 4 & 0 & 0 & 0 \\
\end{array}
\right]
$$

Optimal Matrix

$$
\begin{array}{cccccc}
x_1 & x_2 & x_3 & u_1 & u_2 & b \\
\end{array}
$$
$$
\left[
\begin{array}{ccccc|c}
\frac{1}{2} & 1 & 0 & \frac{3}{2} & -\frac{1}{2} & 15 \\
\frac{1}{2} & 0 & 1 & -\frac{1}{2} & \frac{1}{2} & 5 \\
\hline
-\frac{3}{2} & 0 & 0 & -\frac{5}{2} & -\frac{1}{2} & -65 \\
\end{array}
\right]
$$

A natural question is how much the profit of x_1 should be increased before it becomes profitable to produce, i.e., enter the solution. This can be determined directly from the optimal matrix. The product x_1 would cause a $-\frac{3}{2}$ change in profit if produced under the present conditions, as indicated by the cost coefficient in the optimal matrix. Thus the profit must be increased by $\$\frac{3}{2}$ per unit before the net change in profit becomes zero. This means that the profit per unit must be increased to 2 (present value) $+ \frac{3}{2}$ (present loss) or $\$3\frac{1}{2}$ per unit. This can be verified by checking the loss in profit from making 1 unit of x_1 at the expense of x_1 and x_2.

$$\text{Loss from reduction in } x_1 \text{ and } x_2 = 3(\tfrac{1}{2}) + 4(\tfrac{1}{2})$$

$$= \tfrac{3}{2} + 2 = 3\tfrac{1}{2} \qquad ////$$

EXAMPLE 12-5   In the hypothetical manufacturing plant, it has been determined that proper maintenance procedures will take 3 hours/week for each department. What will this cost in terms of lost production?

Refer to the optimal matrix for this problem. The cost coefficients in the z row indicate that a reduction of 1 hour in available manufacturing time will cost (reduce profit) $\$\frac{1}{4}$ in A, $\$\frac{1}{2}$ in B, and nothing in C. Thus the 3-hour requirement will cause a reduction in profit of $3(\frac{1}{4}) + 3(\frac{1}{2})$, or $\$2\frac{1}{4}$. If the added benefits from better operation are worth this, it should be done.   ////

EFFECT OF CHANGING CONSTRAINT LIMITS

One very practical question that may be raised concerning an optimal linear-programming solution is the effect of increasing or decreasing some limiting resource. This will have an effect not only upon the objective result (profit or cost) but also upon the solution or product mix. Large changes in a limiting or binding resource will even cause a change of the variables in solution. Relatively small changes in constraints that are not limiting will have no effect unless they are decreased to the point of becoming limiting.

In the two-product plant that uses departments A, B, and C, consider the case where some expansion in plant capacity is possible. The first question might be which department should be increased. If the cost of increasing the resource is the same for all three departments, department B should be increased because it has the most negative revised cost coefficient $-\frac{1}{2}$. That is, a unit increase in department B time will result in the largest profit increase. In many cases, the cost coefficients in the revised matrix are called *shadow prices* since they reflect the cost of changing some nonbasic variable.   The values presented in this z row actually indicate the net effect on the objective as a result of increasing a nonbasic variable by 1 unit.   In this problem, u_1, u_2, and u_3 represent the slack or idle time in departments A, B, and C.   Since u_1 and u_2 are zero (no idle time available), it would cost profit to provide idle time due to reduced production.   Increasing the constraint is physically reflected by increasing the production capacity.   In this case idle time is added without reducing the production of products, and this idle time can be used to increase production and thus profits. *Therefore, increasing a constraint value may be viewed as the negative of increasing a slack variable.*   If the profit changes by $-\frac{1}{2}$ to increase u_2, then increasing the production capacity of department B will increase profit by $\frac{1}{2}$.

What is the result on profit of increasing production capacity in department B by 10 units?

$$\text{Profit change} = -(-\tfrac{1}{2})(10) = 5$$

$$\text{Revised profit} = 100 + 5 = 105$$

What are the production rates if department B is increased by 10 units?   In the optimal matrix, row 1 represents the equation

$$1x_1 - 1u_2 = 40 \qquad u_2 = 0$$

Since adding capacity is the negative of increasing slack, an increase of 1 unit of capacity has the equivalent effect of a -1 unit change in u_2.

$$1x_1 - 1(-1) = 40$$

$$x_1 = 40 - 1 = 39$$

Using the same analysis for rows 2 and 3 provides the effect of a 1-unit change in capacity on the other basic variables.

Row 2:

$$x_2 + 1u_2 = 40$$

$$x_2 + 1(-1) = 40$$

$$x_2 = 41$$

Row 3:

$$u_3 + 2u_2 = 40$$

$$u_3 + 2(-1) = 40$$

$$u_3 = 42$$

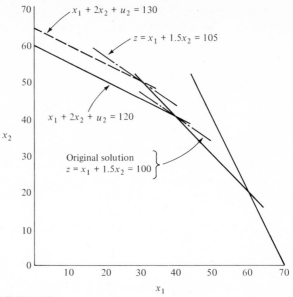

FIGURE 12-4
The effect of increasing department B capacity from 120 to 130.

A change in the capacity of department B (u_2) of 10 units then would give the following product mix:

$$x_1 = 40 - 10(1) = 30$$

$$x_2 = 40 + 10(1) = 50$$

$$x_3 = 40 + 10(2) = 60$$

$$\text{Profit} = 30(1) + 50(1.5) = 105$$

This effect is illustrated graphically in Fig. 12-4.

The next logical question is: How much can the capacity of shop B be profitably increased? Physically it is economically desirable to increase the capacity until shop B is no longer a production limitation. Mathematically, this means to increase capacity until u_2 has a positive value, representing unused slack, and replacing one of the basic variables presently in solution. To find this point, all the restrictions must be evaluated to determine this point.

Row 1:

$$x_1 - 1(-u_2) = 40$$

$$x_1 + u_2 = 40$$

where $-u_2$ is used to represent a capacity increase.   As u_2 increased, x_1 must decrease to maintain the equation.   Thus, u_2 can be increased only until x_1 becomes zero, since no variable is allowed to have a negative value. At

$$x_1 = 0 \qquad u_2 = 40$$

Row 2:

$$x_2 + 1(-u_2) = 40$$
$$x_2 - u_2 = 40$$

Note that as u_2 increases, x_2 must also increase to maintain the equation.   Thus u_2 may be increased without limit.

Row 3:

$$2(-u_2) + u_3 = 40$$
$$u_3 - 2u_2 = 40$$

Note that as u_2 is increased, u_3 must also increase to maintain the equation.   Thus u_2 may be increased without limit.

Thus the capacity in department B may be increased by a maximum of 40 units. At this point, department B will no longer be a limitation on production.   The product mix at this point can be determined as previously illustrated.

$$x_1 - (-u_2) = 40$$
$$x_1 - (-40) = 40$$
$$x_1 = 0$$
$$x_2 + (-u_2) = 40$$
$$x_2 - 40 = 40$$
$$x_2 = 80$$
$$u_3 + 2(-u_2) = 40$$
$$u_3 - 2(40) = 40$$
$$u_3 = 120$$

This result is presented graphically in Fig. 12-5.

EXAMPLE 12-6   If the optimal matrix of a maximization problem is

$$
\begin{array}{cccccc}
x_1 & x_2 & x_3 & u_1 & u_2 & b \\
\end{array}
$$

$$
\left[
\begin{array}{ccccc|c}
\frac{1}{2} & 1 & 0 & \frac{3}{2} & -\frac{1}{2} & 15 \\
\frac{1}{2} & 0 & 1 & -\frac{1}{2} & \frac{1}{2} & 5 \\
\hline
-\frac{3}{2} & 0 & 0 & -\frac{5}{2} & -\frac{1}{2} & -65
\end{array}
\right]
$$

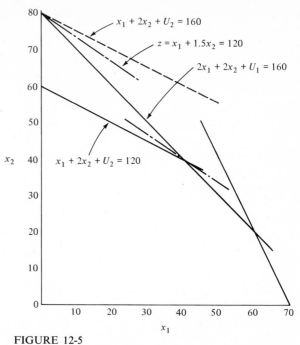

FIGURE 12-5
The effect of increasing department B to maximum capacity.

how much can the restriction in row 1 be increased before it is no longer limiting?
What will the value of the objective function be?

Row 1:

$$x_2 + \tfrac{3}{2}(-u_1) = 15$$

$$x_2 - \tfrac{3}{2}u_1 = 15$$

Since both x_2 and u_1 can increase without changing the value of the equation, this is not limiting.

Row 2:

$$x_3 - \tfrac{1}{2}(-u_1) = 5$$

$$x_3 + \tfrac{1}{2}u_1 = 5$$

Let

$$x_3 = 0$$

$$u_1 = 10$$

A maximum of 5 units can be added to constraint (1). This will increase the value of the objective function by $10(-\tfrac{5}{2}) = -25$ making a total of $-65 - 25 = -90$.

At this point, what would the product mix be?

$$x_2 + \frac{3}{2}(-10) = 15$$

$$x_2 = 30$$

$$x_3 - \frac{1}{2}(-10) = 5$$

$$x_3 = 0$$

Check using the original objective function.

$$-z = 2x_1 + 3x_2 + 4x_3$$
$$= 1(0) + 3(30) + 4(0)$$
$$= 90 + 0 = 90 \qquad ////$$

EFFECT OF CHANGING NONBASIC INPUT COEFFICIENTS

For more complete illustration, the original two-product problem is modified by adding a third product x_3 to the present product mix. This product, x_3, requires 3 hours in department A, 4 hours in department B, and 4 hours in department C; it has a profit of $2 per unit.

Matrix 3   Original Matrix

	x_1	x_2	x_3	u_1	u_2	u_3	b
A	2	2	3	1	0	0	160
B	1	2	4	0	1	0	120
C	4	2	4	0	0	1	280
	1	1.5	2	0	0	0	0

Matrix 4   Optimal Matrix

	x_1	x_2	x_3	u_1	u_2	u_3	b
A	1	0	-1	1	-1	0	40
B	0	1	$\frac{5}{2}$	$-\frac{1}{2}$	1	0	40
C	0	0	3	-3	2	1	40
	0	0	$-\frac{3}{4}$	$-\frac{1}{4}$	$-\frac{1}{2}$	0	-100

The optimal matrix shows $x_1 = 40$, $x_2 = 40$, $u_3 = 40$, and $x_3 = u_1 = u_2 = 0$. Thus it is most profitable not to make product 3. It is suggested that the labor requirements in department B for product 3 are excessive and a methods study may reduce the time required.   How much must this value be reduced before product 3 would be profitable to make?

If product 3 is made, it would require time in all three departments, and so the total effect upon the plant must be considered.   Extra time to manufacture x_3 can be obtained only by reducing the amount of x_1 and x_2 ; that is, some slack time must be made available to assign to the manufacture of x_3.   Department C already has 40 hours of idle time ($u_3 = 40$), and so this department is no problem.   Matrix 4 shows that $c_4 = -\frac{1}{4}$ and $c_5 = -\frac{1}{2}$.   This is the cost in reduced profit of providing 1 unit of slack in departments A (u_1) and B (u_2), respectively.   Thus the cost to profit for the production of 1 unit of x_3 is

$$\text{Profit change} = (-\tfrac{1}{4})(3) + (-\tfrac{1}{2})(4) + 0(4)$$

$$= -2\tfrac{3}{4} \qquad (12\text{-}12)$$

In this equation, the $-\frac{1}{4}$ is the change in profit caused by reducing x_1 and x_2 enough to provide 1 unit of slack in department A (u_1); the 3 is the hours required to produce 1 unit of x_3 ; the $-\frac{1}{2}$ is the profit change required to provide 1 unit of slack in department B (u_2); and the 4 is the time required in department B to make 1 unit of x_3.

The zero coefficient indicates that there is no change in profit as a result of providing time in department C (u_3).   This is apparent because $u_3 = 40$, indicating that 40 units of slack or idle time are now present in department C.   Thus the change in profit as a result of reducing x_1 and x_2 is $2\frac{3}{4}$ for 1 unit of production of x_3. Remembering that the profit per unit of x_3 was \$2/unit, it can be seen that a net change in profit resulting from the production of 1 unit of x_3 is

$$\text{Net change in profit} = 2 - 2\tfrac{3}{4} = -\$\tfrac{3}{4} \text{ per unit} \qquad (12\text{-}13)$$

For x_3 to be considered for production, the net change in profit must, at the very least, be zero; or the decrease in profit from x_1 and x_2 must equal the added profit of 1 unit of x_3.   Equating these values give

$$(-\tfrac{1}{4})(3) + (-\tfrac{1}{2}a_{23}) + 0(4) = \text{profit loss} \qquad (12\text{-}14)$$

where a_{23} is the time to make 1 unit of x_3 in department B.   Setting the profit loss due to reduction of x_1 and x_2 equal to the gain from an added unit of x_3 gives

$$-\tfrac{1}{4}(3) + (-\tfrac{1}{2}a_{23}) + 0(4) = -2 \qquad (12\text{-}15)$$

Solving for a_{23}, we have

$$a_{23} = \frac{2 - \tfrac{3}{4}}{\tfrac{1}{2}} = \frac{5}{2}$$

Note that a -2 is used in this case because a gain in profit is really a minus loss. Thus a_{23}, the time in department B to make 1 unit of x_3, must be $2\frac{1}{2}$ hours instead of 4 hours if the added profit of \$2 per unit is to offset the loss in profit due to x_1 and

x_2. Any reduction in time beyond this would cause x_3 to be favored over one or more of the products now being produced. To obtain a new optimal solution with an $a_{23} < 2/5$, the initial matrix would usually be corrected with a new a_{23} and then reworked to solution.

EXAMPLE 12-7   What is the maximum allowable manufacturing time in department A for x_3 to enter the solution?

$$a_{13}(-\tfrac{1}{4}) + 4(-\tfrac{1}{2}) + 4(0) = -2$$

$$a_{13} = \frac{2-2}{\tfrac{1}{4}} = 0$$

This means that with the other time requirements in departments B and C, the time requirements for department A must be reduced to zero before x_3 would be profitable to consider. Thus it is apparent that the time requirements for department B would be more likely to be adjusted than those in department A.   ////

INTERPRETATION AND FORMULATION OF THE DUAL

A solution to a linear-programming problem with its accompanying formulation is typically called the *primal*. Actually it is possible to formulate any problem in a different context and obtain the same results using a *dual* solution. In some cases this is desirable as it may reduce the work required for solution. In any case, this ability to formulate and interpret the dual problem offers added insight into the problem and as such becomes a useful tool for both analysis and communication. The existence and proof of the dual is well presented in several texts (see the references). This book emphasizes the formulation and the interpretation of both this formulation and the results obtained in economic and physical terms.

In a normal maximization linear-programming problem, it is desired to maximize the objective function without exceeding any stated restrictions. This situation can be modeled on a black-box basis, as suggested in Fig. 12-6. Here we are not concerned with the exact procedures required to convert the inputs into the desired output. Thus this conversion may be received as occuring within a "black box."

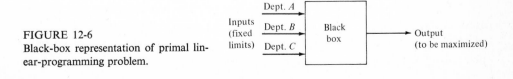

FIGURE 12-6
Black-box representation of primal linear-programming problem.

In the normal case (often called the primal), the solution maximizes the output regardless of the input values as long as these values do not exceed some fixed restrictions. In the hypothetical manufacturing plant the objective is in terms of dollars. The discussion of this problem will be simplified if the following modifications are made.

1 Product x_1 sells for $10, and product x_2 sells for $15.
2 The workers in departments A, B, and C are hired and paid whether they are fully used or not.
3 Accounting practice does not allow determination of a dollar profit per part; thus the objective will be to maximize gross income.

$$z = 10x_1 + 15x_2 = \$/unit \times units + \$/unit \times units = \$$$

Thus the output depicted in Fig. 12-6 is dollars of output to be maximized. The input is the amount of resource put into the system. Due to commitments, perhaps union agreements, the actual resource in man-hours is fixed whether it is used or not. This input is indicated by the restriction inequality for department A.

$$2x_1 + 2x_2 \leq 160$$

$$\frac{\text{Hours}}{\text{Unit}} \times units + \frac{\text{hours}}{\text{unit}} \times units \leq hours(\max)$$

It is the black box, in this case a manufacturing system, which converts these hours of input and dollar per hour cost into a dollar value system. The dollar output is limited by a maximum availability of man-hours. Note that this problem, as presented, implies that these maximum man-hour levels will be available and paid for whether they are used or not. After a solution has been reached, any excess capacity may be used elsewhere or reduced, but as originally posed, this capacity must be considered as available and paid for.

These man-hours may represent potential dollar sales in excess of their actual cost. If this were not true, the firm could not make a profit. If all input resources were perfectly used, the potential dollar-sales value of the input would equal the dollar-sales value of the output. If the input resources were not perfectly used, the potential of the input would be greater than the actual dollars of output.

It is possible to imagine this same problem formulated in a different manner (see Fig. 12-7); i.e., the output has some fixed minimum value and it is desired to minimize the inputs required to achieve that value. Suppose the dual problem is formulated according to the following logic.

The plant now has a fixed amount of capacity in each department, 160 hours in department A, 120 hours in department B, and 280 hours in department C for a total of 560 hours. Management has decided to increase the capacity of the plant incrementally, and present plans are to maintain the same proportion of hours in each

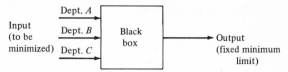

FIGURE 12-7
Black-box representation of dual linear-programming problem.

department.   Thus to add the next unit of capacity to the plant as a whole would require increasing A by $\frac{160}{560}$, B by $\frac{120}{560}$ and C by $\frac{280}{560}$.

At this time, 560 man-hours are used to produce the present dollar value of output.   Thus each total hour of capacity is $\frac{1}{560}$ of the total output value, i.e., dollars divided by output 560.   If one more hour is added incrementally to the gross department capacity while maintaining the same proportion of department capacities, the output dollar value would increase by $\frac{1}{560}$.

Assume that the present accounting practice does not provide information concerning the value of 1 man-hour in any given shop.   Only the gross value of output divided by 560 is known.   A new set of variables must be defined.   Let

w_1 = potential value of one additional man-hour in department A, \$/hour

w_2 = potential value of one additional man-hour in department B, \$/hour

w_3 = potential value of one additional man-hour in department C, \$/hour

Since the output is fixed, the objective is to minimize the potential value of the input. Remember that only when the input resource is perfectly used will the potential input equal the output.   To add 1 man-hour to the total plant would require $\frac{160}{560}$ hour in A, $\frac{120}{560}$ hour in B, and $\frac{280}{560}$ hour in C.   The total potential input value of an incremental increase in input is

$$y = \tfrac{160}{560} w_1 + \tfrac{120}{560} w_2 + \tfrac{280}{560} w_3 \qquad (12\text{-}16)$$

This can be modified to remove the fractions

$$560y = y' = 160w_1 + 120w_2 + 280w_3 \qquad \text{minimize} \qquad (12\text{-}17)$$

Now consider the following logic to formulate the restrictions.   The exact values of w_i are not known.   If the input resource is perfectly used, the *potential* input value will equal the output.   Most likely a mix of products 1 and 2 will be used. However, if only product 1 is made, the potential input value must be at least as much as could be obtained by making only product 1.   Since product 1 has a value of \$10 in sales, the first restriction is

$$2w_1 + w_2 + 4w_3 \geq 10 \qquad (12\text{-}18)$$

In a similar manner, the potential input value must be at least as much as if only product 2 were made.

$$2w_1 + 2w_2 + 2w_3 \geq 15 \qquad (12\text{-}19)$$

Thus the dual problem has been formulated.   Minimize

$$y' = 160w_1 + 120w_2 + 280w_3$$

subject to

$$2w_1 + w_2 + 4w_3 \geq 10$$
$$2w_1 + 2w_2 + 2w_3 \geq 15$$

This can be rewritten by inserting the required slack and artificial variables.   Minimize

$$y' = 160w_1 + 120w_2 + 280w_3$$

subject to

$$2w_1 + w_2 + 4w_3 - u'_1 + a_1 = 10$$
$$2w_1 + 2w_2 + 2w_3 - u'_2 + a_2 = 15$$

The simplex algorithm is used to obtain the solution, as indicated in matrices 5 and 6.

Matrix 5   Original Dual Matrix

	w_1	w_2	w_3	u'_1	u'_2	a_1	a_2	b
	2	1	4	−1	0	1	0	10
	2	2	2	0	−1	0	1	15
y'	160	120	280	0	0	0	0	0
k	−4	−3	−6	1	1	0	0	−25

Matrix 6   Optimal Dual Matrix

	w_1	w_2	w_3	u'_1	u'_2	b
	1	0	3	−1	$\frac{1}{2}$	2.5
	0	1	−2	1	−1	5
	0	0	40	40	40	−1,000

For comparison purposes the primal tables are also presented in matrices 7 and 8.

Matrix 7   Original Primal Matrix

	x_1	x_2	u_1	u_2	u_3	b
	2	2	1	0	0	160
	1	2	0	1	0	120
	4	2	0	0	1	280
	10	15	0	0	0	0

Matrix 8   Optimal Primal Matrix

x_1	x_2	u_1	u_2	u_3	b
1	0	1	-1	0	40
0	1	$-\frac{1}{2}$	1	0	40
0	0	-3	2	1	40
0	0	-2.5	-5	0	$-1,000$

The dual solution says that the potential sales value of an extra man-hour in shop A is \$2.50, in shop B is \$5, and in shop C is zero. The result for shop C is as expected since it already has slack time; thus an additional man-hour there would not increase the output value. The result for A and B is the same as in the primal, which indicated that an incremental increase in A and B would "cost" -2.5 and -5.00 respectively (remember that a minus cost is the same as a positive income).

In the dual solution, the y' row indicates that if w_3 is increased by \$1, it will cost \$40. Since w_3 has units of dollars per hour, this means that there are 40 unused or idle hours in department C. To interpret the values of the slack variables, consider the first restriction.

$$2w_1 + w_2 + 4w_3 \geq 10$$

$$2w_1 + w_2 + 4w_3 - u_1' = 10$$

u_1' is the difference between the combined potential input value of departments A, B, and C required to make 1 unit of product 1 and the value of 1 unit of product 1. In this solution, u_1' is zero, but the y' row indicates that if u_1' were increased by 1 unit from 0 to 1, it would cost \$40 per hour. Since u_1' has a coefficient of 1 (hour/unit) this represents 40 units of x_1. Similarly the 40 below u_2' represents 40 units of x_2 to be made.

MATHEMATICAL ANALOGY; PRIMAL VS. DUAL

The mathematical analogy of the primal and dual formulations is much easier than the physical or economic interpretation of these formulations. As indicated earlier, several texts have excellent developments and proofs of the existence of the dual. This text reviews this material to illustrate directly how the primal can be converted into the dual and vice versa.

In the primal problem, the formulation is as follows. Maximize

$$z = c_1 x_1 + c_2 x_2$$

subject to

$$a_{11}x_1 + a_{12}x_2 \leq b_1$$
$$a_{21}x_1 + a_{22}x_2 \leq b_2$$
$$a_{31}x_1 + a_{32}x_2 \leq b_3$$

The dual requires definition of a new decision variable w_i and then is formulated as follows.   Minimize

$$y' = b_1 w_1 + b_2 w_2 + b_3 w_3$$

subject to

$$a_{11}w_1 + a_{21}w_2 + a_{31}w_3 \geq c_1$$
$$a_{12}w_1 + a_{22}w_2 + a_{32}w_3 \geq c_2$$

The solution provides equivalent information, but the y' row in the dual solution contains the same information found in the b column of the primal solution.   The b column in the dual solution provides the same data as the z row in the primal solution.

EXAMPLE 12-8   The primal is maximize

$$z = 2x_1 + 3x_2$$

subject to

$$2x_1 + 2x_2 \leq 10$$
$$2x_1 + x_2 \leq 6$$
$$x_1 + 2x_2 \leq 6$$

| | *Original Matrix* | | | | | | *Optimal Matrix* | | | | |

x_1	x_2	u_1	u_2	u_3	b	x_1	x_2	u_1	u_2	u_3	b
2	2	1	0	0	10	0	0	1	$-\frac{2}{3}$	$-\frac{2}{3}$	2
2	1	0	1	0	6	1	0	0	$\frac{2}{3}$	$-\frac{1}{3}$	2
1	2	0	0	1	6	0	1	0	$-\frac{1}{3}$	$\frac{2}{3}$	2
2	3	0	0	0	0	0	0	0	$-\frac{1}{3}$	$-\frac{4}{3}$	-10

The dual is minimize

$$y = 10w_1 + 6w_2 + 6w_3$$

subject to

$$2w_1 + 2w_2 + w_3 \geq 2$$
$$2w_1 + w_2 + 2w_3 \geq 3$$

Original Matrix

	w_1	w_2	w_3	u_1'	u_2'	a_1	a_2	b
	2	2	1	-1	0	1	0	2
	2	1	2	0	-1	0	1	3
y	10	6	6	0	0	0	0	0
k	-4	-3	-3	1	1	0	0	-5

Optimal Matrix

	w_1	w_2	w_3	u_1'	u_2'	b
	$\frac{2}{3}$	1	0	$-\frac{2}{3}$	$\frac{1}{3}$	$\frac{1}{3}$
	$\frac{2}{3}$	0	1	$\frac{1}{3}$	$-\frac{2}{3}$	$\frac{4}{3}$
y	2	0	0	2	2	-10

////

REFERENCES

1 WILDE, DOUGLAS J., and CHARLES S. BEIGHTLER: "Foundations of Optimization," Prentice-Hall, Inc., Englewood Cliffs, N.J., 1967.
2 DANTZIG, GEORGE B.: "Linear Programming and Extensions," Princeton University Press, Princeton, N.J., 1963.
3 GARVIN, WALTER W.: "Introduction to Linear Programming," McGraw-Hill Book Company, New York, 1964.

PROBLEMS

12-1 The original problem and optimal solution to a linear-programming problem are given below.

   (*a*) What is the optimal range for the cost coefficient of x_2; that is, what are the largest and smallest value for c_2 which will still result in the optimal solution $x_2 = 3$?

   (*b*) If x_1 is set equal to 1, what will the new solution be? What will the revised z value be?

   (*c*) How large must c_3 be for it to enter the solution?

   (*d*) What would be the result of increasing b_1 to a value of 7?

   (*e*) What value must a_{11} take before x_1 will be a solution candidate?

The *original* problem is to maximize

$$2x_1 + 4x_2 + 3x_3$$

subject to

$$2x_1 + 2x_2 + 3x_3 \le 6$$
$$4x_1 + 2x_2 + 2x_3 \le 8$$

Optimal Solution

$$
\begin{array}{cccccc|c}
x_1 & x_2 & x_3 & u_1 & u_2 & b \\
1 & 1 & \frac{3}{2} & \frac{1}{2} & 0 & 3 \\
2 & 0 & -1 & -1 & 1 & 2 \\
\hline
-2 & 0 & -3 & -2 & 0 & -12
\end{array}
$$

12-2 The following linear-programming problem has been maximized to give the solution indicated. Maximize

$$2x_1 + 4x_2 + 6x_3$$

subject to

$$2x_1 + 2x_2 + 4x_3 \le 12$$
$$x_1 + 4x_2 + 2x_3 \le 8$$
$$4x_1 + 2x_2 + 4x_3 \le 10$$

Solution

$$
\begin{array}{ccccccc|c}
x_1 & x_2 & x_3 & u_1 & u_2 & u_3 & b \\
-2 & 0 & 0 & 1 & 0 & -1 & 2 \\
-\frac{1}{3} & 1 & 0 & 0 & \frac{1}{3} & -\frac{1}{6} & 1 \\
\frac{7}{6} & 0 & 1 & 0 & -\frac{1}{6} & \frac{1}{3} & 2 \\
\hline
-\frac{11}{3} & 0 & 0 & 0 & -\frac{1}{3} & -\frac{4}{3} & -16
\end{array}
$$

(a) What must c_3 be for x_3 to become nonbasic (leave the solution)?

(b) How large can c_2 be before the solution vector changes? What change would occur?

(c) If c_1 is increased from 2 to 3, will x_1 be in solution?

(d) If x_1 is set at $1\frac{1}{2}$, what is the new solution vector?

(e) If b_1 is increased to a value of 14, what effect does this have? Why?

(f) How large must b_2 become before it ceases to be a limiting constraint?

(g) How small must a_{31} be for x_1 to enter solution?

12-3 Feed is to be mixed to meet minimum specifications for nutritional value. The four types of grain available contain varied percentages of the required nutrients A, B, and

Grain type	Cost per bushel	Percent of Nutrient		
		A	B	C
1	$.90	4	15	5
2	1.10	7	8	35
3	1.60	9	20	37
4	1.35	6	13	40

C. The data are tabulated. The mix must meet the following minimum requirements:

$$A \geq 6\% \qquad B \geq 14\% \qquad C \geq 35\%$$

Find the optimal mix and then establish the range of cost for each grain which can be tolerated before the mix must be changed.

12-4 A shop is scheduled for three major products, 1, 2, and 3. These require times in four departments *A, B, C, D.* Time requirements and available hours are tabulated.

Product	Time in department, hours				Estimated contribution/unit
	A	*B*	*C*	*D*	
1	.5	.8	3	1	$2.50
2	2.5	2.5	1.5	0	3.25
3	1.0	3.0	2	3.5	4.50
Available hours	200	240	280	200	

(*a*) If sales exceed production, how many of each should be made? Assume that fractional units may be completed in the next time period and thus constitute a valid answer.

(*b*) Which department has idle time?

(*c*) If you were to increase the capacity in a department by a small amount, which would result in the most added profit per unit increased (assuming equal cost for all departments)?

(*d*) How much could you increase the capacity of department *C* before it would no longer be limiting?

12-5 Given the problem of maximizing

$$2x_1 - 4x_2 + 3x_3 + 7x_4$$

subject to

$$0x_1 + 2x_2 + x_3 + x_4 \geq 20$$

$$x_1 + x_2 + 2x_3 + 3.3x_4 \leq 60$$

$$x_1 + x_2 - x_3 + 6x_4 \leq 50$$

Solution

x_1	x_2	x_3	x_4	u_1	u_2	u_3	b
0	.947	1	0	−.474	.175	−.175	11.228
1	−4.368	0	0	2.684	1.228	−.228	8.597
0	1.053	0	1	−.526	−.175	.175	8.772
0	−5.474	0	0	−.263	−1.754	−.246	−112.28

(*a*) What is the result of adding 2 units of x_2?

(*b*) What range of the cost coefficient for x_2 will not change the solution vector?

(*c*) What must c_2 be for x_2 to be a candidate for solution?

12-6 Using the optimal solution from part (*a*) of Prob. 10-6:

    (*a*) What is the effect of requiring that any size bolt must constitute at least 15 percent of the total package?

    (*b*) If size 3 could be obtained for $10 instead of $12 per pound, would this change the mix?

    (*c*) What is the most you could pay for size 2 and still have the same optimal mix?

12-7 Formulate Prob. 10-9 using the dual instead of a primary format and compare this solution to that obtained previously.

    (*a*) Show that the value attached to time limitations indicates that this is not an important restriction.

    (*b*) How do you interpret the value associated with raw material? Which is the most costly resource, raw material or space?

    (*c*) What value is associated with product 2? What meaning does it have?

12-8 Using the optimal solution from Prob. 10-11:

    (*a*) If a new product *E* were available and it required .1 time unit in Dept. 1, .25 in 2, .15 in 3, and none in 4, what would the contribution to profit have to be for *E* to become an economic alternative (be produced)?

    (*b*) One way to make *E* desirable to manufacture would be to reduce the time requirements for manufacturing in one of the departments. Suppose *E* added only $5 per unit to the profit. Which phase of manufacture would be best to study for time reduction? How much would the time have to be reduced?

    (*c*) If additional time were available on an overtime basis, which department should it be added to? How much could you afford to pay on a premium (added-cost) basis to get overtime? How much can be added before that department is no longer restrictive?

    (*d*) What is the greatest reduction in price (and thus profit contribution) that can be made in product *B* before it becomes an undesirable product?

12-9 Formulate Prob. 10-12 in the dual. Explain your constraints in economic terms.

13

DYNAMIC PROGRAMMING

INTRODUCTION

Of all of the mathematical techniques employed in operations research, dynamic programming is perhaps the simplest in concept and yet one of the most difficult to apply. Unless the student is already at ease with functional notation, learning to use this technique is often difficult. This chapter explains the concept of dynamic programming in simple, straightforward terms.

One of the difficulties in applying dynamic programming is the lack of a clearcut formulation and solution algorithm. As a result, each problem requires basic decisions for formulation. The problem formulation is like working a probability problem or setting up a word problem in algebra. You must understand both the problem and the technique before the solution can begin. There are no simple, easy-to-follow rules that always lead to a correct formulation. As a result, this technique will be demonstrated by working different examples.

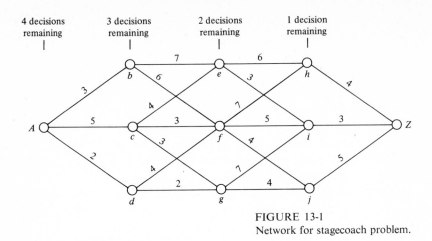

FIGURE 13-1
Network for stagecoach problem.

CONCEPTS OF DYNAMIC PROGRAMMING

Dynamic programming is best suited for the solution of problems requiring inter-related decisions, i.e., decisions which must be made in a sequence and which influence future decisions in that sequence. Concepts developed by Richard Bellman allow partial optimization of a portion of the sequence and then connect the optimized units to the next in line until the whole sequence is optimized. These concepts can be applied to problems containing continuous functions or problems where only integer values are practical. Since the latter are the easiest to visualize, this is where the presentation will begin. The basic concepts of dynamic programming are most easily presented by means of the *stagecoach problem*.

Suppose someone must travel between points A and Z, as indicated by the network shown in Fig. 13-1. Between the terminal points any path may be taken, but the total distance traveled is to be minimized. The distance between junctions is noted on the network.

The total path from A to Z consists of four legs, each having an assigned length. Thus the objective will be to minimize the sum of the four selected legs.

Note that the decision stages are numbered in terms of the number of decisions remaining before the problem is complete. Thus if $i = 2$, this means that the traveler is at a point in the sequence where two more decisions are required. If l_i is the distance of the leg selected with i decisions left, the objective can be expressed in mathematical notation as follows. Minimize

$$\text{Total distance} = l_1 + l_2 + l_3 + l_4 = \sum_{i=1}^{i=4} l_i$$

Thus the problem can be visualized as one of making four decisions in sequence. What complicates the problem is that each decision influences all future decisions.

Dynamic programming works by breaking the problem into a set of smaller, easy to solve problems and then reassembling the results of the analysis. This is referred to as *decomposition*. For example, if one is at station h on the network, there is only one decision available: go directly to Z over a distance of 4 units. Similarly from i and j the lengths are 3 and 5, respectively. Since these are the only paths available, they are minimum. However, if one is at e, two decisions are available, go to h or to i. The total distance from e to Z has two components: (1) the distance resulting from the immediate decision made at that time and (2) the minimum distance resulting from all future decisions required to get to Z. For example, suppose one is at e and makes the decision to go to h. The total distance from e to Z *as a result* of the e to h decision is $6 + 4 = 10$ units. Similarly the decision $e \rightarrow i$ results in a total distance of $3 + 3 = 6$ units. Since $6 < 10$, the optimum decision at e is to go to i for a total distance of 6.

In a similar manner compare the three alternative decisions available at f.

Decision	First distance	Second distance	Total distance
$f \rightarrow h$	7	4	11
$f \rightarrow i$	5	3	8
$f \rightarrow j$	4	5	9

Thus the optimal decision at f is to go to i for a total distance of 8 units. From g the optimal decision will be to go to j, resulting in a total distance of 9 units.

Now let us stop and summarize what has been done. When we were at the last decision point (one decision remaining), we found that the optimal decision at that location was very simple. Next we moved back one stage to the point with two decisions remaining and found that the total distance from any point was the sum of the decision made there and the optimal result from the last decision. This allowed us to determine an optimal path from any point at the third decision stage. This is summarized in the table.

Decision stage $= 2$	Optimal decision	Minimum total distance to Z
e	i	$3 + 3 = 6$
f	i	$5 + 3 = 8$
g	j	$4 + 5 = 9$

It says that if we know what happened previously, we can optimize future decisions since we are already near the end. If this same process is continued, we can back up all the way to the beginning, finding optimal decisions as we go.

Try evaluating the possible decisions at decision stage 3. If we are at b, the possible decisions are $b \rightarrow e$ and $b \rightarrow f$. From b, the total distance to Z is the result of the immediate decision plus the minimum distance resulting from all future decisions (these are already known).

$$b \rightarrow e = \text{total} = 7 + 6 = 13$$

Once we decide to go to e, we know from earlier calculations that the minimum distance from e to Z is 6 units.

$$b \rightarrow f = 6 + 8 = 14$$

Thus of the two possible decisions, $b \rightarrow e$ gives the minimum distance of 13 units. In a similar manner evaluate the possible decisions at c and d where the minimum is printed in boldface type.

Decision	First distance	Minimum remaining distance	Total distance
$c \rightarrow e$	4	6	$4 + 6 = \mathbf{10}$
$c \rightarrow f$	3	8	$3 + 8 = 11$
$c \rightarrow g$	3	9	$3 + 9 = 12$
$d \rightarrow f$	4	8	$4 + 8 = 12$
$d \rightarrow g$	2	9	$2 + 9 = \mathbf{11}$

Finally we can back up to decision stage 4 at A and evaluate the three feasible decisions.

Decision	First distance	Minimum remaining distance	Total distance
$A \rightarrow b$	3	13	16
$A \rightarrow c$	5	10	15
$A \rightarrow d$	2	11	13

From this we know that the minimum total distance from A to Z is 13 units and follows the path $AdgjZ$.

This demonstrates the basic concept of dynamic programming, i.e., breaking a problem into stages and for any given condition optimizing that one stage. Then the results can be combined. In this example, we have shown that the total result is the sum of the result of the immediate decision plus the optimal result from all future decisions that it leads to. In this example, it is expressed as

Total distance = distance from next decision + minimum distance remaining

In a more general form this concept is expressed as

Total return = return from immediate decision

+ optimal returns from all future stages as
a result of immediate decision

Although this concept is not difficult, it may become more complicated with the requirements of any given problem.   Still the same basic rule will always apply.

One other fact should be recognized from this example.   The problem was broken down into a series of single stages wherein each feasible decision was evaluated. For purposes of communication, terminology and finally notation become important. This problem was divided into four parts.   At each part a decision was required.   In terms of dynamic programming, each part will be called a *stage*.   At each stage, at least one decision is made; i.e., one decision variable is optimized.   The output or return at any stage depends on prior decisions, i.e., input conditions to that stage and some objective function.   Mathematically this is expressed

$$r_i = f(d_i, S_i) \qquad (13\text{-}1)$$

This says that the immediate result (return) r_i of a decision at the ith stage depends upon the conditions S_i prevailing at that time and the decision d_i made at that time. As an example, when we were at point f and decided to go to point i, the immediate result r_3 was 5 units because at that time the input conditions said that we were at f, $S_3 = f$, and the decision $d_3 = i$ said that we would go to i next.   The total distance called f_i is the total result due to the decision and input conditions at stage i.

$$f_i = r_i(d_i, S_i) + f_{i-1}^*(d_i, S_i)$$
$$= r_i + f_{i-1}^* \qquad (13\text{-}2)$$

where f^* is the total distance resulting from optimal decisions.   Equation (13-2) says that the *total return* f_i is equal to the *immediate result* at i due to the decision d_i and input conditions S_i *plus* the optimal values from all other stages.   In terms of the example it is the distance as a result of the immediate decision plus the remaining minimum distance.   For example, from c, a decision $c \rightarrow e$ gives

$$f = 4 + 6 = 10$$

EXAMPLE 13-1   An investor has \$6,000 to invest in any of three ventures.   He must invest in units of \$1,000.   The potential return from investment in any one venture depends upon the amount invested, according to the table.

Amount invested	Return from venture		
	A	B	C
0	0	0	0
1	.5	1.5	1.2
2	1.0	2.0	2.4
3	3.0	2.2	2.5
4	3.1	2.3	2.6
5	3.2	2.4	2.7
6	3.3	2.5	2.8

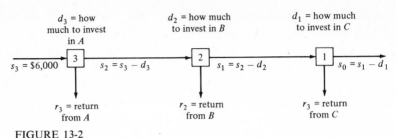

FIGURE 13-2
Investment problem displayed as a dynamic-programming problem, Example 13-1.

This may be posed as a dynamic-programming problem by viewing the decision regarding the amount to invest in each venture as a stage. Thus $N = 3$, the number of decisions to be made; i.e., the number of stages is 3. Graphically this can be displayed as in Fig. 13-2.

Here the problem is visualized as that of the investor having 6,000 initially, then making d_3 regarding how much to invest in A. As an output from this stage he has $6,000 - d_3$ left to invest in B and C. At stage 2, he makes d_2, which determines the amount left to invest in C, $S_1 = S_2 - d_2$. In this case it is obvious that all remaining monies will be invested in C. This problem is most easily worked by using a tabular method. A table of results will be constructed for all possible decisions and input conditions at each stage.

To start, we begin at the end, i.e., with only one decision left to make, $n = 1$. Table 13-1 presents the results of possible decisions d_1 for various input conditions S_1. Note that we have listed as rows all possible values of input conditions which might

Table 13-1 RETURN MATRIX AT $n = 1$

Input conditions, S_1 Monies left to invest	Possible decisions d_1 at stage 1							r_1^*
	0	1	2	3	4	5	6	
0	0	NF†	NF	NF	NF	NF	NF	0
1	0	**1.2**	NF	NF	NF	NF	NF	1.2
2	0	1.2	**2.4**	NF	NF	NF	NF	2.4
3	0	1.2	2.4	**2.5**	NF	NF	NF	2.5
4	0	1.2	2.4	2.5	**2.6**	NF	NF	2.6
5	0	1.2	2.4	2.5	2.6	**2.7**	NF	2.7
6	0	1.2	2.4	2.5	2.6	2.7	**2.8**	2.8

r_1^* = optimal result for input conditions S_1. Note that the boldface answers indicate d_1^*, the optimal decision for that input condition S_1.
† NF = not feasible.

result from prior decisions.   This covers the entire range from $S_1 = 0$ (all funds already spent) to $S_1 = \$6,000$ (no funds invested in A or B).   For example, row 4 indicates that \$4,000 has not yet been invested, $S_1 = 4$.   The values under $d_1 = 0$ to 6 give the results (r_1) if \$0, 1,000, 2,000, ... are invested in venture C.   Note that if only \$4,000 is available $(S_1 = 4)$, it would not be feasible to invest \$5,000 or \$6,000 in venture C.   The r_1^* column gives the optimal result for that input condition.   Since $n = 1$ (one decision remaining), there are no returns from future decisions to include.

Now back up one stage so that there will be two decisions remaining, $n = 2$.   At this stage, the possible input conditions S_2 still range from 0 to \$6,000.   In computing the *total* return from a decision d_2, the return r_2 from stage 2 is added to the best return available from stage 1.

$$f_2 = r_2 + r_1^* \,. \qquad (13\text{-}3)$$

These computations are summarized in Table 13-2.

As an example, in the row $S_2 = 4$, if decision $d_2 = 2,000$, is made the return of stage 2 is \$2,000.   As a result of investing \$2,000 in B, the input to stage 1, S_1, will be \$4,000 − \$2,000 = \$2,000.

$$S_i = S_{i+1} - d_{i+1}$$

In words, the money available at stage i is the amount available at the prior stage minus the amount invested at that prior stage.   Then looking at stage 1, *if* you know $S_1 = \$2,000$, $r_i^* = \$2,400$ from Table 13-1.   The *total* result at stage 2 is the sum of these values:

$$f_2 = r_2 + r_1^* \qquad (13\text{-}3)$$

$$= \$2,000 + \$2,400 = \$2,400$$

Table 13-2   RETURN MATRIX AT $n = 2$

S_2	0	1	2	3	4	5	6	f^*
				d_2				
0	0	—	—	—	—	—	—	0
1	0 + 1.2 = 1.2	1.5 + 0 = **1.5**	—	—	—	—	—	1.5
2	0 + 2.4 = 2.4	1.5 + 1.2 = **2.7**	2.0 + 0 = 2.0	—	—	—	—	2.7
3	0 + 2.5 = 2.5	1.5 + 2.4 = **3.9**	2.0 + 1.2 = 3.2	2.2 + 0 = 2.2	—	—	—	3.9
4	0 + 2.6 = 2.6	1.5 + 2.5 = 4.0	2.0 + 2.4 = **4.4**	2.2 + 1.2 = 3.4	2.3 + 0 = 2.3	—	—	4.4
5	0 + 2.7 = 2.7	1.5 + 2.6 = 4.1	2.0 + 2.5 = 4.5	2.2 + 2.4 = **4.6**	2.3 + 1.2 = 3.5	2.4 + 0 = 2.4	—	4.6
6	0 + 2.8 = 2.8	1.5 + 2.7 = 4.2	2.0 + 2.6 = 4.6	2.2 + 2.5 = **4.7**	2.3 + 2.4 = **4.7**	2.4 + 1.2 = 3.6	2.5 + 0 = 2.5	4.7

Table 13-3   RETURN MATRIX AT $n = 3$

S_3	0	1	2	3	4	5	6	f_3^*
				d_3				
6	$0 + 4.7$ $= 4.7$	$.5 + 4.6$ $= 5.1$	$1.0 + 4.4$ $= 5.4$	$3.0 + 3.9$ $= 6.9$	$3.1 + 2.7$ $= 5.8$	$3.2 + 1.5$ $= 4.7$	$3.3 + 0$ $= 3.3$	6.9

Finally, at stage 3 (three decisions remaining) the input S_3 is known to be $6,000 because that is the total amount of capital available. This input condition must be evaluated over the entire range of feasible decisions. These calculations are summarized in Table 13-3, which shows that the optimal sequence of decisions will result in a total return of $f_3^* = \$6,900$. This optimal sequence of decisions is $d_3^* = 3$ (leaving $S_2 = \$6,000 - \$3,000 = \$3,000$), and at $S_2 = 3, d_2^* = 1$ (leaving $S_3 = \$3,000 - \$1,000 = \$2,000$) and at $S_1 = 2, d_3^* = 2$.   ////

EXAMPLE 13-2   A truck can carry a total of 10 tons of product. Three types of product are available for shipment. Their weights and values are tabulated. Assuming that at least one of each type must be shipped, determine the loading which will maximize the total value.

Type	Value	Weight, tons
A	$20	1
B	50	2
C	60	2

In this case, there are three basic decisions, how many units of A, B, and C, respectively, should be loaded. Thus let each stage represent the decision regarding the number of units of a given product type to be loaded.

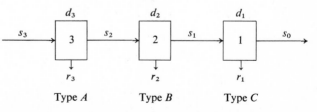

The input will represent the amount of unloaded capacity; thus $S_3 = 10$ tons since no decisions have been made at that time. The input to all other stages will depend on the prior input and decision.

$$S_i = S_{i+1} - d_{i+1}w_i \qquad (13\text{-}4)$$

Table 13-4   ANALYSIS OF EXAMPLE 13-2

$$n = 1$$

	d_1			
S_1	1	2	3	f_1^*
2	1(60) = 60	NF	NF	60
3	1(60) = 60	NF	NF	60
4	60	2(60) = 120	NF	120
5	60	2(60) = 120	NF	120
6	60	120	3(60) = 180	180
7	60	120	180	180

$$n = 2$$

	d_2			
S_2	1	2	3	f_2^*
4	1(50) + 60 = 110	NF	NF	110
5	110	NF	NF	110
6	50 + 120 = 170	2(50) + 60 = 160	NF	170
7	170	160	NF	170
8	50 + 180 = 230	100 + 120 = 220	3(50) + 60 = 210	230
9	50 + 180 = 230	100 + 120 = 220	150 + 60 = 210	230

$$n = 3$$

S_3	1	2	3	4	5	6	f_3^*
10	20 + 230 = 250	2(20) + 230 = 270	3(20) + 170 = 230	4(20) + 170 = 250	5(20) + 110 = 210	6(20) + 110 = 230	270

where w_i is the weight of product i.   The total return at stage i is $f_i = r_i + f_{i-1}^*$, where $r_i = d_i v_i$ (v_i = value of product i).   At stage $n = 1$, the input could vary between $S_1 = 2$ (all space loaded except for 1 unit of c) and $S_1 = 10 - 3 = 7$ (only 1 unit each of items A and B).   Similarly at $n = 2$, the range of S_2 might be $4 \le S_2 \le 9$.   Table 13-4 presents the calculations for this analysis.

The results of the analysis shown in Table 13-4 indicate the following optimum sequence of decisions.

$$d_3^* = 2A \qquad d_2^* = 1B \qquad d_1^* = 3C \qquad f_3^* = \$270 \qquad ////$$

EXAMPLE 13-3   Maximize

$$x_1(x_2 - 1)^2 + (x_3 - 2)^3$$

subject to the constraints

$$x_1 + 2x_2 + x_3 \leq 4$$

$$x_1, x_2, x_3 \geq 0 \text{ and integer}$$

In this problem, consider each variable as a stage. Thus the sequence of decisions is concerned with how much to assign to x_1, x_2, and x_3. The input conditions relate to the constraint. Thus S_i is the amount of unused resource at stage i.

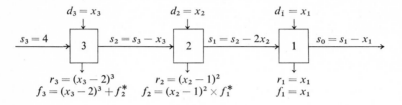

Table 13-5   ANALYSIS OF EXAMPLE 13-3

	$n = 1$					
	x_1					
S_1	0	1	2	3	4	f_1^*
0	0	—	—	—	—	0
1	0	1	—	—	—	1
2	0	1	2	—	—	2
3	0	1	2	3	—	3
4	0	1	2	3	4	4

	$n = 2$			
	x_2			
S_2	0	1	2	f_2^*
0	0	—	—	0
1	$(0-1)^2 1 = 1$	—	—	1
2	$(0-1)^2 2 = 2$	0	—	2
3	$(0-1)^2 3 = 3$	0	—	3
4	$(0-1)^2 4 = 4$	0	$(2-1)^2 0 = 0$	4

	$n = 3$				
	x_3				
S_3	0	1	2	3	4	f_3^*
	$(0-2)^3 + 4 = -4$	$(1-2)^3 + 3 = 2$	$(2-2)^3 + 2 = 2$	$(3-2)^3 + 1 = 2$	$(4-2)^3 + 0 = 8$	8

At the first point in the analysis, note that S_1 may take a range in value from 0 to a maximum of 4 due to the constraint.   This sets the limits of S_1 for the table.

Note that at $n = 2$, S_2 may have a full range of values 0 to 4 but x_2 may only take values of 0, 1, or 2 due to the coefficient in the constraint.   The optimal answer is therefore $x_1 = 0$, $x_2 = 0$, $x_3 = 4$.   ////

EXAMPLE 13-4   The manufacturing department of a company has estimated the work requirements for the next four periods.   Although work could be done ahead of time and stored, it is not desirable to back order work.   Inventory carried into a period will be charged as stored for that period, but it is not charged storage during the period it was made.

Period	Work to be done, man-periods
1	5,000
2	3,000
3	4,000
4	2,000

The cost of direct labor is $5 per man-period, and the cost of changing the work force by hiring or firing is $2 times the square of the change in force.   The cost of storage is $3 per unit-period, where 1 unit is the work done in 1 man-period.   Find the optimum schedule of work if there is no inventory on hand at this time.   The present work force is three men.   Assume that part-time work is not possible and that the men available will be used to produce work (no idle time allowed).

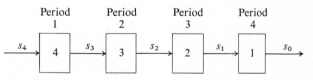

This problem is formulated in four stages with a decision regarding manpower level made at each stage.   There are two input conditions to each stage, one the manpower level from the last stage d_{i+1} and the other the inventory on hand I_i.   The following relationships will hold.

$$r_i = 5d_i + 2(d_{i+1} - d_i)^2 + 3I_i \qquad (13\text{-}5)$$

$$I_i = I_{i+1} + d_{i+1} - w_{i+1} \qquad (13\text{-}6)$$

$$w_{i+1} = \text{work required in } (i+1)\text{st stage}$$

This can be done in tabular form, as shown in Table 13-6. Note that as input conditions for period 4 (stage $n = 1$) both the last decision d_2 and the inventory level I_1 must be considered. Thus in the table there must be enough rows to cover the likely combinations of d_2 and I_1. For example, the first row represents $d_2 = 2$ and $I_1 = 0$. As this table shows, nine combinations are evaluated to ensure that the requirements for computation at $n = 2$ can be covered.

As an example, look at row $d_2 = 3$, $I_1 = 1$. In this case, the first decision, $d_1 = 0$, is not feasible since an inventory level of 1 unit will not fill the demand of 2 units for that time. It is feasible to let $d_1 = 1$ since the manufactured unit plus the unit in inventory would meet the demand. The cost is

$$5(d_1 = 1) + 2(\text{change in work force} = 3 - 1)^2 + 3(\text{inventory level } I_1 = 1)$$

$$= 5(1) + 2(3 - 1)^2 + 3(1) = 16$$

At the decision $d_1 = 2$, the cost is

$$5(d_1 = 2) + 2(d_2 - d_1 = 3 - 2)^2 + 3(1) = 5(2) + 2(3 - 2)^2 + 3(1) = 15 \qquad (13\text{-}7)$$

At $n = 2$, the input conditions to be evaluated cover the same range of combinations, but the possible decisions for d_2 range from 2 to 4. This obviously does not cover all feasible combinations, but it does cover the most likely ones.

As an example, look at row $d_3 = 4$, $I_2 = 1$. The first decision, $d_2 = 2$, is not feasible since the total number of units available would be 2 manufactured + 1

Table 13-6 ANALYSIS OF STAGE 1

				$n = 1$			
Input conditions				Decision d_1 at stage 1			
d_2	I_1	0		1	t	2	f_1^*
2	0	NF		NF		$5(2) + 0 + 0 = 10$	10
	1	NF		$5(1) + 2(1)^2 + 3(1) = 10$		$5(2) + 0 + 3(1) = 13$	10
	2	$0 + 2(2)^2 + 3(2) = 14$		$5(1) + 2(1)^2 + 3(2) = 13$		$5(2) + 0 + 3(2) = 16$	13
3	0	NF		NF		$5(2) + 2(1)^2 + 0 = 12$	12
	1	NF		$5(1) + 2(2)^2 + 3(1) = 16$		$5(2) + 2(1)^2 + 3(1) = 15$	15
	2	$0 + 2(3)^2 + 3(2) = 24$		$5(1) + 2(2)^2 + 3(2) = 19$		$5(2) + 2(1)^2 + 3(2) = 18$	18
4	0	NF		NF		$5(2) + 2(2)^2 + 0 = 18$	18
	1	NF		$5(1) + 2(3)^2 + 3(1) = 26$		$5(2) + 2(2)^2 + 3(1) = 21$	21
	2	$0 + 2(4)^2 + 3(2) = 38$		$5(1) + 2(3)^2 + 3(2) = 29$		$5(2) + 2(2)^2 + 3(2) = 24$	24

inventory $= 3$, which will not meet the demand of 4. At $d_2 = 3$, the decision is feasible.

$$\text{Cost}(d_2 = 3) = 5(3) + 2(4 - 3)^2 + 3(1) + f_1^*(d_2, I_1) \qquad (13\text{-}8)$$

direct labor — change in work force — inventory

Note that the demand is 4 units; 3 units are made $(d_2 = 3)$, and the remaining unit is drawn from inventory. Thus the inventory level for stage 1 is $I_1 = I_2 + d_2 - w_2 = 1 + 3 - 4 = 0$. In Table 13-6 for $n = 1$ in the row $d_2 = 3$ and $I_1 = 0$ find $f_1^*(d_2, I_1) = 12$. Using this value, the total cost at $n = 2$ is

$$f_2(d_2 = 3, I_2 = 1) = 5(3) + 2(4 - 3)^2 + 3(1) + 12 = 32$$

The last decision evaluated, $d_2 = 4$, is costed in a similar manner.

$$f_2(d_2 = 4, I_2 = 1) = 5(4) + 2(4 - 4)^2 + 3(1) + f_1^*(d_2, I_1) \qquad (13\text{-}9)$$

$$I_1 = 1 + 4 - 4 = 1 \qquad (13\text{-}10)$$

$$f_1^*(d_2 = 4, I_1 = 1) = 21 \qquad (13\text{-}11)$$

$$f_2(d_2 = 4, I_2 = 1) = 5(4) + 2(0)^2 + 3(1) + 21 = 44 \qquad (13\text{-}12)$$

Table 13-7   ANALYSIS OF STAGE 2

			$n = 2$		
Input conditions			Decision d_2 at stage 2		
d_3	I_2	2	3	4	f_2^*
2	0	NF	NF	$5(4) + 2(2)^2 + 0 + 18$ $= 46$	46
	1	NF	$5(3) + 2(1)^2 + 3(1) + 12$ $= 32$	$5(4) + 2(2)^2 + 3(1) + 21$ $= 52$	32
	2	$5(2) + 0 + 3(2) + 10$ $= 26$	$5(3) + 2(1)^2 + (3)(2) + 15$ $= 38$	$5(4) + 2(2)^2 + 3(2) + 24$ $= 58$	26
3	0	NF	NF	$5(4) + 2(1)^2 + 0 + 18$ $= 40$	40
	1	NF	$5(3) + 0 + 3(1) + 12 = 30$	$5(4) + 2(1)^2 + 3(1) + 21$ $= 46$	30
	2	$5(2) + 2(1)^2 + 3(2) + 10$ $= 28$	$5(3) + 0 + 3(2) + 15 = 36$	$5(4) + 2(1)^2 + 3(2) + 24$ $= 52$	28
4	0	NF	NF	$5(4) + 0 + 0 = 18 = 38$	38
	1	NF	$5(3) + 2(1)^2 + 3(1) + 12$ $= 32$	$5(4) + 0 + 3(1) + 21 = 44$	32
	2	$5(2) + 2(2)^2 + 3(2) + 10$ $= 34$	$5(3) + 2(1)^2 + 3(2) + 15$ $= 38$	$5(4) + 0 + 3(2) + 24 = 50$	34

At stage 3, the decisions that will be evaluated will be $d_3 = 2$, 3, and 4 to match the input conditions at $n = 1$.

In this case the number of input conditions was greatly reduced due to the problem conditions. For example, if $d_4 = 5$ and $I_4 = 0$ (given), I_3 can only be zero. Since $w_4 = 5$ and $I_4 = 0$, it is not feasible for d_4 to be less than 5; and if $d_4 = 6$, I_3 must $= 1$.

Finally stage 4 can be evaluated at decision levels of $d_4 = 5$ or 6. Remember that $I_4 = 0$ and the original workforce is 3 (given in the problem statement).

$$f_4(d_4 = 5) = 5(5) + 2(5 - 3)^2 + 0 + f_3^*(d_4 = 5, I_3 = 0)$$

$$= 25 + 8 + 0 + 54 = 87 \tag{13-13}$$

$$f_4(d_4 = 6) = 6(5) + 2(6 - 3)^2 + 0 + f_3^*(d_4 = 6, I_3 = 1)$$

$$= 30 + 18 + 0 + 65 = 113 \tag{13-14}$$

Therefore

$$f_4^* = 87$$

The solution provides an optimum workforce over the four periods.

Period	Workforce	Hire/fire	Inventory
1	5	Hire 2	$I_4 = 0$
2	4	Fire 1	$I_3 = 0$
3	3	Fire 1	$I_2 = 1$
4	2	Fire 1	$I_1 = 0$

Minimum cost $= 87$

////

Table 13-8   ANALYSIS OF STAGE 3

		$n = 3$		
Input conditions		d_3		
d_4	I_3	2	3	4	f_3^*
5	0	NF	$5(3) + 2(2)^2 + 0 + 40$ $= 63$	$5(4) + 2(1)^2 + 0 + 32$ $= 54$	54
6	1	$5(2) + 2(4)^2 + (3)(1)$ $+ 46 = 91$	$5(3) + 3(3)^2 + 3(1) + 30$ $= 75$	$5(4) + 2(2)^2 + 3(1) + 34$ $= 65$	65

EXAMPLE 13-5 Consider another integer programming problem posed as a dynamic-programming problem. Maximize

$$4x_1 + 3x_2 + 8x_3$$

subject to

$$(1) \qquad 6x_1 + 4x_2 + 6x_3 \leq 14$$

$$(2) \qquad x_3 \leq 1$$

$$x_1, x_2, x_3 \geq 0$$

This requires a little insight if it is to be formulated without requiring excessive calculation. First recognize that we can consider this as a problem requiring three decisions, the value assigned to x_1, x_2, and x_3. Thus it is a three-stage problem. The decisions are $d_1 = x_1, d_2 = x_2$, and $d_3 = x_3$. Each constraint will be represented by a separate input condition. Thus constraint (1) will be represented by S_{1i} and constraint (2) by S_{2i}.

$$S_{1i} = 14 - \sum_{j=1}^{j=i} a_{1j} d_j \qquad (13\text{-}15)$$

$$a_{11} = a_{13} \qquad \text{from constraint (1)} \qquad (13\text{-}16)$$

$$S_{2i} = 1 - d_1 \qquad (13\text{-}17)$$

Since a_{1j} are all positive and relatively large, it can be deduced from constraint (1) that x_1 and x_3 cannot be greater than 2 and x_2 cannot be greater than 3. Constraint (2) indicates that x_3 cannot exceed 1, thus limiting the available decisions.

Actually these calculations can be greatly reduced by proper grouping of S_{1i}. This has not been done since it tends to complicate the problem. Note that at stage 1, S_{11} could feasibly have values ranging from 0 to 14 (if x_2 and x_3 are zero). Thus at $n = 1$, the tabular method is quite straightforward.

For example, consider the row for $S_1 = 11$. At this value it is feasible to let $x_1 = 0$, which will give a return of $4(0) = 0$. It is also feasible to let $x_1 = 1$ since $6(1) < 11$ so it will not violate the first constraint. The return at $x_1 = 1$ is $4(1) = 4$. However, it will not be possible to allow x_1 to equal 2 since this would exceed S_1; $2(6) > 11$.

The input conditions for stage 2 are actually simpler since x_3 is so tightly bound by the second constraint. As previously mentioned, x_3 must equal either 0 or 1. Thus S_{12} must equal 8 (if $x_3 = 1$, $S_{12} = 14 - 6$) or 14 (if $x_3 = 0$, $S_{12} = 14 - 0$). This greatly reduces the size of this matrix. The range of values that d_2 may have is 0, 1, 2, 3 based on S_{12}.

Consider the row representing input conditions $S_{12} = 14$. Here it is feasible to have $x_2 = 0$, 1, 2, or 3. When $x_2 = 0$, $S_{11} = 14 - 0 = 14$ and $f_1^*(S_{11} = 14) = 8$. When $x_2 = 1$, $S_{11} = 14 - 1(4) = 10$, so that $f_1^*(S_{11} = 10) = 4$. Again when $x_2 = 2$, $S_{11} - 2(4) = 6$ and $f_1^*(S_{11} = 6) = 4$; and if $x_2 = 3$, $S_{11} = 14 - 12 = 2$ and so $f_1^*(S_{11} = 2) = 0$.

For the third stage, $n = 3$, the input conditions are $S_{13} = 14$ and $S_{23} = 1$, and so there are only two feasible decisions to evaluate, $x_3 = 0$ and $x_3 = 1$.

$$f_3(x_3 = 0) = 0 + f_2^*(S_{12} = 14) = 10 \qquad f_3(x_3 = 1) = 1(8) + f_2^*(S_{12} = 8) = 14$$

Thus the optimal decisions can be traced.

Table 13-9   ANALYSIS OF STAGE 1

Input condition S_{11}	Stage 1 decision, $d_1 = x_1$			$f_1^* = 4x_1$
	0	1	2	
0	0	NF	NF	0
1	0	NF	NF	0
2	0	NF	NF	0
3	0	NF	NF	0
4	0	NF	NF	0
5	0	NF	NF	0
6	0	4	NF	4
7	0	4	NF	4
8	0	4	NF	4
9	0	4	NF	4
10	0	4	NF	4
11	0	4	NF	4
12	0	4	8	8
13	0	4	8	8
14	0	4	8	8

Table 13-10   ANALYSIS OF STAGE 2

Input condition S_{12}	Decision at stage 2, $d_2 = x_2$				f_2^*
	0	1	2	3	
8	$0 + 4 = 4$	$1(3) + 0 = 3$	$2(3) + 0 = 6$	NF	6
14	$0 + 8 = 8$	$1(3) + 4 = 7$	$2(3) + 4 = 10$	$3(3) + 0 = 9$	10

Table 13-11

Stage	Decision	f_3^*
3	$x_3^* = 1$	$1(8) + 2(3) = 14$
2	$x_2^* = 2$	
1	$x_1^* = 0$	

Table 13-12

Feasible combinations		S_{11} resulting
x_3	x_2	
0	0	$S_{11} = 14 - 0 - 0 = 14$
0	1	$S_{11} = 14 - 0 - 1(4) = 10$
0	2	$S_{11} = 14 - 0 - 2(4) = 6$
0	3	$S_{11} = 14 - 0 - 3(4) = 2$
1	0	$S_{11} = 14 - 6 - 0 = 8$
1	1	$S_{11} = 14 - 6 - 4 = 4$
1	2	$S_{11} = 14 - 6 - 8 = 0$

In retrospect it is possible to observe that the possible input conditions at stage 1 might be determined ahead of time by considering the feasible combinations of x_2 and x_3. In fact this is probably not worth the time.

Dynamic programming can also be applied to problems involving continuous variables. This greatly reduces the amount of computation but unfortunately usually results in a more complex mathematical form. Although the concepts are identical, the method may appear different due simply to a change in emphasis. Before starting this example, first review the steps we took using the tabular form.

1 Establish the stages, decision variables, and input conditions (sometimes called *state variables*).

2 Determine the return function for each stage.

3 Determine the method of computing the next input conditions as a result of prior decisions and conditions.

4 Find f_1^* as a function of d_1 for a necessary range of input conditions (compute a row in the table $n = 1$).

5 Find $f_2 = r_2 + f_1^*(d_2, S_2)$. Compute the rows in the table $n = 2$, Here we are transferring f_1^* to this table as a result of a given decision (d_2) and input condition (S_2) at stage 2. Again this is done for a range in values of S_2.

6 Repeat step 5 for stages $n = 3, 4, \ldots, N$ until complete.   ////

Note that in every case as we move to a new table, we enter the optimum return from the last table as a result of what happened at the new table, i.e., as a function of S_n and d_n. Now consider this next example.

EXAMPLE 13-6   Maximize

$$x_1^2 + 2x_2^2 + 4x_3$$

subject to

$$x_1 + 2x_2 + x_3 \leq 8$$

$$x_j \geq 0$$

As before, the decision regarding what value to assign each variable will represent a state, and thus it is a three-state problem. The return function and input conditions for each state are displayed in Fig. 13-3.

Now find f_1, that is, optimize at $n = 1$.

$$f_1 = r_1 = x_1^2 \qquad (13\text{-}18)$$

This is obviously maximized when x_1 is as large as possible. Since the constraint cannot be exceeded, x_1 must not exceed S_1, which is the amount of the constraint resource that has not yet been assigned. Thus $x_1 \leq S_1$, and to maximize $x_1 = S_1$

$$f_1^* = S_1^2 \qquad (13\text{-}19)$$

Next go back to stage 2.

$$f_2 = r_2 + f_1^*$$
$$= 2x_2^2 + S_1^2 \qquad (13\text{-}20)$$

Express S_1 in terms of the variables at stage 2, that is, x_2 and S_2. This is done by using the relation $S_1 = S_2 - 2x_2$.

$$f_2 = 2x_2^2 + (S_2 - 2x_2)^2$$
$$= 2x_2^2 + S_2^2 - 4x_2 S_2 + 4x_2^2$$
$$= 6x_2^2 - 4x_2 S_2 + S_2^2 \qquad (13\text{-}21)$$

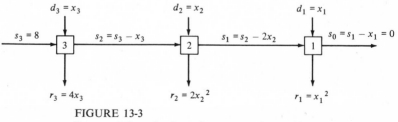

FIGURE 13-3
Representation of a dynamic-programming problem (Example 13-6).

In this stage, x_2 may take any value in the range $0 \leq x_2 \leq S_2/2$ due to the constraint. By taking the partial derivative of f_2 with respect to x_2, both first and second, it can be shown that the *minimum* value of f_2 occurs at $x_2 = \frac{1}{3}S_2$. Since this is within the range of 0 to $\frac{1}{2}S_2$, it means that f_2^* occurs either at $x_2 = 0$ or at $x = \frac{1}{2}S_2$. Both must be evaluated.

At $x_2 = 0$:

$$f_2 = 0 - 0 + S_2^2 = S_2^2 \qquad (13\text{-}22)$$

At $x_2 = \frac{1}{2}S_2$:

$$f_2 = 6\left(\frac{S_2}{2}\right)^2 - 4S_2\frac{S_2}{2} + S_2^2$$

$$= \frac{6S_2^2}{4} - \frac{4S_2^2}{2} + S_2^2$$

$$= \frac{1}{2}S_2^2 \qquad (13\text{-}23)$$

Since $S_2^2 > \frac{1}{2}S_2^2$, $f_2^* = S_2^2$, $x_2^* = 0$.

Finally evaluate at stage 3.

$$f_3 = r_3 + f_2^*$$
$$= 4x_3 + S_2^2 \qquad (13\text{-}24)$$

Remember that $S_2 = S_3 - x_3$ and convert this expression to stage 3 variables only.

$$f_3 = 4x_3 + (S_3 - x_3)^2$$
$$= 4x_3 + S_3^2 - 2x_3 S_3 + x_3^2 \qquad (13\text{-}25)$$

Since $S_3 = 8$, this can be simplified to

$$f_3 = x_3^2 + 4x_3 - 16x_3 + 64$$
$$= x_3^2 - 12x_3 + 64 \qquad (13\text{-}26)$$

The variable x_3 may have any value in the range $0 \leq x_3 \leq 8$. Taking the first and second partial derivatives shows that the *minimum* value for f_3 occurs at $x_3 = 6$, so that x_3 must be evaluated at both extremes of the range.

$$f_3(x_3 = 0) = 0 - 0 + 64 = 64 \qquad (13\text{-}27)$$
$$f_3(x_3 = 8) = 64 - 96 + 64 = 32 \qquad (13\text{-}28)$$

Thus

$$f_3^* = 64 \qquad \text{at } x_3^* = 0 \qquad (13\text{-}29)$$

From this the other values of x_1 and x_2 can be determined.

$$S_3 = 8 \qquad x_3^* = 0$$
$$S_2 = S_3 - x_3 = 8 - 0 = 8 \qquad (13\text{-}30)$$
$$x_2^* = 0$$
$$S_1 = S_2 - 2x_2 = 8 - 0 = 8 \qquad (13\text{-}31)$$
$$x_1^* = S_1 = 8$$

Actually this can be evaluated for any value of S_3. First write f_3 in terms of x_3 and S_3.

$$f_3 = 4x_3 + S_3{}^2 - 2x_3 S_3 + x_3{}^2 \qquad (13\text{-}32)$$

We already know that x_3^* will either be 0 or S_3. To find this point set them equal and solve.

$$
\begin{array}{ll}
x_3 = 0 & f_3 = S_3{}^2 \\
x_3 = S_3 & f_3 = 4S_3 \\
S_3{}^2 = 4S_3 & \\
S_3 = 4 &
\end{array}
$$

This says that if S_3 is 4 or less, set $x_3 = S_3$ and if S_3 is 4 or more, set $x_3 = 0$.

$$
\begin{array}{ll}
0 \le S_3 \le 4 & 4 \le S_3 \le \infty \\
x_3^* = S_3 & x_3^* = 0 \\
S_2 = S_3 - x_3 = 0 & S_2 = S_3 - x_3 = S_3 \\
x_2^* = 0 & x_2^* = 0 \\
S_1 = S_2 - 2x_2 & S_1 = S_2 - x_2 = S_3 - 0 \\
\quad = 0 - 0 = 0 & \\
x_1 = S_1 = 0 & x_1^* = S_1 = S_3 \\
f_3^* = 4S_3 & f_3^* = S_3{}^2
\end{array}
$$

Now review what we have done. After determining how to compute the return and input conditions for each stage, we begin by finding x_1^* and f_1^* in terms of S_1. This is the same as in the tabular method, where we found x_1^* for all values of S_1 which might occur. Actually using the expression for x_1^* and f_1^* one can compute the values for any desired range of S_1 values and thus generate the same results as found with the tabular method. Next we found $f_2 = r_2 + f_1^*$. Then f_1^* was expressed in terms of stage 2 so that f_2 could be optimized. This is the same as in the tabular method, when we added f_1^* to each computation in stage 2. However, since we had already expressed f_1^* in terms of S_2 and x_2, we did not have to look up each discrete value. ////

EXAMPLE 13-7 As another example of the continuous method modify the last example to minimize

$$x_1{}^2 + 2x_2{}^2 + 4x_3$$

subject to

$$x_1 + 2x_2 + x_3 \ge 8$$

$$x_j \ge 0$$

STAGE 1

$$f_1 = r_1 = x_1{}^2 \qquad (13\text{-}33)$$

Obviously x_1 should be as small as possible. Due to the change in the constraint, $x_1 \geq S_1$; so set $x_1 = S_1$.

$$f_1^* = S_1{}^2$$
$$x_1^* = S_1$$

STAGE 2

$$f_2 = r_2 + f_1^* = 2x_2{}^2 + S_1{}^2 \qquad (13\text{-}34)$$
$$S_1 = S_2 - 2x_2 \qquad (13\text{-}35)$$
$$f_2 = 2x_2{}^2 + (S_2 - 2x_2)^2$$
$$= 2x_2{}^2 + S_2{}^2 - 4x_2 S_2 + 4x_2{}^2$$
$$= 6x_2{}^2 - 4x_2 S_2 + S_2{}^2 \qquad (13\text{-}36)$$

Take the first and second partial derivative with respect to x_2.

$$\frac{\partial f_2}{\partial x_2} = 12x_2 - 4S_2 \qquad (13\text{-}37)$$

$$\frac{\partial^2 f_3}{\partial x_2{}^2} = 12 \qquad (13\text{-}38)$$

Since this is positive, the solution of $12x_2 - 4S_2 = 0$ will be a minimum.

$$x_2^* = \tfrac{1}{3}S_2 \qquad (13\text{-}39)$$

Substitute in f_2 to find f_2^*.

$$f_2^* = 6\left(\frac{S_2}{3}\right)^2 - 4\frac{S_2}{3}S_2 + S_2{}^2$$
$$= \tfrac{2}{3}S_2{}^2 - \tfrac{4}{3}S_2{}^2 + S_2{}^2$$
$$= \tfrac{1}{3}S_2{}^2 \qquad (13\text{-}40)$$

STAGE 3

$$f_3 = r_3 + f_2^* = 4x_3 + \tfrac{1}{3}S_2{}^2 \qquad (13\text{-}41)$$
$$S_2 = S_3 - x_3 \qquad (13\text{-}42)$$
$$f_3 = 4x_3 + \tfrac{1}{3}(S_3{}^2 - 2x_3 S_3 + x_3{}^2) \qquad (13\text{-}43)$$

Take the first and second partial derivative with respect to x_3.

$$\frac{\partial f_3}{\partial x_3} = 4 - \tfrac{2}{3}S_3 + \tfrac{2}{3}x_3 \qquad (13\text{-}44)$$

$$\frac{\partial^2 f_3}{\partial x_3^2} = \frac{2}{3} \qquad (13\text{-}45)$$

This says the minimum will occur when $\partial f_3/\partial x_3 = 0$ is evaluated.

$$4 - \tfrac{2}{3}S_3 + \tfrac{2}{3}x_3 = 0 \qquad (13\text{-}46)$$

$$\tfrac{2}{3}x_3 = \tfrac{2}{3}S_3 - 4$$

$$x_3^* = S_3 - 6$$

Since $S_3 = 8$, $x_3^* = 8 - 6 = 2$.

$$f_3^* = 4(2) + \tfrac{1}{3}[64 - 2(2)(8) + 2^2]$$

$$= 8 + \tfrac{1}{3}(64 - 32 + 4) = 20 \qquad (13\text{-}47)$$

Note that if S_3 were less than 6, x_3^* would be negative, which is not feasible; thus for $S_3 < 6$, $x_3^* = 0$ and for $S_3 \geq 6$, $x_3^* = S_3 - 6$.

$$S_3 < 6$$

$$x_3^* = 0 \qquad (13\text{-}48)$$

$$S_2 = S_3 - x_3 = S_3 \qquad (13\text{-}49)$$

$$x_2^* = \tfrac{1}{3}S_2 = \tfrac{1}{3}S_3 \qquad (13\text{-}50)$$

$$S_1 = S_2 - 2x_2 \qquad (13\text{-}51)$$

$$S_1 = S_3 - 2(\tfrac{1}{3}S_3)$$

$$= \tfrac{1}{3}S_3 \qquad (13\text{-}52)$$

$$x_1^* = S_1 = \tfrac{1}{3}S_3 \qquad (13\text{-}53)$$

Thus all values of x_j are expressed in terms of S_3. ////

EXAMPLE 13-8 As a final example of a solution using continuous variables maximize

$$-x_1^2 - 2x_2^2 + 3x_2 + x_3$$

subject to

$$x_1 + x_2 + x_3 \leq 1$$

$$x_1, x_2, x_3 \geq 0$$

First determine the relationships for r_i and S_i.

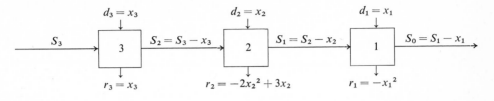

$$d_3 = x_3 \qquad d_2 = x_2 \qquad d_1 = x_1$$

$$S_3 \quad \boxed{3} \quad S_2 = S_3 - x_3 \quad \boxed{2} \quad S_1 = S_2 - x_2 \quad \boxed{1} \quad S_0 = S_1 - x_1$$

$$r_3 = x_3 \qquad r_2 = -2x_2{}^2 + 3x_2 \qquad r_1 = -x_1{}^2$$

STAGE 1

$$f_1 = r_1 = -x_1{}^2 \qquad (13\text{-}54)$$

This is maximized when $x_1 = 0$.

$$f_1^* = 0$$

$$x_1^* = 0$$

STAGE 2

$$f_2 = r_2 + f_1^* = -2x_2{}^2 + 3x_2 + 0 \qquad (13\text{-}55)$$

Use calculus to optimize with respect to x_2.

$$\frac{\partial x_2}{\partial f_2} = -4x_2 + 3 \qquad (13\text{-}56)$$

This will be maximum if $\partial f_2 / \partial x_2 = 0$ is evaluated.

$$-4x_2 + 3 = 0 \qquad (13\text{-}57)$$

$$x_2^* = \tfrac{3}{4}$$

However, x_2 cannot exceed S_2, and so if $S_2 < \tfrac{3}{4}$, f_2 would be maximized by letting x_2 be as large as possible, that is, $x_2 = S_2$.

$$S_2 < \tfrac{3}{4} \qquad\qquad S_2 \geq \tfrac{3}{4}$$

$$x_2^* = S_2 \qquad\qquad x_2^* = \tfrac{3}{4}$$

$$f_2^* = -2S_2{}^2 + 3S_2 \qquad f_2^* = \tfrac{9}{8}$$

STAGE 3

$$f_3 = r_3 + f_2^* = x_3 + f_2^* \qquad (13\text{-}58)$$

This must be done for two conditions since f_2^* depends on how large S_2 is.

Case 1, $S_2 \geq \tfrac{3}{4}$:

$$f_3 = x_3 + \tfrac{9}{8} \qquad (13\text{-}59)$$

This is maximized if x_3 is as large as possible.   How big can x_3 be if $S_2 \geq \frac{3}{4}$?

$$S_2 = S_3 - x_3 = 1 - x_3 \qquad (13\text{-}60)$$

$$\tfrac{3}{4} = 1 - x_3$$

$$x_3^* = \tfrac{1}{4} \qquad (13\text{-}61)$$

and so

$$f_3^* = \tfrac{1}{4} + \tfrac{9}{8} = \tfrac{11}{8} \qquad (13\text{-}62)$$

Case 2, $S_2 < \frac{3}{4}$:

$$f_3 = x_3 + 3S_2 - 2S_2{}^2 \qquad (13\text{-}63)$$

$$S_2 = S_3 - x_3 \qquad (13\text{-}64)$$

$$f_3 = x_3 + 3S_3 - 3x_3 - 2(S_3 - x_3)^2$$

$$= x_3 + 3S_3 - 3x_3 - 2S_3{}^2 + 4x_3 S_3 - 2x_3{}^2$$

$$= +3S_3 - 2x_3 - 2S_3{}^2 + 4x_3 S_3 - 2x_3{}^2 \qquad (13\text{-}65)$$

$$\frac{\partial f_3}{\partial x_3} = 0 - 2 - 0 + 4S_3 - 4x_3 \qquad (13\text{-}66)$$

Since the second partial derivative is -4, the first may be set equal to zero to find a value of x_3 which maximizes

$$4S_3 - 4x_3 - 2 = 0 \qquad (13\text{-}67)$$

$$x_3^* = S_3 - \tfrac{1}{2} = 1 - \tfrac{1}{2} = \tfrac{1}{2} \qquad \text{since } S_3 = 1 \qquad (13\text{-}68)$$

$$f_3^* = 3 - 2(\tfrac{1}{2}) - 2(1)^2 + 4(\tfrac{1}{2})(1) - 2(\tfrac{1}{2})^2$$

$$= 1\tfrac{1}{2} \qquad (13\text{-}69)$$

Now compare case 1 with case 2.   Since $\tfrac{11}{8} < 1\tfrac{1}{2}$,

$$x_3^* = \tfrac{1}{2} \qquad f_3^* = 1\tfrac{1}{2}$$

$$S_2 = S_3 - x_3 = 1 - \tfrac{1}{2} = \tfrac{1}{2} \qquad (13\text{-}70)$$

$$x_2^* = S_2 = \tfrac{1}{2} \qquad (13\text{-}71)$$

$$S_1 = S_2 - x_2 = 0 \qquad (13\text{-}72)$$

$$x_1^* = 0 \qquad (13\text{-}73)$$

$$////$$

DIFFICULTIES IN APPLICATION

Although dynamic programming theoretically can be used to solve an extremely wide range of problems, applications rapidly become very difficult.   The major problem is that of problem size.   In particular, these comments apply to problems having finite or noncontinuous solutions. The size of the problem increases exponentially with an increase in the number of stages. Obviously, the problem size also increases with an increase in the range of possible conditions at each stage. This is a combinatorial problem. If there are 3 stages and 5 possible conditions at each stage, there are $5^3 = 125$ feasible answers. Even if the output for each combination is not computed, the computations in dynamic programming still increase in a similar manner. Even more important, the computer space required also becomes large. Since one cannot intuitively anticipate the final answer, the optimal output for each stage and input condition must be stored. The storage requirements are often more restrictive than the computational requirements.

An even greater problem occurs when more variables are added. Each added dimension expands the space required at a rapid exponential rate. For example, if a 3-stage problem has 2 variables, each having a feasible range of 5 values at each stage, the number of feasible answers becomes $(5 \times 5)^2 = 1,625$.

As a result, practical sized problems are not feasible with more than two or three variables. Several computational tricks can be used to reduce space or time requirements, but even these do not greatly expand the possible size by very much. One of the common techniques is first to determine an optimal answer using a coarse grid to determine the approximate answer. Then, increasingly finer divisions are used until the answer is as accurate as desired. This requires some assumptions concerning modality; however, in most real problems, this is not a major problem.

REFERENCES

1 BELLMAN, R.: "Dynamic Programming," Princeton University Press, Princeton, N.J., 1957.
2 BELLMAN, R., and S. DREYFUS: "Applied Dynamic Programming," Princeton University Press, Princeton, N.J., 1962.
3 HOWARD, R.: "Dynamic Programming and Markov Processes," John Wiley & Sons, Inc., New York, 1960.
4 WILDE, D. J., and C. S. BEIGHTLER: "Foundations of Optimization," Prentice-Hall, Englewood Cliffs, N.J., 1967.

PROBLEMS

13-1   Use dynamic programming to find the minimum-distance path from A to L.

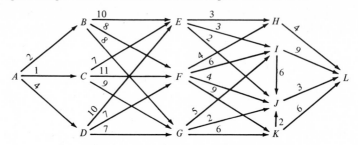

13-2   An airplane is to be loaded to maximize the total income.   Five items will be considered, only one of each is needed.   The shipping company gets 5 cents per pound plus the item bonus.   The plane can carry 2,000 lb.

Item	Weight, lb	Volume, ft^3	Bonus value
1	1,000	70	$70
2	1,100	100	80
3	700	100	110
4	800	80	100
5	500	50	70

(*a*) What items should be carried?
(*b*) If a maximum of 200 ft^3 is also considered, which items should be carried?

13-3   A firm has $10,000 to invest in any of four year-long ventures.   Any money not invested in these ventures may be put into working capital and with the net effect of carrying 10 percent per year.   How should the funds be used?

Venture	Amount to invest	Net worth at end of year
1	$2,000	$2,500
2	3,000	3,800
3	6,000	7,500
4	7,000	8,200

13-4   Obtain an integer solution by dynamic programming.   Minimize

$$3x_1 + 4x_2 + 5x_3$$

subject to

$$x_1 + 2x_2 + x_3 \geq 6$$
$$x_1 - x_2 + 2x_3 \geq 4$$
$$x_j \geq 0$$

13-5 A manufacturing department has to meet the following demand for its product:

Quarter	1	2	3	4
Demand, thousands	4	2	6	3

Assume that products made during the quarter may be used to satisfy the demand that quarter. Storage costs are not incurred during the quarter products are made, but if held over, they will acquire a storage cost since demand effectively occurs at the end of a quarter. It costs $100 to increase production by 1,000 and $150 to decrease production by 1,000. Storage cost are $75 per thousand per quarter stored. Assume that production during the 0 quarter was 4,000 and that there was no inventory on hand. What is the optimal production schedule?

13-6 Obtain a maximum integer solution using dynamic programming

$$1.5x_1 + x_2$$

subject to

$$x_1 + x_2 \leq 10$$
$$4x_1 + x_2 \leq 20$$
$$x_1, x_2 \geq 0$$

13-7 Repeat Prob. 13-6 without restricting it to an integer solution.

13-8 Obtain a maximum solution using dynamic programming

$$x_1{}^2 + 3x_2 - x_1$$

subject to

$$x_1 + 2x_2 \leq 5$$

13-9 A pipeline company realizes a profit of 30, 50 and 40 cents per barrel from oil companies 1, 2, and 3 respectively. The capacity of the available pipeline is 100,000 barrels/day. Requests to ship 50,000, 30,000, and 30,000 barrels have been received from the three oil companies. The pipeline company further realizes a profit of 10 cents per barrel in storage. In order to maximize the profit of the pipeline company, determine the optimal mix using dynamic programming.

13-10 Maximize

$$z = 6x_1 + 2x_2 + 3x_3 + 4$$

subject to

$$x_1 + x_2 \leq 4$$
$$x_2 + 3x_3 \leq 6$$
$$x_1, x_2, x_3 \geq 0$$

13-11 An investor has $500 to invest. He has narrowed his possible alternatives to three small companies. The estimated returns for different amounts of capital invested in each company are tabulated. Zero allocation returns $0. What is the optimal investment policy?

Amount	Company		
	1	2	3
$100	10	20	10
200	10	20	20
300	30	20	20
400	40	30	30
500	40	30	40

APPENDIX A

Summation of terms of Poisson's exponential binomial limit

$1,000 \times$ probability of c or less occurrences of event that has average number of occurrences equal to c' or np'

c' or np'	0	1	2	3	4	5	6	7	8	9
0.02	980	1,000								
0.04	961	999	1,000							
0.06	942	998	1,000							
0.08	923	997	1,000							
0.10	905	995	1,000							
0.15	861	990	999	1,000						
0.20	819	982	999	1,000						
0.25	779	974	998	1,000						
0.30	741	963	996	1,000						
0.35	705	951	994	1,000						
0.40	670	938	992	999	1,000					
0.45	638	925	989	999	1,000					
0.50	607	910	986	998	1,000					
0.55	577	894	982	998	1,000					
0.60	549	878	977	997	1,000					
0.65	522	861	972	996	999	1,000				
0.70	497	844	966	994	999	1,000				
0.75	472	827	959	993	999	1,000				
0.80	449	809	953	991	999	1,000				
0.85	427	791	945	989	998	1,000				
0.90	407	772	937	987	998	1,000				
0.95	387	754	929	984	997	1,000				
1.00	368	736	920	981	996	999	1,000			
1.1	333	699	900	974	995	999	1,000			
1.2	301	663	879	966	992	998	1,000			
1.3	273	627	857	957	989	998	1,000			
1.4	247	592	833	946	986	997	999	1,000		
1.5	223	558	809	934	981	996	999	1,000		
1.6	202	525	783	921	976	994	999	1,000		
1.7	183	493	757	907	970	992	998	1,000		
1.8	165	463	731	891	964	990	997	999	1,000	
1.9	150	434	704	875	956	987	997	999	1,000	
2.0	135	406	677	857	947	983	995	999	1,000	

(*From E. L. Grant and R. S. Leavenworth, "Statistical Quality Control," 4th ed., McGraw-Hill Book Company, New York, 1972. By permission of the publishers.*)

Summation of terms of Poisson's exponential binomial limit. (*Continued*)

c c' or np'	0	1	2	3	4	5	6	7	8	9
2.2	111	355	623	819	928	975	993	998	1,000	
2.4	091	308	570	779	904	964	988	997	999	1,000
2.6	074	267	518	736	877	951	983	995	999	1,000
2.8	061	231	469	692	848	935	976	992	998	999
3.0	050	199	423	647	815	916	966	988	996	999
3.2	041	171	380	603	781	895	955	983	994	998
3.4	033	147	340	558	744	871	942	977	992	997
3.6	027	126	303	515	706	844	927	969	988	996
3.8	022	107	269	473	668	816	909	960	984	994
4.0	018	092	238	433	629	785	889	949	979	992
4.2	015	078	210	395	590	753	867	936	972	989
4.4	012	066	185	359	551	720	844	921	964	985
4.6	010	056	163	326	513	686	818	905	955	980
4.8	008	048	143	294	476	651	791	887	944	975
5.0	007	040	125	265	440	616	762	867	932	968
5.2	006	034	109	238	406	581	732	845	918	960
5.4	005	029	095	213	373	546	702	822	903	951
5.6	004	024	082	191	342	512	670	797	886	941
5.8	003	021	072	170	313	478	638	771	867	929
6.0	002	017	062	151	285	446	606	744	847	916

	10	11	12	13	14	15	16
2.8	1,000						
3.0	1,000						
3.2	1,000						
3.4	999	1,000					
3.6	999	1,000					
3.8	998	999	1,000				
4.0	997	999	1,000				
4.2	996	999	1,000				
4.4	994	998	999	1,000			
4.6	992	997	999	1,000			
4.8	990	996	999	1,000			
5.0	986	995	998	999	1,000		
5.2	982	993	997	999	1,000		
5.4	977	990	996	999	1,000		
5.6	972	988	995	998	999	1,000	
5.8	965	984	993	997	999	1,000	
6.0	957	980	991	996	999	999	1,000

(*From E. L. Grant and R. S. Leavenworth, "Statistical Quality Control," 4th ed., McGraw-Hill Book Company, New York, 1972. By permission of the publishers.*)

Summation of terms of Poisson's exponential binomial limit. (*Continued*)

c'or np' / c	0	1	2	3	4	5	6	7	8	9
6.2	002	015	054	134	259	414	574	716	826	902
6.4	002	012	046	119	235	384	542	687	803	886
6.6	001	010	040	105	213	355	511	658	780	869
6.8	001	009	034	093	192	327	480	628	755	850
7.0	001	007	030	082	173	301	450	599	729	830
7.2	001	006	025	072	156	276	420	569	703	810
7.4	001	005	022	063	140	253	392	539	676	788
7.6	001	004	019	055	125	231	365	510	648	765
7.8	000	004	016	048	112	210	338	481	620	741
8.0	000	003	014	042	100	191	313	453	593	717
8.5	000	002	009	030	074	150	256	386	523	653
9.0	000	001	006	021	055	116	207	324	456	587
9.5	000	001	004	015	040	089	165	269	392	522
10.0	000	000	003	010	029	067	130	220	333	458

	10	11	12	13	14	15	16	17	18	19
6.2	949	975	989	995	998	999	1,000			
6.4	939	969	986	994	997	999	1,000			
6.6	927	963	982	992	997	999	999	1,000		
6.8	915	955	978	990	996	998	999	1,000		
7.0	901	947	973	987	994	998	999	1,000		
7.2	887	937	967	984	993	997	999	999	1,000	
7.4	871	926	961	980	991	996	998	999	1,000	
7.6	854	915	954	976	989	995	998	999	1,000	
7.8	835	902	945	971	986	993	997	999	1,000	
8.0	816	888	936	966	983	992	996	998	999	1,000
8.5	763	849	909	949	973	986	993	997	999	999
9.0	706	803	876	926	959	978	989	995	998	999
9.5	645	752	836	898	940	967	982	991	996	998
10.0	583	697	792	864	917	951	973	986	993	997

	20	21	22
8.5	1,000		
9.0	1,000		
9.5	999	1,000	
10.0	998	999	1,000

(*From E. L. Grant and R. S. Leavenworth, "Statistical Quality Control," 4th ed., McGraw-Hill Book Company, New York, 1972. By permission of the publishers.*)

Summation of terms of Poisson's exponential binomial limit. (*Continued*)

c' or np' \ c	0	1	2	3	4	5	6	7	8	9
10.5	000	000	002	007	021	050	102	179	279	397
11.0	000	000	001	005	015	038	079	143	232	341
11.5	000	000	001	003	011	028	060	114	191	289
12.0	000	000	001	002	008	020	046	090	155	242
12.5	000	000	000	002	005	015	035	070	125	201
13.0	000	000	000	001	004	011	026	054	100	166
13.5	000	000	000	001	003	008	019	041	079	135
14.0	000	000	000	000	002	006	014	032	062	109
14.5	000	000	000	000	001	004	010	024	048	088
15.0	000	000	000	000	001	003	008	018	037	070

	10	11	12	13	14	15	16	17	18	19
10.5	521	639	742	825	888	932	960	978	988	994
11.0	460	579	689	781	854	907	944	968	982	991
11.5	402	520	633	733	815	878	924	954	974	986
12.0	347	462	576	682	772	844	899	937	963	979
12.5	297	406	519	628	725	806	869	916	948	969
13.0	252	353	463	573	675	764	835	890	930	957
13.5	211	304	409	518	623	718	798	861	908	942
14.0	176	260	358	464	570	669	756	827	883	923
14.5	145	220	311	413	518	619	711	790	853	901
15.0	118	185	268	363	466	568	664	749	819	875

	20	21	22	23	24	25	26	27	28	29
10.5	997	999	999	1,000						
11.0	995	998	999	1,000						
11.5	992	996	998	999	1,000					
12.0	988	994	997	999	999	1,000				
12.5	983	991	995	998	999	999	1,000			
13.0	975	986	992	996	998	999	1,000			
13.5	965	980	989	994	997	998	999	1,000		
14.0	952	971	983	991	995	997	999	999	1,000	
14.5	936	960	976	986	992	996	998	999	999	1,000
15.0	917	947	967	981	989	994	997	998	999	1,000

(*From E. L. Grant and R. S. Leavenworth,* "*Statistical Quality Control,*" *4th ed., McGraw-Hill Book Company, New York, 1972. By permission of the publishers.*)

Summation of terms of Poisson's exponential binomial limit. (*Continued*)

c' or np' \ c	4	5	6	7	8	9	10	11	12	13
16	000	001	004	010	022	043	077	127	193	275
17	000	001	002	005	013	026	049	085	135	201
18	000	000	001	003	007	015	030	055	092	143
19	000	000	001	002	004	009	018	035	061	098
20	000	000	000	001	002	005	011	021	039	066
21	000	000	000	000	001	003	006	013	025	043
22	000	000	000	000	001	002	004	008	015	028
23	000	000	000	000	000	001	002	004	009	017
24	000	000	000	000	000	000	001	003	005	011
25	000	000	000	000	000	000	001	001	003	006

	14	15	16	17	18	19	20	21	22	23
16	368	467	566	659	742	812	868	911	942	963
17	281	371	468	564	655	736	805	861	905	937
18	208	287	375	469	562	651	731	799	855	899
19	150	215	292	378	469	561	647	725	793	849
20	105	157	221	297	381	470	559	644	721	787
21	072	111	163	227	302	384	471	558	640	716
22	048	077	117	169	232	306	387	472	556	637
23	031	052	082	123	175	238	310	389	472	555
24	020	034	056	087	128	180	243	314	392	473
25	012	022	038	060	092	134	185	247	318	394

	24	25	26	27	28	29	30	31	32	33
16	978	987	993	996	998	999	999	1,000		
17	959	975	985	991	995	997	999	999	1,000	
18	932	955	972	983	990	994	997	998	999	1,000
19	893	927	951	969	980	988	993	996	998	999
20	843	888	922	948	966	978	987	992	995	997
21	782	838	883	917	944	963	976	985	991	994
22	712	777	832	877	913	940	959	973	983	989
23	635	708	772	827	873	908	936	956	971	981
24	554	632	704	768	823	868	904	932	953	969
25	473	553	629	700	763	818	863	900	929	950

	34	35	36	37	38	39	40	41	42	43
19	999	1,000								
20	999	999	1,000							
21	997	998	999	999	1,000					
22	994	996	998	999	999	1,000				
23	988	993	996	997	999	999	1,000			
24	979	987	992	995	997	998	999	999	1,000	
25	966	978	985	991	994	997	998	999	999	1,000

(*From E. L. Grant and R. S. Leavenworth, "Statistical Quality Control," 4th ed., McGraw-Hill Book Company, New York, 1972. By permission of the publishers.*)

APPENDIX B

Areas under the normal curve

Proportion of total area under the curve that is under the portion of the curve from $-\infty$ to $\dfrac{X_i - \bar{X}'}{\sigma'}$. ($X_i$ represents any desired value of the variable X)

$\frac{X_i-\bar{X}'}{\sigma'}$	0.09	0.08	0.07	0.06	0.05	0.04	0.03	0.02	0.01	0.00
−3.5	0.00017	0.00017	0.00018	0.00019	0.00019	0.00020	0.00021	0.00022	0.00022	0.00023
−3.4	0.00024	0.00025	0.00026	0.00027	0.00028	0.00029	0.00030	0.00031	0.00033	0.00034
−3.3	0.00035	0.00036	0.00038	0.00039	0.00040	0.00042	0.00043	0.00045	0.00047	0.00048
−3.2	0.00050	0.00052	0.00054	0.00056	0.00058	0.00060	0.00062	0.00064	0.00066	0.00069
−3.1	0.00071	0.00074	0.00076	0.00079	0.00082	0.00085	0.00087	0.00090	0.00094	0.00097
−3.0	0.00100	0.00104	0.00107	0.00111	0.00114	0.00118	0.00122	0.00126	0.00131	0.00135
−2.9	0.0014	0.0014	0.0015	0.0015	0.0016	0.0016	0.0017	0.0017	0.0018	0.0019
−2.8	0.0019	0.0020	0.0021	0.0021	0.0022	0.0023	0.0023	0.0024	0.0025	0.0026
−2.7	0.0026	0.0027	0.0028	0.0029	0.0030	0.0031	0.0032	0.0033	0.0034	0.0035
−2.6	0.0036	0.0037	0.0038	0.0039	0.0040	0.0041	0.0043	0.0044	0.0045	0.0047
−2.5	0.0048	0.0049	0.0051	0.0052	0.0054	0.0055	0.0057	0.0059	0.0060	0.0062
−2.4	0.0064	0.0066	0.0068	0.0069	0.0071	0.0073	0.0075	0.0078	0.0080	0.0082
−2.3	0.0084	0.0087	0.0089	0.0091	0.0094	0.0096	0.0099	0.0102	0.0104	0.0107
−2.2	0.0110	0.0113	0.0116	0.0119	0.0122	0.0125	0.0129	0.0132	0.0136	0.0139
−2.1	0.0143	0.0146	0.0150	0.0154	0.0158	0.0162	0.0166	0.0170	0.0174	0.0179
−2.0	0.0183	0.0188	0.0192	0.0197	0.0202	0.0207	0.0212	0.0217	0.0222	0.0228
−1.9	0.0233	0.0239	0.0244	0.0250	0.0256	0.0262	0.0268	0.0274	0.0281	0.0287
−1.8	0.0294	0.0301	0.0307	0.0314	0.0322	0.0329	0.0336	0.0344	0.0351	0.0359
−1.7	0.0367	0.0375	0.0384	0.0392	0.0401	0.0409	0.0418	0.0427	0.0436	0.0446
−1.6	0.0455	0.0465	0.0475	0.0485	0.0495	0.0505	0.0516	0.0526	0.0537	0.0548
−1.5	0.0559	0.0571	0.0582	0.0594	0.0606	0.0618	0.0630	0.0643	0.0655	0.0668
−1.4	0.0681	0.0694	0.0708	0.0721	0.0735	0.0749	0.0764	0.0778	0.0793	0.0808
−1.3	0.0823	0.0838	0.0853	0.0869	0.0885	0.0901	0.0918	0.0934	0.0951	0.0968
−1.2	0.0985	0.1003	0.1020	0.1038	0.1057	0.1075	0.1093	0.1112	0.1131	0.1151
−1.1	0.1170	0.1190	0.1210	0.1230	0.1251	0.1271	0.1292	0.1314	0.1335	0.1357
−1.0	0.1379	0.1401	0.1423	0.1446	0.1469	0.1492	0.1515	0.1539	0.1562	0.1587
−0.9	0.1611	0.1635	0.1660	0.1685	0.1711	0.1736	0.1762	0.1788	0.1814	0.1841
−0.8	0.1867	0.1894	0.1922	0.1949	0.1977	0.2005	0.2033	0.2061	0.2090	0.2119
−0.7	0.2148	0.2177	0.2207	0.2236	0.2266	0.2297	0.2327	0.2358	0.2389	0.2420
−0.6	0.2451	0.2483	0.2514	0.2546	0.2578	0.2611	0.2643	0.2676	0.2709	0.2743
−0.5	0.2776	0.2810	0.2843	0.2877	0.2912	0.2946	0.2981	0.3015	0.3050	0.3085
−0.4	0.3121	0.3156	0.3192	0.3228	0.3264	0.3300	0.3336	0.3372	0.3409	0.3446
−0.3	0.3483	0.3520	0.3557	0.3594	0.3632	0.3669	0.3707	0.3745	0.3783	0.3821
−0.2	0.3859	0.3897	0.3936	0.3974	0.4013	0.4052	0.4090	0.4129	0.4168	0.4207
−0.1	0.4247	0.4286	0.4325	0.4364	0.4404	0.4443	0.4483	0.4522	0.4562	0.4602
−0.0	0.4641	0.4681	0.4721	0.4761	0.4801	0.4840	0.4880	0.4920	0.4960	0.5000

(*From E. L. Grant and R. S. Leavenworth, "Statistical Quality Control," 4th ed., McGraw-Hill Book Company, New York, 1972. By permission of the publishers.*)

Areas under the normal curve. (*Continued*)

$\dfrac{X_i - \bar{X}'}{\sigma'}$	0.00	0.01	0.02	0.03	0.04	0.05	0.06	0.07	0.08	0.09
+0.0	0.5000	0.5040	0.5080	0.5120	0.5160	0.5199	0.5239	0.5279	0.5319	0.5359
+0.1	0.5398	0.5438	0.5478	0.5517	0.5557	0.5596	0.5636	0.5675	0.5714	0.5753
+0.2	0.5793	0.5832	0.5871	0.5910	0.5948	0.5987	0.6026	0.6064	0.6103	0.6141
+0.3	0.6179	0.6217	0.6255	0.6293	0.6331	0.6368	0.6406	0.6443	0.6480	0.6517
+0.4	0.6554	0.6591	0.6628	0.6664	0.6700	0.6736	0.6772	0.6808	0.6844	0.6879
+0.5	0.6915	0.6950	0.6985	0.7019	0.7054	0.7088	0.7123	0.7157	0.7190	0.7224
+0.6	0.7257	0.7291	0.7324	0.7357	0.7389	0.7422	0.7454	0.7486	0.7517	0.7549
+0.7	0.7580	0.7611	0.7642	0.7673	0.7704	0.7734	0.7764	0.7794	0.7823	0.7852
+0.8	0.7881	0.7910	0.7939	0.7967	0.7995	0.8023	0.8051	0.8079	0.8106	0.8133
+0.9	0.8159	0.8186	0.8212	0.8238	0.8264	0.8289	0.8315	0.8340	0.8365	0.8389
+1.0	0.8413	0.8438	0.8461	0.8485	0.8508	0.8531	0.8554	0.8577	0.8599	0.8621
+1.1	0.8643	0.8665	0.8686	0.8708	0.8729	0.8749	0.8770	0.8790	0.8810	0.8830
+1.2	0.8849	0.8869	0.8888	0.8907	0.8925	0.8944	0.8962	0.8980	0.8997	0.9015
+1.3	0.9032	0.9049	0.9066	0.9082	0.9099	0.9115	0.9131	0.9147	0.9162	0.9177
+1.4	0.9192	0.9207	0.9222	0.9236	0.9251	0.9265	0.9279	0.9292	0.9306	0.9319
+1.5	0.9332	0.9345	0.9357	0.9370	0.9382	0.9394	0.9406	0.9418	0.9429	0.9441
+1.6	0.9452	0.9463	0.9474	0.9484	0.9495	0.9505	0.9515	0.9525	0.9535	0.9545
+1.7	0.9554	0.9564	0.9573	0.9582	0.9591	0.9599	0.9608	0.9616	0.9625	0.9633
+1.8	0.9641	0.9649	0.9656	0.9664	0.9671	0.9678	0.9686	0.9693	0.9699	0.9706
+1.9	0.9713	0.9719	0.9726	0.9732	0.9738	0.9744	0.9750	0.9756	0.9761	0.9767
+2.0	0.9773	0.9778	0.9783	0.9788	0.9793	0.9798	0.9803	0.9808	0.9812	0.9817
+2.1	0.9821	0.9826	0.9830	0.9834	0.9838	0.9842	0.9846	0.9850	0.9854	0.9857
+2.2	0.9861	0.9864	0.9868	0.9871	0.9875	0.9878	0.9881	0.9884	0.9887	0.9890
+2.3	0.9893	0.9896	0.9898	0.9901	0.9904	0.9906	0.9909	0.9911	0.9913	0.9916
+2.4	0.9918	0.9920	0.9922	0.9925	0.9927	0.9929	0.9931	0.9932	0.9934	0.9936
+2.5	0.9938	0.9940	0.9941	0.9943	0.9945	0.9946	0.9948	0.9949	0.9951	0.9952
+2.6	0.9953	0.9955	0.9956	0.9957	0.9959	0.9960	0.9961	0.9962	0.9963	0.9964
+2.7	0.9965	0.9966	0.9967	0.9968	0.9969	0.9970	0.9971	0.9972	0.9973	0.9974
+2.8	0.9974	0.9975	0.9976	0.9977	0.9977	0.9978	0.9979	0.9979	0.9980	0.9981
+2.9	0.9981	0.9982	0.9983	0.9983	0.9984	0.9984	0.9985	0.9985	0.9986	0.9986
+3.0	0.99865	0.99869	0.99874	0.99878	0.99882	0.99886	0.99889	0.99893	0.99896	0.99900
+3.1	0.99903	0.99906	0.99910	0.99913	0.99915	0.99918	0.99921	0.99924	0.99926	0.99929
+3.2	0.99931	0.99934	0.99936	0.99938	0.99940	0.99942	0.99944	0.99946	0.99948	0.99950
+3.3	0.99952	0.99953	0.99955	0.99957	0.99958	0.99960	0.99961	0.99962	0.99964	0.99965
+3.4	0.99966	0.99967	0.99969	0.99970	0.99971	0.99972	0.99973	0.99974	0.99975	0.99976
+3.5	0.99977	0.99978	0.99978	0.99979	0.99980	0.99981	0.99981	0.99982	0.99983	0.99983

(*From E. L. Grant and R. S. Leavenworth, "Statistical Quality Control," 4th ed., McGraw-Hill Book Company, New York, 1972. By permission of the publishers.*)

APPENDIX C

Random numbers*

10	09	73	25	33	76	52	01	35	86	34	67	35	48	76	80	95	90	91	17	39	29	27	49	45
37	54	20	48	05	64	89	47	42	96	24	80	52	40	37	20	63	61	04	02	00	82	29	16	65
08	42	26	89	53	19	64	50	93	03	23	20	90	25	60	15	95	33	47	64	35	08	03	36	06
99	01	90	25	29	09	37	67	07	15	38	31	13	11	65	88	67	67	43	97	04	43	62	76	59
12	80	79	99	70	80	15	73	61	47	64	03	23	66	53	98	95	11	68	77	12	17	17	68	33
66	06	57	47	17	34	07	27	68	50	36	69	73	61	70	65	81	33	98	85	11	19	92	91	70
31	06	01	08	05	45	57	18	24	06	35	30	34	26	14	86	79	90	74	39	23	40	30	97	32
85	26	97	76	02	02	05	16	56	92	68	66	57	48	18	73	05	38	52	47	18	62	38	85	79
63	57	33	21	35	05	32	54	70	48	90	55	35	75	48	28	46	82	87	09	83	49	12	56	24
73	79	64	57	53	03	52	96	47	78	35	80	83	42	82	60	93	52	03	44	35	27	38	84	35
98	52	01	77	67	14	90	56	86	07	22	10	94	05	58	60	97	09	34	33	50	50	07	39	98
11	80	50	54	31	39	80	82	77	32	50	72	56	82	48	29	40	52	42	01	52	77	56	78	51
83	45	29	96	34	06	28	89	80	83	13	74	67	00	78	18	47	54	06	10	68	71	17	78	17
88	68	54	02	00	86	50	75	84	01	36	76	66	79	51	90	36	47	64	93	29	60	91	10	62
99	59	46	73	48	87	51	76	49	69	91	82	60	89	28	93	78	56	13	68	23	47	83	41	13
65	48	11	76	74	17	46	85	09	50	58	04	77	69	74	73	03	95	71	86	40	21	81	65	44
80	12	43	56	35	17	72	70	80	15	45	31	82	23	74	21	11	57	82	53	14	38	55	37	63
74	35	09	98	17	77	40	27	72	14	43	23	60	02	10	45	52	16	42	37	96	28	60	26	55
69	91	62	68	03	66	25	22	91	48	36	93	68	72	03	76	62	11	39	90	94	40	05	64	18
09	89	32	05	05	14	22	56	85	14	46	42	75	67	88	96	29	77	88	22	54	38	21	45	98
91	49	91	45	23	68	47	92	76	86	46	16	28	35	54	94	75	08	99	23	37	08	92	00	48
80	33	69	45	98	26	94	03	68	58	70	29	73	41	35	53	14	03	33	40	42	05	08	23	41
44	10	48	19	49	85	15	74	79	54	32	97	92	65	75	57	60	04	08	81	22	22	20	64	13
12	55	07	37	42	11	10	00	20	40	12	86	07	46	97	96	64	48	94	39	28	70	72	58	15
63	60	64	93	29	16	50	53	44	84	40	21	95	25	63	43	65	17	70	82	07	20	73	17	90
61	19	69	04	46	26	45	74	77	74	51	92	43	37	29	65	39	45	95	93	42	58	26	05	27
15	47	44	52	66	95	27	07	99	53	59	36	78	38	48	82	39	61	01	18	33	21	15	94	66
94	55	72	85	73	67	89	75	43	87	54	62	24	44	31	91	19	04	25	92	92	92	74	59	73
42	48	11	62	13	97	34	40	87	21	16	86	84	87	67	03	07	11	20	59	25	70	14	66	70
23	52	37	83	17	73	20	88	98	37	68	93	59	14	16	26	25	22	96	63	05	52	28	25	62
04	49	35	24	94	75	24	63	38	24	45	86	25	10	25	61	96	27	93	35	65	33	71	24	72
00	54	99	76	54	64	05	18	81	59	96	11	96	38	96	54	69	28	23	91	23	28	72	95	29
35	96	31	53	07	26	89	80	93	54	33	35	13	54	62	77	97	45	00	24	90	10	33	93	33
59	80	80	83	91	45	42	72	68	42	83	60	94	97	00	13	02	12	48	92	78	56	52	01	06
46	05	88	52	36	01	39	00	22	86	77	28	14	40	77	93	91	08	36	47	70	61	74	29	41
32	17	90	05	97	87	37	92	52	41	05	56	70	70	07	86	74	31	71	57	85	39	41	18	38
69	23	46	14	06	20	11	74	52	04	15	95	66	00	00	18	74	39	24	23	97	11	89	63	38
19	56	54	14	30	01	75	87	53	79	40	41	92	15	85	66	67	43	68	06	84	96	28	52	07
45	15	51	49	38	19	47	60	72	46	43	66	79	45	43	59	04	79	00	33	20	82	66	95	41
94	86	43	19	94	36	16	81	08	51	34	88	88	15	53	01	54	03	54	56	05	01	45	11	76
98	08	62	48	26	45	24	02	84	04	44	99	90	88	96	39	09	47	34	07	35	44	13	18	80
33	18	51	62	32	41	94	15	09	49	89	43	54	85	81	88	69	54	19	94	37	54	87	30	43
80	95	10	04	06	96	38	27	07	74	20	15	12	33	87	25	01	62	52	98	94	62	46	11	71
79	75	24	91	40	71	96	12	82	96	69	86	10	25	91	74	85	22	05	39	00	38	75	95	79
18	63	33	25	37	98	14	50	65	71	31	01	02	46	74	05	45	56	14	27	77	93	89	19	36
74	02	94	39	02	77	55	73	22	70	97	79	01	71	19	52	52	75	80	21	80	81	45	17	48
54	17	84	56	11	80	99	33	71	43	05	33	51	29	69	56	12	71	92	55	36	04	09	03	24
11	66	44	98	83	52	07	98	48	27	59	38	17	15	39	09	97	33	34	40	88	46	12	33	56
48	32	47	79	28	31	24	96	47	10	02	29	53	68	70	32	30	75	75	46	15	02	00	99	94
69	07	49	41	38	87	63	79	19	76	35	58	40	44	01	10	51	82	16	15	01	84	87	69	38

* This table is reproduced with permission from tables of the RAND Corporation.

(From E. L. Grant and R. S. Leavenworth, "Statistical Quality Control," 4th ed., McGraw-Hill Book Company, New York, 1972. By permission of the publishers.)

INDEX